THE ENCYCLOPEDIA OF COOKING

© Rebo International b.v., Lisse, The Netherlands
1997 Published by Rebo Productions Ltd., London

translation: First Edition Translations, Cambridge, U.K.
typesetting: Hof&Land Typografie, The Netherlands
coverdesign: Librairie Grund, Paris, France

recipes: Ceres-Verlag Rudolf-August Oetker KG, Bielefeld, Germany

Photography Germany:

Ludwig Bartling, Bielefeld
Fotostudio Büttner, Bielefeld
Thomas Diercks, Hamburg
Gruner & Jahr, Hamburg
Friederun Köhnen, Sprockhövel
Fotodesign Bernd Lippert, Bielefeld
Herbert Maas, Hamburg
Orbis Verlag, Munich
Christiane Pries, Borgholzhausen
Fotostudio Teubner, Füssen
Brigitte Wegner, Bielefeld
Arnold Zabert, Hamburg

A 0002UK

ISBN 1 901094 13 8

printed in Slovenija

THE ENCYCLOPEDIA
OF COOKING

REBO
PRODUCTIONS

STARTERS AND ENTREMETS

Sweet or savoury, perfect as the start to any meal or as a snack.

Page 9

POTATOES

Popular as an accompaniment, potatoes can also take pride of place on any table.

Page 43

PASTA

Countless varieties of pasta offer an endless source of imaginative dishes.

Page 61

VEGETABLES

Cooked according to traditional recipes, flavoursome vegetables complement meat, poultry and fish.

Page 83

SALADS

Refreshing and packed with vitamins,
eat your fill of crisp, fresh salads.

Page 115

MEAT

You need never lack ideas with
inventive recipes for all types of meat dish, whether simple or sumptuous.

Page 135

FISH

Varied methods and interesting accompaniments to satisfy any fish-lover.

Page 239

GAME

Try the unique flavour of game for a superb celebration meal. Easy-to-follow recipes for guaranteed success.

Page 277

POULTRY

Reserve a special place at your table for poultry, whether roast, as kebabs or escalopes, or thinly sliced.

Page 307

STEWS AND CASSEROLES

Traditional recipes and regional specialities for simple, convivial meals.

SAVOURY BAKES

Crisp and tasty, savoury bakes delight hearty appetites and gourmets alike.

DESSERTS

Hard to resist and a feast for the eyes.

and cook over a low heat until toasted. Gently fold the crème fraîche into the soup and scatter toasted pine kernels over the top. You can also mix together the pine kernels and crème fraîche and serve separately. Pumpkin soup can also be served chilled.

CREAM OF CARROT SOUP

Serves 4

400 g (13 oz) carrots	1-2 knobs of butter
2 large potatoes	½ tub crème fraîche
1 celeriac	1 tbsp fresh dill, chopped
2-3 onions	salt and pepper

Peel and dice the carrots, onions, potatoes and celeriac. Melt the butter in a saucepan, add the onions and fry gently until transparent, then add the chopped root vegetables to the pan and brown them.

Add 1 litre (1¾ pints) water to the saucepan, season the soup with salt and pepper, bring it to the boil, simmer for 12 minutes, then purée it using a hand blender or food processor.

Gently fold the crème fraîche into the soup, then adjust the seasoning. Just before serving, stir in the chopped dill and top the soup with dots of butter.

CREAM OF SWEET PEPPER SOUP

Serves 4

3-4 red, green or yellow	3-4 tbsp white wine
sweet peppers	125 ml (4 fl oz) double
4 onions	cream
200 g (7 oz) pickled	salt
cabbage or sauerkraut	pepper
2-3 tbsp oil	
1 litre (1w pints) meat stock	

Slice the peppers in half, remove the cores and seeds. Thinly slice the peppers. Peel and dice the onions. Loosen the pickled cabbage using two forks.

Heat the oil in a saucepan and gently fry the onions in it until transparent. Add the sliced peppers and pickled cabbage and warm them through. Add the stock and bring the soup to the boil. Simmer for 20 minutes. Season with salt and pepper.

Purée the soup using a hand blender or food processor, then add the white wine and double cream, return the soup to the pan and reheat gently without boiling.

PUMPKIN SOUP

Serves 4-6

1 kg (2 lb) beef bones	1 kg (2 lb) pumpkin flesh
1 leek	30 g (1 oz) butter
1 carrot	50 g (2 oz) pine kernels
1 turnip	1 tbsp fresh dill, chopped
1 stick of celery	100 g (3½ oz) crème
fresh parsley	fraîche
2 bay leaves	salt
1 tbsp black peppercorns	pepper
100 g (3½ oz) onions	

In a large saucepan bring 12 litres (22 pints) of salted water to the boil. Rinse the beef bones thoroughly in cold water, place them in the pan of boiling water, bring to the boil again and skim. Wash and peel the vegetables and chop coarsely, and add them to the stock with the bay leaves, black peppercorns and parsley. Bring the soup to a slow boil and simmer, uncovered, skimming as necessary. Allow the stock to reduce by about one third, then strain it through a sieve.

Peel and thinly slice the onions. Chop the pumpkin flesh into 1 cm (½ inch) cubes. Melt the butter in a saucepan and sweat the onions in it until transparent, add the cubed pumpkin to the pan and brown it over a low heat. Add the hot beef stock to the mixture, bring the pan to the boil and simmer the soup over a low heat for 15 minutes, until the pumpkin flesh starts to break up. Remove the pan from the heat, pour the soup into a blender or food processor and purée roughly. Season the soup with salt and pepper and add the chopped dill. Place the pine kernels in the frying pan without any fat

CHEESE AND ONION SOUP

Serves 4

40 g (1½ oz) butter
40 g (1½ oz) flour
1 litre (1w pints) meat stock
200 g (7 oz) Gouda cheese,
diced

2 tbsp crème fraîche
1 bunch spring onions
knob of butter
grated nutmeg
salt
freshly ground pepper

Melt the butter in a saucepan until foaming, add the flour and cook to form a white roux. Add the meat stock, whisking the roux all the time to prevent lumps forming. Bring the stock to the boil and simmer for 5 minutes. Add the diced cheese and crème fraîche to the stock, bring the soup gently to the boil and simmer, stirring constantly until the cheese has melted completely. Season the soup with salt, freshly ground pepper and grated nutmeg.

Trim the spring onion stalks to 15 cm (6 ins) lengths and then slice the spring onions into rounds.
Melt the knob of butter in a saucepan and fry the spring onions gently until soft. Scatter the fried spring onions over the cheese soup immediately before serving.

CREAM OF AVOCADO SOUP

Serves 3-4

30 g (1 oz) butter
40 g (1½ oz) flour
750 ml (1¼ pints) meat
stock
1 ripe avocado
125 ml (4 fl oz) champagne

100 g (3½ oz) cream,
whipped until stiff
1 tsp fresh dill, finely
chopped
salt
pepper

Melt the butter in a saucepan, add the flour and cook gently to form a roux. Add the meat stock to the roux, whisking all the time to prevent lumps forming. Bring the stock to the boil and simmer for 3 minutes.

Slice the avocado in half, remove the stone and scrape out the flesh. Mash the flesh to a pulp and add it to the soup. Do not let the soup boil. Season the soup with salt and pepper. Add the champagne to the soup and serve immediately, garnished with whipped cream and chopped dill.

Below: *Cream of avocado soup*
Left: *Pumpkin soup*

them dry, then cut them into thin ribbons. Peel the garlic clove and onion or shallots, then dice them finely. Add the sorrel, garlic and onion to the soup with the chopped chives, parsley, and a little grated nutmeg. Season the soup with salt and pepper and bring to the boil.

Beat together the egg yolk and crème fraîche, then add to the soup to bind it. Reheat the soup over a gentle heat. Do not allow it to boil. Pour the soup into the bowls, on top of the croutons, and serve immediately.

Above:
Cream of tomato soup

CREAM OF TOMATO SOUP

Serves 3-4

400 g (13 oz) tomatoes	stock
60 g (2½ oz) bacon	2 tbsp tomato purée
1 onion	fresh oregano
2 cloves of garlic	4 tbsp crème fraîche
40 g (1½ oz) flour	fresh dill, chopped
750 ml (1¼ pints) meat	

Dice the bacon, place in a heat-proof casserole dish or a saucepan and fry until brown. Chop the onion and garlic. Fry them gently in the bacon fat. Sprinkle the flour over the bacon and onions and allow to cook.

Wash and finely dice the tomatoes and add them to the bacon mixture. Add the stock to the pan. Chop the oregano and add it to the soup with the tomato purée, stirring well. Cover the soup and leave to simmer for 10 minutes, then pass it through a sieve. Whip the crème fraîche. When serving the soup, place a spoonful of crème fraîche gently in each bowl, on top of the soup, and sprinkle with chopped dill.

SORREL SOUP

Serves 4

2 slices of bread	1 tbsp fresh chives,
1 carrot	chopped
1 piece of celeriac	1 tbsp fresh parsley,
2 leeks	chopped
40 g (1½ oz) butter	grated nutmeg
1 tbsp flour	1 egg yolk
100 g (3½ oz) sorrel	1 tbsp crème fraîche
1 clove of garlic	salt, pepper
2 shallots or 1 small onion	

Melt 3 knobs of butter in a frying pan. Cut the bread into small dice and fry them in the melted butter until crisp and golden. Divide the croutons amongst 4 soup bowls. Peel the carrot and celeriac, rinse the leeks thoroughly, then trim them, retaining only the white and 10 cm (4 ins) of the green. Wash and thinly slice the vegetables. Place 1 litre (1¾ pints) of cold water in a saucepan, add the chopped vegetables to the water, bring the saucepan to the boil and simmer the vegetables for 30 minutes. Strain the stock through a sieve.

In another saucepan, melt the remaining butter, add the flour, stirring all the time, and cook to form a roux. Add the vegetable stock to the roux, whisking thoroughly to prevent lumps forming, then bring the stock to the boil. Remove the sorrel stalks, wash the sorrel leaves and pat

CREAM OF BRUSSELS SPROUT SOUP

Serves 4

500 g (1 lb) Brussels sprouts	knob of butter
1 meat stock cube	cayenne pepper
1 tsp cornflour	fresh parsley, chopped
3 tbsp crème fraîche	salt
	pepper

Wash and trim the Brussels sprouts. Bring 250 ml (8 fl oz) salted water to the boil, add the sprouts to the saucepan, bring to the boil again and simmer for 10 minutes. Remove 10 sprouts from the pan, cut them into quarters and reserve them. Purée the soup using a hand mixer or food processor. Return the soup to the saucepan, add 500 ml (18 fl oz) boiling water and the beef stock cube to the pan and bring it to the boil. Mix the cornflour with a little cold water, add the crème fraîche to the cornflour and then whisk the mixture into the soup. Reheat the soup over a low heat. Add the knob of butter. Adjust the seasoning with salt and cayenne pepper.

Add the reserved sprouts to the soup, heat through gently, then sprinkle the soup with chopped parsley.

HOLSTEIN BEER SOUP

Serves 3-4

150 g (5 oz) bread
½ stick of cinnamon
juice and zest of ½ an unwaxed lemon
125 g (4 oz) sugar

100 g (3½ oz) raisins
2 apples
500 ml (18 fl oz) beer
1 egg
salt

Dice the bread. Place 500 ml (18 fl oz) water in a saucepan, add the diced bread to the pan, and bring it to the boil, then purée the soup through a sieve. Return the soup to the saucepan. Add the cinnamon, juice and zest of the lemon, salt, raisins and 75 g (3 oz) of the sugar.

Peel the apples, core and quarter them, then slice them. Bring the soup to the boil again, stirring all the time. Add the sliced apples and the beer to the soup and allow it to simmer for 10 minutes. Lightly beat the egg yolk, then add it to the pan to bind the soup.

To make the meringue garnish: whisk the egg white with the remaining sugar until glossy and the mixture forms soft peaks. Dot spoonfuls of meringue mixture on top of the piping hot soup. Cover and leave for 3-4 minutes to set.

Below: *Holstein beer soup*

CHICKEN CONSOMMÉ

Serves 5-6

250 g (8 oz) dark chicken meat, chopped
500 g (1 lb) white chicken meat
1 leek
1 carrot
1 turnip
1 stick of celery
200 g (7 oz) asparagus tips, cooked
100 g (3½ oz) petit pois, tinned or frozen
fresh parsley, chopped
salt

Place 1½ litres (2½ pints) cold, salted water in a saucepan, add the chicken meat, bring the saucepan to the boil and skim the stock. Peel the carrot and turnip, wash and trim the leek and celery, chop them into small pieces, add them to the chicken stock and simmer for 20 minutes.

Strain the stock through a sieve and return it to the saucepan. Add the asparagus and peas to the stock and heat through gently. Season the consommé with salt, and sprinkle with chopped parsley just before serving.

CONSOMMÉ WITH VERMICELLI

Serves 4

1 litre (1w pints) meat stock
40 g (1½ oz) vermicelli
1 tbsp fresh parsley, chopped
salt

Place the stock in a saucepan and bring it to the boil. Add the vermicelli, stir well and leave the stock to simmer for 10-15 minutes. Season the consommé with salt and serve sprinkled with chopped parsley. The vermicelli may also be cooked separately in boiling, salted water and added to the consommé a few minutes before serving.

LENTIL SOUP

Serves 4-6

200 g (7 oz) lentils
1½ litres (2½ pints) meat stock
1 leek
1 carrot
1 turnip
1 stick of celery
1 onion
2-3 coarse, meaty sausages
1 tsp cornflour
fresh thyme and parsley, chopped
1 tbsp fresh chives, finely chopped
salt

Wash the lentils, then leave them to soak in the meat stock for 12-24 hours. Place the stock and lentils in a saucepan and bring them to the boil, simmer for 45 minutes Peel and finely chop the carrot and turnip; wash, trim and finely chop the leek and celery. Peel and dice the onion. Slice the sausages into rounds. After 45 minutes, add the chopped vegetables and sliced sausage to the soup. Simmer for a further 45 minutes. Blend the cornflour with a teaspoon of cold water and add it to the

Right: Fish soup with fennel
Below: Chicken consommé

soup to thicken it. Season the soup with salt and add the chopped thyme and parsley. Just before serving, sprinkle the chopped chives over the soup.

FISH SOUP WITH FENNEL

Serves 4

500 g (1 lb) fillet of turbot or salmon	fresh parsley, chopped
1 kg (2 lb) fish bones	1 clove of garlic
juice of 1 lemon	4 tbsp olive oil
4-5 bulbs of fennel	100 g (3½ oz) long grain rice
4 onions	1 tsp green peppercorns, crushed
2 bay leaves	250 g (8 oz) tomatoes
1 leek	2 tbsp fresh parsley, chopped
1 carrot	
1 turnip	
1 stick of celery	salt

Place 2 litres (3½ pints) cold, salted water in a saucepan, add the fish bones, and bring to the boil. Simmer for 15 minutes. Strain the stock, discarding the bones. Cut the fish fillets into small pieces, drizzle with lemon juice and leave to rest for 15 minutes. Remove and reserve the green fennel fronds, wash the fennel bulbs, and cut them into eight pieces. Peel and dice the onions, carrot and turnip; wash, trim and dice the leek and celery. Chop the garlic. Heat the olive oil in a large saucepan or casserole dish, add the chopped fennel, onions, other vegetables, parsley, garlic and rice and cook for 5 minutes. Then add the fish stock, crushed green peppercorns and bay leaves. Cover the pan and simmer the soup for 20 minutes, skimming occasionally if necessary.

Blanch the tomatoes in boiling water for 1 minute, then refresh them in cold water, skin and dice them. Add the chopped fish and tomatoes to the soup. Cook gently, uncovered, for 8-10 minutes, but do not allow the soup to boil. Season with salt. Wash, dry and chop the fennel fronds and add them to the soup, together with the chopped parsley, just before serving

WHITE ROUX

Serves 4

40 g (1½ oz) butter	40 g (1½ oz) flour

Melt the butter in a saucepan. Blend the flour into the melted butter, stirring all the time, until it is cooked and a roux forms. Continuing to stir, add 1 litre (1w pints) water. Bring the stock to the boil and simmer for approximately 10 minutes. Season according to taste.

BEEF CONSOMMÉ

Serves 6-8

250 g (8 oz) beef bones
375 g (12 oz) beef
1 leek: 1 turnip: 1 carrot

1 onion: 1 stick of celery
knob of butter
stock cube: salt

Wash and chop the beef bones (or get your butcher to chop them for you). Put 2 litres (3½ pints) cold, salted water into a saucepan with the meat and beef bones, and bring it to the boil. Peel the onion and slice it into rings. Melt the knob of butter in a frying pan and gently fry the onion in the butter until golden. Peel and chop the carrot and turnip; wash, trim and chop the leek and celery. Add the chopped vegetables and fried onion to the stock and simmer it for 2½-3 hours. Strain the consommé, season with salt, and add the stock cube. Serve with cheese straws.

PEKINESE TAIFUN SOUP

Serves 4

1 carton of frozen spiced
Pekinese soup
100 g (3½ oz) pumpkin
2 tbsp natural yoghurt

ground ginger
cayenne pepper
soy sauce

Prepare the Pekinese soup according to the instructions on the packet. Dice the pumpkin flesh and add it to the soup. Simmer for 15 minutes. Add the yoghurt, ground ginger, cayenne pepper and soy sauce.

Above: *Spicy soup*
Left: *Pekinese Taifun soup*

SPICY SOUP

Serves 4-6

250 g (8 oz) beef
250 g (8 oz) pork
3-4 tbsp oil
250 g (8 oz) shallots
2 tbsp tomato purée
ground paprika
fresh oregano, chopped

250 ml (8 fl oz) red wine
2-3 tomatoes
1 large leek
340 g (11½ oz) tinned
sweetcorn
salt and pepper

Cut the meat into pieces. Heat the oil in a saucepan, brown the meat in the hot oil, turning so that the meat is sealed and browned on all sides. Peel the shallots, cut them in half and add them to the meat with the tomato purée, paprika and oregano. Season the meat and vegetable mixture with salt and pepper. Deglaze the pan with 750 ml (1¼ pints) water and 250 ml (8 fl oz) red wine and bring the liquid to the boil. Simmer the soup for 45 minutes.

Blanch the tomatoes in boiling water for one minute, then refresh them in cold water, skin and dice them. Wash the leek and slice it into rings. Add the tomatoes, sliced leek and tinned sweetcorn, together with its liquor, to the soup. Season with salt and pepper, add more paprika and simmer for a further 15 minutes.

PIGEON SOUP

2 oven-ready pigeons	1 turnip
1 leek	1 stick of celery
1 carrot	salt

Place 2½ litres (4½ pints) cold water in a saucepan and season it with salt. Peel and chop the carrot and turnip; wash, trim and chop the leek and celery. Place the pigeons, together with the giblets, in the pan of water and add the chopped vegetables. Bring the saucepan to the boil and simmer for 1 hour. Remove the pigeons from the soup, take the meat off the bones and chop it into small pieces. Purée the soup through a sieve. Return the soup to the saucepan, add the chopped pigeon meat and reheat thoroughly before serving.

ONION SOUP

Serves 4

375g (12 oz) onions	butter until golden
75 g (3 oz) butter	70 g (3 oz) Gruyère cheese,
1 litre (1¾ pints) meat stock	grated
4 tbsp white wine	salt
cubes of bread fried in	pepper

*P*eel the onions and slice them into rings. Melt the butter in a saucepan, and fry the onion rings in the melted butter until golden brown. Add the stock to the pan and bring to the boil. Season the soup with salt and pepper and add the white wine. Simmer for 15-20 minutes. Pour the soup into heat-resistant bowls, scatter the croutons over and top with grated cheese. Bake under a hot grill or in the oven until the cheese browns.

VEAL CONSOMMÉ

Serves 4

250 g (8 oz) breast of veal	fresh parsley, chopped
250 g (8 oz) veal bones,	stock cube
chopped	100 g (3½ oz) asparagus
1 leek	tips, cooked
1 carrot	100 g (3½ oz) peas, frozen
1 turnip	or tinned
1 stick of celery	

*P*lace the breast of veal and bones in 1½ litres (2½ pints) of cold, salted water and bring them to the boil. Skim the stock as necessary. Peel and finely chop the carrot and turnip; wash, trim and chop the leek and celery. Add them to the veal stock with the parsley. Simmer the soup

for about 1½ hours. Then strain the consommé, season it with salt, add the stock cube, asparagus tips and peas and reheat it.

Above: *Spicy oxtail soup*
Left: *Onion soup*

SPICY OXTAIL SOUP

Serves 4

1 onion	pinch of paprika
1 tbsp oil	1 tin of oxtail soup
1 small gherkin	red wine
1 tsp honey	brandy
pinch of curry powder	double cream

***P**eel* and dice the onion. Heat the oil in a saucepan and fry the onion in the oil until brown. Thinly slice the gherkin. Add the gherkin, honey, curry powder and paprika to the onion. Cook gently for a minute to combine the flavours. Prepare the oxtail soup according to the instructions on the tin, and pour the tinned soup over the onion mixture. Bring to the boil, stirring carefully, and remove the saucepan from the heat as soon as the soup boils. Add the red wine and brandy and enrich the soup with a little double cream.

SPRING VEGETABLE SOUP

Serves 4

125 g (4 oz) cauliflower
2 carrots
4 asparagus spears
1 leek
125 g (4 oz) celeriac
2 tomatoes
1 litre (1¾ pints) meat stock

1 meat stock cube
2 tbsp fresh parsley,
chopped
salt
pepper

*S*eparate the cauliflower florets, scrape the carrots, wash and trim the asparagus, leeks and celeriac. Slice the carrots, asparagus and leek into rounds, thinly slice the celeriac.

Wash and dice the tomatoes. Place the meat stock in a saucepan and bring it to the boil. Add the vegetables, season with salt and pepper, add the stock cube and simmer for 20 minutes.

Serve the soup, garnished with chopped parsley.

TOMATO SOUP

Serves 3-4

375 g (12 oz) tomatoes
1 onion
50 g (2 oz) fatty bacon
30 g (1 oz) butter
40 g (1½ oz) flour
1 tsp fresh basil, chopped

½ meat stock cube
ground paprika
tomato purée
Tabasco sauce
fresh parsley, chopped
salt and pepper

*W*ash the tomatoes and chop them into small pieces. Peel the onion. Dice the onion and the bacon. Fry the bacon in a saucepan or casserole dish until the fat runs, add the butter, flour and onion to the pan and cook to form a roux.

Add 750 ml (1¼ pints) water to the pan, season with salt, then add the tomatoes, chopped basil and stock cube. Bring the soup to the boil and simmer it for 20 minutes. Purée the soup through a sieve, season with salt and pepper, add the tomato purée, then season with paprika and Tabasco sauce. Garnish with chopped parsley.

Variation: You can substitute 3 tablespoons of condensed tomato soup per litre (1¾ pints) water for the fresh tomatoes.

MUSHROOM AND RICE SOUP

Serves 4-5

500 g (1 lb) shin, fore rib, thick or thin rib of beef	50 g (2oz) rice
	125 g (4 oz) asparagus tips, cooked
250 g (8 oz) button mushrooms	fresh tarragon, chopped
knob of butter	salt

*P*lace the meat in a saucepan with 1½ litres (2½ pints) cold, salted water and bring it to the boil. Simmer the meat for 2 hours, skimming as necessary. Then remove the meat and bones from the stock, take the meat off the bones, cut it into small pieces and reserve it.

Peel and thinly slice the mushrooms. Melt the knob of butter in a saucepan and fry the mushrooms until golden. Season them with salt and chopped tarragon and cook for a further 10 minutes so that the flavours can combine.

Bring the stock to the boil, add the rice to it and simmer for 12-15 minutes. The rice should still be slightly al dente. Chop the asparagus tips and add them to the stock with the chopped meat and mushrooms. Reheat for 1-2 minutes. Instead of button mushrooms you could use ceps, or chanterelle mushrooms.

Opposite: *Spring vegetable soup*
Below: *Mushroom and rice soup*

CHILLED CHERRY SOUP WITH SEMOLINA DUMPLINGS

Serves 4

750 g (1½ lb) cherries
250 ml (8 fl oz) red or white wine
zest of 2 unwaxed lemons
1 tbsp lemon juice
1 stick of cinnamon

1 clove
100-125 g (3½-4 oz) sugar
20 g (¾ oz) cornflour
500 ml (18 fl oz) milk
150 g (5 oz) semolina
1 egg, beaten
salt

Wash and stone the cherries. In a saucepan, mix the wine with 750 ml (1¼ pints) water, the zest of 1 lemon and the lemon juice. Add the cinnamon and clove, 75-100 g (3-3½ oz) sugar, and bring the mixture to the boil. Add the cherries to the wine mixture and leave them to infuse for about 8 minutes. The syrup should not boil, but simmer very gently. In a bowl, blend the cornflour with a little cold water, add to the syrup and bring it to the boil, then remove immediately from the heat. Remove the cinnamon stick and clove, then leave the cherry mixture in the refrigerator to cool.

To make the semolina dumplings: In a saucepan mix together the milk, the remaining lemon zest and 25 g

(1 oz) sugar and a pinch of salt. Bring it to the boil, then remove the pan from the heat. Incorporate the semolina, stirring briskly, leave it to cook for 1 minute, then mix the beaten egg into the mixture. The semolina should come away from the sides of the saucepan and form a firm ball. Bring a pan of salted water to the boil.
Shape portions of semolina dough into dumplings using two teaspoons. Plunge the dumplings into the boiling water and poach them for 5-7 minutes in the simmering water. Serve the dumplings with the chilled cherry soup.

VIENNESE FRUIT SALAD

Serves 4-6

750 g (1½ lb) berry fruits,
e.g. strawberries,
redcurrants, raspberries,
bilberries or
cranberries, blackberries
150 g (5 oz) caster sugar

2 tbsp lemon juice
1 tbsp Grand Marnier
pinch of ground cinnamon
1 litre (1¾ pints) soured milk
vanilla ice-cream

Sort the raspberries and wash the other fruit. Pat them dry and hull them. Add the caster sugar, lemon juice, Grand Marnier and cinnamon to the fruit, stir well, cover, and leave to marinate for 30 minutes. Stir the sour milk into the fruit mixture. Serve with vanilla ice-cream.

MERINGUE SNOWFLAKES

Serves 4

2 egg whites
2 tsp caster sugar
chocolate, grated or

caster sugar
cinnamon

Whisk the egg whites until stiff and gently fold in the caster sugar. Shape the meringue into little blobs. Plunge them into very hot sugar syrup or boiling water, leave them to firm up for 5 minutes, then garnish them with grated chocolate or caster sugar and cinnamon.

FRUIT SOUP WITH GARLIC

Serves 4

2 tbsp shelled almonds
5-6 tbsp fresh
breadcrumbs
2-3 cloves of garlic, finely
chopped or   crushed

2-3 tbsp oil
200 g (7 oz) grapes
200 g (7 oz) melon
salt
pepper

Opposite: *Chilled cherry soup*

Place the almonds, breadcrumbs and garlic in a food processor, gradually add the oil, processing the mixture a little each time, and add a generous 250 ml (8 fl oz) water. Process everything thoroughly. Season with salt and pepper. Wash and dry the grapes, cut them in half and remove the pips. Slice the melon in half, remove the seeds then, using a spoon, scoop out the flesh and dice it. Add the grapes and melon to the almond mixture. Serve the soup very cold, with ice cubes if desired.

Above: *Fruit soup with garlic*

RED WINE SOUP

Serves 4-5

1 stick of cinnamon	750 ml (1¼ pints) red wine
2 cloves	2 tbsp lemon juice
1 small apple	100 g (3½ oz) sugar
40 g (1½ oz) tapioca	

Peel and core the apple. Cut it into quarters, then slices. Put approximately 350 ml (10 fl oz) water in a saucepan with the cinnamon and cloves and bring them to the boil. Add the sliced apple and tapioca to the pan, stir well, bring to the boil again, simmer for 10-15 minutes, then remove the cinnamon and cloves. Add the red wine to the mixture and heat it through thoroughly, without boiling. Add the sugar and lemon juice, stirring carefully. Red wine soup can be served hot or cold as liked. You can use rice instead of tapioca (20-30 minutes cooking time).

RHUBARB AND RED FRUIT SOUP

Serves 6-8

500 g (1 lb) rhubarb
140 g (5 oz) caster sugar
250 ml (8 fl oz) white wine
250 g (8 oz) raspberries,
fresh or frozen

500 g (1 lb) strawberries
1 egg white
1 tsp ground cinnamon
5 tsp caster sugar

Remove any string from the rhubarb and cut it into small pieces. In a saucepan, gently cook 10 g (¼-½ oz) caster sugar until it starts to caramelize, then deglaze with the white wine. Heat this mixture, stirring all the time. Add the rhubarb and raspberries to the syrup, boil for 10 minutes, then strain. Slice the strawberries in half and add them to the syrup. Whisk the egg white until stiff, then gently fold in the remaining caster sugar. Shape the meringue into little dumplings. Bring a saucepan of water to the boil and plunge the meringues into the boiling water, cover the pan and leave the meringues to

set for 5 minutes, then remove them and place them on top of the soup. Mix together the ground cinnamon and 5 teaspoons of caster sugar and dust over the meringues. This soup can be made the day before and served chilled, the meringues should then be added just before serving.

MILK SOUP

Serves 4

1 sachet vanilla or almond
flavour custard mix
60 g (2½ oz) sugar
1 egg, separated

1 litre (1¾ pints) milk
zest of 1 unwaxed lemon
1 tsp caster sugar
1 tsp salt

Mix the contents of the packet with the sugar, a pinch of salt and the egg yolk. Add 6 tablespoons of cold milk and mix well. In a saucepan bring the remaining milk to the boil with the lemon zest. Add the packet mixture to the hot milk, stir well and bring to the boil again. Whisk the egg white until stiff, then gently fold in the caster sugar. Using a teaspoon, shape the meringue mixture into little balls and drop them into the boiling custard mixture.

CHILLED RHUBARB SOUP

Serves 4

375 g (12 oz) rhubarb
150 g (5 oz) sugar
1 sachet cherry or lemon flavour

custard mix
3-4 tbsp white wine
100 g (3½ oz) strawberries

Wash the rhubarb and chop it into small pieces. Bring 1¼ litres (2¼ pints) of water to the boil in a saucepan, add the rhubarb and sugar, bring to the boil again and remove from the heat immediately. Blend the contents of the sachet with 4 tablespoons of cold water and add to the rhubarb to thicken it. Add the white wine to the soup, and more sugar if necessary. Chill the soup in the refrigerator.
Serve garnished with halved strawberries.

CHILLED KIWI FRUIT SOUP

Serves 4

500 ml (18 fl oz) sweet white wine
2 tbsp caster sugar
4 cloves
1 stick of cinnamon

4 tbsp maple syrup
5 kiwi fruit
100 g (3½ oz) crème fraîche
a few mint leaves

Mix together the white wine, caster sugar, cloves and cinnamon stick. Bring them to the boil in a saucepan and add the maple syrup, stirring gently. Allow the soup to cool, then strain it. Peel the kiwi fruit and slice into rounds. Reserve a few slices for a garnish, and purée the rest with a hand blender or food processor. Strain the purée to remove the seeds. Add the wine mixture to the kiwi purée, then add the crème fraîche, beating it into the soup. Leave the soup in the refrigerator to chill.
To serve, garnish with sliced kiwi fruit and mint leaves.

Below: *Chilled kiwi fruit soup*
Left: *Rhubarb and red fruit soup*

RUSSIAN CREAM SOUP

Serves 4-6

500 ml (1 pint) cucumber
juice,
freshly squeezed
500 ml (1 pint) crème
fraîche
½ cucumber
½ red pepper
½ green pepper

200 g (7 oz) beetroot,
cooked
2 hard-boiled eggs, shelled
2 bunches of fresh chives
3 tbsp vodka
salt
freshly ground pepper

Mix together the cucumber juice and crème fraîche. Wash the cucumber. Remove the cores and seeds from the peppers. Drain the beetroot. Chop all the vegetables into small pieces. Mash the hard-boiled eggs. Chop the chives. Add everything to the cucumber juice and stir well. Add the vodka to the soup, season it with salt and pepper. Russian cream soup should be served cold.

CHILLED COURGETTE AND TOMATO SOUP

Serves 4-5

2-3 small courgettes
450 g (15 oz) natural
yoghurt
150 g (5 oz) crème fraîche
125 ml (4 fl oz) milk
300 g (10 oz) tomatoes,
skinned and diced
1 tbsp fresh mint or
tarragon, chopped

1 tsp fresh dill, chopped
1 tsp fresh parsley,
chopped
a few lettuce leaves
1 hard-boiled egg
(optional)
1-2 cloves of garlic
salt and pepper
fresh mint for garnish

Above: *Cream of white wine soup*
Opposite: *Russian cream soup*

Slice the courgettes in two lengthways and then slice each half thinly. Steam the sliced courgette for 10 minutes, until soft. Add the yoghurt and crème fraîche to the milk, mix them all together, then add the courgettes and tomatoes, mint or tarragon, dill and parsley. Finely slice the garlic and add it to the soup. Season with salt and pepper. Leave in the refrigerator for several hours to infuse.
Line a salad bowl with the lettuce leaves and pour the soup into the salad bowl. Sprinkle the soup with chopped hard-boiled egg, if liked, and garnish it with a few sprigs of mint.

CREAM OF WHITE WINE SOUP

Serves 4

1 stick of cinnamon
2-3 drops of lemon oil
30 g (1 oz) cornflour
2 tsp caster sugar

750 ml (1¼ pints) white
wine
1 egg, separated
100 g (3½ oz) sugar

*P*lace 300 ml (½ pint) water in a saucepan with the cinnamon stick and bring it to the boil. Blend the cornflour with 2 tablespoons of cold water. Remove the water and cinnamon from the heat, add the cornflour, then return the pan to the heat and boil the soup for a few moments. Add the white wine and heat the soup without letting it boil.

Then add the egg yolk and sugar to enrich and thicken the soup.

To make the meringues: briskly whisk the egg white until stiff. Sprinkle the caster sugar onto the egg white and fold it in gently. Using a damp teaspoon, shape the meringue into little dumplings.

Bring a saucepan of water to the boil, drop the meringue dumplings into the boiling water, cover the saucepan and leave the dumplings to firm up for 5 minutes. Then add the meringues to the soup.

TROUT TERRINE EN CROÍTE

Serves 6-8

2 trout, filleted
1 onion
1 tbsp fresh chives, finely chopped
100 ml (3½ fl oz) white wine
5 tbsp oil
300 g (10 oz) flour
5 eggs
100 g (3½ oz) lard
500 g (1 lb) fillet of sole,
frozen
1 heaped tsp fresh dill, finely chopped
2 tbsp breadcrumbs
zest of 1 unwaxed lemon, grated
150 g (5 oz) crème fraîche
50 g (2 oz) butter
½ tbsp milk
salt
pepper

*P*lace the trout fillets in a dish. Peel and slice the onion. Mix together the onion, white wine, chives and oil. Pour the marinade over the trout fillets, cover them and leave to marinate in a cool place for 4-5 hours or overnight.

To make the pastry: Sieve the flour and make a well in the centre. Add 1 whole egg plus ½ the yolk and ½ the white of another egg, 1 tablespoon of cold water and a pinch of salt. Mix these ingredients together, using a wooden spatula, gradually incorporating the flour. Chop the lard into small pieces. When a thick batter has formed, add the chopped lard and cover it with the remaining flour from the sides of the bowl. Knead quickly to form a smooth dough. Shape the pastry into a ball and leave it to rest for 4-5 hours or overnight.

Defrost the sole fillets at room temperature, then mince them in a food processor. Melt the butter. Mix the minced sole with 2 eggs, the dill, breadcrumbs, grated lemon zest, the crème fraîche and melted butter. Season generously with salt and pepper.

Preheat the oven to 175⁰-200⁰C (350ß-400ßF, Gas Mark 4-6). Knead the pastry again. Take two-thirds of the pastry and roll it out on a floured work surface. Butter a loaf tin measuring 30 x 11 cm (12 x 4½ ins), and line it with pastry. Use some of the remaining egg white to seal the seams. Make sure that the corners are properly lined and that there are no gaps. Drain the trout fillets and pat

FORELLENHOF TROUT PLATTER

Serves 1

1 leaf of broad-leaved
endive
1 chicory leaf
1 slice of orange
1 smoked trout fillet
2 tsp lemon juice
1 tbsp crème fraîche

1 tsp fresh dill, finely
chopped
1 tsp grated horseradish,
from a jar
salt
pepper

Wash the salad leaves and pat them dry. Remove the skin from the trout fillet. Arrange the salad leaves, trout fillet and slice of orange on a salad plate and sprinkle with the lemon juice.

Mix together the crème fraîche, dill and a few drops of lemon juice, season with salt and pepper. Pour the sauce over the trout fillet and serve the grated horseradish on the side.

Left: *Forellenhof trout platter*
Below: *Trout terrine en croûte*

them dry. Spread half of the sole paté over the pastry base, then place a layer of trout on top. Spread the remaining sole mixture over the trout fillets and press it down lightly. Trim the pastry lining to the shape of the tin, leaving a 1 cm (½ inch) border. Roll out the remaining pastry and cut out a lid. Place the pastry lid on top of the sole paté, brush the edges with egg white and seal them. Make two or three holes, 2-3 cm (¾-1 inch) in diameter, in the pastry lid to allow steam to escape during cooking.

Use the pastry trimmings to decorate the pastry lid, sticking them down with egg white. Place the terrine in the oven and bake for 30 minutes.

Mix together the remaining egg yolk and ½ tablespoon of milk. After 30 minutes, remove the terrine from the oven and brush the lid with the egg and milk mixture, then return the terrine to the oven for a further 45 minutes. Remove the terrine from the oven, carefully loosen the pastry case from the sides of the tin, then leave to cool before turning out.
The terrine will keep for several days in the refrigerator, wrapped in foil.

HERRING FILLETS WITH DILL

Serves 6-8

10 herring fillets	375 ml (12 fl oz) red wine
2-3 red onions	vinegar
5-6 tbsp fresh dill, chopped	2 bay leaves

Peel and thinly slice the onions. Alternately layer the herring fillets, dill and onions in a lidded jar. Place the red wine vinegar and bay leaves in a saucepan, bring them to the boil, then leave to cool.

When the marinade is cool, pour it into the jar over the herring and onions. Close the jar tightly. Leave the herring to marinate in a cool place (but not in the refrigerator) for 2 days.

HERRINGS IN ASPIC

Serves 4

500 g (1 lb) fresh herrings	125 ml (4 fl oz) vinegar
1 leek	1 sachet of white gelatine
1 carrot	1 medium tomato
1 turnip	1 egg, hard boiled
1 stick of celery	1 gherkin
1 onion	oil
3 chillies	salt
1 bay leaf	1 egg white, if necessary,
fresh parsley	to clear the stock

Peel and chop the carrot, onion and turnip; wash, trim and chop the leek and celery. Put 500 ml (18 fl oz) water in a saucepan and bring it to the boil. Add the salt, chillies, bay leaf, parsley, chopped vegetables and onions to the water and simmer for about 15 minutes.

Gut the herrings, remove the heads and rinse the fish under cold, running water. Add the herrings to the vegetable stock and poach them for 10-15 minutes. Then take them out of the stock, remove the skin, take the flesh off the bones and leave it to cool. Strain the stock through a sieve. Reserve 375 ml (12 fl oz) of stock, adding water, if necessary, to make up the required amount.

Add the vinegar to the stock and season it with salt. (If the stock is cloudy, clear it as follows: crush an egg shell and mix it with an egg white and 3 tablespoons of cold water. Add the egg mixture to the stock. Heat the stock through again, stirring briskly all the time, but do not allow it to boil. In this way the egg white thickens and congeals the particles in the stock. Leave the stock to settle until it is completely clear.) Skim the stock and strain it through a muslin cloth. Dissolve the gelatine powder in 5 tablespoons of cold water. Leave it to rest for 10 minutes. Add the gelatine to the hot stock, stirring until the gelatine has completely dissolved.

Brush a mould with oil. Pour a little stock into the mould and put it in the refrigerator to set. Slice the tomato, hard-boiled egg and gherkin into rings and arrange them in the mould on top of the aspic. Pour a few tablespoons of stock over the vegetables and return the mould to the refrigerator to set again. Dice the cold herrings, arrange them on top of the layer of aspic, and pour the remaining aspic, which should already have started to thicken, on top of them. Leave the mould in the refrigerator to set.

Before serving, dip the mould in hot water to loosen the aspic, and then run a knife around the edge before turning out.

Opposite: *Herring fillets with dill*
Right: *Herrings in cream*

HERRING COCKTAIL

Serves 4-6

4 herring fillets
200 g (7 oz) French beans, cooked
2 tsp oil
2 tsp vinegar
2 tsp fresh dill, chopped
a few lettuce leaves
2 tbsp mayonnaise

2 tbsp white wine
2 tbsp crème fraîche
1 tbsp horseradish, from a jar
3 tbsp tomato ketchup
fresh dill
salt
pepper

Drain the French beans, pat them dry and chop into small pieces. Mix together the oil, vinegar and dill. Season with salt and pepper. Pour the dressing over the French beans and mix well. Gently rinse the herring fillets and dry them. Cut the fillets into thin strips. Garnish 4-6 individual cocktail dishes with salad leaves and divide the French beans and herring strips amongst them. Mix together the mayonnaise, white wine, crème fraîche, horseradish and tomato ketchup. Pour the dressing over the herring cocktails, and decorate them with a little ketchup and a few sprigs of dill.

HERRINGS IN CREAM

Serves 6-8

6 marinated herrings
1 small onion
250 g (8 oz) cream

juice of 1 lemon
or vinegar
salt and pepper

Cut the herrings into thin strips. Peel and grate the onion. Mix together the cream, onion, salt and pepper. Adjust the seasoning to taste with the lemon juice or vinegar. Pour the cream mixture over the herring strips and leave to marinate for several hours.

CRAB MAYONNAISE

Serves 4

375 g (12 oz) crab meat,
fresh or frozen
1 egg, separated
1 tbsp lemon juice
1 tbsp tomato ketchup
125 ml (4 fl oz) oil
a few lettuce leaves

slices of lemon
cocktail cherries
fresh fines herbes (parsley,
chervil,
tarragon, chives), chopped
salt

Place the egg yolk, lemon juice, tomato ketchup and salt in a basin and whisk like a mayonnaise, adding the oil to the egg mixture in a slow, steady stream, whisking all the time.

Line 4 individual salad plates with lettuce leaves. Divide the crab meat amongst the dishes and pour the mayonnaise over the meat. Garnish the salads, as desired, with lemon slices, cocktail cherries and fresh, chopped herbs.

PRAWN COCKTAIL

Serves 2-3

300 g (10 oz) Dublin Bay
prawn tails, cooked
2 knobs of butter
1 clove of garlic
½ bunch fresh dill,
chopped

150 g (5 oz) crème fraîche
3 tbsp sherry
Worcester sauce
1 tsp lemon juice
4 lettuce leaves
salt and pepper

Melt the butter in a frying pan. Peel and crush the garlic and add it to the frying pan with the chopped dill and prawns. Brown the mixture quickly over a high heat, season with salt. Leave to cool.

Mix together the crème fraîche, sherry, a few drops of Worcester sauce and the lemon juice. Season the dressing with salt and pepper. Line 4 individual salad plates with lettuce, arrange the prawns on top and cover with the dressing. Sprinkle chopped dill over the prawn cocktails.

MACKEREL MARINATED IN DILL

Serves 6-8

1 kg (2 lb) mackerel fillets
2-3 red onions
125 ml (4 fl oz) vinegar
10 peppercorns
2 bay leaves

a few juniper berries
1 bunch of fresh dill,
chopped
salt

Peel the onions and slice them into rings. Arrange the mackerel fillets in a salad bowl, cover them with the onion rings.

In a saucepan mix together the vinegar, 250 ml (8 fl oz) water, the peppercorns, bay leaves, juniper berries, and salt, and bring them to the boil. After simmering for 5 minutes, remove the marinade from the heat and leave to cool. Then pour the marinade over the fish fillets and leave to marinate for 1-2 days. Just before serving, sprinkle chopped dill over the mackerel.

PAUPIETTES DE SOLE À LA NICOISE

Serves 4

800 g (1½ lb) fillets of sole
or 12 fillets
125 ml (4 fl oz) white wine
6 peppercorns
4 tbsp wholegrain mustard
4 tbsp vinegar
12 artichoke hearts, tinned
2-3 large tomatoes

1 egg yolk
125 ml (4 fl oz) oil
4 tbsp cream
1 tbsp fresh chives,
chopped
1 tbsp fresh parsley,
chopped
salt and pepper

Below: *Crab mayonnaise*
Right: *Paupiettes de sole à la nicoise*

Roll up the fillets of sole and secure them with cocktail sticks. In a saucepan mix together the white wine, 125 ml (4 fl oz) water, the peppercorns and 3 tablespoons of mustard, 2 tablespoons of vinegar, salt and a pinch of pepper and bring them to the boil. Add the sole rolls to the liquid and poach them for 5 minutes, them remove them and leave them to cool. Remove the cocktail sticks from the sole rolls.

To make the herb dressing: mix together the egg yolk, 2 tablespoons of vinegar, 1 tablespoon of mustard, oil, cream, chives and parsley; season with salt and pepper. Drain the artichoke hearts, sprinkle them with salt. Wash the tomatoes and slice them into rings.

Spread the dressing over the serving dish, put the artichoke hearts on top, then a slice of tomato on top of each heart and finish with a paupiette of sole. Secure the layers with a cocktail stick.

GERONA TOMATO SALAD

Serves 3-4

500 g (1 lb) tomatoes
2 large onions
2 cloves of garlic
1 egg, hard boiled
3 tbsp oil
2 tbsp vinegar

½ tsp mustard
75 g (3 oz) bacon
2-3 tbsp fresh basil, chopped
salt and pepper

Bring a saucepan of water to the boil. Blanch the tomatoes in the boiling water for a few seconds, then refresh them in cold water. When cold, slice into rings. Peel the onions, slice into rings and place them in a salad bowl with the tomatoes.

Peel and finely chop the garlic. Shell the hard-boiled egg, dice the white and reserve it, mash the yolk until smooth. Mix together the oil, vinegar, mustard, salt, pepper, garlic and egg yolk and pour the dressing over the tomatoes and onions. Grill the bacon until crisp, then chop it into small pieces. Mix the grilled bacon with the diced egg white and scatter the mixture over the tomato salad. Sprinkle fresh, chopped basil over the salad.

MIXED SALAD

Serves 6-8

1 small lettuce
1 red pepper
1 green pepper
4 large tomatoes
3-4 small onions
½ cucumber
1 small tin sweetcorn
250 g (8 oz) tin tuna in brine

300 g (10 oz) crème fraîche
2-3 tbsp tomato ketchup
2-3 tbsp milk
fresh parsley, chopped
fresh dill, chopped
fresh chives, chopped
salt
pepper

Wash the lettuce. Tear the large leaves into smaller pieces. Slice the peppers in half, remove the cores and seeds and slice the flesh thinly. Slice the tomatoes into rings. Peel and slice the onions. Slice the cucumber very thinly. Drain the sweetcorn and tuna. Place all these ingredients in a large salad bowl and mix them together.

Mix together the crème fraîche, tomato ketchup and milk; season the dressing with salt and pepper and pour it over the salad. Sprinkle with fresh, chopped parsley, dill and chives.

TOMATO AND TUNA SALAD

Serves 4-5

500 g (1 lb) tomatoes
200 g (7 oz) tuna in oil
2 large red onions
3 tbsp oil
2 tbsp red wine vinegar

2 tbsp fresh parsley, chopped
salt
pepper

Slice the tomatoes. Peel and slice the onions. Drain the tuna and add it to the salad, flaking the flesh with a fork. Mix together the oil, vinegar, salt and pepper. Pour the vinaigrette dressing over the salad and sprinkle with fresh, chopped parsley.

Mix together the crème fraîche and Pernod; season the dressing with salt and pepper.

Line 4 individual glass dishes with lettuce leaves. Divide the salad amongst the dishes and pour the dressing on top. Garnish the salads with the reserved broccoli florets and chopped pistachio nuts.

GRATED CARROT AND WALNUT SALAD

Serves 6-8

750 g (1¼ lb) carrots
5-6 tbsp lemon juice
4 tbsp walnut oil
75 g (3 oz) walnuts

a few lettuce leaves
a few slices of unwaxed lemon
salt
pepper

Peel and grate the carrots. Mix together the lemon juice and oil, season with salt and pepper and pour the dressing over the grated carrots. Coarsely chop the walnuts, mix them into the carrots and leave the salad for approximately 15 minutes for the flavours to combine.

Line a large salad bowl, or individual dishes, with lettuce. Divide the carrot salad amongst the bowls and garnish with lemon slices.

Opposite: *Gerona tomato salad*
Below: *Broccoli salad*

BROCCOLI SALAD

Serves 4

250 g (8 oz) broccoli
3 tomatoes
125 g (4 oz) Gruyëre cheese
150 g (5 oz) crème fraîche

1 glass of Pernod, approx.
200 ml (7 fl oz)
a few lettuce leaves
pistachio nuts, chopped
salt and pepper

Bring a saucepan of salted water to the boil. Wash the broccoli. Immerse it in the boiling water, cook for 10-12 minutes, then drain it and leave it to cool. When it is cool, break the broccoli up into small florets, reserving a few for the garnish.
Bring another saucepan of water to the boil and blanch the tomatoes in the boiling water for a few seconds, then remove them and refresh them in cold water. Skin and dice the tomatoes. Chop the cheese into small cubes.

POTATO SALAD

Serves 6-8

750 g (1½ lb) potatoes,
boiled in their skins
200 g (7 oz) boiled beef
1 leek
150 g (5 oz) chanterelle
mushrooms

3-4 tomatoes
1 large onion
6 tbsp oil
3 tbsp vinegar
1 tsp mustard
salt and pepper

Peel and slice the potatoes whilst still hot. Dice the beef.
Wash and trim the leek, cut in half lengthways and cut
into thin strips. Melt a little butter in a frying pan and fry
the chanterelle mushrooms until brown. Drain them and
cut them in half, if necessary. Bring a saucepan of water
to the boil. Blanch the tomatoes in the boiling water for a
few seconds, refresh them in cold water, then skin,
deseed and dice them. Mix together the potatoes, meat,
leek, mushrooms and tomatoes. Peel and dice the onion.

Mix together the oil, vinegar and mustard, add the onion,
season the dressing with salt and pepper. Pour the
vinaigrette dressing over the salad, toss the salad, and
leave it to rest for 1 hour before serving.

CHINESE LEAF SALAD

Serves 5-6

600 g (1¼ lb) Chinese leaf
1 small onion
3 tbsp oil

2 tbsp vinegar
2 tbsp tomato ketchup
1 tsp mustard
salt and pepper

Slice the Chinese leaf into thin ribbons. Peel and dice the
onion, and mix it with the oil, vinegar, tomato ketchup
and mustard. Season the dressing with salt and pepper.
Pour the vinaigrette dressing over the salad and toss to
coat the Chinese leaf thoroughly. Serve immediately.

ENDIVE WITH MUSHROOMS

Serves 2-4

½ a broad leaf endive
2-3 sticks of celery
200 g (7 oz) mushrooms
4 anchovy fillets
3 tbsp oil

2 tbsp wine vinegar
1 tbsp crème fraîche
1 tbsp shelled nuts
salt and pepper

Remove the outer leaves from the endive, then slice it into thin ribbons. Wash the celery, remove any string and chop the celery finely. Slice the mushrooms thinly. Mix everything together in a salad bowl.

Mash the anchovy fillets. Mix together the oil, vinegar, crème fraîche, salt, pepper and shelled nuts. Pour the dressing over the salad and garnish it with the mashed anchovies.

SPANISH ENDIVE AND PEPPER SALAD

Serves 5-6

1 broad leaf endive	4 tbsp olive oil
2 green or red peppers	3 tbsp vinegar
10 stuffed green olives	paprika
1 onion	mustard, salt, pepper
1 egg, hard boiled	

Wash the endive and cut it into thin ribbons. Cut the peppers in half, remove the stalks, cores and seeds. Slice the peppers thinly. Slice the olives. Mix all the salad ingredients together. Peel and finely dice the onion. Shell the hard-boiled egg, separate the white from the yolk and mash each separately.

Mix together the diced onion, egg yolk, olive oil, vinegar, salt, pepper, mustard and paprika. Pour the dressing over the salad, then scatter the mashed egg white on top. Serve immediately.

RED CABBAGE AND TUNA SALAD

Serves 4-5

250 g (8 oz) red cabbage	3 tbsp oil
200 g (7 oz) tin tuna in brine	2-3 tbsp vinegar
3 eggs, hard boiled	salt
	pepper

Separate the red cabbage leaves from the stalk, wash them and pat them dry. Drain and mash the tuna. Slice the hard-boiled eggs. Place them all together in a salad bowl. Mix together the oil, vinegar, salt and pepper. Pour the dressing over the red cabbage, tuna and eggs and mix well. If necessary, adjust the seasoning.

STUFFED AVOCADOS

Serves 4

2 ripe avocados	sugar
juice of ½ lemon	150 g (5 oz) crème fraîche
250 g (8 oz) strawberries	1-3 tbsp Grenadine
1 kiwi fruit	

Cut the avocados in half, remove the stone, and cut out the flesh without damaging the skin. Dice the flesh and sprinkle it with lemon juice. Wash the strawberries and pat them dry, hull them and cut the biggest ones in half. Slice the kiwi fruit. Mix together the fruit and diced avocado and sprinkle sugar on top. Stuff the avocado shells with this mixture.

Mix together the crème fraîche and Grenadine. Set the avocados on a bed of ice cubes and pour the sauce over the top.

Below: *Red cabbage and tuna salad*
Left: *Endive with mushrooms and Spanish endive and pepper salad.*

ARTICHOKE HEARTS WITH PRAWNS

Serves 6-8

14-16 artichoke hearts,
tinned
juice of 1 lemon
Worcester sauce
250-300 g (8-10 oz) prawns,
frozen
a few lettuce leaves

4-5 tbsp tomato ketchup
3 tbsp crème fraîche
1 tbsp brandy
stuffed olives
salt
pepper

Line a serving dish with lettuce leaves. Drain the artichoke hearts, arrange them on the serving dish and sprinkle them with a few drops of lemon juice and Worcester sauce. Divide the prawns amongst the artichoke hearts.

Mix together the tomato ketchup, crème fraîche and brandy. Season the dressing with salt and pepper. Pour the dressing over the prawns. Slice the olives and use them to decorate the artichoke hearts and prawns.

MUSHROOM STUFFED TOMATOES

Serves 4

4 medium tomatoes
150 g (5 oz) mushrooms
juice of 1 lemon
white wine
knob of butter

2 tbsp crème fraîche
2 slices boiled ham
fresh chives, snipped
salt
pepper

Slice the tops off the tomatoes and scoop out the seeds. Sprinkle salt and pepper inside them. Thinly slice the mushrooms and drizzle them with lemon juice. Pour a little white wine into a pan and heat it, add the mushrooms to the pan and poach them until tender. Remove the pan from the heat and leave the mushrooms to cool. Melt the butter in a frying pan, add the mushrooms and crème fraîche to the pan, stirring all the time. Bring the mushroom mixture briefly to the boil. Finely chop the ham, add it to the mushroom mixture and season with salt and pepper if necessary. Fill the tomatoes with the mushroom and ham mixture, dotting the tops with butter. Place the tomatoes under a hot grill or in a hot oven for about 15 minutes until brown. Sprinkle with chopped chives before serving.

HAWAIIAN ASPARAGUS SALAD

Serves 5-6

500 g (1 lb) asparagus tips, tinned	2 tbsp crème fraîche
250 g (8 oz) prawns, frozen	1 tbsp sherry
5 tbsp mayonnaise	juice of 1 lemon
	2 oranges

Drain the asparagus thoroughly and defrost the prawns at room temperature. Mix together the asparagus and prawns.

Mix together the mayonnaise, crème fraîche and sherry. Slice the oranges in half, scoop out the flesh and chop it finely. Add the chopped orange to the asparagus and prawns, and fill the orange shells with the mixture. Pour the dressing over the top and serve chilled.

GREEK TOMATO SALAD

Serves 5

500 g (1 lb) tomatoes	3 mint leaves, chopped
15 olives	or 1 tbsp fresh fines herbes
150 g (5 oz) feta cheese	(parsley,
3 tbsp oil	chervil, tarragon chives),
2 tbsp lemon juice	chopped
1 onion	salt and pepper

Slice the tomatoes thinly. Dice the feta cheese. Arrange the tomatoes on a dish with the olives and diced feta cheese. Mix together the oil and lemon juice, season the dressing with salt and pepper. Peel and dice the onion, add it to the dressing with the mint or fines herbes. Pour the dressing over the salad. Leave to marinate for 15 minutes before serving.

SPICY RED CABBAGE SALAD

Serves 4-5

500 g (1 lb) red cabbage	1 tsp mustard
1 onion	salt
1-2 tbsp golden syrup	pepper
2-3 tbsp vinegar	

PSlice the red cabbage very finely. Peel and thinly slice the onion. Mix together the golden syrup, vinegar and mustard; season the dressing with salt and pepper. Pour the dressing over the cabbage and onion, coat the cabbage and onion thoroughly in the dressing and serve immediately.

SPRING SALAD WITH EGGS

Serves 2

1 black radish	1 tbsp sherry
½ cucumber	1 egg, hard boiled
2 tomatoes	1 tbsp fresh chives,
a few lettuce leaves	chopped
4 tbsp cream	salt
1 tsp mild mustard	pepper

Slice the radish, cucumber and tomatoes into rounds. Make a bed of lettuce in 2 individual dishes and arrange the sliced radish, cucumber and tomato on top. Mix together the cream, mustard and sherry, season the dressing with salt and pepper. Pour the dressing over the salad. Shell the egg and cut it into 4. Arrange the slices of egg on top of the salads. Sprinkle fresh, chopped chives over the salad.

Left: *Mushroom stuffed tomatoes*
Below: *Spring salad with eggs*

BEEF SALAD WITH CHÂTELAINE DRESSING

Serves 4

200 g (7 oz) boiled beef
100 g (3½ oz) lean raw ham
1 tbsp capers
1 onion
2 gherkins
4 eggs, hard boiled
4 tbsp fresh chives,
snipped

Worcester sauce
125 ml (4 fl oz) cream
4 tbsp mayonnaise
2 tbsp mustard
90 g (3½ oz) lumpfish roe
a few lettuce leaves
salt

Dice the beef, ham and the gherkins. Peel and slice the onion. Drain the capers. Shell and finely chop the eggs. Place all these ingredients in a salad bowl and mix well. Add the chopped chives, season the mixture with salt and a little Worcester sauce.

Mix together the cream, mayonnaise, mustard and some of the lumpfish roe. Place a bed of lettuce in the bottom of 4 individual salad bowls, divide the salad mixture amongst the dishes, and pour some of the dressing on top of each.

Decorate the salads with the remaining lumpfish roe. Serve the remaining dressing separately.

LOBSTER SALAD LOREN

Serves 2

450 g (15 oz) lobster meat,
cooked
2 tomatoes
½ tin of sweetcorn
12 stuffed olives
1 carton of natural yoghurt

1 tbsp fresh fines herbes
(parsley, chervil, tarragon,
chives) chopped fresh dill
salt
pepper

Flake the lobster meat. Bring a saucepan of water to the boil, blanch the tomatoes in the boiling water for a moment or two, then remove them and refresh them in cold water. Skin and deseed them and chop the flesh into thin strips. Drain the sweetcorn and slice the olives.

Mix together the yoghurt and herbs; season the dressing with salt and pepper. Arrange all the ingredients in individual dishes and pour the dressing over the top. Garnish the salads with sprigs of fresh dill.

GREEN DRESSING

Serves 4

1 bunch of fresh parsley	cress
1 bunch of fresh chives	1 small onion
1 bunch of fresh chervil	150 g (5 oz) crème fraîche
1 bunch of fresh dill	125 g (4 oz) low fat cream
1 bunch of fresh borage	cheese
1 bunch of fresh tarragon	salt
1 bunch of fresh basil	pepper
½ box of mustard and	

Wash the herbs and dry them in a tea towel. Peel the onion. Coarsely chop the herbs and onion, then put them in a food processor with the crème fraîche and cream cheese. Process for several minutes. Season the dressing with salt and pepper.

Serve with a vegetable terrine.

Opposite: *Beef salad with châtelaine dressing*
Below: *Green dressing*

POTATOES IN THEIR SKINS

Serves 4-5

Wash 1 kilogram (2 lb) potatoes, all the same variety and roughly the same size. Fill a saucepan with cold water, add some salt and the potatoes, and a teaspoon of cumin if liked. Bring the saucepan to the boil and simmer the potatoes for 25-30 minutes. When the potatoes are cooked, drain and peel them.

Tip: You can sauté the boiled potatoes in a little oil or butter in a frying pan.

POTATOES IN CHIVE SAUCE

Serves 4-5

1 kg (2 lb) potatoes
30 g (1 oz) butter
30 g (1 oz) flour
250 ml (8 fl oz) milk

½ stock cube
2 tbsp fresh chives,
chopped
salt

Wash the potatoes. Fill a saucepan with water, add the potatoes and salt, bring the pan to the boil and cook the potatoes for 20-30 minutes. Drain the potatoes, peel them whilst still hot, and leave them to cool. Slice them into rounds.

STEAMED POTATOES

Serves 4-5

1 kg (2 lb) potatoes	75 g (3 oz) fatty bacon

Wash, peel and dice the potatoes. Dice the bacon. Fry the bacon in a frying pan until brown, then add the potatoes, season the mixture with salt, cover the pan and cook the bacon and potato mixture for 20-30 minutes. At the end of cooking time, remove the lid from the pan and allow the potatoes to brown.

POTATOES IN MILK

Serves 4-5

1 kg (2 lb) potatoes	125 g (4 oz) lean bacon
600 ml (1 pint) milk	3 onions
45 g (1½ oz) cornflour	salt

Wash and peel the potatoes and cut them into small pieces. Fill a saucepan with salted water, bring it to the boil, add the chopped potatoes and simmer them until cooked. Bring the milk to the boil in a large saucepan. Drain the potatoes, mash two-thirds of them, then add the mashed potato and whole pieces to the boiling milk. Bring the mixture to the boil again. Blend the cornflour with a little water, then use it to thicken the potato mixture. Peel and dice the onions, dice the bacon, then fry the bacon in a frying pan, add the diced onion, and cook them both until golden brown. Arrange the potato mixture on a serving dish, top with fried onions and bacon. Accompany the potato mixture with grilled sausages and a salad.

Above: *Potatoes in chive sauce*
Right: *Potatoes in milk*

To make the chive sauce: Melt the butter in a saucepan, add the flour, stirring all the time, until cooked. Add the milk and ½ stock cube. Whisk the sauce to prevent lumps forming. Bring the sauce to the boil. Season it with salt, add the potatoes and chives and simmer for 10 minutes. Adjust the seasoning if necessary.

POTATO RAGOUT

Serves 4-5

1 kg (2 lb) potatoes
500 ml (18 fl oz) meat stock
knob of butter

1 tbsp fresh parsley,
chopped
salt

Peel, wash and dice the potatoes. Pour the meat stock into a saucepan, add the diced potatoes, bring the pan to the boil, and simmer the potatoes in the stock for 15-20 minutes. Season the stock with salt and add the knob of butter and chopped parsley. Serve the potatoes with fish dishes, uncooked ham or meat in a sauce.
Variation: You can add thinly sliced carrots to the potato mixture.

MASHED POTATO

Serves 4-5

1 kg (2 lb) potatoes
250 ml (8 fl oz) milk

75 g (3 oz) butter nutmeg,
freshly grated and salt

Below: *Potatoes with Gruyère*

Wash, peel and chop the potatoes. Bring a pan of salted water to the boil, add the potatoes and cook them for 20 minutes. When the potatoes are cooked, drain them and mash them immediately using a potato masher or potato ricer. Pour the milk into a saucepan, bring it to the boil, and add it to the mashed potato with the butter.

Return the saucepan to the heat and stir the mashed potato until smooth. Season the potato mixture with salt, if necessary, and add a little grated nutmeg. Mashed potato can also be served topped with fried onion rings or toasted breadcrumbs.

POTATOES WITH GRUYÈRE

IN THE PRESSURE COOKER

Serves 4-5

1 kg (2 lb) potatoes
50 g (2 oz) fatty bacon
2 onions
100 g (3½ oz) Gruyère,
grated

fresh marjoram, chopped
250 ml (8 fl oz) meat stock
2 tbsp fresh chives,
chopped
salt, pepper

Wash and peel the potatoes, then slice them into rounds. Dice the bacon, peel and thinly slice the onions. Fry the diced bacon in the unlidded pressure cooker, then add the sliced onions and fry them both until brown. Add the sliced potatoes. Sprinkle the potato mixture with grated cheese. Season the mixture with salt, pepper and marjoram. Add the stock, put the lid on the pressure cooker and cook the potatoes for 12 minutes. Sprinkle with chopped chives.

POTATOES IN BÉCHAMEL SAUCE

Serves 4-5

1 kg (2 lb) potatoes
2 small onions
40 g (1½ oz) raw ham
30 g (1 oz) butter or
margarine
30 g (1 oz) flour
250 ml (8 fl oz) milk

250 ml (8 fl oz) water
½ stock cube
nutmeg, grated
2 tbsp fresh parsley,
chopped
salt
pepper

Wash the potatoes. Bring a saucepan of salted water to the boil, add the potatoes and cook them for 20-30 minutes. Drain the potatoes and peel them immediately. Leave the potatoes to cool then slice them into rounds.

To make the béchamel sauce: Peel and finely chop the onions, finely chop the ham. Melt the butter in a

saucepan, brown the ham in it and then brown the onions. Add the flour, stirring the mixture all the time, until cooked. Add the milk, water and ½ stock cube. Whisk the sauce to prevent lumps forming, bring it to the boil and cook it for about 5 minutes. Add the sliced potatoes to the sauce, bring it to the boil again, then season it with salt, pepper, nutmeg and chopped parsley.

HERBED MASHED POTATO WITH SCRAMBLED EGGS AND HAM

Serves 4-5

1 kg (2 lb) potatoes	*150 g (5 oz) boiled ham*
50-75 g (2-3 oz) herb butter	*20 g (scant 1 oz) butter or*
250 g (8 oz) butter	*margarine*
nutmeg, grated	*salt and freshly ground*
6 eggs	*pepper*

Above: *Herbed mashed potato with scrambled eggs and ham*

*P*eel, wash and chop the potatoes. Add them to a saucepan of salted water, bring it to the boil and cook the potatoes for about 20 minutes. When cooked, drain the potatoes and mash them immediately with a potato masher or ricer. In a saucepan bring the milk to the boil, then add it to the potatoes with the herb butter. Return the saucepan to the heat and stir the potato mixture until it is smooth. Season the potatoes with salt, pepper and grated nutmeg. Keep the mashed potato warm.

Mix the eggs with a little water, but do not beat them. Season with salt and pepper. Cut the ham into strips. Melt the butter in a frying pan, add the eggs to the pan, and then the ham.

Stir the egg mixture as soon as it starts to set, and cook it for about 5 minutes. The scrambled eggs should be soft and light, but not too dry. Serve the eggs and ham with the herbed mashed potato.

ITALIAN SALAD

Serves 2-3

125 g (4 oz) potatoes,
boiled
100 g (3½ oz) carrots,
boiled
125 g (4 oz) apples
125 g (4 oz) cold cooked
meat or boiled ham
125 g (4 oz) pickled
gherkins
2 anchovy fillets
1 onion
1 tsp fresh parsley,

chopped
1 tsp fresh dill, chopped
1 tsp garlic, chopped
1 tsp fresh salad burnet,
chopped
1 egg yolk
1 tbsp vinegar
1 tsp mustard
100 ml (3½ fl oz) oil
2 tbsp yoghurt
salt

Slice the potatoes and carrots into rounds. Peel and core the apples, then cut them into thin strips. Do the same with the gherkins and meat. Chop the anchovy fillets. Peel and finely chop the onion.

To make the mayonnaise: Using an electric mixer, or whisk, beat together the egg yolk, vinegar, mustard and salt until they form a thick dressing. Add the oil, a couple of tablespoons at a time, and whisk it into the egg mixture. Then add the yoghurt.

Mix together the salad ingredients in a large bowl. Add the mayonnaise, mix to coat the meat and vegetables, then add the chopped herbs. Season the salad with salt and vinegar. Garnish with sliced tomatoes, gherkins and hard-boiled egg.

PARSLEY POTATOES

Serves 4-5

1 kg (2 lb) potatoes, small
and evenly sized, if possible
40 g (1½ oz) butter or
margarine

2 tbsp fresh parsley,
chopped
salt

Wash the potatoes. Bring a saucepan of salted water to the boil, add the potatoes and cook them for 20-30 minutes. As soon as they are cooked, drain and peel them. Leave the potatoes to cool, then slice them into

rounds. Melt the butter in a frying pan, add the potatoes, salt and parsley and fry until the potatoes are golden. (New potatoes are perfect for this dish).

POTATOES WITH MUSTARD SAUCE

Serves 4-5

1 kg (2 lb) potatoes	2 tbsp ready-made
30 g (1 oz) butter or	mustard, e.g. Dijon
margarine	vinegar
30 g (1 oz) flour	salt

Wash the potatoes. Bring a saucepan of salted water to the boil and add the potatoes. Cook them for 20-30 minutes. As soon as they are cooked, drain and peel them. Leave the potatoes to cool, then slice them into rounds.

To make the mustard sauce: Melt the butter in a saucepan, add the flour, stirring all the time, and cook for 1-2 minutes. Add 500 ml (18 fl oz) water and whisk the sauce to prevent lumps from forming. Bring the sauce to the boil and simmer it for 5 minutes. Add the mustard, salt and potatoes and simmer the sauce for a further 10 minutes. Season with vinegar.

POTATO AND CUCUMBER SALAD

Serves 5

750 g (1½ lb) potatoes	yoghurt
1 cucumber	3 tbsp double cream
1 onion	2 bunches fresh dill
150 g (5 oz) natural	salt and pepper

Wash the potatoes. Bring a saucepan of salted water to the boil, add the potatoes, and cook them for 20-30 minutes. Drain them and peel them immediately. Leave the potatoes to cool, then slice them into rounds. Wash and thinly slice the cucumber. Peel and finely chop the onion. Mix all three ingredients together.

In a bowl, mix together the cream and yoghurt, season the mixture well with salt and pepper. Wash and pat dry the dill, then chop it finely and add it to the dressing. Pour the dressing over the potato and cucumber mixture and adjust the seasoning. This salad should be eaten as soon as possible after preparation as the cucumber soon wilts.

Left: *Potato and cucumber salad*
Above: *Potato and herring salad*

POTATO AND HERRING SALAD

Serves 4

4 herring fillets	gherkin
250 g (8 oz) potatoes,	1 egg yolk
cooked in their skins	1-2 tsp mustard
2 eggs, hard boiled	1 tbsp vinegar
200 g (7 oz) smoked	100 ml (3½ fl oz) oil
sausage, cooked	3 tbsp yoghurt
1 apple	salt and pepper
1 large sweet pickled	

Drain the herring fillets and pat them dry. Peel the potatoes and shell the eggs. Skin the sausage. Peel, quarter and core the apple. Dice all these ingredients, as well as the sausage and gherkin. Mix everything together. **To make the mayonnaise:** Using an electric mixer, or whisk, beat together the egg yolk, vinegar, mustard and salt and pepper until they form a thick dressing. Add the oil, a couple of tablespoons at a time, and whisk it into the egg mixture. Then add the yoghurt. Mix the dressing together thoroughly, then pour it over the salad and coat the ingredients in the dressing.

OMELETTE FORESTIÈRE

Serves 2

250 g (8 oz) boiled potatoes
50 g (2 oz) bacon
1 onion
100 g (3½ oz) button
mushrooms

3 eggs
100 ml (3½ fl oz) milk
bunch of fresh chives,
chopped
salt

Dice the boiled potatoes and bacon. Render the bacon in a frying pan. Peel and thinly slice the onion and mushrooms. Add them to the pan with the bacon and fry until golden brown. Then add the potatoes and fry until brown. Beat together the eggs and milk, season with salt, and add the chopped chives. Pour the egg mixture over the potatoes and allow it to set. Add a little butter to the frying pan to prevent the omelette becoming too dry. Once the bottom of the omelette is cooked and the top is set, slide the omelette out of the frying pan onto a warmed plate.

SAUTÉ POTATOES

Serves 4-5

1 kg (2 lb) potatoes   50 g (2 oz) butter, salt

Wash the potatoes. Bring a saucepan of salted water to the boil, add the potatoes to the pan and cook them for 20 minutes. When cooked, drain the boiled potatoes and peel them immediately. Leave them to cool, and when cold, dice them.Melt the butter in a frying pan and add the diced potato. Season the potatoes with salt. Fry the potatoes for about 10 minutes or until golden brown.

Above: *Potato croquettes*
Opposite: *Omelette forestière*

POTATO CROQUETTES

Serves 4

750 g (1½ lb) potatoes
2 egg yolks
1 whole egg
1 heaped tsp cornflour

nutmeg, grated
50 g (2 oz) breadcrumbs
vegetable oil
salt

Wash and peel the potatoes. Bring a saucepan of salted water to the boil, add the potatoes and cook them for 20 minutes. When cooked, drain the potatoes and mash

CRISPS

Serves 2-3

500 g (1 lb) potatoes   *oil, salt*

them immediately, using a potato masher or ricer. Leave the mashed potato to cool.

Beat the two egg yolks and the cornflour into the mashed potato. Season with salt and a little grated nutmeg.

Using your hands, shape the mashed potato into little sausages or balls. Beat the remaining egg, place the breadcrumbs in a shallow plate, then dip the potato croquettes first in the beaten egg, then in the breadcrumbs. Heat the vegetable oil until very hot. Deep fry the potato croquettes in the hot oil for 2-3 minutes until crisp and golden. You can substitute 100 g (3½ oz) of ground almonds for the breadcrumbs.

Peel the potatoes, wash them and slice them very thinly. Divide the potato slices into several piles and pat them dry. Heat the oil until very hot, then immerse the potato slices in the hot oil for 1-2 minutes. As soon as the potato slices start to turn brown, remove them and drain them. When they have gone cold, return them to the oil for a further 3 minutes until they are golden brown and crisp. Drain the crisps in a colander. When they have cooled, sprinkle them with salt.

COUNTRY BREAKFAST

Serves 4

750 g (1½ lb) potatoes
4 small onions
200 g (7 oz) lean bacon
30 g (1 oz) butter or
margarine
3 eggs

3 tbsp milk
paprika
grated nutmeg
2 tbsp fresh chives, finely
chopped
salt and pepper

Wash the potatoes. Bring a saucepan of salted water to the boil, add the potatoes and cook them for 20-25 minutes. When they are cooked, drain them and peel them whilst still hot. Leave them to cool, then slice them. Peel and dice the onion. Dice 75 g (3 oz) of bacon, then render it in a frying pan. Add the butter to the pan and the onions. Fry the onions until brown, add the potatoes and fry until golden. Beat together the eggs and milk. Season the egg mixture with salt, paprika, nutmeg and

pepper. Add the chopped chives and remaining bacon to the egg mixture, then pour it over the fried potatoes. Leave it to set for 10 minutes. Serve the omelette piping hot.

POTATO OMELETTE

Serves 3

500 g (1 lb) potatoes
2 small onions
75 g (3 oz) fatty bacon
120 ml (4 fl oz) milk
3 eggs

1 tbsp fresh parsley,
chopped
1 tbsp fresh chives,
snipped
salt

Wash the potatoes. Bring a saucepan of salted water to the boil and cook the potatoes for about 20 minutes. When cooked, drain them and peel them whilst still hot. Allow them to cool, then slice them. Peel and finely chop the onions. Dice the bacon, and fry it in a frying pan until brown. Add the potatoes and onions and fry them in the

Left:
Potato omelette
Below:
Country breakfast

bacon fat until golden. Beat together the eggs and milk. Season the egg mixture with salt, then add the chopped parsley and chives. Pour the egg mixture over the fried potato, and cook it for 10 minutes until the bottom of the omelette is golden and the top is set. Slide the omelette out of the pan onto a warmed plate. Serve with a green salad.

then add the chips, and fry them until half cooked (for about 2 minutes). (Don't cook too many chips at once or you won't be able move them around in the pan and you will cool down the oil too much).

As soon as the chips are golden brown, remove them with a skimming spoon or slotted spoon, put them in a colander, drain them and leave them to cool. When they are cold, return them to the hot oil and fry them again until crisp (about 4-5 minutes). Sprinkle the chips with salt and serve immediately.

CHIVE PANCAKES STUFFED WITH FROMAGE FRAIS

Serves 4

1 kg (2 lb) potatoes	1 tbsp lemon juice
2 small onions	1 small clove of garlic
1-2 tbsp flour	125 g (4 oz) boiled ham
3 eggs	1 bunch of parsley
1 bunch fresh chives	150 g (5 oz) lard, or use oil
500 g (1 lb) fromage frais	salt and pepper
100 ml (3½ fl oz) milk	

Peel, wash and grate the potatoes and onions. Add the flour, eggs and salt to the potato and onion mixture. Rinse, pat dry and finely chop the chives. Add half of the chopped chives to the potato mixture.

Season the fromage frais with salt and pepper. Add the remaining chives to the fromage frais with the milk and lemon juice. Peel the clove of garlic and chop or crush it. Dice the ham. Wash, pat dry and finely chop the parsley.

Add the garlic, ham and parsley to the fromage frais.

Melt the lard in a frying pan, then place a tablespoon full of potato mixture in the frying pan and flatten it down to form a small pancake. Make several pancakes in this way and add them to the pan. Fry the pancakes on both sides for 6-8 minutes. Remove the pancakes from the frying pan and arrange them on a serving dish. Spread the fromage frais over half the potato pancakes and top the filling with the remaining pancakes.

BAKED POTATOES

Serves 4

8 medium-sized potatoes	butter
aluminium foil	

Preheat the oven to 200-225⁰C (400-425⁰F, Gas Mark 6-7). Wash the potatoes and dry them. Wrap each one individually in aluminium foil. Place the potatoes on a baking sheet and bake them in the oven for 40-60 minutes. When they are cooked, open the foil parcel, cut a cross in the top of each potato, turn back the corners of the foil and loosen the centre of each potato. Place a knob of butter in the centre of each.

Accompany the jacket potatoes with yoghurt or sour cream flavoured with herbs, tomatoes and salad.

CHIPS

Serves 4

1 kg (2 lb) potatoes	salt
oil	

Peel the potatoes, wash them, and cut them into sticks. Dry them in a tea towel. Put sufficient oil in a pan to immerse the chips completely. Heat the oil until very hot,

Above: *Baked potatoes*
Right: *Chive pancakes stuffed with fromage frais.*

POTATO DOORMATS

Serves 4

1 kg (2 lb) potatoes	40 g (1½ oz) butter, salt

Wash the potatoes. Bring a saucepan of salted water to the boil, add the potatoes to the pan and cook them for about 3 minutes. Drain them and peel them immediately. Leave them to cool, then grate them. Melt the butter in a frying pan and add half the grated potato, flattening it out over the base of the frying pan, season with salt and cook it for 10 minutes until golden brown. Turn the doormat out onto a plate and slide it back into the frying pan the other way up, so that the raw side cooks for 10 minutes. Add a little oil to the pan if necessary. Once the doormat is crisp and golden, remove it from the pan and keep it warm. Make a second doormat with the remaining grated potato. The potato doormat makes a very good accompaniment to thinly sliced meat in gravy or a sauce and a green salad.

POTATO FRITTERS

Serves 5-6

1 kg (2 lb) potatoes	2 tsp salt
500 g (1 lb) flour	150 ml (¼ pint) milk
1 sachet dried yeast	250 g (8 oz) raisins
2 eggs	200 ml (7 fl oz) oil

Sieve the flour into a large bowl and mix it carefully with the yeast. Peel, wash and grate the potatoes. Heat the milk in a saucepan. Add the potatoes to the flour with the eggs, salt and hot milk. Mix everything together, then pour the batter into a food processor and process, first of all slowly, then on a high speed, to mix the batter thoroughly. Turn the batter out of the food processor into a large bowl, stir the raisins gently into the batter, then leave it in a warm place until doubled in volume. Return

the batter to the processor and mix again on a high speed. Heat a little oil in a frying pan, and place spoonfuls of batter in the hot oil. Cook the fritters on each side until golden brown, then remove them from the frying pan and sprinkle them with salt.

POTATO PIZZA BASE

Serves 4-6

1½ kg (3½ lb) potatoes
250 ml (8 fl oz) double cream
4 eggs, beaten
2 tsp fresh oregano, chopped
100 g (3½ oz) Parmesan

cheese, grated
knob of butter
500 g (1 lb) tomatoes
300 g (10 oz) mozzarella
100 g (3½ oz) salami, sliced
salt and pepper

Above: *Potato fritters*
Left: *Potato doormats*

Preheat the oven to 200-225⁰ C (400-425⁰ F, Gas Mark 6-7). Peel and wash the potatoes. Mix together the cream and beaten eggs. Grate the potatoes and add them immediately to the beaten eggs. Add the Parmesan and oregano to the egg mixture. Butter a baking sheet. Pour the potato mixture onto the baking sheet and place it in the oven on as high a shelf as possible. Cook the potato pizza for about 20 minutes. Wash and slice the tomatoes. Cut the mozzarella into slices. Garnish the pizza base with the tomatoes and sliced salami. Season the base with salt and top with the mozzarella. Return the pizza to the oven, this time on as low a shelf as possible, and cook it for 20 minutes. Switch off the oven and leave the pizza to cool for 5 minutes. Sprinkle the pizza with pepper before serving.

GRATIN DAUPHINOIS

Serves 4

1 kg (2 lb) potatoes
1 tbsp fresh parsley,
chopped
½ tsp fresh thyme,
chopped
knob of butter

1 clove of garlic
100 g (3½ oz) cheese,
grated
400 ml (14 fl oz) cream
salt and pepper

Preheat the oven to 225-250°C (425-475°F, Gas Mark 7-9). Peel and wash the potatoes. Slice them thinly. Sprinkle the sliced potato with salt, pepper, parsley and thyme. Butter a large gratin dish. Peel and chop

or crush the garlic clove and scatter it across the base of the gratin dish. Layer the potato slices in the dish and top them with grated cheese. Pour the cream over the potatoes. Place the dish in the oven for 30-40 minutes and cook the potatoes until crisp and brown on top.

Tip: Gratin dauphinois can either accompany roast meats or be served as a dish on its own.

CUMIN POTATOES

Serves 6

1 kg (2 lb) new potatoes	cumin
1 tbsp oil	salt

Below:
Gratin dauphinois
Opposite:
Cumin potatoes

*P*reheat the oven to 200°C (400°F, Gas Mark 6). Carefully wash the potatoes but do not peel them. If necessary, cut them in half. Dip them in the oil and toss them in the salt, then in the cumin. Put them all on a large sheet of aluminium foil. Wrap the potatoes up in the aluminium foil and bake them in the oven, on a middle shelf, for 30 minutes.

TYROLEAN PASTA WITH CABBAGE

Serves 4-5

1 white cabbage, approx.
1 kg (2 lb) in weight
2 large onions
75 g (3 oz) lard

250 g (8 oz) pasta
250 g (8 oz) garlic sausage
salt and pepper

Cut the cabbage into thin strips, wash them and drain them thoroughly. Peel and finely dice the onions. Melt the lard in a cast-iron casserole dish, add the onions to the casserole dish, then the cabbage. Season the vegetables with salt and pepper. Cover the dish and cook the vegetables for 25 minutes until tender, stirring them from time to time.

In a saucepan bring 2-3 litres (3½-5 pints) salted water to the boil, add the pasta to the pan and cook it for 10 minutes, stirring from time to time. Drain the pasta. Remove the skin from the sausage and cut it into small pieces. Mix together the cabbage, pasta and garlic sausage. Return the casserole dish to the heat and heat through again, stirring frequently. Adjust the seasoning.

PASTA WITH HERBS

Serves 3

250 g (8 oz) green ribbon
pasta, e.g. tagliatelle
40 g (1½ oz) butter
300 g (10 oz) tomatoes
300 g (10 oz) crème fraîche
nutmeg, grated

1 tbsp fresh chervil,
chopped
Parmesan cheese, grated
fresh basil
salt and pepper

PASTA WITH MUSSELS

Serves 6

250 g (8 oz) pasta
500 g (1 lb) mussels, from a jar
1 tbsp oil
80 g (3 oz) butter
2 cloves of garlic

250 g (8 oz) button mushrooms
1 bunch of fresh parsley
1 clove of garlic
salt and pepper

*I*n a saucepan bring 2-3 litres (3½-5 pints) salted water to the boil. Add the oil and then the pasta. Cook the pasta for about 15 minutes. Drain it into a colander, rinse it under cold, running water and leave it to drain.

Melt 40 g (1½ oz) butter in a saucepan and toss the pasta in the butter. Turn the pasta out into a large bowl and keep it warm. Peel and finely chop all 3 cloves of garlic. Wipe the mushrooms, then slice them thinly. Wash, pat dry and finely chop the parsley. Drain the mussels, reserving the liquid.

Melt 40 g (1½ oz) butter in a frying pan, add two-thirds of the garlic, then the mushrooms and parsley and brown them in the butter for 5 minutes. Add a little of the liquid from the mussels, then cover the frying pan with a lid and simmer the mushrooms and garlic for about 10 minutes. Add the mussels and heat them through. Season the mixture with salt, pepper and the remaining chopped garlic. Pour the mussel mixture over the pasta and serve immediately

Above: *Tyrolean pasta with cabbage*
Opposite: *Pasta with mussels*

*B*ring a saucepan with 1½ litres (2½ pints) salted water to the boil. Add the pasta to the pan and cook it for 8-10 minutes, stirring occasionally. Drain the pasta.

Wash and drain the tomatoes. Bring a saucepan of water to the boil, blanch the tomatoes in the boiling water for a few moments, then refresh them in cold water, and skin, de-seed and dice them.

Melt 40 g (1½ oz) butter and toss the pasta in the butter. Add the tomatoes and crème fraîche and heat them through, stirring all the time. Season the pasta with salt and pepper. Sprinkle a little grated nutmeg over the pasta. Just before serving, sprinkle the pasta with your choice of grated Parmesan, chopped chervil and basil leaves.

PASTA WITH LEMON

Serves 6

400 g (13 oz) ribbon pasta
1 unwaxed lemon
500 ml (18 fl oz) double
cream
3-4 tbsp aquavit

juice of 1 lemon
60 g (2½ oz) Parmesan,
grated
salt and pepper

*I*n a saucepan bring 3-4 litres (5-7 pints) salted water to the boil, add the pasta and cook it for 8-10 minutes, stirring from time to time. Drain the pasta and keep it hot.

To make the sauce: Wash and dry the lemon, grate the zest and reserve it. Remove the pith from the lemon, finely dice the lemon flesh and mix it with the cream and aquavit.
Pour the cream mixture into a saucepan, bring it to the boil and simmer it for 5 minutes. Add the lemon juice and simmer the sauce for a further 5 minutes. Season the sauce with salt and pepper. Mix the pasta with the sauce and grated parmesan. Arrange the pasta on a serving dish and garnish with the lemon zest.

Tip: Pasta with lemon makes a wonderful accompaniment to escalopes and grilled chicken breasts.

PASTA WITH SALMON

Serves 4-5

300 g (10 oz) tomatoes
100 g (3½ oz) smoked
salmon, sliced
2 cloves of garlic
60 g (2½ oz) black olives,
stoned
3 tbsp olive oil

300 g (10 oz) crème fraîche
1 tsp fresh mint, chopped
½ tsp fresh oregano,
chopped
400 g (13 oz) thin pasta
salt and pepper

*B*ring a saucepan of water to the boil. Blanch the tomatoes in the boiling water for a few moments, then refresh them in cold water. Skin, halve and de-seed them; mash the flesh. Cut the smoked salmon into thin strips. Peel and finely chop the garlic.

Finely chop the stoned olives. Heat the oil in a frying pan and brown the garlic in it. Add the chopped olives and salmon strips, stirring gently. Leave the salmon and olives to cook for 2-3 minutes. Add the cream, stirring all the time, then add the tomato pulp. Season the mixture with salt, pepper, chopped mint and oregano. Keep the sauce hot. Bring a saucepan with 3-4 litres (5-7 pints) salted water to the boil. Cook the pasta in the boiling water for 8-10 minutes, stirring occasionally.
Drain the pasta. Arrange the pasta on a serving dish, pour the sauce over the pasta, and garnish with strips of smoked salmon and black olives.

PASTA WITH PARSLEY
IN THE PRESSURE COOKER
Serves 3

250 g (8 oz) pasta
oil
50 g (2 oz) butter
20 g (¾ oz) breadcrumbs

1 tbsp fresh parsley,
chopped
salt

heat everything through, stirring well, so that the pasta is coated in butter, breadcrumbs and chopped parsley.

PASTA VERDE WITH MUSHROOMS

Serves 4-5

400 g (13 oz) pasta verde	*mushrooms*
1 tbsp oil	*75 g (3 oz) herb butter*
1 clove of garlic	*1 tsp black peppercorns,*
250 g (8 oz) spring onions	*crushed*
750 g (1½ lb) button	*salt*

*I*n a saucepan bring 3 litres (5 pints) salted water to the boil. Add the pasta and oil to the pan. Peel the clove of garlic, chop it finely or crush it and add it to the saucepan. Boil the pasta for 8-10 minutes, stirring occasionally. Drain the pasta, cool it under cold, running water and leave it to drain.

Trim the spring onions, leaving about 15 cm (6 ins) green. Wash and chop them. Wipe the mushrooms.

Melt 50 g (2 oz) butter in a saucepan. Add the spring onions to the pan and brown them, then add the mushrooms and sweat them for 10-15 minutes. Add the pasta to the pan with the mushrooms and peppercorns and season. Add a further 25 g (1 oz) butter to the pan. Toss the pasta in the butter and serve immediately.

Above: *Pasta with lemon*
Right: *Pasta verde with mushrooms*

*P*lace 1½ litres (2½ pints) water in a pressure cooker. Salt the water, then add the pasta and a drop of oil. Close the pressure cooker and cook the pasta until the valve starts to hiss. Remove the pressure cooker from the heat and allow the steam to escape slowly. Drain the pasta, rinse it under cold, running water and leave it to drain.

Melt the butter in the unlidded pressure cooker and fry the breadcrumbs in the melted butter until crisp and golden brown. Add the pasta and parsley to the pan, and

CLASSIC LASAGNE

Serves 4

250 g (8 oz) lasagne verde
80 g (3 oz) butter
300 g (10 oz) minced meat
100 g (3½ oz) celery
2 carrots
1 onion
5 cloves of garlic
150 ml (¼ pint) red wine
70 g (3 oz) tomato purée

50 g (2 oz) flour
400 ml (14 fl oz) meat stock
250 g (8 oz) double cream
70 g (3 oz) Parmesan,
grated
nutmeg, grated
salt
pepper

*I*n a saucepan bring 2 litres (3½ pints) salted water to the boil. Cook the sheets of lasagne in the boiling water, one by one, for about 5 minutes each, then immerse them in cold water and leave them there.

To make the filling: Melt 30 g (1 oz) butter in a frying pan and brown the minced meat in it. Peel the carrots and celery, wash and grate them. Peel the onion and cloves of garlic, finely chop the onion and crush the garlic. Add them to the meat with the vegetables, allow them to brown, then add the wine. Season the filling with salt and pepper. Add the tomato purée.

To make the béchamel sauce: Melt 50 g (2 oz) butter in a saucepan. Add the flour, stirring all the time, until the flour is cooked and takes on a little colour. Add the stock and cream to the sauce. Whisk the sauce to prevent lumps forming, and bring it to the boil. Simmer the sauce for 10 minutes. Add the grated nutmeg and Parmesan.

Preheat the oven to 225-250°C (425-475°F, Gas Mark 7-9). Butter a gratin dish well, and layer the pasta, filling and béchamel sauce in the dish, with the final layer being béchamel sauce. Sprinkle grated Parmesan on top and dot with several knobs of butter. Bake the lasagne in the oven for 25-30 minutes.

PASTA WITH FROMAGE FRAIS AND HERBS

Serves 3-4

250 g (8 oz) pasta
1 tbsp oil
150 g (5 oz) fromage frais
150 g (5 oz) crème fraîche
3 eggs
1 tbsp garlic, thinly sliced

1 tbsp fresh parsley,
chopped
1 tbsp lemon balm,
chopped
50 g (2 oz) streaky bacon
salt, pepper

Below: *Pasta with fromage frais and herbs*

Preheat the oven to 200-225ßC (400-425ßF, Gas Mark 6-7). In a saucepan, bring 2-3 litres (3½-5 pints) salted water to the boil, add the oil and pasta, and cook the pasta for about 10 minutes. Drain the pasta, rinse it under cold, running water and leave it to drain.

To make the sauce: Mix together the fromage frais, cream and eggs, then add the garlic, parsley and lemon balm. Season the mixture with salt and pepper. Stir the cheese mixture into the pasta. Butter a gratin dish, put the pasta in the dish, and cover the pasta with slices of bacon. Bake the pasta in the oven for 40 minutes.

PASTA AL LIMONE

Serves 4-5

400 g (13 oz) pasta
200 ml (7 fl oz) cream
200 g (7 oz) fromage frais
4 tbsp lemon juice

10 citronella leaves
2 tbsp Parmesan, grated
salt

In a saucepan bring 3 litres (5 pints) salted water to the boil, add the pasta to the boiling water and cook it for 8-10 minutes, stirring occasionally. Drain the pasta, rinse it under cold, running water and leave it to drain.

In a saucepan, heat the cream and add the fromage frais, a spoonful at a time, stirring all the time. Add the lemon juice, beating vigorously, so that the mixture combines well, then simmer until the sauce is creamy. Pour the sauce over the pasta.

Wash the citronella leaves and dry them carefully on a tea towel or kitchen paper. Reserve a few leaves for decoration. Chop the remaining leaves into thin strips and add them to the pasta with the Parmesan, stirring gently. Garnish the pasta with whole citronella leaves.

FRESH PASTA WITH PESTO

Above: *Fresh pasta with pesto*
Right: *Strangozze with artichokes*

Serves 6

500 g (1 lb) flour
4 eggs whites
5 bunches of fresh basil
20 pine kernels
3 cloves of garlic
300 ml (½ pint) cold pressed olive oil

30 g (1 oz) Parmesan, grated
15 g (½ oz) pecorino, grated or use all pecorino instead of Parmesan
knob of butter
salt and pepper

Sieve the flour into a bowl, then make a well in the middle. Add the egg whites and 150 ml (¼ pint) water, and mix them into the flour until a thick, smooth dough forms. Using your hands, knead this dough for a further 8-10 minutes. The dough must be elastic. If the dough sticks, add a little flour. Roll it out as thinly as possible. Cut it into several rectangles, dust them with flour, roll them up to form sausages and cut them horizontally into very thin strips. In a saucepan bring 3 litres (5 pints) salted water to the boil. Cook the pasta in the boiling water, stirring occasionally, for no longer than 5 minutes, because the pasta should still be al dente. Drain the pasta, rinse it under cold, running water, and leave it to drain.

To make the pesto: Wash the basil and pat it dry with a tea towel or kitchen paper. Remove the leaves from the stalks. Brown the pine kernels in a frying pan, then leave them to cool. Roughly chop the pine kernels and basil leaves, or crush them with a pestle and mortar. Peel and crush the garlic and add it to the basil mixture. Add the olive oil, a little at a time, stirring constantly. Then add the grated Parmesan and pecorino; season with pepper. Melt a little butter in a saucepan, add the pasta and heat it through, tossing it gently in the butter. Then pour the pesto over the pasta.

STRANGOZZE WITH ARTICHOKES

Serves 6

500 g (1 lb) flour
4 egg whites
125 g (4 oz) artichoke
hearts, tinned
6 tbsp olive oil

1 bunch of fresh parsley
3 cloves of garlic
1 small green pepper
knob of butter
salt

Sift the flour into a bowl, then make a well in the middle. Add the egg whites and 150 ml (¼ pint) water, and mix them into the flour until a thick, smooth dough forms. Using your hands, knead this dough for a further 8-10 minutes. The dough must be elastic. If the dough sticks, add a little flour. Roll it out as thinly as possible. Cut it into several rectangles, dust them with flour, roll them up to form sausages and cut them horizontally into very thin strips. In a saucepan bring 3 litres (5 pints) salted water to the boil. Cook the pasta in the boiling water, stirring occasionally, for no longer than 5 minutes, because the pasta should still be al dente. Drain the pasta, rinse it under cold, running water, and leave it to drain.

To make the artichoke sauce: Finely chop the artichoke hearts. Heat the oil in a saucepan and brown the artichoke hearts in the oil. Wash the parsley, pat it dry with a tea towel or kitchen paper, and chop it. Peel and chop or crush the garlic. Cut the pepper in half, core and de-seed it, wash and finely chop it. Add the parsley, garlic and pepper to the artichokes, and fry them for about ten minutes. Melt a little butter in a saucepan, add the pasta to the pan and heat it through, tossing it in the butter. Arrange the pasta on a serving dish and pour the artichoke mixture over it.

Above: *Spinach lasagne*

SPINACH LASAGNE

Serves 4

300 g (10 oz) spinach, frozen	tomatoes, tinned
70 g (3 oz) butter	2-3 tbsp mustard
nutmeg, grated	fresh thyme, chopped
250 g (8 oz) ribbon pasta, e.g.	fresh oregano, chopped
tagliatelle	100 g (3½ oz) Parmesan, grated
1 tbsp oil	30 g (1 oz) flour
1 onion	500 ml (18 fl oz) milk
125 g (4 oz) minced beef	2-3 tbsp white wine
125 g (4 oz) minced pork	250 g (8 oz) Gruyère, thinly sliced
1 clove of garlic	salt and pepper
250 g (8 oz) peeled	

*P*lace the frozen spinach in a saucepan with a little water and a knob of butter and cook it over a low heat until defrosted. Season the spinach with salt, pepper and a little grated nutmeg. In a saucepan, bring 3 litres (5 pints) salted water to the boil, add a little oil and the pasta, and cook the pasta for about 8 minutes, stirring occasionally. Do not cook the pasta for any longer than 8 minutes if you want it to be al dente. Drain the pasta, rinse in warm water, drain well again and keep it warm.

Peel and finely chop the onion. Melt 20 g (1 oz) butter in a frying pan, and fry the onion until brown. Add the minced meats and fry them, breaking up any large lumps. Peel and chop or crush the garlic and add it to the meat. Drain and roughly chop the tomatoes. Add the tomatoes and their juice to the meat.

Put a lid on the frying pan and simmer the meat sauce until it thickens. Season the sauce generously with mustard, salt, pepper, nutmeg, thyme and oregano.

To make the sauce: Melt 30 g (1 oz) butter in a saucepan, sprinkle the flour into the melted butter and cook it over a high heat. Add the milk and wine and whisk the sauce to prevent lumps forming. Bring the sauce to the boil and simmer it for 5 minutes. Add the grated Parmesan and stir it in until completely melted. Season the sauce with pepper and grated nutmeg.

Preheat the oven to 225⁰C (425⁰F, Gas Mark 7). Butter a gratin dish and layer the pasta and béchamel sauce in the following order: half the pasta first, the minced meat mixture, half the sauce, the spinach, the remaining pasta and finish with the remaining sauce. Level out the sauce and top it with the thin slices of Gruyère. Bake the lasagne in the oven for about 30 minutes.

LASAGNE AL FORNO

Serves 4

250 g (8 oz) sheets of lasagne (about 15 sheets)	fresh oregano, chopped
1 clove of garlic, peeled	fresh thyme, chopped
1 large onion	150 g (5 oz) crème fraîche
2 tbsp oil	150 ml (¼ pint) milk
125 g (4 oz) minced beef	40 g (1½ oz) Parmesan, grated
125 g (4 oz) minced pork	2 knobs of butter
3 tbsp tomato purée	salt, pepper
fresh rosemary, chopped	

*B*ring a saucepan with 1½ litres (2½ pints) salted water to the boil and cook the sheets of pasta in the boiling water, one by one, for about 2 minutes each. When cooked, immerse them in cold water and leave them there.

Crush the garlic. Peel and finely chop the onion. Heat the oil in a frying pan and brown the onion and garlic in it. Add the minced meats and fry them with the onion, then add the tomato purée, cover the frying pan and leave the meat mixture to simmer. Season the meat mixture with salt, pepper, rosemary, oregano and thyme. If the meat sauce is reducing too much, add a little water as necessary.

To make the sauce: Mix together the cream, milk and Parmesan cheese. Drain the pasta. Preheat the oven to 200-225⁰C (400-425⁰F, Gas Mark 6-7). Butter a gratin dish and alternately layer the pasta, meat sauce and cream sauce, finishing with a layer of cream sauce. Dot the top of the lasagne with butter. Bake the lasagne in the oven for about 30 minutes.

Opposite: *Lasagne al forno*

Sieve the flour into a large bowl and make a well in the centre. Beat together the eggs, salt and 100 ml (3½ fl oz) water, add the liquid to the flour a little at a time and gradually work it in to form a dough, taking care to prevent lumps forming. Work the dough with a spoon until it starts to come together.

Bring a saucepan of water to the boil. Take a colander with fairly large holes, put the dough in the colander, and then, holding the colander over the pan of boiling water, force the dough through the holes using a wooden spoon. (You can also roll the dough out on a chopping board and, using a knife, slice off little strips and drop them into the boiling water.) The spétzle should drop into the pan of boiling water and, when cooked, should float to the surface. When the spétzle have surfaced, leave them to cook for a few minutes more, then remove them from the pan with a slotted spoon, put them in a sieve and rinse them under cold water.

Leave them to drain. Melt the butter in a saucepan, add the spétzle and heat them through for 3-4 minutes, tossing them in the melted butter.

SPÉTZLE VERDE

Serves 4-6

200 g (7 oz) spinach, frozen	50 g (2 oz) butter
400 g (13 oz) flour	1 heaped tsp salt
4 eggs	

Defrost the spinach at room temperature. Sift the flour into a large bowl and make a well in the centre. Beat together the eggs, salt and 100 ml (3½ fl oz) water, add the liquid to the flour a little at a time and gradually work it in to form a dough, taking care to prevent lumps forming. Work the dough with a spoon until it starts to come together. Drain the spinach thoroughly and add it to the dough, working it in until the dough turns green.

Bring a saucepan of water to the boil. Take a colander with fairly large holes, put the dough in the colander, and then, holding the colander over the pan of boiling water, force the dough through the holes using a wooden spoon. The spétzle should drop into the pan of boiling water and, when cooked, should float to the surface. When the spétzle have surfaced, leave them to cook for a few minutes more, then remove them from the pan with a slotted spoon, put them in a sieve and rinse them under cold water. Leave them to drain. Melt the butter in a saucepan, add the spétzle and heat them through, tossing them in the melted butter.

Tip: Serve the spétzle with a Bolognese sauce.

SPÉTZLE

Serves 4-6

400 g (13 oz) flour	50 g (2 oz) butter
4 eggs	1 heaped tsp salt

SPÉTZLE AU GRATIN

Serves 2

½ packet or 125 g (4 oz) spétzle	2 eggs
100 g (3½ oz) Gruyère, grated	150 g (5 oz) double cream
	nutmeg, grated
	knobs of butter
	salt and pepper

Cook the spétzle according to the instructions on the packet. Rinse them in cold water and leave them to drain in a sieve. Mix together the grated Gruyère, eggs and cream. Season the cream mixture with salt, pepper and a little grated nutmeg.

Preheat the oven to 200-225°C (400-425°F, Gas Mark 6-7). Combine the spétzle and cream mixture. Butter a gratin dish and fill it with the spétzle mixture. Dot the spétzle with a few knobs of butter and bake it in the oven for 25-30 minutes. Accompany the spétzle with a green salad and grilled meat.

GIPSY SPÉTZLE

Serves 4-5

375 g (12 oz) flour	50 g (2 oz) butter
3 eggs	salt
75 g (3 oz) paprika	freshly ground pepper

Sift the flour into a large bowl and make a well in the centre. Beat together the eggs, paprika and 100 ml (3½ fl oz) water, add the liquid to the flour a little at a time and gradually work it in to form a dough, taking care to prevent lumps forming. Work the dough with a spoon until it starts to come together.

Bring a saucepan of water to the boil. Take a colander with fairly large holes, put the dough in the colander, and then, holding the colander over the pan of boiling water, force the dough through the holes using a wooden spoon. The spétzle should drop into the pan of boiling water and, when cooked, should float to the surface. When the spétzle have surfaced, leave them to cook for a few minutes more, then remove them from the pan with a slotted spoon, put them in a sieve and rinse them under cold water. Leave them to drain. elt the butter in a saucepan, add the spétzle and heat them through for 3-4 minutes, tossing them in the melted butter. Season the spétzle with salt and pepper.

SPÉTZLE WITH PARSLEY

Serves 4-6

50 g (2 oz) fresh parsley	50 g (2 oz) butter
3 eggs	1 heaped tsp salt
400 g (13 oz) flour	pepper

Wash the parsley, pat dry in a tea towel and finely chop it. Beat together the eggs and parsley in a large bowl. Add the flour, salt, pepper and 100 ml (3½ fl oz) water. Mix the ingredients thoroughly, taking care to prevent lumps forming. Work the dough with a spoon until it starts to come together.

Bring a saucepan of water to the boil. Take a colander with fairly large holes, put the dough in the colander, and then, holding the colander over the pan of boiling water, force the dough through the holes using a wooden spoon. The spétzle should drop into the pan of boiling water and, when cooked, should float to the surface. When the spétzle have surfaced, leave them to cook for a few minutes more, then pour them into a sieve and rinse them under cold water. Leave them to drain. Melt the butter in a saucepan, add the spétzle and heat them through, tossing them in the melted butter.

Left: Spétzle verde / Below: Spétzle au gratin

TORTELLINI VERDE WITH WALNUTS

Serves 4-5

500 g (1 lb) tortellini verde
200 g (7 oz) walnuts,
shelled
2-3 cloves of garlic
100 ml (3½ fl oz) olive oil

150 ml (¼ pint) double
cream
2 tbsp fresh marjoram,
chopped
salt

Finely chop two-thirds of the walnuts. Peel and finely chop the garlic. Heat the oil in a saucepan and gently fry the garlic in it, then add the chopped and whole walnuts. Add the cream, and season the sauce with salt. Add the chopped marjoram. Bring a saucepan with 3-4 litres (5-7 pints) salted water to the boil, put the tortellini in the boiling water and simmer for 20-30 minutes.

Drain the tortellini in a sieve, rinse them in cold water and leave them to drain. Arrange the tortellini on a serving dish, pour the sauce over the top, and stir the tortellini to coat them in the sauce.

Below: *Tortellini verde with walnuts*

TORTELLINI MARIO

Serves 2

125 g (4 oz) tortellini
125 g (4 oz) mushrooms
1 stock cube
1 onion
knob of butter
100 ml (3½ fl oz) dry white

wine
150 g (5 oz) crème fraîche
fresh herbes de Provence
mix, chopped
salt
pepper

Bring a saucepan with 1 litre (1¾ pints) water to the boil, crumble the stock cube into the water and, when it is dissolved, add the tortellini to the boiling water. Cook the tortellini for about 20 minutes. Drain the pasta, rinse it in cold water, then drain it again. Wipe the mushrooms and slice them thinly. Peel and finely chop the onion.

Melt the butter in a saucepan. Add the chopped onion to the pan and brown it in the butter, then add the mushrooms. Add the wine and simmer the sauce for 2 minutes. Add the cream to the saucepan and simmer the sauce for a further 2 minutes. Season with salt and pepper. Stir the cooked tortellini into the sauce and leave them to heat through for a few minutes over a low heat. Serve sprinkled with herbes de Provence.

TORTELLINI CINDERELLA

Serves 2

125 g (4 oz) tortellini
1 stock cube
1 clove of garlic
150 g (5 oz) crème fraîche
2-3 tbsp milk
nutmeg, grated

beef stock concentrate (e.g.
Bovril)
100 g (3½ oz) ham, sliced
fresh chives, chopped
salt and pepper

Bring a saucepan with 1 litre (1¾ pints) water to the boil, dissolve the stock cube in the water, then add the tortellini to the stock and simmer for about 20 minutes. Drain the tortellini. Peel the garlic and use it to rub the base and sides of a saucepan, then put the cream and milk in the pan, bring them to the boil and simmer for a few minutes. Add the tortellini to the cream sauce. Season the pasta with salt and pepper, add a little grated nutmeg and flavour the sauce with a little beef concentrate. Simmer the sauce for a few minutes over a low heat. Cut the ham into strips and add it to the pasta with the chopped chives. Serve the pasta immediately.

Above:
Tortellini Cinderella

PASTA WITH MIDNIGHT SAUCE

Serves 4-6

400 g (13 oz) pasta
1 large onion
250 g (8 oz) tomatoes
250 g (8 oz) baby
courgettes
1 green pepper
200 g (7 oz) prunes

100 ml (3½ fl oz) olive oil
1 tsp fresh mint, chopped
1 tsp fresh basil, chopped
1 tbsp oil
salt, pepper

Peel the onion. Wash the tomatoes and remove the stalks. Wash and top and tail the courgettes. Wash the green pepper, remove the stalk and core. Finely dice all these ingredients. Wash the prunes, slice them in half and remove the stones.

Heat the olive oil in a saucepan, add the diced vegetables and halved prunes to the pan, season with salt and pepper, then leave to sweat for 30-45 minutes. Add the chopped mint and basil to the pan. Bring a saucepan with 5-6 litres (9-10½ pints) salted water to the boil, add the pasta to the boiling water, and a tablespoon of oil, and cook the pasta for about 10 minutes. Drain the cooked pasta in a sieve, add it to the vegetable and prune mixture, coat well in the sauce and serve immediately.

CANNELLONI ROSANELLA

Serves 3

250 g (8 oz) cannelloni	beef concentrate, e.g.
125 g (4 oz) minced beef	Bovril
125 g (4 oz) minced pork	fresh basil, chopped
2 slices stale bread	1 tbsp Parmesan, grated
fresh oregano, chopped	butter
fresh thyme, chopped	salt
150 g (5 oz) crème fraîche	pepper
6 tbsp milk	

*T*o make the filling, soak the stale bread in cold water. Squeeze it out well and mix it with the minced meats. Season the mixture with salt, pepper, oregano and thyme. Stuff the cannelloni with this mixture, using a piping bag or the handle of a wooden spoon. Butter a gratin dish and arrange the cannelloni in the dish side by side. Preheat the oven to 175-200⁰ C (350-400⁰ F, Gas Mark 4-6).

To make the sauce: Mix together the cream and milk in a saucepan. Bring them to the boil; season the sauce with salt, pepper, a little beef concentrate and the chopped basil. Pour the sauce over the cannelloni (they must be completely covered in sauce). Sprinkle grated Parmesan over the cannelloni and dot with knobs of butter. Bake the cannelloni in the oven for about 30 minutes.

CANNELLONI AU GRATIN

Serves 4

250 g (8 oz) cannelloni	50 g (2 oz) streaky bacon
150 g (5 oz) spinach, frozen	1 tbsp flour
250 g (8 oz) minced beef	70 g (3 oz) tomato purée
2 onions	fresh basil, chopped
2 cloves of garlic	400 ml (14 fl oz) meat stock
2 tbsp oil	a little Gruyère, grated
2 tbsp Parmesan, grated	butter
1 tbsp double cream	salt
1 egg	pepper
fresh oregano, chopped	

*T*o make the stuffing, defrost the spinach at room temperature. Peel one onion and one clove of garlic and finely chop them. Heat a tablespoon of oil in a frying pan, and fry the garlic and onion. Add the defrosted spinach to the frying pan and allow it to cook for a few minutes. Remove the spinach mixture from the frying pan and reserve it in a bowl.

Melt a knob of butter in the frying pan and fry the minced beef until brown. Add the beef to the spinach and sprinkle the grated Parmesan over the mixture. Beat together the cream and egg, and season the mixture with some of the oregano, salt and pepper. Pour the cream mixture over the meat and spinach, mix well, then use this mixture to stuff the cannelloni.

To make the tomato sauce: Peel the remaining onion and clove of garlic. Finely dice the onion and bacon, crush the garlic. Heat a little oil in a frying pan and fry the bacon, add the onion and garlic and brown all three in the oil. Then add the flour and tomato purée. Season the mixture with salt, pepper, basil and the remaining oregano. Add the stock to the sauce and combine thoroughly. Bring the sauce to the boil and simmer it for about 10 minutes.

Preheat the oven to 175⁰ C (350⁰ F, Gas Mark 4). Butter a gratin dish. Pour a little of the tomato sauce over the base of the dish, arrange the cannelloni side by side on top, then pour the remaining tomato sauce over. Sprinkle grated Gruyére on top of the cannelloni and dot with a few knobs of butter. Bake the cannelloni in the oven for about 30 minutes.

Opposite: *Cannelloni Rosanella*

Above: *Cannelloni on a bed of spinach*

CANNELLONI ON A BED OF SPINACH

Serves 4

600 g (1¼ lb) spinach, frozen
125 g (4 oz) cannelloni
2 tbsp oil
1 onion
nutmeg, grated
120 g (4 oz) butter
100 g (3½ oz) flour

850 ml (approx. 1½ pints) milk
250 g (8 oz) crème fraîche
120 g (4 oz) Parmesan, grated
250 g (8 oz) fromage frais
salt and pepper

Heat the oil in a saucepan. Peel the onion, chop finely and fry it in the oil. Add the frozen spinach to the pan with the chopped onion and a little water and leave it to simmer for about 15 minutes. Season the spinach with salt, pepper and a little grated nutmeg, then drain it.

Butter a gratin dish and line the base of it with the cooked spinach.

To make the sauce: In a saucepan melt 100 g (3½ oz) butter , then add the flour. Stir the flour until it takes on a slight coloration, then add 750 ml (1¼ pints) milk. Whisk the sauce to prevent lumps forming. Bring the sauce to the boil and simmer it for 2 minutes. Season with salt and pepper, then add the grated Parmesan. Take one third of the sauce and mix it with the fromage frais. Adjust the seasoning.

Using a piping bag, stuff the cannelloni with the fromage frais mixture. Pour half of the remaining basic sauce over the spinach and arrange the stuffed cannelloni on top. Preheat the oven to 225°C (425°F, Gas Mark 7). Mix the remaining basic sauce with 100 ml (3½ fl oz) milk and pour it over the cannelloni. Sprinkle Parmesan over the sauce and dot the cannelloni with several knobs of butter. Bake the spinach and cannelloni in the oven for 30 minutes.

SPAGHETTI BOLOGNESE

Serves 4

400 g (13 oz) spaghetti
500 g (1 lb) peeled tomatoes, tinned
125 g (4 oz) minced beef
125 g (4 oz) minced pork

2 onions
1-2 cloves of garlic
2 tbsp olive oil
paprika
70 g (3 oz) tomato purée

100 ml (3½ oz) red wine or water
1 tsp fresh thyme, chopped
1 tbsp fresh basil, chopped

1 tbsp oil
a little Parmesan, grated
salt
pepper

To make the sauce, peel and finely chop the onions and garlic. Heat the olive oil in a saucepan and fry the onion and garlic in the oil until brown. Add the minced meat and fry it for 5 minutes, stirring all the time, and breaking up large lumps of meat. Season the meat with salt, pepper and paprika. Add the tomatoes and their juice, breaking up large pieces of tomato. Add the tomato purée and the wine. Combine all the ingredients thoroughly and bring the sauce to the boil. Simmer the sauce for about 15 minutes. Add the chopped thyme and basil.

To prepare the spaghetti: Bring a saucepan with 3 litres (5 pints) salted water to the boil. Add a tablespoon of oil, and the spaghetti, and cook the spaghetti for 10 minutes. Empty the spaghetti into a colander and leave it to drain. Pour the sauce over the spaghetti, sprinkle grated Parmesan on top and serve it immediately.

Left: *Spaghetti Bolognese*
Below: *Spaghetti with asparagus*

SPAGHETTI WITH ASPARAGUS

Serves 6

500 g (1 lb) asparagus
400 g (13 oz) spaghetti
250 g (8 oz) boiled ham
1 onion
1 clove of garlic

knob of butter
3 eggs
100 g (3½ oz) Parmesan, grated
salt

Prepare the asparagus, taking care to remove the woody parts and not to damage the tips. Wash and finely chop the asparagus.
Bring a saucepan with 2 litres (3½ pints) salted water to the boil, put the asparagus in the boiling water and simmer it for 15 minutes. Drain the asparagus and keep it hot.

Bring a saucepan of salted water to the boil, add the spaghetti to the pan and cook it for about 10 minutes, stirring occasionally. Pour the spaghetti into a colander, rinse it in warm water and keep the spaghetti hot. Peel and finely chop the onion and garlic. Dice the ham. Melt the butter in a frying pan and fry the onion and garlic in it. In a bowl, beat together the eggs and Parmesan, then add the ham and the cooked asparagus. Pour the egg mixture over the onion and garlic.
Allow the egg mixture to set, stirring occasionally with a wooden spoon. Combine the cooked spaghetti and asparagus omelette.

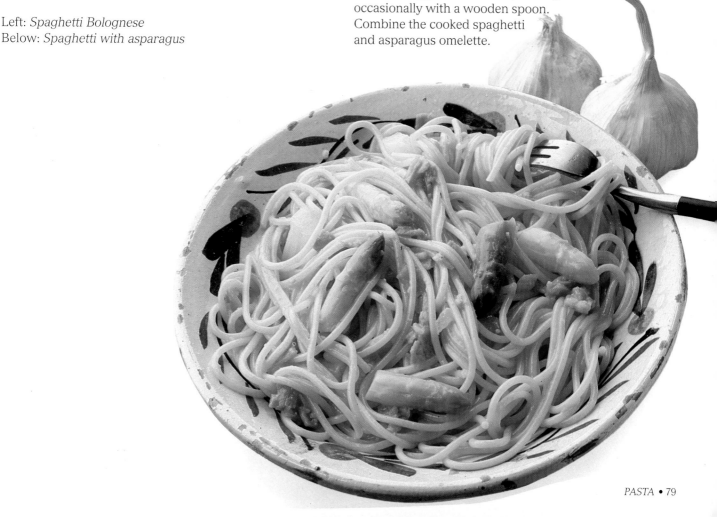

SPAGHETTI WITH MUSHROOMS

Serves 4

400 g (13 oz) spaghetti
750 g (1½ lb) mushrooms
250 g (8 oz) lean bacon
125 g (4 oz) crème fraîche
100 g (3½ oz) Parmesan,
freshly grated
2 bunches fresh basil

2 bunches fresh chives
1 clove of garlic
1 tbsp oil
50 g (2 oz) butter
4 egg yolks
salt
pepper

Wipe the mushrooms and slice them very thinly. Finely dice the bacon and render it in a frying pan. Add the mushrooms to the pan. Season them with salt and pepper and cook them for about 20 minutes.

Mix together the cream and grated Parmesan. Wash the basil and chives, pat them dry, finely chop them and stir them into the cream mixture. Add the cream to the mushrooms and simmer the mushroom sauce for 10 minutes.

Peel the garlic and slice it in half. Bring a saucepan with 4 litres (7 pints) salted water to the boil, add the tablespoon of oil and the garlic, then add the spaghetti to the pan and cook it for about 10 minutes. Pour the spaghetti into a colander, rinse it in cold water and drain it. Melt the butter in a saucepan, sauté the spaghetti in it, then divide the spaghetti amongst four plates and pour the mushroom sauce over. Top each plate with an egg yolk.

SPAGHETTI WITH TOMATO AND MUSSELS

Serves 4-6

400 g (13 oz) spaghetti
250 g (8 oz) tomatoes
150-200 g (5-7 oz) mussels,
from a jar
375 g (12 oz) tuna, tinned

4 cloves of garlic
2 tbsp olive oil
2-3 tbsp fresh parsley,
chopped
salt, pepper

To make the sauce, bring a saucepan of water to the boil and quickly blanch the tomatoes in the boiling water, then refresh them in cold water. Skin and destalk them, then chop them.

Drain the mussels, reserving the liquid. Drain and roughly flake the tuna. Peel and chop the garlic. Heat the olive oil in a frying pan and fry the garlic in it. Add the chopped tomatoes to the pan and cook them for 5 minutes. Then add the mussels, the tuna and a little of the liquid from the mussels. Heat everything through thoroughly. Season the mussel and tomato mixture with salt, pepper and chopped parsley.

Bring a saucepan with 3 litres (5 pints) salted water to the boil, add the spaghetti to the pan and cook it for 10 minutes, stirring occasionally. Pour the spaghetti into a colander and leave it to drain. Arrange the spaghetti on a serving dish and pour the mussel and tomato sauce over the top.

Opposite: *Spaghetti with tomatoes and mussels*
Below: *Spaghetti with herbs*

SPAGHETTI WITH HERBS

Serves 4-6

400 g (13 oz) spaghetti	6 eggs
2 tbsp oil	30 g (1 oz) butter
1 bunch of fresh parsley	1 clove of garlic
1 bunch of fresh dill	nutmeg, grated
1 bunch of fresh basil	150 g (5 oz) ham
1 bunch of fresh chives	salt
250 ml (8 fl oz) double	pepper
cream	

*B*ring 3 litres (5 pints) salted water to the boil in a saucepan, add the oil, then the spaghetti and cook it for about 10 minutes. Drain the spaghetti into a colander, rinse it in warm water and leave it to drain.

Wash the herbs, pat them dry in a tea towel and roughly chop them. Peel and chop the garlic, beat the eggs, then mix together the herbs, cream, eggs, butter and garlic. Season the sauce with salt and pepper and a little grated nutmeg.

Heat the spaghetti and sauce together, in a saucepan, over a gentle heat, stirring all the time, until the sauce is smooth and creamy. Arrange the spaghetti on a serving dish. Cut the ham into ribbons, arrange them on top of the spaghetti and serve it immediately.

ASPARAGUS IN VINAIGRETTE

Serves 4

1 kg (2 lb) white or green asparagus
4 tbsp oil
3 tbsp vinegar
1 tsp mustard
salt
pepper

The tips of the asparagus should be tender, the stalks should snap easily and be juicy at the break. Peel the asparagus from top to bottom, taking care to remove all the peel, without damamging the spears. Cut all the asparagus to the same length, wash it and tie it up with kitchen thread in bundles of 8 stalks.

In a saucepan bring 2 litres (3½ pints) salted water to the boil, put the asparagus in the boiling water, bring the pan to the boil again and cook the asparagus for about 20 minutes or until tender. Fold a tea towel in four and use it to cover a plate. Carefully remove the cooked asparagus from the pan using a slotted spoon and drain the asparagus on the tea towel. Untie the bundles of asparagus stalks. Serve the asparagus warm or cold with a vinaigrette dressing made with the oil, vinegar, mustard, salt and pepper.

Variation: Coat the asparagus in a crème fraîche or hollandaise sauce (see page 93). Sprinkle with fresh, chopped fines herbes.

LEEKS A LA CRÈME

Serves 4-6

1¾ kg (4 lb) leeks
40 g (1½ oz) butter
125 ml (4 fl oz) water
nutmeg, grated
2 tbsp crème fraîche
1 tbsp fresh parsley, chopped

Trim and wash the leeks and cut them into chunks. Melt the butter in a saucepan and sweat the leeks in the butter. Add the water, salt and freshly grated nutmeg and leave the leeks to simmer for about 10 minutes. Add the crè85 îche to the pan and coat the leeks in it. Add more salt and grated nutmeg as necessary. Serve the leeks, garnished with fresh chopped parsley.

Below: *Leeks á la crème*
Opposite: *Asparagus in vinaigrette*

ASPARAGUS Á L'IMPÊRIALE

Serves 4

1 kg (2 lb) asparagus
125 ml (4 fl oz) white wine
2 egg yolks
1 tsp cornflour
150 g (5 oz) crème fraîche
1 tbsp fresh parsley,

chopped
8 slices Parma ham,
weighing approx. 175 g
(6 oz)
knob of butter
salt and pepper

Peel the asparagus from top to bottom, taking care to remove all the skin and the hard parts without damaging the spears. Bring a saucepan with 2 litres (3½ pints) salted water to the boil. Put the asparagus in the pan, bring it to the boil again and simmer for about 25 minutes. Drain the asparagus and leave it to cool.

Put the white wine, egg yolks, butter, cornflour and salt in a saucepan, and bring them to the boil, stirring constantly. As soon as the mixture has boiled, remove it from the heat and leave it to cool, stirring it from time to time. Whip the crème fraîche until it forms soft peaks. Fold it into the egg mixture. Season the dressing with salt and pepper. Divide the asparagus amongst 4 plates, garnish each one with 2 slices of Parma ham and chopped parsley. Pour the dressing over the asparagus or serve it separately.

FENNEL IN WHITE SAUCE

Serves 3-4

750 g (1½ lb) fennel
125 ml (4 fl oz) meat stock

2 tbsp cornflour
4 tbsp cold milk
salt

Remove the stalks and any brown parts from the fennel. Wash the fennel bulbs and slice them. Bring a saucepan with 500 ml (18 fl oz) salted water to the boil, add the fennel and cook it for about 20 minutes. When it is cooked, drain the fennel, reserving half the cooking liquid.

To make the sauce: In a saucepan bring the reserved cooking liquid to the boil. Add the meat stock and cornflour, then the milk. Simmer the sauce for sveral minutes, stirring all the time. Fold the sliced fennel into the white sauce.

Below: *Asparagus A l'Impèriale*
Right: *Cucumber braised in curry sauce*

CUCUMBER BRAISED IN CURRY SAUCE

Serves 4

2-3 cucumbers, weighing
approx.
800 g (approx. 1½ lb)
1 onion
2 tbsp lemon juice
½ tsp zest of an unwaxed
lemon, grated
8 tbsp cream, whipped

curry powder
juice of 1 lemon ora little
white wine
fresh lemon balm, chopped
or fresh parsley
butter
salt
white pepper

Peel the cucumbers and cut them in half lengthways.
Scoop out the seeds using a spoon. Chop the flesh into
1 cm (½ inch) dice. Peel and dice the onion.

Melt the butter in a saucepan and fry the diced onion.
Add the chopped cucumber. Incorporate 2 tablespoons
of lemon juice and the grated lemon zest. Season the
cucumber with salt and pepper. Put a lid on the pan and
fry the cucumber for 7 minutes. Add the whipped cream,
then the curry powder and lemon juice or white wine to
the cucumber mixture. Taste the sauce and adjust the
seasoning as necessary. Serve the cucumber garnished
with lemon balm.

PETIT POIS WITH HAM

Serves 2

300 g (10 oz) packet frozen
petit pois
1 small onion
50 g (2 oz) boiled ham
25 g (1 oz) butter

packet of white sauce mix
4 tbsp whipped cream
nutmeg, grated
salt
pepper

Bring a saucepan with 125 ml (4 fl oz) salted water to the
boil, add the petit pois, bring the pan to the boil again
and simmer the petit pois for 8 minutes. Drain them and
reserve the cooking liquid. Peel and thinly slice the
onion, dice the ham.

Melt the butter in a frying pan and add the sliced onion
and diced ham. Fry them for 5 minutes.

In a saucepan mix together the whipped cream and half
the packet of white sauce mix. Add the cooking liquid
from the petit pois and whisk until smooth. Bring the
sauce to the boil and season with pepper and grated
nutmeg. Fold the fried onion and ham into the white
sauce. Serve the sauce with the petit pois.

HARICOT BEANS WITH BACON

Serves 4

740 g (1½ lb) shelled
haricot beans or 3 kg (7 lb)
with the pods
sprig of fresh savory
100 g (3½ oz) bacon

2-3 onions
1 tbsp fresh chives, finely
chopped
salt

Wash the beans and the savory. Dice the bacon. Peel and slice the onions. In a saucepan, fry the bacon until the fat runs, then add the sliced onion and fry both until golden brown. Add the beans, the sprig of savory and 150 ml (5 fl oz) salted water.

Put a lid on the saucepan and simmer the beans for 20-30 minutes until the beans are tender. Season the beans to taste with salt, and sprinkle with chopped chives just before serving. The beans can be accompanied by grilled bacon rashers.

BROAD BEAN STEW

Serves 4

600 g (1¼ lb) broad beans,
shelled or 2½ kg (5½ lb)
with pods
¼ stale baguette
2 onions
1 egg
250 g (8 oz) smoked
sausage meat
125 g (4 oz) minced beef

125 g (4 oz) minced pork
50 g (2 oz) lean bacon
1 tbsp oil
500 g (1 lb) tomatoes
40 g (1½ oz) flour
2 tbsp tomato purée
2 tbsp fresh parsley,
chopped
paprika
salt

Bring a saucepan of water to the boil. Add the broad beans to the pan, drain them, then remove the skins. Put the beans in a saucepan with 500 ml (18 fl oz) salted water, bring them to the boil and simmer them for 10-12 minutes. Drain the beans, reserving the cooking liquid. Soak the stale bread in a little cold water to soften it, then squeeze it out well. Peel and finely dice one of the onions. Beat the egg.

Mix together the sausage meat, minced beef and pork, diced onion, bread and beaten egg, binding them all together thoroughly. Season the mixture with salt, pepper and paprika. Shape the meat mixture into little balls. In a saucepan, bring the cooking liquid from the beans to the

FRENCH BEANS WITH PARMESAN

IN THE PRESSURE COOKER
Serves 4

500 g (1 lb) French beans
150 g (5 oz) button
mushrooms
200 g (7 oz) tomatoes
50 g (2 oz) bacon
1 onion
½ tsp fresh savory,

chopped
½ tsp fresh oregano,
chopped
150 ml (5 fl oz) meat stock
40 g (1½ oz) Parmesan,
grated
salt and pepper

Top and tail the French beans, wash and chop them. Peel, wash and quarter the mushrooms. Skin and dice the tomatoes. Dice the bacon. Peel and dice the onion. Render the bacon in the unlidded pressure cooker, then fry the diced onion in the bacon fat until translucent. Add the beans, mushrooms and tomatoes to the pan. Season the vegetables with salt, pepper, oregano and savory. Pour the stock over the vegetables, close the pressure cooker and cook the vegetables for 4 minutes. Before serving, adjust the seasoning as necessary and sprinkle the beans with grated Parmesan.

Above: *French beans with Parmesan*
Right: *Broad bean stew*

boil again, and drop the meatballs into the boiling liquid. Gently simmer the meatballs for 5-7 minutes then remove them from the cooking liquid. Make up the liquid with 500 ml (18 fl oz) water, and reserve it. Dice the bacon. Heat the oil in a frying pan and fry the bacon in it. Peel and thinly slice the other onion and fry it with the bacon.

Chop 300 g (10 oz) of tomatoes and add them to the pan with the bacon and onion. When the tomatoes are half cooked, sprinkle the flour over the tomatoes and stir it into the mixture. When the tomatoes are fully cooked, add the cooking liquid from the meatballs to the pan. Stir the liquid until thoroughly combined, bring the sauce to the boil and simmer it for 5 minutes, then strain it.

Season the sauce with salt, pepper and paprika. Add the tomato purée. Warm the sauce through, then add the broad beans and meatballs to the sauce. Slice and de-seed the remaining tomatoes, add them to the stew and simmer it over a medium heat. Before serving, sprinkle the stew with chopped parsley.

PARSLEYED TOMATOES

Serves 3-4

750 g (1½ lb) medium-sized firm tomatoes	salt
50 g (2 oz) butter	freshly ground pepper
	1 tbsp fresh parsley or chives, chopped

Bring a saucepan of water to the boil, blanch the tomatoes in the boiling water for a moment, then remove them and refresh them under cold water. This will make them easier to skin. Skin the tomatoes, then melt the butter in a frying pan and arrange the whole tomatoes side by side in the pan. Season them with salt and pepper.

Cover the pan and sweat the tomatoes for about 10 minutes. Sprinkle the cooked tomatoes with chopped parsley or chives and serve them immediately.

RED CABBAGE WITH APPLES

Serves 4

1 kg (2 lb) red cabbage
1 large onion
3 cooking apples
60 g (2½ oz) lard or
goose fat

1 bay leaf
2 tbsp vinegar
a few cloves
salt and pepper

Remove the outler leaves from the cabbage. Cut the cabbage into quarters and remove the stalk. Wash the cabbage and slice it into thin strips or grate it. Peel and dice the onion. Peel, quarter, core and finely dice the apples.

Melt the lard or goose fat is a large saucepan. Add the onion to the pan, put the lid on the saucepan and sweat the onion in the covered pan until translucent. Add the cabbage to the pan, cover it again and sweat it, then add the chopped apple, bay leaf, and cloves. Season the cabbage to taste with salt, vinegar and pepper. Then add 150 ml (5 fl oz) water to the pan and braise the cabbage over a medium heat for about 30 minutes.

Variation: You can substitute red or white wine for the water.

STEAMED MILAN CABBAGE

Serves 4

1 Milan cabbage (or curly
kale)
1 onion
60 g (2½ oz) butter or lard

1-2 tbsp corn flour
1 tbsp fresh parsley,
chopped
salt

Remove the outer leaves from the cabbage, cut the cabbage into 8 pieces, remove the stalk, then wash the pieces of cabbage and cut them into thin strips. Peel and dice the onion. Melt the butter or lard in a saucepan, add the onion to the pan and sweat the onion in the butter until translucent. Add the cabbage to the pan with 150 ml (5 fl oz) water and steam the cabbage for 30 minutes or until soft.
Blend the cornflour with 1 tablespoon cold water and add the cornflour to the cabbe to thicken it. Bring the pan with the cabbage to the boil. Season it cabbage to taste and sprinkle it with chopped parsley.

Variation: For white cabbage, when steaming it with the onion, add a teaspoon of cumin to the pan, then follow the recipe as before.

Below: *Red cabbage with apples*

CAULIFLOWER IN WHITE SAUCE

Serves 4

1 cauliflower, weighing	margarine
about 750 g	20 g (¾ oz) flour
(1½ lb)	1 egg yolk
20 g (¾ oz) butter or	1 tbsp lemon juice, salt

Remove the cauliflower leaves, trim any damaged florets and remove the stalk. Wash the cauliflower under running water, then separate the florets. Bring a saucepan with 1 litre (1¾ pints) salted water to the boil, add the cauliflower florets to the pan and simmer them for 25-30 minutes. Drain the cauliflower, reserving the cooking liquid, and keep the cauliflower hot.

To make the sauce: Melt the butter or margarine in a saucepan. Add the flour to the pan and cook it, stirring all the time, until a light yellow paste forms. Gradually add 125 ml (4 fl oz) of the cauliflower water, whisking all the time to prevent lumps forming. When the sauce thickens, simmer it on a gentle heat for about 5 minutes. In a bowl beat together the egg yolk and 2 tablespoons of cold water. Then beat the egg mixture into the sauce. Season the sauce with salt and the lemon juice. Coat the cauliflower in the white sauce.

Variation: As an alternative to white sauce, melt 60 g (2½ oz) butter in a frying pan and heat it until it foams, then add 1 tablespoon of breadcrumbs to the pan and fry them in the hot butter. Then pour the hot butter and fried breadcrumbs over the cauliflower.

Above: *Cauliflower in white sauce*

FRENCH BEANS WITH BACON

Serves 3

500 g (1 lb) French beans	chopped
150 g (5 oz) streaky bacon	butter
2 shallots	salt
2-3 tbsp fresh parsley,	pepper

Top, tail and wash the beans. Dice the bacon. Melt the butter in a saucepan and fry the bacon in it until brown. Peel and finely chop the shallots. Add them to the pan with the bacon, cover the pan with a lid and sweat the shallots until translucent. Add the beans to the pan and season them to taste with salt and pepper. Add 125 ml (4 fl oz) water to the pan and simmer the beans for 5-7 minutes, stirring occasionally. Add the chopped parsley to the beans. Serve the beans with steak or other pan-fried or grilled meats.

SWEDE

Serves 4

1 kg (2 lb) swede	chopped
60 g (2½ oz) margarine	1 tbsp cornflour
1 tsp sugar	salt and pepper
1 tsp fresh parsley,	

Peel the swede and cut it into sticks 4 cm (1½ ins) in length. Melt the margarine in a saucepan, add the sugar and cook it until caramelized. Add the swede to the pan and brown it in the caramelized sugar. Add 150 ml (5 fl oz) water to the pan, put the lid on the saucepan and steam the swede for 30 minutes. Blend the cornflour with 1 tablespoon of cold water, and use it to thicken the swede. Season the dish with salt, pepper and chopped parsley.

CHINESE LEAVES A LA CR'ME

Serves 3-4

1 kg (2 lb) Chinese leaves	1 tbsp cornflour
1 small onion	2 tbsp crème fraîche
50-60 g (2-2½ oz) butter	salt

Divide the Chinese leaves, remove the ribs and reserve them. Carefully wash the leaves. Put a little water in a saucepan, bring it to the boil, add the leaves, cover the pan and steam the leaves for a few minutes until tender. Remove them from the pan, roughly chop and reserve them. Peel and dice the onion. Melt 40 g (1½ oz) butter in a saucepan and sweat the onion in the butter until translucent. Then add the cooked Chinese leaves, season them with salt, and sweat them in the pan with the onion for about 10 minutes. Blend the cornflour with 2 tablespoons of cold water and add it to the Chinese leaf mixture. Then fold in the crème fraîche.

Chop the ribs into chunks and steam them or cook them in boiling, salted water until tender. Drain and reserve them. Melt 1-2 tbsp butter in a

pan and toss the steamed ribs in the melted butter. Serve them with the chopped leaves.

Variation: Serve the Chinese leaf ribs in a white sauce flavoured with 1 tablespoon of grated cheese.

BUTTERED BRUSSELS SPROUTS

Serves 4

1 kg (2 lb) Brussels sprouts	nutmeg, grated
40 g (1½ oz) butter or margarine	salt

Remove any wilted or damaged outer leaves from the sprouts, cut away the base of the stalk, score a cross in the base and wash them. Melt the butter in a saucepan, add the sprouts and season wthem with salt and grated nutmeg. Add a little water to the saucepan then cover it and sweat the sprouts for 15-20 minutes.

Variation: Steam or boil the Brussels sprouts, then toss them in melted butter immediately before serving.

FRENCH BEANS WITH CHANTERELLE MUSHROOMS

Serves 3

500 g (1 lb) French beans	250 g (8 oz) chanterelle mushrooms
2 or 3 sprigs of savory	
100 g (3½ oz) streaky bacon	400 g (13 oz) tomatoes
	butter
1 onion	salt and pepper

Top, tail and wash the French beans. In a saucepan, bring a little salted water to the boil, add the beans and savory to the pan, bring it to the boil again, cover and simmer for 5 minutes. Drain the beans and reserve them. Peel and dice the onion. Dice the bacon. Melt the butter in a saucepan, add the diced onion and bacon and fry them until translucent. Carefully trim and wipe the mushrooms and add them to the onion and bacon mixture. Season the mixture with salt and pepper, cover and sweat it for about 5 minutes.

Bring a saucepan of water to the boil. Blanch the tomatoes in the boiling water for a few moments, then refresh them in cold water and skin them. Cut them into quarters and add them to the mushroom mixture with the cooked beans, folding in lightly. Fry the mixture over a gentle heat for about 15 minutes.

Opposite: *Buttered Brussels sprouts*
Right: *Broccoli in Hollandaise sauce*

BROCCOLI IN HOLLANDAISE SAUCE

Serves 4

750 g (1½ lb) broccoli
1 clove of garlic
200 g (7 oz) butter
4 egg yolks
1-2 tsp lemon juice
3 tbsp white wine
2 tbsp fresh parsley, chopped

2-3 tbsp fresh chives, finely chopped
2-3 tbsp fresh fennel, chopped
1 tbsp fresh thyme, chopped
2-3 tbsp basil, chopped
salt and pepper

Remove the broccoli leaves, trim the stalks and score a cross in the stalks down to the base of the florets. Wash the broccoli. Peel and crush the clove of garlic. Bring 2 litres (3½ pints) of salted water to the boil and put the crushed garlic in the pan with the broccoli and a knob of butter. Cook the broccoli for 8-10 minutes, then drain it. Arrange the broccoli on a warmed serving dish and keep warm.

To make the hollandaise sauce: Melt the butter in a small saucepan, skim it until clarified. In another saucepan, beat together the egg yolks, lemon juice and white wine. Season with salt and pepper. Heat this sauce in a double saucepan or in a bowl over a saucepan of simmering water, whisking constantly with an electric whisk for about 5 minutes until light and foaming. Then gradually trickle in the melted butter, stirring all the time, until a creamy sauce forms.

Add the parsley, chives, fennel, thyme and basil. Mix thoroughly. Season the sauce to taste with salt and pepper and serve it with the broccoli.

BROCCOLI MIMOSA

Serves 4

1 kg (2 lb) broccoli
grated nutmeg
75 g (3 oz) butter

2 hard-boiled eggs
salt

Remove the leaves from the broccoli, trim the stalks and score a cross in the stalks down to the base of the florets. Wash the broccoli. Bring to the boil 1 litre (1¾ pints) of water, to which salt and grated nutmeg have been added. Put the broccoli into the pan, bring the pan to the boil again and simmer the broccoli for about 10 minutes.

Carefully remove the broccoli from the pan using a slotted spoon, arrange it on a warmed serving dish and keep it warm. Melt the butter and pour it over the broccoli. Sprinkle the finely chopped hard-boiled eggs over.

ARTICHOKES WITH VINAIGRETTE DRESSING

Serves 4

4 artichokes	1 tbsp fresh chives, finely
7 tbsp vinegar	chopped
8 tbsp oil	1 sprig fresh chervil
1 tsp mustard	1 sprig fresh basil
1 tbsp fresh parsley,	salt
chopped	pepper

Peel the artichokes by removing the damaged leaves and cutting off the tips of the others. Blanch them in salted water and leave them to drain. Then cook them for 30-40 minutes in 3-4 litres (5-7 pints) of salted, boiling water with 4 tablespoons of vinegar added to it. (They are cooked when the leaves can be separated easily from the heart.) Remove them from the water, turn them upside down and leave them to drain.

To make the vinaigrette: Whisk together the oil, remaining vinegar and mustard. Then add the parsley, chives, chervil and basil. Season to taste with salt and pepper. Serve the dressing as an accompaniment to the artichokes.

Variation: Place each artichoke on a plate. Carefully spread out the leaves, taking care not to separate them from the base. With a spoon, carefully remove the choke covering the heart and fill the space with vinaigrette.

Below: *Artichokes with vinaigrette dressing*
Opposite: *Broccoli with vinaigrette dressing*

Blanch the broad beans for 4 minutes, drain them and remove the skins. Cook them for 15 minutes in boiling, salted water in a covered pan. Drain them. Peel and finely dice the onions. Sweat them in melted butter until translucent. Add the broad beans, cover the pan and sweat them for about 10 minutes.

Incorporate the crème fraîche and cook the broad beans for a minute or two longer so that they soak up the crème fraîche. Season the beans with salt and pepper. Add the herbs and full fat yoghurt.

Tip: Serve the broad beans with pork or lamb chops.

BROCCOLI WITH VINAIGRETTE DRESSING

Serves 4

800 g (1½ lb) broccoli
4 tbsp oil
3 tbsp vinegar
1 tsp mustard
1 tbsp fresh chives, chopped
1 tbsp fresh parsley, chopped
1 tbsp fresh lemon balm, chopped
1 tbsp fresh tarragon, chopped
salt
pepper

Remove the broccoli leaves, trim the stalks and score a cross in the stalks down to the base of the florets. Wash the broccoli. Add the broccoli to boiling, salted water. Bring the pan to the boil again, cover it, and cook the broccoli for 8-10 minutes. Drain the broccoli.

To make the vinaigrette: Whisk together the oil, vinegar and mustard with the chopped herbs and season with salt and pepper. Arrange the broccoli on a serving dish and drizzle the vinaigrette over the broccoli so that it soaks up the dressing.

BROAD BEANS WITH SOUR CREAM

Serves 3

500 g (1 lb) shelled broad beans or 2 kg (4½ lb) with the pods
2-3 onions
2 knobs of butter
150 g (5 oz) crème fraîche
150 g (5 oz) full fat natural yoghurt
1 tbsp fresh marjoram, finely chopped
1 tbsp fresh savory, finely chopped
salt
pepper

Below: *Broccoli with almonds*

BROCCOLI WITH ALMONDS

Serves 4

800 g (1½ lb) broccoli
50-75 g (2-3 oz) butter
50 g (2 oz) flaked almonds

Remove the leaves from the broccoli. Trim the stalks and score a cross in the stems down to the base of the florets. Wash it and cook it for 10 minutes in boiling, salted water. Drain the broccoli. Sauté the flaked almonds in melted butter until golden. Pour the almonds over the broccoli and serve immediately.

Broccoli with almonds is delicious served with steak accompanied by sautéed potatoes.

STEAMED PETIT POIS

Serves 4

*1 kg (2 lb) shelled petit pois
or 2.5 kg (5½ lb) unshelled
40 g (1½ oz) butter or
margarine
sugar*

*1 tbsp fresh parsley,
chopped
salt*

Wash the petit pois. Melt the butter or margarine and sweat the peas in it. Add 150 ml (5 fl oz) water, season with salt and sugar to taste and simmer in a covered pan for 10-15 minutes. Sprinkle chopped parsley over the peas just before serving.

Serve with steak or any other grilled meat.

MANGETOUT WITH ALMONDS

Serves 3

*600 g (1¼ lb) mangetout
50 g (2 oz) butter*

*40 g (1½ oz) flaked almonds
salt and pepper*

Prepare the mangetout (top and tail and remove any string), wash them and immerse them in boiling, salted water. Bring the pan to the boil again, cover and simmer

Below: *Steamed petit pois*

for about 5 minutes. Drain the peas. Sauté the flaked almonds in the melted butter until golden. Add the mangetout and toss them in the almond butter, coating thoroughly. Season with salt and pepper and serve immediately.

Serve with steak or any other grilled meat.

PURÊE OF SPLIT PEAS

Serves 2

*400 g (13 oz) split peas
1 fresh bouquet garni
1 onion
20 g (¾ oz) butter*

*50 g (2 oz) streaky bacon,
diced
salt
pepper*

Rinse the split peas and soak them for 24 hours. Cook the peas in the soaking liquid for 2½ hours. Wash and carefully pick over the bouquet garni and add it to the split peas after 1½ hours.

At the end of the cooking time, strain off the herbs. Reheat the pea purée and beat it until a smooth creamy mass forms. Season with salt and pepper. Peel and slice the onion. Brown the sliced onion in the butter with the diced bacon. Add the bacon and onions to the split peas just before serving.

Serve with pork chump chops or salt beef.

PARSLEYED MUSHROOMS

Serves 4

1 kg (2 lb) mushrooms
(button or boletus
mushrooms)
2 onions
40 g (1½ oz) streaky bacon

30 g (1 oz) butter
1 tbsp fresh parsley,
chopped
salt and pepper

Remove the mushroom stalks and wipe the mushrooms. Peel and dice the onions, dice the bacon. Render the bacon, add 30 g (1 oz) butter and sweat the onions in the bacon fat and butter until translucent.

Add the mushrooms, season with salt and pepper, cover and cook for 10-15 minutes. Adjust the seasoning as necessary and sprinkle with chopped parsley.

MACEDOINE OF VEGETABLES

Serves 4-6

250 g (8 oz) petit pois,
shelled or 750 g (1½ lb),
unshelled
250 g (8 oz) carrots
250 g (8 oz) asparagus
½ kohl-rabi
½ cauliflower

40 g (1½ oz) butter or
margarine
1 tbsp fresh parsley,
chopped
salt

Shell the peas. Peel and dice the carrots. Peel and chop the asparagus. Peel and slice the kohl-rabi. Clean the cauliflower and divide it into florets. Wash and drain all

the vegetables. Melt 40 g (1½ oz) butter or margarine and sauté all the vegetables in it. Add 150 ml (5 fl oz) water, season with salt, cover and steam the vegetables for 1-1½ hours. Sprinkle chopped parsley over the vegetables before serving.

Tip: The vegetables retain their colour and shape better if steamed separately and then tossed in butter.

MANGETOUT IN LEMON DRESSING

Serves 3

600 g (1¼ lb) mangetout
2 tbsp oil
150 g (5 oz) crème fraâche
2 tbsp natural yoghurt

grated zest of 1 unwaxed
lemon
1-2 tbsp fresh lemon balm,
chopped
salt and pepper

Prepare the mangetout (top and tail them and remove any string), wash them and immerse them in boiling, salted water.
Add the oil to the pan and bring it to the boil again, then simmer on a medium heat for 5-7 minutes. Drain the mangetout, arrange them on a warmed serving dish and keep warm.

To make the lemon dressing: Mix together the crème fraîche and yoghurt. Season to taste with salt and pepper and add the grated lemon zest and chopped lemon balm. Serve with the mangetout.

Serve with chops or steak.

GLAZED CARROTS

Serves 2-3

500 g (1 lb) baby carrots	fresh mint, chopped
50 g (2 oz) butter	salt
3 tbsp sugar	pepper

Remove the leaves from the carrots, leaving 1 cm (½ inch) stalk. Scrape the carrots, wash them and immerse them in boiling, salted water. Cook them for 7 minutes and then drain them.

Melt the butter and sweat the carrots in the covered pan for a few minutes. Add the sugar, stir well, and continue cooking the carrots in a covered pan for 10 minutes. Season with pepper and sprinkle with chopped mint.

CREAMED SPINACH

Serves 3

1 kg (2 lb) spinach	2 tbsp double cream
1 small onion	grated nutmeg
40 g (1½ oz) butter	salt
1 tsp cornflour	pepper

Pick over the spinach and wash it carefully, changing the water 5 or 6 times. Then cook it without adding any water and chop it or purée it. Peel and finely dice the onion. Melt the butter, add the onion and sweat it until it is translucent. Add the spinach, season with salt and pepper and add grated nutmeg. Cover the pan and cook for about 10 minutes. Blend the cornflour with a tablespoon of cold water and add it to the spinach mixture to bind it. Adjust the seasoning and incorporate the double cream, mixing well.

Serve with fried eggs and boiled potatoes.

Tip: If the spinach seems bitter to you, throw away the juice produced during cooking and substitute as much milk as the spinach will soak up.

BABY CARROTS

Serves 4-5

1 kg (2 lb) baby carrots	2 tbsp crème fraîche
1 onion	2 tbsp fresh fines herbes,
2-3 knobs of butter	chopped
250 ml (8 fl oz) meat stock	1 hard-boiled egg
30 g (1 oz) butter	lemon juice
30 g (1 oz) flour	salt and pepper

Clean, wash and scrape the carrots. Slice or dice them. Peel and dice the onion. Melt the butter and sweat the carrots and the onion in it. Add the stock, cover the pan and simmer for 20 minutes until the vegetables are tender. Reserve the cooking liquid for the sauce.

To make the sauce: Cook the flour in the butter. Add 400 ml (14 fl oz) of the vegetable stock, made up to the right volume with water. Whisk the sauce to prevent lumps, bring it to the boil and simmer it for about 5 minutes.

Below: *Creamed spinach*
Right: *Glazed carrots*

Incorporate the crème fraîche and stir. Season with salt and pepper. Add the lemon juice and fines herbes and stir. Then add the carrots and reheat them over a medium heat. Chop the hard-boiled egg and sprinkle it over the vegetables.

FRENCH BEANS WITH CHEESE

Serves 4

800 g (1½ lb) French beans
fresh or dried savory

2 portions cheese spread
4 slices boiled ham
knob of butter

*T*op and tail the beans, wash them and immerse them in a saucepan of boiling, salted water with the savory. Cook them for about 30 minutes on a medium heat, then drain the beans and divide them into four portions on a warmed serving dish. Keep them warm.

Melt the cheese in a double saucepan, stirring all the time. Melt the butter and fry the slices of boiled ham in it. Arrange the slices of ham on top of each portion of beans and top with melted cheese.

Serve with grilled tomatoes and sautéed potatoes.

BUTTERED FRENCH BEANS

Serves 4

1 kg (2 lb) French beans
(thin, well-rounded string
beans or
bigger, flatter mangetout)
1 medium onion

40 g (1½ oz) butter
salt and pepper
1 tbsp fresh parsley,
chopped

*T*op, tail and wash the beans. Peel and dice the onion. Melt the butter, add the onion and sweat until it is translucent. Add the beans, brown them, then add 150 ml (5 fl oz) water. Season with salt and pepper.

Cover the pan and cook the beans for 25-30 minutes. Adjust the seasoning, sprinkle with chopped parsley and serve.

Variation: Add 250 g (8 oz) chopped tomatoes 10 minutes before the end of cooking time.

LENTILS WITH VINEGAR

Serves 4

400 g (13 oz) lentils
1 fresh bouquet garni
1 onion
50 g (2 oz) bacon, diced

2-3 tbsp vinegar
sugar
salt

*R*inse the lentils and soak them for 12-24 hours in 750 ml (1¼ pints) water. Clean the bouquet garni, wash it, chop it and cook it with the lentils for about 25 minutes in the soaking liquid, which has been salted and brought to the boil.

Peel and dice the onion. Render the bacon, then add the onion and brown it in the bacon fat. Add the bacon and onion to the lentils and continue cooking. Season the lentils with salt, add the vinegar and adjust the seasoning with a little sugar.

Serve with black or white pudding or sausages.

CARAMELIZED BABY ONIONS

Serves 3-4

500 g (1 lb) baby onions
2 tbsp oil
60 g (2½ oz) brown sugar
200 ml (7 fl oz) red wine
6 tbsp red wine vinegar

2 tbsp tomato purée
2 tsp ground cinnamon
cayenne pepper
salt

Peel the onions. Heat the oil in a large frying pan. Add the onions and sweat them until translucent. Season with salt, sprinkle with brown sugar and leave them to caramelize.

Mix together the red wine, red wine vinegar and tomato purée. Pour this mixture over the onions. Stir well, season with cinnamon and cayenne pepper, cover and cook for 15 minutes, stirring occasionally. Remove the onions from the pan and boil the cooking liquid for about 10 minutes until thickened and reduced. Return the onions to the pan, heat them through and adjust the seasoning if necessary with vinegar and cinnamon.

This dish is a perfect accompaniment to lamb, game or fondue bourguignonne.

ONIONS IN PORT

Serves 6-7

1 kg (2 lb) medium-sized
onions
250 ml (8 fl oz) red wine
vinegar
250 g (8 oz) sugar
2 tsp salt
8 small, fresh sage leaves
4 bay leaves

20 g (¾ oz) root ginger,
peeled and
 sliced
5 cloves
10 black peppercorns
1 stick of cinnamon
zest of 1 organic lemon

Peel the onions and cook them for 10 minutes in boiling water. Remove them from the pan and immerse them in cold water for 10 minutes, then drain them. Bring the red wine vinegar to the boil with 100 g (3½ oz) sugar and the salt. Put the remaining sugar in a saucepan and stir it until caramelized.

Then add the hot vinegar mixture and stir until the caramel dissolves. Carefully rinse the sage leaves, pat them dry with kitchen paper and add them to the vinegar and caramel mixture with the onions.

Opposite: *Onions in port*
Above: *Caramelized baby onions*

Bring this mixture to the boil and simmer it for 5 minutes. Add the port. Put the onions and herbs and spices into glass jars, cover with the port-flavoured cooking liquid, close the jars tightly and keep them in a cool place.

Serve these onions in port with fondue bourguignonne or grilled meats.

ONIONS IN WHITE WINE

Serves 4-5

800 g (1½ lb) onions
50 g (2 oz) butter
125 ml (4 fl oz) instant meat stock

150 ml (5 fl oz) white wine
2 tbsp crème fraîche
1 tbsp fresh parsley, chopped
salt

Peel the onions, slice them in half, then slice them thinly. Melt the butter and brown the onions in it. Add the stock and white wine to the pan, cover and cook the onions for 10-15 minutes. Season with salt, add the crème fraîche, and sprinkle with chopped parsley.

ITALIAN-STYLE VEGETABLES

Serves 2

1 large green pepper
2 small tomatoes
60 g (2½ oz) chanterelle mushrooms
1 large onion
knob of butter
a little meat stock

1 tbsp cornflour
1 tbsp tomato purée
1 clove of garlic, chopped
1 tbsp crème fraîche
fresh parsley, chopped
salt
pepper

Remove the stalk from the pepper, slice it in half, remove the core and seeds. Wash the pepper and dice it roughly. Blanch the tomatoes, then rinse them immediately in cold water. Skin the tomatoes and cut into quarters.
Slice the biggest mushrooms in half. Peel and dice the onion and fry it until golden in the butter. Add the green pepper and the mushrooms, fry them quickly until brown, then add the stock, cover the pan and simmer for about 10 minutes. Then add the quartered tomatoes, cover the pan again and cook for 2-3 minutes. Blend together the cornflour and 2-3 tablespoons cold water and add this mixture to the vegetables to bind them. Bring the vegetable mixture to the boil. Season with the tomato purée and garlic, salt and pepper. Add the crème fraîche and sprinkle with chopped parsley just before serving.

BUTTERED FENNEL

Serves 4

1 kg (2 lb) fennel bulbs   salt
75 g (3 oz) butter

Make a cut in the fennel stems and open them out a little to remove the tough centre section, remove any damaged leaves, trim the tips and wash the fennel. Bring 1 litre (1¾ pints) salted water to the boil, add the fennel and cook it for about 20 minutes. Then cut the fennel bulbs into quarters and arrange them on a warmed serving dish. Keep them warm. Melt the butter until foaming and pour it over the fennel quarters.

Below: *Italian-style vegetables*

crème fraîche. Pour this mixture over the bottom of the oven-proof dish. Bake the aubergines for 40 minutes at 200-225°C (400-425°F, Gas Mark 6-7). Blend the cornflour with 150 ml (5 fl oz) cold water and add it to the cooking juices to bind them. Adjust the seasoning. Add the chopped herbs. Spoon the cooking juices over the aubergines and top them with grated cheese. Brown them in the oven or under a hot grill for 8-10 minutes.

STUFFED ONIONS

Serves 4

4 large onions (about 800 g (1½ lb) total weight)	sausage meat
15 g (½ oz) butter	2 tbsp fresh parsley, chopped
3 tbsp crème fraîche	salt
400 g (13 oz) smoked	

Peel the onions and immerse them in boiling, salted water. When they are half cooked, slice a lid off the top and remove some of the flesh from the inside. Dice this onion flesh. Melt the butter in an oven-proof dish and brown the diced onion in it. Add the crème fraîche to the fried onion, season with salt and arrange the onion shells on top of this mixture.

Mix the smoked sausage meat with 1 tbsp chopped parsley and use it to stuff the onions. Bake the onions in the oven at 200-225°C (400-425°F, Gas Mark 6-7) for about 30 minutes. Sprinkle the onions with chopped parsley just before serving.

TOMATOES STUFFED WITH TUNA

Serves 4

8 large firm tomatoes	3 tbsp mayonnaise
400 g (13 oz) tin tuna in brine	grated zest of 1 unwaxed lemon
40 g (1½ oz) long grain rice	fresh basil, chopped
1-2 tbsp fresh parsley, chopped	salt and pepper

Cook the rice. Wash the tomatoes, slice off the tops to make lids, then scoop out the flesh and seeds using a teaspoon. Season the insides with salt and turn them upside down on kitchen paper to drain.
Drain the tuna, flake it and mix it with the cooked rice, chopped parsley, mayonnaise, grated lemon zest, pepper and basil. Stuff the tomatoes with this mixture and put the tomato lids on top.

STUFFED AUBERGINES

Serves 4

2 large or 4 small aubergines (about 800 g (1½ lb) total weight)	250 ml (8 fl oz) crème fraîche
1 onion	2-3 tbsp cornflour
125 g (4 oz) minced beef	1 tbsp fresh parsley, chopped
125 g (4 oz) minced pork	1 tbsp fresh chives, finely chopped
1 egg	100 g (3½ oz) Gruyère cheese, grated
1 slice of stale bread	
50 g (2 oz) butter	
3-4 tomatoes	salt and pepper

Wash and dry the aubergines. Cut them in half lengthways. Sprinkle the cut sides with salt and turn them upside down. Leave them to drain for about 30 minutes. Scoop out the flesh, leaving about 1 cm (½ inch) thickness. Finely chop the flesh and mix it with the minced meat and a diced onion. Bind this mixture with the beaten egg and the bread soaked in water and squeezed out thoroughly. Season with salt and pepper and use this mixture to stuff the aubergines.

Melt the butter in an oven-proof dish and put the aubergines in the dish. Blanch the tomatoes and rinse them under cold water to remove the skins, then chop them finely. Mix together the chopped tomatoes and

Above: *Stuffed aubergines*
Left: *Stuffed onions*

CABBAGE PARCELS

Serves 4-5

1 white cabbage or head of kale	200 g (7 oz) minced beef
	200 g (7 oz) minced pork
1 slice of stale bread	75 g (3 oz) butter
1 medium onion	1-2 tbsp cornflour
1 egg	salt and pepper

*I*mmerse the cabbage in salted, boiling water for a moment, until the outer leaves come off. Repeat this step until all the leaves have come off. Leave them to drain and remove any thick ribs.

Soften the bread in cold water and squeeze it out well. Peel and dice the onion. Mix together these ingredients and the minced meat, binding them with the beaten egg. Season with salt and pepper. Place 2 or 3 large cabbage leaves on top of each other, place a portion of the stuffing on top, roll up the cabbage leaves and secure them with kitchen string or cocktail sticks. Melt the butter and fry the cabbage parcels in it until brown on all sides. Add 250-500 ml (8-18 fl oz) boiling water and braise the parcels for 35-45 minutes, turning them from time to time and adding more water to the pan if necessary.

When the parcels are cooked, remove the kitchen string or cocktail sticks and arrange the parcels on a warmed serving dish. Blend together the cornflour and 3 tablespoons of cold water and add this to the cooking liquid to thicken it. Adjust the sauce's seasoning to taste.

STUFFED CABBAGE

Serves 4-6

8 large tomatoes	2 tsp cornflour
100 g (3½ oz) Bleu d'Auvergne	2 eggs, separated
or any other soft, crumbly, tart- flavoured blue cheese	salt and pepper
150 ml (5 fl oz) milk	1 tsp fresh tarragon, finely chopped

Remove the cabbage leaves (if they are very tightly closed, plunge the cabbage into boiling water several times, as in the previous recipe). Remove the biggest stalks and immerse the cabbage leaves in boiling water to soften them. Butter a heat-proof mould or basin and line it with the biggest cabbage leaves. Soak the bread in cold water, then squeeze it out well. Peel and dice the onion. Mix together the bread, onion and minced meat, binding it with the beaten egg and seasoning it with salt and white pepper.

Layer the stuffing mixture and cabbage leaves in the mould, finishing with a layer of cabbage. Cover the mould with a saucepan lid or plate, then put it in a covered casserole dish filled with boiling water. Steam the cabbage for 1 hour.

The stuffed cabbage can also be cooked in a tea towel. Butter the centre of the tea towel, line it with cabbage leaves, then alternate layers of stuffing and cabbage leaves, finishing with a layer of cabbage.
Secure the tea towel by knotting the two opposite corners. Then suspend the tea towel from a wooden spoon resting across a saucepan or casserole dish containing boiling water, and steam it this way.

The stuffed cabbage may be served surrounded by braised, sliced tomatoes, or with a tomato or caper sauce.

TOMATOES WITH BLUE CHEESE

Serves 4

1 white cabbage or head of kale	1 egg
3 knobs of butter	250 g (8 oz) minced pork
1 slice of stale bread	salt
1 small onion	freshly ground white pepper

Wash and dry the tomatoes. Slice off the tops to make lids, scoop out the flesh and seeds, then leave them to drain upside down on kitchen paper. Heat the milk. Crumble the cheese, add it to the milk and stir until a smooth, creamy sauce forms.

Blend together the cornflour and 2 tablespoons of cold water, then add it to the cheese sauce to thicken it. Allow the sauce to cool a little. Beat the 2 egg yolks and add them to the cheese sauce. Whisk the egg whites until very stiff, then fold them into the cheese sauce and season the mixture with salt and pepper. Add the tarragon and stir it into the cheese sauce. Fill the tomato shells with the cheese sauce. Put the lids on the tomatoes and arrange them on a buttered, oven-proof dish. Bake them in the oven at 225°C (425°F, Gas Mark 7) for about 15 minutes.

Left: *Cabbage parcels*
Below: *Tomatoes with blue cheese*

LEEKS WITH HAM

Serves 4

4 leeks	fraîche
4 slices boiled ham, about	1 tsp cornflour
90 g (3 ½ oz) in total	grated nutmeg
150 ml (5 fl oz) crème	salt

Carefully wash and trim the leeks. Cut them into chunks roughly equal in length to the width of the slices of ham. Cook the leeks for about 10 minutes in 500 ml (18 fl oz) boiling, salted water, then drain them.

Wrap a slice of ham around each chunk of leek. Arrange them on a well-buttered serving dish. Cover the dish either with its lid or with foil and place it in the oven at 225-250⁰C (425-475⁰F, Gas Mark 7-9) for about 20 minutes.

Arrange the cooked leeks on a warmed dish. Blend together the cornflour and 1 tablespoon of cold water and add it to the cooking liquid for the leeks to thicken it. Bring the sauce to the boil. Pour this sauce over the leeks.

SALSIFY AU GRATIN

Serves 4

1 kg (2 lb) salsify	40 g (1½ oz) flour
4 thin slices beef (about	grated nutmeg
400 g (13 oz) total weight)	fresh fennel or dill fronds,
2 heaped tbsp flour	chopped
4 tbsp vinegar	50 g (2 oz) Gouda
40 g (1½ oz) butter	salt and pepper

Scrub, scrape and wash the salsify under running water until nice and white. Blend the 2 heaped tablespoons of flour with 1 litre (1¾ pints) cold water and immerse the salsify in the water for a moment. Remove the salsify and leave it to drain. Cut the biggest pieces in half lengthways. Bring 4 litres (7 pints) water to the boil and add 4 tablespoons of vinegar. Plunge the salsify into the water and simmer it for about 10 minutes. Remove the salsify with a slotted spoon. Wrap 4-8 slices of meat around the salsify and arrange on a buttered oven-proof dish. Reserve 4 litres (7 pints) of the salsify cooking liquid.
To make the sauce: Melt the butter in a small saucepan and add the 40 g (1½ oz) flour, stirring it carefully into the butter. Add the salsify cooking liquid and whisk it carefully to prevent lumps forming. Bring the sauce gently to the boil and simmer it for about 5 minutes over a gentle heat, stirring all the time, then season it with salt and pepper, nutmeg and chopped fennel or dill fronds.

Pour this sauce over the salsify. Sprinkle the grated Gouda on top. Put the salsify in an oven preheated to 200-225⁰C (400-425⁰F, Gas Mark 6-7) and bake for 20-25 minutes.

Below: *Salsify au gratin*

Left: *Leeks with ham*

AUBERGINES AU GRATIN

Serves 6

6-8 aubergines
3 cloves of garlic
500 ml (18 fl oz) olive oil
250 g (8 oz) tomato purée
a few small basil leaves

100 g (3½ oz) mozzarella
150 g (5 oz) boiled ham
60 g (2½ oz) Parmesan, grated
salt and pepper

Wash the aubergines and slice them lengthways. Sprinkle the slices with salt and leave them to drain for about 30 minutes. Rinse the aubergine slices and pat them dry. Crush the garlic. Heat 4 tablespoons of oil and brown the garlic in it. Add the tomato purée. Season with salt and pepper. Rinse and thoroughly dry the basil and chop it finely, then add it to the sauce. Simmer the sauce over a low heat. In a frying pan heat the remaining oil and fry the aubergine slices until golden, then drain them on kitchen paper. Slice the mozzarella and ham.

Alternately layer the aubergine slices, tomato sauce, mozzarella and ham in a buttered oven-proof dish. Finish with a layer of tomato sauce and sprinkle grated Parmesan on top. Bake the aubergines in an oven preheated to 175-200°C (350-450°F, Gas Mark 4-6) for about 30 minutes. This dish may also be eaten cold.

CHANTERELLES WITH PARMESAN

Serves 2-3

400 g (13 oz) chanterelle mushrooms
1 red onion
3-4 knobs of butter

4 slices of brown bread
1 tbsp Parmesan, grated
fresh parsley, chopped
salt and pepper

Carefully wipe the mushrooms. Peel and thinly slice the onion and fry it in the melted butter until translucent. Then add the mushrooms, cover the pan and sweat them for about 15 minutes. Season with salt and pepper. Butter the slices of bread and divide the mushroom mixture amongst them.

Sprinkle grated Parmesan over each slice of bread and mushrooms, then toast the slices under a preheated grill for about 5 minutes, until the cheese melts. Sprinkle chopped parsley over the mushrooms on toast just before serving.

Peel and finely dice the onions. Dice the bacon and fry it in a dry frying pan to render the fat. Add the butter and the diced onions to the pan. Sweat the onions until translucent, then add the mushrooms to the pan. Season the mushroom mixture with salt and pepper, cover the pan and sauté the mushrooms for about 20 minutes. Sprinkle chopped parsley over the mushrooms just before serving.

Serve with scrambled eggs and crusty bread.

SAUTÊED MUSHROOMS

Serves 4-6

500 g (1 lb) boletus mushrooms
250 g (8 oz) button mushrooms
125 g (4 oz) chanterelle mushrooms
125 g (4 oz) ceps
100 g (3½ oz) streaky

bacon
2 knobs of butter
1-2 tbsp fresh parsley, chopped
2 onions
salt
pepper

Below:
Sautéed mushrooms

Wipe the mushrooms. Leave the smallest mushrooms whole and slice the biggest in half, or chop them.

Left: *Chanterelles with Parmesan*

CHINESE LEAVES AU GRATIN

Serves 4

1 head of Chinese leaves
1 litre of meat stock
1-3 knobs of butter
50 g (2 oz) Gruyère, grated
125g (4 oz) cream

1 tbsp fresh parsley,
chopped
1 small onion
salt and pepper

Clean the head of Chinese leaves, slice it in half, then into quarters (it should not fall apart). Bring the stock to the boil and cook the Chinese leaves in it for about 10 minutes. Drain the Chinese leaves, then arrange on a buttered oven-proof dish, layering them with the butter and half the grated cheese.

To make the sauce: Peel and dice the onion and mix together the diced onion and cream. Add the chopped parsley and season with salt and pepper. Pour this mixture over the Chinese leaves and sprinkle the remaining grated cheese on top. Bake the Chinese leaves in the oven at 200-225°C (400-425°F, Gas Mark 6-7) for about 15 minutes. If necessary, brown the Chinese leaves under a hot grill.

CHINESE LEAF PARCELS

Serves 4-6

2 firm heads of Chinese
leaves (about 500 g (1 lb)
total weight
2 spring onions
1 large carrot
50 g (2 oz) button
mushrooms
4 tbsp beansprouts
200 g (7 oz) chicken breast

or turkey escalope
300 ml (½ pint) oil plus 1
tablespoon
soy sauce
4 tbsp dry sherry
1 tbsp lemon juice
1 tsp honey
salt and pepper

Remove any damaged outer leaves from the Chinese leaves and separate 16 medium-sized leaves. Remove the large ribs. Quickly blanch the leaves (30 seconds) to soften them, then refresh them in cold water immediately and drain them on kitchen paper.

To make the stuffing: Clean the onions, retaining 15 cm (6 inches) of the green, wash them and cut them into rounds. Peel and dice the carrot. Rinse the beansprouts and drain them. Wipe the mushrooms and chop them finely. Heat 1 tablespoon of oil and sweat the onions, carrot, beansprouts and mushrooms in it for 2-3 minutes. Finely dice the chicken breast or turkey escalope and add

Above: *Chinese leaf parcels*

it to the vegetables. Season the mixture with salt, pepper and soya sauce, cover the pan and braise the mixture for a further 1-2 minutes.

Arrange one Chinese leaf on top of another in the shape of a cross. Place a portion of stuffing mixture in the middle of the leaves (reserve the juices). Roll up the leaves and tie them with kitchen string. Repeat until all the leaves are used up. Heat 300 ml (½ pint) oil and brown the parcels on all sides, then remove them from the pan, drain them on kitchen paper and keep them warm.

Mix together the sherry, lemon juice, honey and a little soy sauce. Add the meat juices from the stuffing mixture, mix all the ingredients well and pour the sauce over the Chinese leaf parcels.

Serve the parcels immediately with buttered rice or a mixed salad.

Opposite: *Chinese leaves au gratin*

ingredients with the kohl-rabi flesh and the minced meats. Season the mixture with salt, pepper and nutmeg.

Fill the kohl-rabi with this stuffing and put the lids back on top. Melt the butter in a casserole dish and lay the kohl-rabi side by side in it to seal them. Add the meat stock, cover the casserole dish and braise the kohl-rabi for about 45 minutes. Then put the kohl-rabi on a warmed dish and keep them hot. Blend together the cornflour and cream and add it to the kohl-rabi cooking liquid to thicken it. Adjust the seasoning and pour the sauce over the kohl-rabi. Sprinkle finely chopped chives over the top.

ONIONS IN CREAM SAUCE

Serves 3-4

500 g (1 lb) onions	4 slices of sandwich bread
250 ml (8 fl oz) crème fraîche	3-4 knobs of butter
	salt and pepper
150 g (5 oz) Gruyère, grated	fresh thyme, chopped

Peel the onions and slice them thinly. Melt 1-2 knobs of butter and add the onions to it. Sweat the onions until translucent, then season them with salt, pepper and thyme. Divide the onions amongst 4 small individual dishes. Season the cream with salt and pour it over the onions until they are just covered. Sprinkle grated cheese over the onions.

Remove the crusts from the bread and cut it into small cubes. Divide the cubed bread between the dishes of onions. Use 2 knobs of butter to dot on top of the bread cubes. Bake the onion dishes in the oven for 20-30 minutes at 200°C (400°F, Gas Mark 6).

CAULIFLOWER IN BATTER

Serves 4-5

1 cauliflower	75 g (3 oz) flour
1 egg	grated nutmeg
5 tbsp oil	salt

STUFFED KOHL-RABI

Serves 6-8

8 medium-sized kohl-rabi (approx. 1.2 kg (3lb) total weight)	50 g (2 oz) minced beef
	50 g (2 oz) minced pork
1 slice of stale bread	grated nutmeg
1 onion	240 ml (8 fl oz) meat stock
1 tomato	50 g (2 oz) butter
125 g (4 oz) chanterelle mushrooms	2 tsp cornflour
	150 g (5 oz) cream
1 hard-boiled egg	fresh chives, finely chopped
1 large sausage	salt and pepper

Peel the kohl-rabi. Slice off the tops to make lids and scoop out the flesh (reserve 2 tablespoons of flesh to add to the stuffing and the rest, if liked, to make soup).

To make the stuffing: Soak the stale bread in cold water to soften it, then squeeze it out well. Peel and dice the onion. Blanch the tomato quickly, then refresh it under cold water, skin and dice it. Finely chop the chanterelle mushrooms. Chop the hard-boiled egg. Remove the skin from the sausage and slice it thinly. Mix all these

Above left: *Onions in cream sauce*
Right: *Cauliflower in batter*

Wash the cauliflower thoroughly and divide it into medium-sized florets. Cook the florets for about 10 minutes in boiling, salted water. Drain them well. Beat together the egg, flour and about 100 ml (3½ fl oz) cold water to form a thick but liquid batter. Season the batter to taste with salt and nutmeg. Heat 4-5 tablespoons of oil in a frying pan. Coat the cauliflower florets in the batter and fry them for about 15-20 minutes in the hot oil until crisp.

SALAD OF LAMB'S LETTUCE WITH EGGS

Serves 4

250 g (8 oz) lamb's lettuce
2 hard-boiled eggs
1 clove of garlic
1 shallot or small onion
3 tbsp oil

1-2 tbsp vinegar
fresh chives, chopped
salt
pepper

Clean the lamb's lettuce. Wash it carefully and drain it.
Shell the eggs and cut them into quarters. Divide the
lettuce and eggs between 4 plates.

To make the dressing, cut the clove of garlic in half and
crush it. Peel and thinly slice the shallot. Combine the
oil, vinegar, salt and pepper to make a vinaigrette
dressing. Add the chives. Toss the salad thoroughly in
the dressing and serve.

SALAD OF LAMB'S LETTUCE WITH TOMATOES AND MUSHROOMS

Serves 4

150 g (5 oz) lamb's lettuce
3 medium tomatoes
150 g (5 oz) button
mushrooms
juice of ½ lemon

1 avocado
2 onions
4 tbsp oil
3 tbsp herb vinegar
salt and white pepper

Carefully wash the cleaned lamb's lettuce and drain it.
Wash the tomatoes, skin them, if preferred, and slice
them. Wipe and slice the mushrooms. Pour the lemon
juice over all the salad ingredients.
Chop the avocado flesh into small pieces and sprinkle
lemon juice over it. Arrange the salad on plates. Peel and
thinly slice the onions. Pour the vinaigrette over and stir
the salad.

COS LETTUCE SALAD WITH PAPRIKA AND PEPPERS

Serves 4

1 good head of cos or romaine lettuce	fresh parsley, chopped
1 small green pepper	3-4 tbsp oil
1 small red pepper	3-4 tbsp vinegar
½ cucumber	1 tsp mustard
fresh chives, chopped	salt and pepper

Wash and drain the lettuce leaves. Remove the cores and seeds from the peppers and cut them into thin strips. Wash the cucumber and slice it thinly. Clean the chives and parsley. Mix these ingredients in a salad bowl. Make a vinaigrette dressing with the remaining ingredients and toss the salad in it.. Toss the salad in the dressing.

Left-hand page: Salad of lamb's lettuce with eggs and Salad of lamb's lettuce with tomatoes and mushrooms.

Opposite: *Salad of lamb's lettuce with onions and bacon*
Below: *Cos lettuce salad with paprika and peppers*

SALAD OF LAMB'S LETTUCE WITH ONIONS AND BACON

Serves 4

300 g (10 oz) lamb's lettuce	3 tbsp herb vinegar
2 onions	1 tsp mustard
margarine	salt
75 g (3 oz) bacon	pepper
4 tbsp olive oil	

Wash and drain the lamb's lettuce. Peel and slice the onions. Melt the margarine and brown the slices of bacon in it. Arrange the salad on plates. Make a vinaigrette dressing with the remaining ingredients and pour it over the salad.

APPLE SALAD

Above: *Cos lettuce salad with cream dressing*
Opposite: *Lettuce with lardons*

Serves 4

½ head of cos or romaine lettuce	2 tbsp crème fraîche
2-3 stalks of celery	4 tbsp orange juice
2 medium eating apples	ground ginger
5 tbsp lemon juice	1 tbsp ground hazelnuts.
	salt and white pepper

Clean and wash the lettuce. Clean and finely chop the celery sticks. Peel and finely chop the apples and add a tablespoon of lemon juice to them.

To make the dressing: Mix together the crème fraîche, orange juice, ginger and 4 tablespoons of lemon juice. Season with salt and pepper and sprinkle on 1 tablespoon of ground hazelnuts.

LETTUCE WITH LARDONS

Serves 4

1 Batavia or cos lettuce
2 tbsp oil
6 tbsp single cream
2 tbsp lemon juice
salt
pepper
paprika

2 tbsp fresh parsley, chopped
1 onion
100 g (3½ oz) streaky bacon
margarine

Wash and drain the lettuce.

To make the dressing: Mix together the oil, cream and lemon juice and season with salt, pepper and paprika. Add the chopped parsley. Pour the dressing over the lettuce.

Peel and dice the onion. Dice the streaky bacon. Melt the margarine and fry the onion and bacon in it until brown. Scatter them over the lettuce.

COS LETTUCE SALAD WITH CREAM DRESSING

Serves 4

1 small cos lettuce
1 apple
1 tbsp lemon juice
200 g (7 oz) cooked ox tongue
1 orange

125 g (4 oz) black grapes
150 g (5 oz) crème fraîche
150 g (5 oz) natural yoghurt
2 tbsp lemon juice
salt and pepper

Clean the lettuce. Cut the heart into four, then cut the leaves into ribbons. Peel the apple, remove the pips and core and slice it. Sprinkle the sliced apple with lemon juice. Dice the ox tongue. Peel and segment the orange. Wash the grapes, drain them and cut each one in half, taking care to remove the pips. Arrange the ingredients in a salad bowl.

To make the dressing: Mix together the cream, yoghurt, lemon juice and seasoning. Pour the dressing over the salad ingredients. Carefully toss the salad in the dressing.

SUMMER SALAD

Serves 4

1 lettuce
1 bunch of radishes
½ cucumber
20 Spanish olives, stuffed
with pimentoes
50 g (2 oz) Roquefort
cheese
2 tbsp crème fraîche

3 tbsp olive oil
2 tbsp vinegar
1 tbsp fresh mixed herbs,
chopped: parsley,
tarragon, chives, sorrel
salt
freshly ground black
pepper

Clean, wash and drain the lettuce. Wash the radishes and cut them into quarters lengthways. Wash the cucumber and cut it in half. Remove the seeds and cut the cucumber flesh into 5 cm (2 inch) sticks. Chop half the olives and slice the rest in half.

To make the dressing: Mash the Roquefort and blend it with the cream, olive oil and vinegar. Season with salt and pepper. Add the mixed herbs. Pour the dressing over the salad.

Tip: As the tenderest leaves are delicate, arrange the washed lettuce leaves in a bowl and coat them in a little of the dressing, then continue to garnish the lettuce with the other ingredients and pour over more dressing.

FRUIT SALAD

Serves 4

½ Batavia or cos lettuce	2 tbsp lemon juice
1 grapefruit	2 tbsp vinegar
1 orange	50 g (2 oz) chopped nuts
2 kiwi fruit	salt
4 tbsp oil	pepper

Remove the lettuce leaves, wash and drain them. Peel the grapefruit and orange. Remove the pith and segment the fruit. Chop the segments. Peel and slice the kiwi fruit.

To make the dressing: Make a vinaigrette with the oil, lemon juice, vinegar and seasoning. Arrange the salad in a bowl and pour the dressing over it. Garnish as liked with chopped nuts. Serve immediately.

Opposite: *Summer salad*
Below: *Fruit salad*

CHICORY SALAD

Serves 4

4 medium heads of chicory	4 tbsp oil
	2 tbsp vinegar
1 sharp apple	salt and pepper

Trim the chicory, then slice it. Wash and drain the slices. Peel, quarter, core and thinly slice the apple.

To make the dressing: Make a vinaigrette with the remaining ingredients and toss the chicory and apple in it. Serve immediately.

BANANA SALAD

Serves 4

4 ripe bananas
4 tbsp grapefruit juice
100 g (3½ oz) boiled veal
tongue
50 g (2 oz) celery
1 tbsp milk
150 g (5 oz) crème fraîche

1 tsp sugar
1 tsp fresh rosemary,
chopped
few drops soy sauce
vinegar
salt
freshly ground pepper

Peel and slice the bananas. Pour the grapefruit juice over the bananas. Slice the tongue to accompany the salad. Wash and finely chop the celery.

To make the dressing: Mix together the milk, crème fraîche, rosemary, soy sauce and vinegar. Season the dressing with salt and pepper, then pour it over the salad.

NORDIC LETTUCE

Serves 4

1 lettuce
1 tbsp oil
2-3 tbsp vinegar
4 tbsp crème fraîche
1 small onion, diced

1-2 tbsp fresh mixed
herbs, chopped
salt and freshly ground
pepper

Separate the lettuce leaves. Wash them carefully and drain them.

To make the dressing: Mix together the oil, vinegar and crème fraîche and add the herbs and diced onion. Season the salad with salt and pepper immediately before serving.

WATERCRESS SALAD

Serves 4

200 g (7 oz) watercress
2-3 tbsp oil
2 tbsp vinegar

1 tbsp fresh mixed herbs,
chopped
salt

Carefully pick over the watercress and wash it in plenty of water, without bruising it. Drain the watercress. Make a vinaigrette with the oil, vinegar and salt and add the chopped herbs. Toss the watercress in the dressing.

Below: *Nordic lettuce*

Right:
Banana salad

GOURMET SALAD WITH KIWI FRUIT DRESSING
Serves 4

1 bulb of fennel	2 tbsp brandy
1 red pepper	1 tsp honey
1-2 courgettes	pinch of ground
3 small white onions	cinnamon
6 kiwi fruit	1 egg yolk
1 tbsp walnut oil	4 tbsp crème fraîche
1 tbsp lemon juice	salt

Wash the fennel root, drain and finely chop it. Then wash the bulb and chop it. Slice the pepper in half and remove the core and seeds. Wash the pepper and cut it into thin strips. Wash and thinly slice the courgettes. Peel and thinly slice the onions, reserving a little of the stalk. Peel and slice 4 kiwi fruit. Arrange the ingredients in a salad bowl or on individual salad plates.

To make the dressing: Peel the 2 remaining kiwi fruit and chop them. Mash the flesh. Mix together the oil, lemon juice, brandy, honey and cinnamon. Add the kiwi fruit flesh, egg yolk and cream. Season with salt and toss the salad in the dressing.

PEPPER SALAD WITH TOMATO AND CUCUMBER

Serves 4

3 green peppers	4 tbsp oil
1 small cucumber	4 tbsp vinegar
375 g (12 oz) firm	fresh dill, finely chopped
tomatoes	salt and pepper

Slice the peppers in half and remove the cores and seeds. Wash and thinly slice them. Peel and thinly slice the cucumber. Wash and slice the tomatoes.

To make the dressing: Make a vinaigrette dressing and add the finely chopped dill. Toss the salad ingredients in the dressing. Season with salt and pepper.

Variation: Peel and slice a medium onion, chop 125 g (4 oz) white cabbage and add these ingredients to the salad.

Below: *Pepper salad with tomato and cucumber*
Left: *Gourmet salad with kiwi fruit dressing*

CAULIFLOWER SALAD

Serves 4

1 cauliflower
2 hard-boiled eggs
1 egg white
125 ml (4 fl oz) oil
2 tbsp vinegar or lemon
juice
1 tsp mustard
2 tbsp fresh mixed herbs,
chopped
salt
pepper

Clean and carefully wash the cauliflower and divide it into florets. Put them into boiling, salted water, bring to the boil and cook them until tender.

To make the remoulade dressing: Shell the hard-boiled eggs, mash the yolks and mix them with the raw white of an egg. Season with salt and mix again. Then add half the oil, drop by drop. As soon as the sauce has taken on an even, creamy consistency, add the vinegar or lemon juice and mustard, then the remaining oil. Finely dice the egg whites. Add the herbs to the dressing. Season with salt and pepper. Coat the cauliflower florets in the dressing.

Below: *Cauliflower salad*

ASPARAGUS SALAD WITH PRAWNS

Serves 4

500 g (1 lb) cooked
asparagus spears
250 g (8 oz) frozen prawns
5 tbsp mayonnaise
2 tbsp double cream,
whipped
1 tbsp sherry
juice of ½ lemon
lettuce leaves

Drain the asparagus. Add the defrosted prawns to the asparagus. Mix together the mayonnaise, cream, sherry and lemon juice and add to the asparagus and prawns. Arrange the asparagus salad on well-washed lettuce leaves.

Variations: Peel and segment an orange. Fillet the orange segments and finely dice the flesh. Add it to the salad. Or: Use the asparagus salad to fill 4 hollowed-out orange shells, and serve as a starter with Melba toast.

CUCUMBER SALAD

Serves 4

1 cucumber, weighing
about 750 g (1½ lb)
3 tbsp oil
2 tbsp vinegar
1 medium onion

2 tbsp fresh mixed herbs,
chopped
salt
freshly ground pepper

Wash and thinly slice the cucumber.

To make the dressing: Make a vinaigrette dressing,
add the peeled and diced onion and the herbs. Pour the
dressing over the salad just before serving.

Above: *Onion salad with oranges*

ONION SALAD WITH ORANGES

Serves 4

300 g (10 oz) red onions
3 medium oranges
3 tbsp oil
1 tbsp white wine vinegar

2 tbsp sherry
salt and pepper
1 tbsp fresh dill, chopped

Peel and slice the onions. Peel the oranges, remove the
pith and slice them. Arrange the oranges and onions in a
bowl.

To make the dressing: Make a vinaigrette dressing
with the oil, vinegar, sherry, salt and pepper. Pour the
dressing over the salad. Add the chopped dill. Serve
immediately.

PEPPER SALAD

Serves 4

4 peppers, weighing about 600 g (1¼ lb)	2-3 tbsp herb vinegar
1-2 onions	1 tbsp fresh tarragon, chopped
3 tbsp oil	salt and pepper

Remove the cores and seeds from the peppers and cut them into thin strips. Peel and slice the onions.

To make the dressing: Make a vinaigrette dressing in the usual way. Season the dressing to taste and pour it over the salad.

KOHL-RABI SALAD

Serves 4

4 small kohl-rabi	1 tbsp fresh mixed herbs, chopped
2-3 bunches of radishes	
3 tbsp oil	salt and freshly ground pepper
4 tbsp vinegar	

Peel the kohl-rabi, wash and grate them. Wash the radishes and slice them thinly. Combine them with the kohl-rabi.

To make the dressing: Make a vinaigrette dressing in the usual way. Season the dressing to taste and toss the salad in it.

SALAD OF SPINACH WITH ORANGES

Serves 4

250 g (8 oz) spinach	salt and pepper
½ unwaxed orange	sugar
2 tbsp lemon juice	dried thyme
2 tbsp oil	

Pick over the spinach, wash and drain it.

To make the dressing: Peel the orange and make a julienne with the zest. Place the julienne in water and boil it for about 3 minutes. Remove the zest from the water and drain it. Make a vinaigrette dressing in the usual way and add the thyme.

Chop the orange and add it to the dressing with the julienne of zest. Toss the spinach in the orange vinaigrette and serve.

SALAD OF FRENCH BEANS WITH PINE KERNELS

Serves 4

1 kg (2 lb) mangetout	dried oregano
8 tbsp oil	1 clove of garlic
100 g (3½ oz) pine kernels	salt and pepper
3 tbsp herb vinegar	

Wash and top and tail the mangetout. Put them in boiling, salted water, bring to the boil again and cook them for 20 minutes. Drain them and leave them to cool. Heat 2 tablespoons of the oil and toast the pine kernels in it, then leave them to cool.

To make the dressing: Make a vinaigrette dressing with the remaining oil, the herb vinegar, oregano and garlic, season it to taste and pour it over the salad, mixing well. Add the pine kernels.

Opposite: *Kohl-rabi salad*
Right: *Salad of spinach with oranges*

TOMATO AND ONION SALAD

Serves 4

500 g (1 lb) tomatoes
250 g (8 oz) onions
2 tbsp vinegar
3 hard-boiled eggs
1 tbsp fresh parsley,
chopped
1 egg yolk

1 small tsp mustard
125 ml (4 fl oz) oil
2 tbsp natural yoghurt
1 tbsp fresh mixed herbs,
chopped
salt and pepper

Peel and slice the onion. Bring 500 ml (18 fl oz) salted water to the boil with 1 tablespoon of vinegar. Cook the onions in the water and drain them. Wash the tomatoes. Shell the eggs. Slice the eggs and tomatoes. Arrange them in layers with the sliced onion. Sprinkle parsley on top and season with salt.

To make the mayonnaise dressing: Mix together 1 tablespoon of vinegar, the egg yolk and mustard. When the mixture has reached an even, smooth consistency, add the oil, 1-2 tablespoons at a time, to prevent the egg yolk curdling. Add the yoghurt and the mixed herbs. Pour the mayonnaise over the salad and refrigerate it.

FENNEL SALAD

Serves 4

2 bulbs of fennel,
weighing 400 g (13 oz)
3 oranges or 4 mandarins
150 g (5 oz) boiled ham
150 g (5 oz) tub of natural
yoghurt

2 tbsp crème fraîche
1-2 tbsp white wine
vinegar
salt
pepper

Wash and slice the fennel. Peel the oranges, remove the pith and chop the flesh. Cut the ham into thin strips.

To make the dressing: Make a vinaigrette dressing with the yoghurt and crème fraîche. Season the dressing to taste and pour it over the salad.

COURGETTE AND TOMATO SALAD

Serves 4

3 courgettes, 500 g (1 lb)
weight in total
4 medium tomatoes
2 green peppers
1 onion
8-10 pitted olives
4 tbsp oil
2 tbsp vinegar

1 tsp mustard
salt
pepper
2 hard-boiled eggs
150 g (5 oz) goat's cheese
2 tbsp fresh mixed herbs,
chopped

Peel and thinly slice the courgettes. Steam them to soften them. Blanch the tomatoes and refresh them in cold water. Peel and thinly slice them. Remove the cores and seeds from the peppers and cut them into thin strips. Peel and thinly slice the onion. Dice the olives.

To make the dressing: Make a vinaigrette dressing with the oil, vinegar, mustard, salt, pepper and mixed herbs and incorporate it into all the salad ingredients. Slice the shelled hard-boiled eggs into eight sections. Add the eggs and the crumbled goat's cheese to the rest of the salad.

Right: *Beansprout salad*
Above left: *Courgette and tomato salad*

BEANSPROUT SALAD

Serves 4

125 g (4 oz) mayonnaise
(see recipe on
page 130)
1-2 tbsp dark soy sauce
1 tsp ground ginger
1 tbsp mild mustard

300 g (10 oz) petit pois,
shelled
250 g (8 oz) beansprouts
200 g (7 oz) smoked
salmon

Mix together the mayonnaise and soya sauce, then add the ginger and mustard. Put the peas and the beansprouts in a colander and rinse them under running water. Drain them and stir them into the mayonnaise. Roll up the slices of smoked salmon and slice thinly to make little pinwheels. Use them to garnish the salad.

TOMATO AND LEEK SALAD

Serves 4

2 leeks, weighing approx.
300 g (10 oz)
3 tomatoes
1 onion
3 tbsp oil

1 tbsp vinegar
1 tsp mustard
1 hard-boiled egg
salt and pepper

Wash the leeks and trim the dark green part to 10 cm (4 inches). Slice the leeks into rounds. Put them in boiling, salted water and cook them for 1 minute. Drain and reserve them. Blanch the tomatoes, then rinse them in cold water. Skin them and cut them into eight pieces.

To make the dressing: Make a vinaigrette dressing and shell the hard-boiled egg. Separate the white and yolk and chop them. Add the egg yolk to the dressing, pour the dressing over the salad and garnish it with finely chopped pieces of egg white.

ORANGE AND FENNEL SALAD

Serves 4

2 tbsp oil	garlic granules
4 tbsp vinegar	500 g (1 lb) fennel
3 tbsp gin	3 oranges
1 tbsp sugar	salt and white pepper

Make the dressing by mixing together all the ingredients except the fennel and oranges. Wash the fennel and slice thinly. Dip the slices of fennel in the dressing.

Peel the oranges, separate the segments and chop them. Layer the fennel and chopped orange in a salad bowl and pour the dressing over.

POT POURRI SALAD

Serves 4

3 small onions	segments
50 g (2 oz) button	4 tbsp olive oil
mushrooms	3 tbsp lemon juice
1 bunch of radishes	3 tbsp fresh mixed herbs,
1 red-skinned apple	chopped
2 hard-boiled eggs	salt
200 g (7 oz) mandarin	pepper

Peel and slice the onions. Wipe and slice the mushrooms, wash the radishes and apple and slice them. Shell and dice the hard-boiled eggs. Combine all these ingredients and add the mandarin segments.

To make the dressing: Make a vinaigrette dressing and sprinkle the chopped herbs on top. Toss the salad in the dressing. Leave to rest a little.

SERBIAN SALAD

Serves 4

1 large onion	2 tbsp oil
1 green pepper	1 tbsp vinegar
2-3 tomatoes	salt and pepper

Peel and slice the onion. Slice the green pepper in half and remove the core and seeds. Wash it and cut it into thin strips. Wash and slice the tomatoes. Layer the onion, pepper and tomato in a glass bowl.

Make a vinaigrette dressing and pour it over the salad.

Left: *Orange and fennel salad*

TOMATO SALAD IN MUSTARD DRESSING

Servings - see note

500 g (1 lb) firm tomatoes	2 tbsp strong mustard
1 onion	salt
3 tbsp crème fraîche	pepper

Wash the tomatoes, drain and slice them. Arrange them on a large serving dish and season them with salt and pepper. Blend together the crème fraîche and mustard to make a dressing. Pour the dressing over the tomatoes.

Below: *Serbian salad*

MARINATED RUMP OF BEEF IN HERB AND MUSTARD SAUCE

Serves 6

1 kg (2 lb) chuck steak	300 ml (½ pint) oil
1 leek	125 ml (4 fl oz) meat stock,
1 carrot	skimmed
1 turnip	½ bunch of fresh basil
1 stick of celery	bunch of fresh chervil
1 chicken stock cube	½ bunch of fresh parsley
1 bouquet garni	1 onion
1 clove of garlic	salt and freshly ground
140 g (5 oz) mustard	pepper

Put the meat into 1½ litres (2½ pints) water. Peel, wash and roughly chop the vegetables. Add them to the meat with the stock cube and bouquet garni. Gently simmer the meat in the stock for 2-2½ hours. Don't let the stock boil. Once the meat is cooked, remove the pan from the heat and leave the meat to rest for about 24 hours.

To make the marinade: Peel and crush the garlic, add it to the mustard and season it with pepper. Slowly trickle the oil into the mustard mixture, whisking it all the time so

Above: *Rump of beef with herb and mustard sauce*

BEEF WITH HORSERADISH GRAVY

IN THE PRESSURE COOKER
Serves 4

500 g (1 lb) brisket of beef	500 ml (18 fl oz) meat
4 marrow bones	stock
1 onion	2 heaped tbsp horseradish
1 turnip	lemon juice
1 stick of celery	salt
55 g (2 oz) butter	
40 g (1½ oz) flour	

Put the marrow bones in the pressure cooker pan, cover them with 1½ litres (2½ pints) cold water, bring it to the boil. Peel and slice the onion, sauté it in a knob of butter until golden. Peel, wash and roughly chop the turnip and celery, add them to the stock with the meat and onion and simmer for several minutes, skimming frequently. Then put the lid on the pressure cooker and steam for 45 minutes. At the end of cooking time, slice the meat and keep it hot. Strain the stock.

To make the horseradish gravy: Melt the remaining butter in the pressure cooker, add the flour and stir until the flour is cooked. Add the meat stock to the pan, whisking all the time to prevent lumps forming. Bring the gravy to the boil and simmer it for 5 minutes. Add the horseradish, stirring all the time and season the gravy with salt and lemon juice. Pour the gravy over the meat.

Serve with steamed potatoes, garnished with chopped parsley and chives, glazed carrots or a mixed salad.

Below: *Beef with horseradish gravy*

that the marinade is smooth. Still whisking all the time, add the skimmed meat stock. Slice the meat thinly, then layer the slices of meat and marinade. Leave to marinate for at least 5 hours or overnight, then lightly score the meat with a knife. Wash the basil, chervil and parsley, remove the stalks, roughly chop the leaves and add them to the marinade. Put the marinade and herbs in a blender and process until the sauce has a smooth consistency and is bright green in colour. Peel and thinly slice the onion. Arrange the slices of meat on a serving dish, garnish with sliced onion and pour a little sauce on top. Serve the remaining sauce separately.

Serve with potatoes sautéed in bacon and onions and seasoned with fresh, chopped marjoram.

BEEF WITH LOVAGE

Serves 8-10

2½ kg (5½ lb) brisket of beef
3 veal bones
2 carrots
2 leeks
1 celeriac

1 stick of celery
1 onion
4 sprigs fresh lovage
2 bay leaves
2 cloves
salt
a few peppercorns

Put the meat and the bones into a pan with 2½ litres (4½ pints) of salted water. Bring it to the boil and skim. Peel the carrots and celeriac, cut the leeks in half lengthways. Wash and dice the carrots, leeks, celeriac and celery. Peel the onion, carefully wash the lovage and add it to the meat with the vegetables, onion, bay leaves, cloves and seasoning. Bring the pan to the boil again and simmer for 2½-3 hours. Add a little boiling water to the pan from time to time if necessary.

Take the meat out of the stock, slice it and arrange it on a warm serving dish. Strain the stock through a sieve, pour a little over the meat and use the rest for soup.

Serve the meat with steamed potatoes and a mixed salad.

OXTAIL STEW WITH CARAMELIZED ONIONS

Serves 6-8

1½ kg (3½ lb) oxtail, cubed
2 onions
1 bay leaf
2 cloves
5 chilli seeds (or 1 tsp chilli paste)
60 g (2½ oz) butter
60 g (2½ oz) flour

125 ml (4 fl oz) red wine
5 tbsp Madeira
1 kg (2 lb) baby onions or shallots
2 knobs of butter
1 level tbsp sugar
125 ml (4 fl oz) meat stock
salt
pepper

Put the meat into a pan with 1 litre (1¾ pints) salted, boiling water. Peel and quarter the 2 onions and add them to the meat with the bay leaf, cloves and chilli seeds. Bring the pan to the boil and cook for about 2 hours, skimming as necessary. Take the meat out of the pan and remove the bones and cartilage.

To make the gravy: Strain the stock through a sieve, reserving 500 ml (18 fl oz). Melt the butter, add the flour and stir until the flour is cooked. Gradually add the reserved stock to the roux, whisking all the time, to prevent lumps forming. Bring the gravy to the boil and simmer for 10 minutes. Add the Madeira and red wine to the gravy and season it with salt and pepper, then add the meat to the pan and heat it through.

To make the caramelized onions: Peel the baby onions. Melt two knobs of butter, add the sugar and cook until it turns golden. Then add the stock and continue stirring until all the sugar has dissolved. Add the onions, season with salt, cover the pan and cook, stirring frequently. When the onions are cooked, remove the lid and allow the liquid to reduce, stirring it from time to time.

Arrange the stew on a serving dish, surrounded by a ring of onions. Serve with mashed potato.

OX TONGUE STEW

Serves 6-8

1¼ kg (3 lb) ox tongue
1 leek
1 carrot
1 turnip
1 stick of celery
fresh parsley, chopped
50 g (2 oz) minced meat
1 egg yolk
knob of butter
2 tbsp breadcrumbs

100 g (3½ oz) butter
100 g (3½ oz) flour
1 litre (1¾ pints) ox tongue stock
125 ml (4 fl oz) red wine
300 g (10 oz) whole button mushrooms, tinned
little puff pastry crescents
salt and pepper

Rinse the tongue in cold water and put it into 2½ litres (4½ pints) of boiling, salted water. Bring the pan to the boil and skim. Add the vegetables. Cook the tongue for about 2½ hours (it is cooked when the tip of a knife slides easily into the meat). Rinse the tongue under cold water. Remove the skin whilst the tongue is still warm, then slice or cube it. Strain the stock, reserving

1 litre (1¾ pints), and put the meat into the remaining hot stock.

To make the meatballs: Work together a knob of butter, the minced meat, egg yolk and breadcrumbs and season with salt and pepper. Combine all the ingredients together thoroughly. Dampen your hands and shape the meat mixture into little balls. Put them in boiling, salted water and cook them over a low heat.

To make the gravy: Make a roux with the butter and flour. Add the reserved tongue stock and whisk the gravy to prevent lumps forming. Bring the gravy to the boil and simmer it for 5 minutes. Put the sliced or cubed tongue and meatballs into the gravy and heat them through. Season the stew with salt and pepper. Add the wine and drained, quartered mushrooms. Garnish the dish with the puff pastry crescents.

Below: *Ox tongue stew*

MARINATED BEEF

Serves 6

1 kg (2 lb) fore or hind shin	½ tsp cayenne pepper
1 medium onion	3 cloves
1 leek	1 bay leaf
1 carrot	125 ml (4 fl oz) vinegar
1 turnip	50 g (2 oz) margarine
1 stick of celery	flour
15 white peppercorns	salt
5 cayenne pepper seeds or	pepper

Put the meat in a deep dish. To make the marinade, peel and slice the onion. Wash and finely chop the vegetables and add them to the meat with the peppercorns, bay leaf and cloves. Pour the vinegar, to which 500 ml (18 fl oz) water has been added, on top. (The meat must be totally immersed in the marinade.) Cover the meat and leave it to marinate for 1-2 days in a cool place. Turn the meat occasionally.

Take the meat out of the marinade and pat it dry. Brown it on all sides in the margarine, season with salt and pepper, add the vegetables from the marinade, draining them well. Add half the marinade to 500 ml (18 fl oz) water and pour a little of it over the meat. Braise the meat for 2½ hours, turning it from time to time and adding a little marinade as necessary. When the meat is cooked, slice it and keep it hot. Strain the gravy through a sieve, add marinade to taste. Blend the flour with a little cold water and add it to the gravy to thicken it. Bring the gravy to the boil and season it with salt and pepper.
Variation: You can finish the gravy with raisins soaked in the marinade, flaked toasted almonds and crème fraîche.

Serve with potato croquettes and red cabbage.

Below:
Marinated beef

BRAISED BEEF WITH CELERY

Serves 4-5

750 g (1½ lb) beef
4 tbsp oil
1 leek
1 carrot
1 turnip
1 stick of celery
1 tsp paprika

250 ml (8 fl oz) meat stock
125 ml (4 fl oz) beer
2 carrots
500 g (1 lb) celery
250 g (8 oz) baby onions
125-250 ml (4-8 fl oz)
double cream
salt

Season the meat with salt and pepper. Heat the oil in a casserole dish, add the meat and brown it all over. Wash and peel the vegetables and brown them in the casserole dish. Add the paprika. Remove the vegetables and keep them hot. Add a little stock and beer to the meat and braise it for 1½ hours, turning it from time to time. Keep adding stock and beer as necessary.

Peel and dice the carrots. Trim and wash the sticks of celery, remove any stringy parts and trim the ends. Cut the sticks of celery into pieces. Peel the baby onions. Add the vegetables to the meat and braise them for a further 45 minutes.
Take the meat out of the casserole dish and slice it. Arrange the sliced meat on a warmed serving dish and surround it with the vegetables. De-glaze the casserole dish with the double cream, bring the gravy to the boil, allow it to reduce a little, season it with salt and pepper and add a little paprika if necessary. The gravy can be either poured over the meat and vegetables or served separately.

Above: *Braised beef with celery*

BRAISED BEEF WITH HERBS

Serves 6-8

1½ kg (3½ lb) beef
100 g (3½ oz) fatty bacon,
sliced
1 litre (1¾ pints) red wine
2 carrots
200 g (7 oz) celeriac
3 onions

4 tomatoes
fresh rosemary, chopped
fresh marjoram, chopped
1 clove of garlic, sliced
4 tbsp oil
2 tbsp tomato purée
2 tbsp crème fraîche
salt and pepper

Put the meat in a deep dish and cover it in red wine. Cover and leave to marinate for 24 hours, turning the meat from time to time. Scrape, wash and finely chop the carrots. Peel, wash and finely chop the celeriac. Peel and dice the onions. Blanch the tomatoes in boiling water, then refresh them in cold water, skin and quarter them.

Take the meat out of the marinade and pat it dry. Season it with salt and pepper, add the rosemary, marjoram and garlic. Heat the oil in a casserole dish and seal the meat on all sides, then cover it with the slices of bacon. Add the vegetables and tomato purée to the dish. Add 500 ml (18 fl oz) marinade and braise the meat for 2½ hours, basting frequently with marinade.
Arrange the meat on a warmed serving dish and keep it hot. Strain the gravy and vegetables through a sieve, season with salt, pepper, rosemary and marjoram to taste, then incorporate the cream.

Serve with steamed potatoes, French beans or broccoli.

COLD ROAST BEEF WITH PIQUANT DRESSING

Serves 6-8

1½ kg (3½ lb) beef for
braising,
e.g. brisket, silverside, top
rump
5 tbsp oil
2 onions
1 clove of garlic
2 tbsp tomato purèe
1 head of celery

2 hard-boiled eggs
125 ml (4 fl oz) tomato
ketchup
2 tbsp vinegar
1 tbsp green peppercorns,
ground
2 tomatoes
salt and pepper

Season the meat with salt and pepper. Heat 3
tablespoons of oil in a casserole dish and brown the meat
in it on all sides. Peel the onions and garlic, dice them
and add them to the meat. Add 250 ml (8 fl oz) water and
the tomato purée and cook the meat for 2½-3 hours,
turning it from time to time and adding more liquid as
necessary. Then leave it to cool.

When the meat has cooled, slice it and arrange the slices
on a large serving dish. Strain the gravy through a sieve
and leave it to cool.

Trim the celery, removing any string and cutting off the
ends of the stalks and leaves. Wash the sticks of celery
and reserve the leaves. Put the sticks of celery in boiling,
salted water. Bring to the boil and simmer for 5 minutes.

Below: *Cold roast beef with piquant dressing*

Remove the celery and immerse it immediately in ice-cold
water to retain the colour, drain it, and add it to the meat.
Garnish the dish with the reserved celery leaves.

To make the dressing: Shell the hard-boiled eggs and
chop them finely. Add the chopped egg to the cold gravy
with the ketchup, vinegar, 2 tablespoons of oil and
ground green pepper. Wash the tomatoes and cut them
in half. De-seed them, then dice the flesh. Add the
chopped tomatoes to the dressing and season with salt.
Serve the dressing with the meat.

Cold roast beef with piquant dressing goes well with
sautéed potatoes and a mixed salad.

RUSTIC ROAST BEEF

Serves 6

1 kg (2 lb) beef, larded
with bacon
1 calf's foot
250 g (8 oz) veal bones
2 carrots
2 tomatoes
3 onions
50 g (2 oz) butter
1 tbsp flour

125 ml (4 fl oz) white wine
1 bay leaf
fresh thyme, chopped
2 cloves of garlic
Worcester sauce
1 tbsp fresh parsley,
chopped
salt and pepper

Season the meat with salt and pepper. Rinse the calf's
foot and veal bones in cold water and pat them dry. Peel
and dice the carrots. Blanch the tomatoes in boiling
water, then refresh them in cold water, peel and slice
them. Peel and dice the onions.
Brown the meat, bones and calf's foot in the butter, add
the carrots, tomatoes and onions. Sprinkle the flour on
top and add the white wine and 125 ml (4 fl oz) water,
then add the bay leaf, thyme and garlic. Season with salt
and pepper, cover the casserole dish and cook for about
2 hours, turning the meat occasionally. Baste the meat
with the juices. Add a little more wine if necessary.
As soon as the meat is cooked, take it out of the dish,
slice it and arrange the slices on a warm plate.

To make the gravy: Strain the cooking liquid and
vegetables through a sieve, add a little water if necessary
and bring the gravy to the boil. Season with salt and
pepper. Sprinkle a little Worcester sauce over the meat
and scatter chopped parsley on top.

Serve with steamed potatoes, baked tomatoes or peas.

Above: *Rustic roast beef*

GOULASH WITH APRICOTS

Serves 4

750 g (1½ lb) beef, thick flank or sirloin	pickled
1 large onion	250 g (8 oz) tinned apricots in syrup
4 tbsp oil	150 g (5 oz) crème fraîche
375 ml (12 fl oz) white wine	cinnamon
1 tbsp green peppercorns,	salt
	pepper

Cut the meat into 3 cm (1¼ ins) cubes. Peel and dice the onion. Heat the oil until very hot, brown the meat and onion in it and season with salt and pepper. Add the white wine, green peppercorns and 250 ml (8 fl oz) water. Simmer for 55 minutes.

Drain the apricots, mash half of them to a pulp and cut the remaining apricots in half. Fifteen minutes before the end of cooking time, add the apricots to the meat with the crème fraîche. Season to taste with salt, pepper and cinnamon.

Below, left: *Goulash with apricots*
Right: *Chinese beef stir-fry*

CHINESE BEEF STIR-FRY

Serves 4-5

600 g (1¼ lb) thick flank of beef	250 g (8 oz) bamboo shoots, tinned
4 tbsp soy sauce	1-2 tbsp Chinese mushrooms, soaked in water
2 tbsp rice wine	
2-3 tbsp cornflour	ground ginger
250 ml (8 fl oz) oil	salt
1 leek	

Cut the meat into thin slices, then into very thin strips. Blend together the soy sauce and rice wine. Put the strips of meat into the marinade and leave them to marinate for 30 minutes. Take the meat out of the marinade, drain it well, then toss it in the cornflour. Reserve the marinade. Heat the oil and deep fry the meat in batches. As soon as the meat has browned, take it out of the oil, drain it and keep it hot.

Reserve 5 tablespoons of the oil and dispose of the remainder. Trim and wash the leek, then slice it into rounds. Drain the bamboo shoots and cut them into thin strips. Brown the leek and bamboo shoots in the reserved oil, adding the marinade and 250 ml (8 fl oz) boiling water. Add the mushrooms and heat them through.

Return the meat to the pan, simmer it for a few minutes, then season to taste with salt and ginger. Serve with rice.

Opposite: *Beef olives with paprika*

BEEF OLIVES WITH PAPRIKA

Serves 4

4 slices of beef, each
weighing about 200 g (7
oz)
mustard
paprika
1 large pickled gherkin
60 g (2½ oz) bacon, sliced
2 onions
2 tbsp lard
1 leek

1 carrot
1 turnip
1 stick of celery
fresh parsley, chopped
125 ml (4 fl oz) red wine
or meat stock
1-2 tbsp crème fraîche
brandy
salt and pepper

Gently flatten the slices of beef, spread them with
mustard and sprinkle with salt, pepper and paprika to
taste. Cut the pickled gherkin in 4 lengthways. Peel and
slice the onions. Arrange the slices of bacon, gherkin and
onions on top of the slices of meat, then roll them up,
starting from the shortest side. Tie them up with kitchen
thread to secure them. Melt the lard and brown the beef
olives on all sides, then add a little boiling water and
braise the olives for 30 minutes.

Clean, wash and finely chop the vegetables, then add
them with the parsley to the meat. Braise for a further
30 minutes, stirring occasionally. As the liquid in the
meat dish evaporates, add the red wine or stock.
Take the beef olives out of the dish and remove the string.
Strain the gravy and vegetables through a sieve.
Add the crème fraîche to the gravy, bring it to the boil
and season to taste with salt, pepper, paprika and a little
brandy.

Serve with pasta and a mixed salad.

ROAST BEEF Á LA BOURGUIGNONNE

Above: *Roast beef á la bourguignonne*
Right: *Beef in red wine*

Serves 4

750 g (1½ lb) beef for roasting e.g. fillet, sirloin, topside
3 tbsp oil
1 kg (2 lb) onions
6 bay leaves
250 ml (8 fl oz) red wine

200 g (7 oz) crème fraîche
1 tbsp wholegrain mustard
1-2 tbsp gravy granules
salt
freshly ground pepper

Brown the meat on all sides in the hot oil, and season it with salt and pepper. Peel and dice the onions. Add them to the meat with the bay leaves, browning them and gradually adding the red wine. Cover and cook the meat for 30 minutes. When the meat is cooked, remove it from the roasting tin, wrap it in foil and keep it hot.

Add the crème fraîche and mustard to the gravy, stir until they are completely incorporated and season with salt and pepper. Add the gravy granules, then bring the gravy to the boil. Slice the meat and serve coated in the onion gravy.

Serve with sautéed potatoes.

PROVENÇALE BEEF STEW

Serves 3-4

500 g (1 lb) beef: rump,
sirloin, etc.
3 tbsp oil
2 onions
4 tomatoes, skinned
170 g (6 oz) mushrooms,

tinned
300 g (10 oz) crème
fraîche
paprika
herbes de Provence
salt and pepper

Cut the meat into 1 cm (½ inch) slices. Heat the oil, brown the meat in it, and season with salt and pepper. Remove the meat from the pan and keep it hot. Peel and dice the onions, dice the tomatoes, add them to the pan with the meat juices, cover and sweat them for 5 minutes. Add the mushrooms and the liquid from the tin to the crème fraîche, stir well, season with salt and pepper, then add this mixture to the meat juices, with paprika and herbes de Provence to taste. Cover and simmer for 8 minutes until the sauce reduces and thickens. Adjust the seasoning.

Serve the slices of
meat coated in
the sauce.

BEEF IN RED WINE

Serves 5-6

1 kg (2 lb) beef
6 shallots
40 g (1½ oz) butter
1 clove of garlic
1 bay leaf

fresh thyme, chopped
2 tbsp flour
500 ml (18 fl oz) red wine
salt and pepper

Cut the meat into 5-6 cm (2-2½ inch) cubes. Peel the shallots. Melt the butter and brown the meat in it on all sides.

Add the shallots, garlic, bay leaf and thyme, season with salt and pepper and sauté for a minute or two. Then sprinkle the flour over the meat and add the red wine to the pan, stirring all the time. The meat should be completely covered with wine. Cover and cook for 1½ hours.

PEPPERED POTTHAST

Serves 4

750 g (1½ lb) brisket of beef
500 g (1 lb) onions
2 tbsp lard
pinch ground chilli

1 bay leaf
1 tbsp lemon juice
500 ml (18 fl oz) beef stock
salt
peppercorns

Cut the meat into 3 cm (1¼ ins) cubes. Peel and dice the onions. Melt the lard and brown the meat in it, then take the meat out of the pan and brown the onions in the meat juices.

Put the meat back into the pan with salt, pepper and ground chilli to taste, and the bay leaf. Add the lemon juice and stock and simmer for 1 hour.

Serve with boiled potatoes.

BRAISED BEEF

Serves 4

800 g (1½ lb) beef
4 tbsp olive oil
2 cloves of garlic
1 tsp dried oregano
4-6 tomatoes
1 bay leaf

125 ml (4 fl oz) white wine
125 ml (4 fl oz) meat stock
500 g (1 lb) onions
2 knobs of butter
3 tbsp fresh parsley, chopped
salt and pepper

Cut the meat into cubes. Heat the oil and brown the meat on all sides. Peel and finely chop the garlic, add it to the meat with the oregano and season with salt. Fry the garlic for about 2 minutes, then season with pepper.

Blanch the tomatoes in boiling water, then refresh them in cold water. Skin them, cut them in half, then dice them and add them to the meat with the bay leaf. Add the white wine and stock to the meat, cover and cook for about 1 hour. Peel and slice the onions, sauté them in the butter and scatter them on top of the meat stew. Sprinkle fresh, chopped parsley on top.

Right: *Braised beef*
Below: *Peppered potthast*

HUNGARIAN GOULASH

IN THE PRESSURE COOKER
Serves 4-6

750 g (1½ lb) stewing beef	1 green pepper
2 tbsp oil	1 red chilli
600 g (1¼ lb) large onions	salt
1 heaped tsp sweet	pepper
paprika	
1 red pepper	

Heat the oil in the pressure cooker, add the meat and brown it on all sides, then season with salt and pepper. Peel and dice the onions, add them to the meat and brown them. Stir the paprika into the meat and onion mixture.

Slice the peppers in half, remove the cores and seeds, then wash and chop them. Slice the chilli in half, scrape out the seeds and slice it very thinly. Add the peppers and chilli to the meat and brown them. Add 125 ml (4 fl oz) water, then put the lid on the pressure cooker, and cook for 15-20 minutes. Take the pressure cooker off the

heat, run cold water over it, then open the lid. Taste the goulash and, if necessary, adjust the seasoning.

Serve with macaroni or spaghetti and a mixed salad.

Variation: Gently sauté some finely diced garlic and 70 g (3 oz) tomato purée with the onions.

BEEF OLIVES WITH CHICORY

Serves 4

4 small heads of chicory	250 ml (8 fl oz) medium-
4 slices of beef, each	dry white wine
weighing about 175 g	cayenne pepper
(6 oz)	2 tsp flour
paprika	3 tomatoes
4 slices streaky bacon	2 tbsp double cream
4 tbsp oil	salt and freshly ground
	white pepper

Clean the chicory, scoop out the base to avoid a bitter taste. Sprinkle the slices of meat with salt, pepper and paprika to taste. Place a slice of bacon on top of each slice of meat, then put a whole head of chicory on top. Roll up the slices of beef, starting from the short side and wrapping them round the chicory, then tie them up with kitchen string to secure them. Heat the oil and brown the beef olives on all sides, then de-glaze with a little of the white wine and braise for about 1¼ hours, adding more wine, as necessary, from time to time. Take the olives out of the pan and remove the string.

To make the gravy: Blanch the tomatoes in boiling water for a few seconds, then refresh them in cold water. Skin them, slice them in half, de-seed them, purée the flesh and add it to the meat juices. Sprinkle the flour over the gravy and stir in the crème fraîche. Stir thoroughly until all the flour is incorporated, then season with salt and pepper.

Serve with spétzle or potatoes.

Above: *Hungarian goulash*
Right: *Goulash with feta cheese*

GOULASH WITH FETA CHEESE

Serves 6

1 kg (2 lb) lean beef	stick of cinnamon
6 tbsp olive oil	800 g (1½ lb) shallots
4 tbsp tomato purée	125 g (4 oz) feta cheese
3 tbsp wine vinegar	salt
½ tsp ground cumin	pepper

Cut the meat into 2 cm (¾ inch) cubes. Heat the oil, brown the meat on all sides, then add 750 ml (1¼ pints) water. Add the tomato purée, wine vinegar, cumin and cinnamon stick, then season with salt and pepper. Peel the shallots, blanch them in boiling water for 1 minute, strain them, add them to the meat, cover and simmer for 1¼-1½ hours.

When the meat is cooked, cut the feta cheese into cubes and scatter them across the meat. Season with salt and pepper.

N.B.: Feta is a Greek cheese with a crumbly texture, very salty, made from sheep's milk or a mixture of sheep's, goat's and cow's milk. It matures after 4-6 weeks in brine. It is a rindless cheese, white or yellowish-white in colour, piquant and acidic in flavour.

GOULASH WITH ONIONS AND TOMATOES

Serves 3-4

600 g (1¼ lb) beef, off the bone	tinned
2 tbsp oil	1 tbsp flour
250 g (8 oz) onions	sweet paprika
400 g (13 oz) tomatoes,	drop of Tabasco sauce
	salt, pepper and spices

Cut the meat into cubes. Heat the oil and brown the cubed meat in it. Peel the onions, cut them in half, slice thinly and add them to the meat. Season with salt, pepper and spices. De-glaze the meat with the juice from the tomatoes and 375 ml (12 fl oz) boiling water. Add the tomatoes and simmer the meat for 1-1½ hours, adding more water as necessary. Slake the flour with a little cold water and add it to the sauce to thicken it. Adjust the seasoning to taste with salt, paprika and Tabasco sauce.

Below: *Goulash with onions and tomatoes*

GRANNY'S BEEF OLIVES

IN THE PRESSURE COOKER
Serves 4

4 slices of beef, each weighing about 150 g (5 oz)	60 g (2½ oz) bacon
	2 onions
	2 knobs of lard
mustard	125 ml (4 fl oz) beer
paprika	125 ml (4 fl oz) meat stock
4 slices boiled ham	1 tbsp flour
1 large gherkin	salt and pepper

Gently flatten the slices of beef, then spread them with the mustard and sprinkle with salt, pepper and paprika. Place a slice of boiled ham on top of each slice of beef. Cut the gherkin in 4 lengthways, slice the bacon thinly. Peel and thinly slice the onions. Divide the gherkin, bacon and onions amongst the slices of beef.

Roll up the beef, working from the short side, and tie them up with kitchen string to secure them. Melt the lard in the pressure cooker and brown the beef olives on all sides. De-glaze with the beer and stock, put the lid on the pressure cooker and cook for about 15 minutes.

When the beef is cooked, take it out of the pressure cooker and remove the string. Arrange the beef olives on a warm plate and keep them hot. Slake the flour with 2 tablespoons of cold water, add it to the gravy and stir well until the flour is incorporated and the gravy thickens. Season the gravy to taste with salt and pepper and pour it over the beef olives.

Serve with potato croquettes and red cabbage.

Right: *Granny's beef olives.*

OXTAIL WITH CELERY

Serves 4

200 g (7 oz) smoked pork belly
1 kg (2 lb) oxtail
4 sticks of celery
1 onion
1 clove of garlic

250 ml (8 fl oz) white wine
1 kg (2 lb) tomatoes, tinned
meat stock
salt
pepper

Dice the pork and render it in a frying pan. Cut the oxtail into 3 cm (1¼ inch) pieces, wash under running water and pat them dry with kitchen paper. Fry the oxtail in the pork fat then take the meat out of the frying pan. Trim and wash the celery, then cut it into 2 cm (¾ inch) pieces. Peel and finely dice the onion and garlic. Fry the celery, onion and garlic in the bacon fat, then de-glaze with the white wine, add the meat and simmer for about 1 hour.

Drain the tomatoes and cut them into quarters, then add them to the meat together with the juice, cover and simmer for a further hour, stirring occasionally and adding meat stock as necessary. Serve with boiled potatoes.

FORERIB OF BEEF WITH OLIVES

Serves 4

600 g (1¼ lb) chuck
steak
4 tbsp oil
2 onions
750 ml (1¼ pints)
meat stock
250 g (8 oz)
carrots
2 kohl-rabi, each
weighing about
200 g (7 oz)
dried marjoram
horseradish
fresh parsley,
chopped
salt and pepper

Sprinkle the meat
with pepper. Peel
and dice the onion.
Heat the oil and seal the
meat on both sides. Add
the onions and olives and
fry for a few minutes, then
add the stock and green
peppercorns and braise.

Blanch the tomatoes in boiling water for a
few seconds, then refresh them in cold water.
Skin them and cut them into eight. Ten minutes
before the end of cooking time, add them to the meat.
Remove the meat from the pan, sprinkle with salt and
keep it warm. Strain the gravy and add the flour and
crème fraîche, stirring all the time, to thicken the gravy.
Serve the meat with the tomatoes, olives, onion and
peppercorns.

Above: *Forerib of beef with olives*
Left: *Oxtail with celery*

POTÊE DU NORD (NORTHERN STEW)

Serves 3-4

2 foreribs of beef, each
weighing about 600 g (1¼
lb)
1 onion
4 tbsp oil
2 tbsp green peppercorns,
pickled
750 ml (1¼ pints) meat

stock
2 tomatoes
1 tbsp flour
15 stuffed green olives
100 g (3½ oz) crème fraîche
salt and pepper

Cut the meat into thin strips. Heat the oil and brown the
meat in it, then season with salt and pepper. Peel and dice
the onions and brown them in the pan with the meat. De-
glaze with the stock and simmer for about 30 minutes.

Scrape and wash the carrots, cut them in half lengthways,
then into small pieces. Peel the kohl-rabi, cut them in half,
then into small pieces.

Add the carrots and kohl-rabi to the meat with the
marjoram and simmer for a further 30 minutes. Season
with salt and pepper and add the horseradish. Sprinkle
with fresh, chopped parsley.

FILLET OF BEEF STUFFED WITH HERBS AND GORGONZOLA

Serves 6

1 kg (2 lb) fillet of beef
50 g (2 oz) pine kernels
1 onion
4 cloves of garlic
4 tbsp oil
150 g (5 oz) crème fraîche
125 g (4 oz) Gorgonzola
cheese
2 tbsp herbes de Provence
2 tbsp fresh, mixed herbs,
chopped
salt
pepper

*T*oast the pine kernels in a dry frying pan until golden, leave them to cool and then purée them in a mixer. Peel the onion and 1 clove of garlic and chop them finely. Heat 1 tablespoon of oil and fry the onion and garlic in it until golden, then add the mashed pine kernels and crème fraîche, stir gently, and season with salt and pepper. Add 1 tablespoon of herbes de Provence and 1 tablespoon of chopped fresh, mixed herbs to the mixture and stir thoroughly. Cut the fillet of beef in half

To make the Gorgonzola cream: Beat the crème fraîche with a balloon whisk. Mash the Gorgonzola until a smooth paste forms and stir it gently into the whipped cream. If you prefer a very smooth cream, you can process it in a blender. Serve with assorted crudités.

STEAK IN MUSTARD

Serves 4

500 g (1 lb) fillet of beef	chopped
2 onions	2 tbsp crème fraîche
2-4 tbsp English mustard	2 heaped tbsp flour
powder	2 knobs of butter
2 eggs	salt and pepper
2 tbsp fresh parsley,	

Cut the meat into 4 slices, flatten them gently, and sprinkle them with salt and pepper. Peel and dice the onions. Combine the mustard, eggs, diced onion, chopped parsley, crème fraîche and flour to make a smooth batter. Dip the slices of beef in the batter, turning them to make sure they are completely covered.

Heat the butter and cook the slices of beef in it for about 3 minutes on each side.

Above: *Fillet of beef stuffed with herbs and Gorgonzola*
Right: *Steak in mustard*

lengthways, stuff the cavity with the herb mixture, then carefully tie up the fillet and put it in an oven-proof dish. Peel and slice the 3 remaining cloves of garlic, mix them with the remaining oil and season with salt and pepper. Add the fresh herbs and herbes de Provence, baste the meat all over with the oil and herb mixture, then cover it and leave it to rest.

After 2 hours take the lid off the dish and roast the meat at 225-250°C (425-475°F, Gas Mark 7-9). Turn the meat two or three times during cooking. Leave the roast to cool, take off the string and slice the fillet. Garnish with sprigs of fresh herbs.

BEEF WELLINGTON

Serves 4-5

750 g (1½ lb) fillet of beef
100 g (3½ oz) butter
100 g (3½ oz) onions
500 g (1 lb) whole button
mushrooms,
tinned
125 ml (4 fl oz) double

cream
300 g (10 oz) frozen puff
pastry
1 egg, separated
1 tbsp milk
salt and pepper

Melt half the butter and brown the meat on all sides, then season it with salt and pepper. Take the meat out of the pan and leave it to cool. Peel and dice the onions and fry them in the remaining butter. Quarter the mushrooms and add them to the onions with the cream. As soon as the sauce comes to the boil, take the pan off the heat, season the sauce with salt and pepper and leave it to cool. Defrost the pastry at room temperature. Roll out the pastry in a square, until it is twice the width of the meat. You can reserve a little pastry for decoration, if you like.

Spread the mushroom and onion sauce down the centre of the pastry, put the meat on top of the sauce, then spread the remaining sauce over the pastry on either side of the meat. Whisk the egg white until stiff and brush the edges of the pastry with it, then encase the fillet of beef in the pastry, sealing the edges.

Put the beef Wellington on an oven-proof dish. Decorate it with the reserved pastry, and make three small holes, at equal distances from each other, in the top. Beat together the egg yolk and milk and glaze the top of the beef Wellington with this mixture. Bake at 200-225⁰C (400-425⁰F, Gas Mark 6-7) for 40-50 minutes.

Right: *Roast fillet of beef*
Below: *Beef Wellington*

ROAST FILLET OF BEEF

Serves 6

1 kg (2 lb) fillet of beef	salt
oil	pepper

Brush the fillet of beef with oil. Put the beef in a roasting tin and roast it in the oven at 225-250⁰C (425-475⁰F, Gas Mark 7-9) for about 30 minutes. Turn the meat occasionally during cooking. When the meat is cooked, leave it to rest for about 10 minutes, so that the juices are absorbed back into the meat, then slice it and arrange it on a warmed serving dish.

Serve with broccoli and duchesse potatoes.

Above: *Sautéed beef*
Right: *Forerib of beef with onions.*

SAUTÊED BEEF

Serves 2

300 g (10 oz) beef, rump	knob of butter
steak, fillet steak or sirloin	150 g (5 oz) crème fraîche
1 onion	1 tsp tomato purèe
2 cucumbers	½ tsp mustard
2-3 tomatoes	½ stock cube
1 clove of garlic	salt and pepper

Cut the meat into thin slices, then into very thin strips. Peel the onion and cucumber. Blanch the tomatoes in boiling water, then refresh them in cold water and skin them. Dice the onion, cucumber and tomatoes finely.

Peel the clove of garlic and rub the base of a frying pan with it. Melt the butter in the frying pan and brown the meat in it for 8 minutes, then season with salt and pepper. Take the meat out of the pan and keep it warm. Fry the onion, cucumber and tomato in the meat juices. Leave them to cook for a few minutes. Combine the crème fraîche, tomato purée, mustard and stock cube, add this mixture to the vegetables, heat it through and season it with salt and pepper. Return the meat to the pan, reheat it and serve the beef with sautéed potatoes.

MEATBALLS

Serves 3-4

300 g (10 oz) minced beef	1 egg
300 g (10 oz) minced pork	sweet paprika
2 onions	50 g (2 oz) margarine
3 slices of stale bread	salt and pepper

Soak the bread in water to soften it, then squeeze it out well. Peel and finely dice the onions. Mix together the minced meat, onion, egg and bread, season with salt and pepper, and shape portions of the meat into small, oval-shaped patties. Melt the margarine and fry the meatballs for 5 minutes on each side.

FORERIB OF BEEF WITH ONIONS

Serves 4

4 foreribs of beef, each
weighing about 150 g
(5 oz)
500 g (1 lb) onions
2 tbsp oil

dried rubbed thyme
½ stock cube
1 glass of beer
salt
pepper

Peel and slice the onions and fry them in the hot oil.
Remove the onions from the oil and drain them. Cook
the foreribs in the frying pan for 3-4 minutes on each
side, then season them to taste with salt, pepper and
rubbed thyme. Take the meat out of the pan, spread the
onions over the meat and keep it hot.

Add the stock cube and beer to the frying pan, bring the
gravy to the boil, simmer it for a few minutes, then pour it
over the meat.

STEAK
WITH GREEN PEPPERCORNS

Serves 2

300 g (10 oz) fillet of beef
knob of butter
2 tbsp brandy

150 g (5 oz) crème fraîche
1 tbsp green peppercorns
salt and pepper

Cut the meat into two slices, gently flatten them and sprinkle them with salt and pepper. Heat the butter and fry the steaks over a high heat, for about 5 minutes each side. Transfer them to a warmed serving dish and keep them warm. De-glaze the frying pan with the brandy, add the crème fraîche and season the sauce with salt and

TURKISH MEATBALLS

Serves 4

250 g (8 oz) minced beef	ground cumin
250 g (8 oz) minced pork	cayenne pepper
2 onions	1 kg (2 lb) spinach
2 eggs	2 onions
1 clove of garlic	grated nutmeg
2-4 knobs of butter	2 tubs natural yoghurt
ground cinnamon	salt
ground ginger	pepper

Peel and finely chop the onions, then blanch them for 1-2 minutes and drain them. Peel and crush the garlic. Carefully mix together the garlic, onions, minced meat and eggs with the cinnamon, ginger and cumin to taste. Season the mixture with salt and pepper and add the cayenne pepper. The mixture should be highly spiced.

Dampen your hands and shape the meat mixture into about twenty little balls. Melt 1-2 knobs of butter and fry the meatballs in it for 10-15 minutes.

Carefully pick over the spinach, wash and drain it. Melt 1-2 knobs of butter, add the spinach, cover the pan and sweat the spinach for about 10 minutes. Drain off the juices, season with salt, pepper and nutmeg. Arrange the spinach on a warm serving dish.

Mix together both pots of yoghurt, with salt and pepper to taste. Arrange the meatballs on top of the spinach, pour the yoghurt dressing on top and dust with cayenne pepper.

Above: *Steak with green peppercorns*
Right: *Turkish meatballs*

pepper. Add the green peppercorns, bring the sauce to the boil and, as soon as it boils, pour it over the steaks.

Serve with jacket potatoes, topped with a cream and herbes de Provence dressing.

FILLET OF BEEF LUCULLUS

Serves 2

2 fillet steaks, each
weighing about 180 g
(6 oz)

fresh marjoram, chopped
1 tsp tomato purée
salt and pepper

Season the steaks with salt and pepper. Sprinkle fresh marjoram over them, spread them with the tomato purée, then wrap them in foil and roast them in the oven at 250⁰C (475⁰F, Gas Mark 9) for about 10 minutes. Open up the foil and roast the steaks for another 6 minutes to brown them.

Serve with sautéed potatoes and green salad.

Tip: You could cook sliced mushrooms and skinned, quartered tomatoes in the foil envelopes with the steaks.

ROAST BEEF

Serves 6

1 kg (2 lb) beef for
roasting e.g. fillet, rump,
sirloin

a few knobs of butter
salt
pepper

Gently score the surface of the meat and season it with salt and pepper. Butter a roasting tin and put the joint of beef in it. Dot the meat with a few knobs of butter. Cook the meat at 225-250⁰C (425-475⁰F, Gas Mark 7-9) for 35-45 minutes, turning it occasionally.
When the meat is cooked, leave it to rest for 10 minutes before slicing it, to allow the juices to be absorbed back into the meat. Arrange the sliced meat on a warm serving dish.

Below: *Fillet of beef Lucullus*

Above: *Meatballs Stroganoff*

MEATBALLS STROGANOFF

Serves 6

375 g (12 oz) minced beef
375 g (12 oz) minced pork
1 slice of stale bread
2 onions
3 eggs
grated nutmeg
50 g (2 oz) butter
375 g (12 oz) button

mushrooms
200 g (7 oz) onions
250 ml (8 fl oz) double
cream
2 tsp mustard
2 large gherkins in brine

salt and pepper

Soak the stale bread in cold water to soften it, then squeeze it out. Peel and finely dice the 2 onions. Mix together the minced meat, onions, eggs and bread and season the mixture with salt, pepper and grated nutmeg.

Dampen your hands and shape the meat mixture into 12 balls. Melt the butter and fry the meatballs for 10-12 minutes. Remove them from the pan and keep them warm.

To make the sauce: Wipe the mushrooms, then slice them thinly. Peel and slice the onions. Gently fry the onions and mushrooms in the juices from the meatballs, then add the mustard and cream. Heat the sauce gently until it starts to boil, stirring all the time, then season it with salt and pepper. Drain the gherkins, slice them thinly and add them to the sauce. Heat the gherkins through gently, then pour the sauce over the meatballs.

Serve with boiled potatoes sprinkled with fresh, chopped parsley and a cucumber salad.

BEEF AND MUSHROOM STEW

Serves 4

500 g (1 lb) fillet of beef	125 ml (4 fl oz) white wine
2 tbsp flour	250 ml (8 fl oz) crème
2 onions	fraîche
60 g (2½ oz) butter	salt
200 g (7 oz) mushrooms	pepper

Cut the meat into thin strips and toss them in the flour. Peel and dice one onion. Brown half the meat and half the onion in 25 g (1 oz) melted butter, stirring frequently to make sure the meat is sealed and browned all over (about 2 minutes). Then remove the meat and onions from the pan and keep warm. Repeat the process with the remaining meat and half onion. Peel and dice the second onion. Wipe the mushrooms, cutting the big ones in half. Melt a knob of butter and sweat the onion and mushrooms in it for about 10 minutes. Add the wine, crème fraîche and meat to the pan and season the mixture with salt and pepper. Reheat the meat for about 6 minutes, then serve immediately, accompanied by jacket potatoes garnished with a creamy dressing and a bouquet of baby vegetables.

RUMP STEAK

Serves 4

4 slices of rump steak,   *50 g (2 oz) margarine*
each weighing 150 g (5 oz)   *salt and pepper*

Score the layer of fat along the edge of the steaks. Melt the margarine, brown the steaks in it for 3-4 minutes each side, basting frequently during cooking to ensure the steaks stay tender, then season them with salt and pepper. Arrange the steaks on a warm serving dish and pour the cooking juices over them.

Variation: Garnish the steaks with fried onion rings and serve with grated horseradish.

LIVER WITH MUSHROOMS AND ONIONS

Serves 4

4 slices of calf's, pig's or   *250 g (8 oz) onions*
ox liver, each weighing   *200 g (7 oz) button*
150 g (5 oz)   *mushrooms*
1 tbsp flour   *salt and pepper*
50 g (2 oz) butter

Dredge the slices of liver in the flour. Fry them in 40 g (1½ oz) butter, season them with salt and pepper and keep them warm. Peel and slice the onions. Brown them in the remaining butter, stirring from time to time. Add the mushrooms and cook them for 5 minutes, season the mixture with salt and pepper and pour it over the slices of liver.

Serve with mashed potato or baked apples.

PEPPERED STEAK

Serves 4

4 slices of fillet of beef,   *4 tsp black peppercorns*
each 2 cm (¾ inch) thick   *knob of butter*

Crush the peppercorns. Press the steaks down onto the peppercorns to make them stick. Melt a knob of butter in a frying pan and fry the steaks for 3-4 minutes on each side.

Tip: Serve the peppered steaks with sweetcorn and tomatoes.

Opposite: *Beef and mushroom stew*
Below: *Peppered steak*

Above: *Tournedos with corn on the cob*

TOURNEDOS WITH CORN ON THE COB

Serves 4

4 tournedos from the beef
fillet, each weighing 150 g
(5 oz)
4 tbsp oil
4 tsp green peppercorns

4 cobs of corn, each
weighing 200 g (7 oz)
160 g (5½ oz) roll of
parsley butter

*H*eat 1 tablespoon of oil in a frying pan and brown the tournedos for 3 minutes on each side. Add the green peppercorns, sweat them, then take the meat out of the pan and keep it warm. Strip the leaves and silk from the cobs of corn, wash them, then sauté them for about 10 minutes, turning frequently, in 3 tablespoons of oil. Cut the parsley butter into 8 slices and arrange them on top of the steak and corn.

RUMP STEAK WITH SHALLOTS

Serves 4

4 slices of rump steak
750 g (1½ lb) shallots
40 g (1½ oz) butter
6 tbsp white wine

1 tsp green peppercorns
2 tbsp oil
salt
freshly ground pepper

Peel the shallots, cut them in half if they are too big, and sweat them in 40 g (1½ oz) butter. Add 4 tablespoons of white wine and the green peppercorns. Season with salt and pepper and leave to sweat for about 10 minutes, stirring occasionally. Heat the oil in a frying pan, fry the meat for 3 minutes on each side and season it with salt and pepper. Remove the meat from the pan, arrange it on a warm serving dish and keep it hot. De-glaze the meat juices with the remaining wine, pour the juices over the meat and serve with the shallots.
Serve with sautéed potatoes and green salad.

Below: *Fillet of beef with bananas and onions.*

FILLET OF BEEF WITH BANANAS AND ONIONS

Serves 2

2 slices of fillet of beef,
each weighing 150 g (5 oz)
200 g (7 oz) onions
50 g (2 oz) butter

2 bananas
salt and freshly ground
pepper

Peel and slice the onions thinly. Brown the meat on both sides in 30 g (1 oz) butter, season with salt and pepper, remove it from the pan and keep it warm.
Fry the onions until golden in 20 g (¾ oz) butter. Peel the bananas and slice them into thin rounds. Fry them with the onions, taking care not to mash them. Season lightly with salt and pepper.

Serve the banana and onion mixture with the steak, accompanied by gratin dauphinois (p. 58) and a watercress salad.

CALF'S LIVER

Serves 4

4 slices of calf's liver
oil
1 orange, sliced

cranberry jelly
salt
freshly ground pepper

Season the slices of liver with pepper, brush them with oil and grill them for about 3 minutes on each side. Season them with salt and serve with the slices of orange and the cranberry jelly.

Serve with boiled potatoes or potato croquettes and a chicory salad.

RUMP STEAK WITH HORSERADISH

Serves 4

4 slices of rump steak, each weighing 150 g (5 oz)
100 ml (3½ fl oz) whipping cream
1 tbsp grated horseradish

oil
sweet paprika
salt and freshly ground pepper

Whip the cream until it forms soft peaks, fold in the grated horseradish and season with salt. Grill the meat on a griddle for 3 minutes on one side and 2 minutes on the other. Baste the meat with oil after it has been cooking for 1 minute. Season to taste with salt, pepper and paprika.
Serve with the horseradish sauce, accompanied by sautéed potatoes and lamb's lettuce.

SHASHLIK WITH SPICY SAUCE

Serves 2-3

100 g (3½ oz) fillet of pork
100 g (3½ oz) veal escalope
100 g (3½ oz) pig's or ox liver
75 g (3 oz) smoked streaky bacon
6 tbsp tomato ketchup
2 tbsp oil

2 tbsp mild mustard
1 tbsp anchovy butter
1 small onion
fresh parsley, chopped
sweet paprika
salt
freshly ground pepper

Blend together the tomato ketchup, oil, mustard and anchovy butter. Add the peeled and thinly sliced onion, parsley and salt. Cut the pieces of meat into large cubes, about 2½ cm (1 inch) in size and spear them on skewers. Baste the meat with a little oil and grill the kebabs for about 10 minutes, turning them occasionally. Then season the meat with salt, pepper and paprika and serve with the spicy sauce.

GRILLED OX LIVER

Serves 4

4 slices of ox liver
6 tbsp olive oil
2 tbsp lemon juice
mustard

watercress
salt
freshly ground pepper

To make the marinade, mix together the olive oil, lemon juice, salt, pepper and mustard. Put the meat in the marinade, cover and leave to marinate for 1 hour. Drain the slices of meat and grill them on the barbecue for 5-7 minutes, turning them frequently. Garnish the serving plates with watercress.

Serve with slices of orange and raw onion rings.

Variation: You can also cook the liver on a conventional grill, but it will not have the same smoky flavour.

Left: *Calf's liver*
Right: *Grilled ox liver*

FLAMBÉED CALF'S KIDNEYS WITH OLIVES

Serves 4-6

750 g (1½ lb) calf's kidneys	60 g (2½ oz) stuffed green olives
500 ml (18 fl oz) milk	1 tbsp fresh parsley, chopped
1 tsp flour	
2 shallots (or 1 onion)	2 tbsp brandy
4 thin slices of bacon	salt
2 knobs of butter	freshly ground pepper

Prepare the kidneys by removing the cores, then rinse them. Soak them in the milk for 1 hour. Pat them dry and cut them into 3 cm (1¼ inch) dice. Coat them in the flour. Peel and finely chop the shallots or onion. Cut the bacon into small pieces, render it and reserve it. Melt the butter in a frying pan, fry the kidneys for about 4 minutes, then add the shallots. In a bowl, mix together the olives, parsley and bacon; season the mixture with salt and pepper. Warm the brandy, pour it over the kidneys, set light to it and serve the flambéed kidneys immediately. Serve with rice, green salad or endive and potatoes.

CALF'S BRAIN

Serves 3-4

600 g (1¼ lb) calf's brain	butter
1 tbsp vinegar	salt and pepper
1 bunch of fresh parsley, chopped	

Rinse the calf's brain until no more blood runs from it. Remove the skin and veins. Put the brain into 500 ml (18 fl oz) boiling water to which salt and vinegar have been added, bring to the boil and simmer for 5-6 minutes. Skim the cooking liquid, add the parsley to the pan, leave it to infuse for a few minutes, then drain the brain and arrange it on a warm serving dish. Melt some butter and pour it over the calf's brain.
Serve with tomato salad and toast.

Variation: Cook the brain as above, leave it to cool in the stock, then drain it. Season it with salt and pepper, coat it in flour, beaten egg and breadcrumbs and sauté it in margarine.

Right: *Saltimbocca*
Below: *Flambéed calf's kidneys with olives.*

SALTIMBOCCA

IN THE PRESSURE COOKER
Serves 4

8 thin veal escalopes, each
weighing 75-100 g
(3-3½ oz)
1 tbsp lemon juice
8 sage leaves
8 small slices raw ham
50 g (2 oz) butter
100 ml (3½ fl oz) Marsala

or white wine
2 tbsp crème fraîche
flour
soy sauce or Bovril
salt
freshly ground pepper

Gently stretch the escalopes, brush them with the lemon juice and season them with salt and pepper. Carefully rinse the sage leaves, dry them and place one on each escalope. Cover each sage leaf with a slice of ham, roll up the escalopes and secure each with a cocktail stick.

Melt the butter in the pressure cooker, brown the veal olives on all sides for about 6 minutes, then add 100 ml (3½ fl oz) water and the Marsala or white wine, put the lid on the pressure cooker and braise for a further 6 minutes. Take out the cocktail sticks, put the veal olives on a warm serving dish and keep them warm.
Add the crème fraîche to the liquid in the pressure cooker and thicken it with a little flour and cold water blended together. Season with salt, pepper and soy sauce or Bovril, then coat the veal olives in the gravy and garnish them with sage leaves.
Serve with rice or noodles and salad.

OSSO BUCCO

Serves 6-8

2 kg (4½ lb) veal shank
flour
2 tbsp olive oil
100 ml (3½ fl oz) white
wine
100 ml (3½ fl oz) chicken
stock
3 carrots
1 piece celeriac
4 onions

2 knobs of butter
500 g (1 lb) tomatoes,
tinned
1 bay leaf
fresh basil, chopped
fresh thyme, chopped
fresh parsley, chopped
salt
freshly ground pepper

Ask your butcher to cut the veal shank into pieces, 4-6 cm (1½-2½ inches thick). Season the meat with salt and pepper and dredge it in the flour. Heat the olive oil, brown the meat in it, then take the meat out of the pan and keep it warm. De-glaze the pan with the white wine and stock.
Peel and wash the carrots, celeriac and onions. Chop them into small dice and sauté them in the butter, stirring occasionally, until golden. Roughly chop the tomatoes and add them to the vegetables with the juice, bay leaf, basil, thyme and parsley and season with salt and pepper. Arrange the pieces of veal shank on top of the vegetables, pour the cooking juices over the top, cover and cook for about 1¼ hours.

BLANQUETTE DE VEAU

Serves 4

600 g (1¼ lb) veal, boned
1 onion
1 bay leaf
3 cloves
30 g (1 oz) butter

35 g (1 generous oz) flour
1 egg yolk
2 tbsp cold milk
lemon juice
salt
freshly ground pepper

Dice the meat and put it into 750 ml (1¼ pints) boiling, salted water, bring it to the boil and skim it. Peel the onion and spike it with the cloves and bay leaf, add it to the meat and cook for 45-60 minutes. Remove the meat from the pan, strain the stock and reserve 500 ml (18 fl oz). To make the gravy, melt the butter, add the flour, stirring all the time and cook until the roux turns brown. Add the reserved stock, and whisk the gravy to prevent lumps forming. Bring the gravy to the boil and simmer it for 5 minutes. Then add the meat to the gravy and reheat it. Beat together the egg yolk and milk, take the pan off the heat and add the beaten egg mixture to the gravy. Season the gravy with lemon juice, salt and pepper.

Serve with rice (turned out of a ring mould).

VEAL STEW

Serves 4

600 g (1¼ lb) breast of
veal, boned
6 carrots
6 potatoes

3 turnips
3 leeks
a few sticks of celery
salt

Put the meat into 1½ litres (2½ pints) salted, boiling water. Bring it to the boil, add the prepared vegetables and cook it for about 1½ hours. Slice the meat, arrange it on a warm serving dish and garnish it with the vegetables.

Serve with creamed horseradish and boiled potatoes or parsleyed new potatoes and seasonings.

Variation: Instead of breast you could use boned whole shoulder.

VEAL STEW WITH MUSHROOMS

Serves 4

500 g (1 lb) veal, boned
2 tbsp flour
2 onions
3 knobs of butter or margarine
200 g (7 oz) button

mushrooms
125 ml (4 fl oz) white wine
250 ml (8 fl oz) whipping cream
salt and white pepper

Above:
Veal stew with mushrooms

Cut the meat into very thin slices and dredge them in flour. Peel and dice one of the onions. Melt 2 knobs of butter in a frying pan and fry half of the meat and onion for 2 minutes, stirring frequently. Take the meat and onion out of the pan and repeat the process with the other half. Keep the meat and onions hot. Peel and dice the remaining onion and sauté it in a knob of butter with the thinly sliced mushrooms. Add the meat, white wine and cream. Season the meat with salt and pepper and cook over a high heat for about 5 minutes, then serve it immediately.

Serve with potato galettes and salad.

Tip: You could substitute chanterelle mushrooms or ceps for the button mushrooms.

MEATBALLS WITH PAPRIKA

Serves 4-6

750 g (1½ lb) minced beef
1 large onion
knob of butter
paprika

salt
freshly ground pepper

Peel and finely chop the onion. Mix it thoroughly with the minced beef, melted butter and a drop of water. Add salt, pepper and paprika to taste.

Dampen your hands and shape the meat mixture into little balls. Flatten them gently into patties, then grill or barbecue them for 5 minutes each side. Serve when nice and brown.

Opposite: *Blanquette de veau*

Above: *Veal shank with lentils and tomatoes*
Right: *Loin of veal*

VEAL SHANK WITH LENTILS AND TOMATOES

Serves 6-8

1½ kg (3½ lb) veal shank, in 5 cm (2 inch) slices	1 tbsp fresh rosemary, chopped
200 g (7 oz) lentils	125 ml (4 fl oz) chicken stock
6 tbsp oil	500 g (1 lb) tomatoes, tinned
4 cloves of garlic	
150 g (5 oz) onions	200 ml (7 fl oz) red wine
3 carrots	1 bunch of fresh parsley, finely chopped
3 potatoes	
1 leek	salt
1 turnip	
2 tsp hot paprika	

Rinse the lentils, put them in 750 ml (1¼ pints) cold, salted water, bring them to the boil, cover and simmer for 30 minutes. Gently score the meat. Season it with salt and brown it in oil in a large roasting tin, then put it to one side. Peel and finely chop the garlic. Peel and dice the onions, carrots, potatoes, leek and turnip.

Fry half the garlic, the onions and vegetables in the meat juices. Add the lentils, paprika and rosemary. Stir thoroughly and add the stock. Drain and roughly chop the tomatoes and add them to the roasting tin with the meat and red wine. Cover the roasting tin and braise the meat for 1½-2 hours. Just before serving add the finely chopped parsley and remaining garlic.

BRAISED SHOULDER OF VEAL

Serves 5-6

750 g (1½ lb) whole shoulder of veal, boned	1 stick of celery
	1 bay leaf
50 g (2 oz) margarine	5 peppercorns
fresh rosemary, chopped	flour
4 carrots	3 level tbsp crème fraîche
4 potatoes	salt
2 turnips	freshly ground pepper
2 leeks	

Seal the meat on all sides in the margarine. Season it with salt and pepper and add the rosemary, the chopped vegetables, the bay leaf and peppercorns. Brown them in the meat juices for a few minutes, then add 250 ml (8 fl oz) hot water, cover and braise the meat for about 2 hours, turning it from time to time and adding more liquid as necessary. Slice the meat, put it on a warm serving dish

with the vegetables and keep them warm. Strain the cooking juices, skim off the fat and reserve the volume you require to make the gravy. Bring the reserved gravy to the boil, then thicken it with flour and cold water blended together. Add the crème fraîche, season it with salt and pepper and serve the gravy separately.

LOIN OF VEAL

Serves 6-8

1 kg (2 lb) loin of veal	5 dried mushrooms
1 onion	zest of ½ an unwaxed lemon
1 carrot	
2 tomatoes	flour
3 tbsp oil	salt
1 bay leaf	white pepper

Season the veal with salt and pepper. Heat the oil in a casserole dish and brown the veal on all sides. Add the peeled and diced onion and carrot, and skinned, diced tomatoes. Leave the vegetables to brown for 5 minutes. De-glaze the pan with 250 ml (8 fl oz) hot water and add the bay leaf, mushrooms and lemon zest. Braise the meat for 1½-1¾ hours, occasionally basting it with the juices.

Slice the meat and keep it warm. De-glaze the cooking juices with a little water, strain them through a sieve and thicken them with a little flour slaked with water. Serve the gravy separately.

Above: *Roast veal with grapes and almonds*

ROAST SHANK OF VEAL

Serves 6-8

1½ kg (3½ lb) shank of
veal
2 tbsp oil
2 tsp fresh thyme,
chopped

1 tsp salt
100 ml (3½ fl oz) beer
250 g (8 oz) baby onions
or shallots

Mix together the oil, thyme and salt and brush the veal
shank with this mixture. Put the meat in a roasting tin
with a little water and roast it for 2-2½ hours at 200-225°C
(400-425°F, Gas Mark 6-7). Combine 100 ml (3½ fl oz)
water and the beer and pour it over the meat as soon as
the meat juices start to brown.

After 30 minutes' cooking time, add the peeled onions.
Take the meat and onions out of the tin and keep them
warm, reduce the cooking juices and adjust the seasoning
as necessary.

Serve *with potatoes and cabbage.*

ROAST VEAL WITH GRAPES AND ALMONDS

Serves 4

600 g (1¼ lb) veal for
roasting, e.g. shoulder,
loin
2 tbsp oil
knob of butter
250 ml (8 fl oz) chicken
stock
lemon juice

250 g (8 oz) white grapes
100 g (3½ oz) blanched
almonds
fresh lemon balm, finely
chopped
salt and freshly ground
pepper

Season the veal with salt and pepper and seal it on all
sides in the oil. Add the butter and fry it for 18-20
minutes over a low heat. Then take the meat out of the
pan, wrap it in foil and keep it hot.
De-glaze the pan with the stock, bring the gravy to the
boil, season it with salt, pepper and lemon juice. Wash
and drain the grapes, slice them in half and remove the
pips, then add them to the gravy with the almonds and
cook them for 10 minutes. Then add the lemon balm to
the gravy. Take the meat out of the foil, slice it and serve
it with the gravy, accompanied by boiled rice.

Variation: You could substitute pork for the veal.

VEAL SHANK

IN A CHICKEN BRICK OR EARTHENWARE DISH
Serves 6-8

2 kg (4½ lb) veal shank
4 tomatoes
2 onions
fresh rosemary, chopped
fresh parsley, chopped

butter or margarine
3 tsp flour
salt
freshly ground pepper

Season the meat with salt and pepper and spread the
butter over it. Peel the onions. Slice the onions and
tomatoes into 8 pieces. Rinse out a chicken brick and
arrange the onions and tomatoes on the base with the
rosemary.

Add the veal shank, cover and roast in the oven for
2-2½ hours at 200-225°C (400-425°F, Gas Mark 6-7).
Thirty minutes before the end of cooking time, take the
lid off the dish so that the meat is well browned.
Take the meat off the bone, slice it and arrange it on a
warm serving dish. Bind the juices with flour slaked
with cold water. Season the gravy with salt and pepper.

Serve the veal shank with boiled rice or potatoes.

Right: *Veal shank in an earthenware dish*

Below: *Veal ragout in clam shells*
Right: *Brochettes*

VEAL RAGOUT IN CLAM SHELLS

Serves 5-6

300 g (10 oz) boiled calf's tongue	mushrooms
175 g (6 oz) boiled calf's brain	2 egg yolks
	2 tbsp cold milk
250 g (8 oz) stewed veal, boned	2 tbsp lemon juice
	1 tbsp white wine
40 g (1½ oz) butter	Worcester sauce
50 g (2 oz) flour	2 tbsp breadcrumbs
500 ml (18 fl oz) chicken stock	3 tbsp Gruyère cheese, grated
100 g (3½ oz) button	salt
	freshly ground pepper

Cut the meat into small dice. To make the sauce, melt the butter, add the flour and cook the roux, stirring all the time, until it browns. Add the stock, whisking the sauce to prevent lumps forming, then bring the sauce to the boil and simmer it for 5 minutes.

Blanch the mushrooms and drain them, chop them finely, add them to the sauce with the meat and cook them for a few minutes.

Take the ragout off the heat. Beat together the egg yolks and milk and add them to the ragout, then season it with lemon juice, white wine, salt, pepper and Worcester sauce.

Divide the ragout amongst 12 clam shells or ramekins, sprinkle breadcrumbs and grated Gruyère on top and dot them with butter. Brown them in the over for 10-15 minutes at 225-250°C (425-475°F, Gas Mark 7-9).

STUFFED VEAL ESCALOPES

Serves 4

4 veal escalopes	250 ml (8 fl oz) whipping cream
200 g (7 oz) dried apricots	
250 ml (8 fl oz) sherry	salt and freshly ground pepper
4 tbsp flour	
6 tbsp oil	

Soak the dried apricots in the sherry for 2-3 hours, drain them and reserve the liquor. Cut a flap in each escalope widthways, season the inside with pepper and stuff them with the apricots, reserving a few for decoration. Roll up the escalopes and secure them with cocktail sticks. Season the escalopes with salt and pepper and coat them in the flour, fry them for 6-8 minutes on each side in the oil, then take them out of the pan and keep them hot. Deglaze the pan with the liquor from the apricots and the whipping cream, simmer it for a few minutes, season it with salt and pepper and add more sherry to taste. Add the escalopes to the sauce, braise them for 10 minutes, serve them on a warmed serving dish and garnish with the reserved apricots.
Serve with rice and lamb's lettuce.

BROCHETTES

Serves 4

4 slices of pork fillet, each weighing 50-60 g (2-2½ oz)	100 ml (3½ fl oz) olive oil
	butter
	salt
4 slices of veal fillet	black pepper
4 slices of beef fillet	

Marinate the meat in the olive oil and pepper for 1 hour in a covered dish. Spear pieces of pork, veal and beef alternately on 4 skewers. Put them on a lightly buttered grill and grill them for 8 minutes, turning them frequently. Season them with salt and serve immediately. Serve with asparagus, blanched young dandelion leaves, steamed spring onions and hollandaise sauce (see page 93).

CALF'S LIVER WITH PEACHES

Serves 4

4 slices of calf's liver
400 g (13 oz) peach
halves, tinned in syrup
3 tbsp sugar
1 tbsp wine vinegar
250 ml (8 fl oz) chicken

stock
1-2 tsp redcurrant jelly
4 knobs of butter
1-2 tbsp Grand Marnier
salt
freshly ground pepper

Carefully drain the peaches and reserve the syrup. Caramelize the sugar in a saucepan, add the peach syrup, vinegar and stock, cook until the sauce thickens and then add the redcurrant jelly. Sauté the slices of liver in the butter in a frying pan for about 6 minutes on each side. Season the liver with salt and pepper, take it out of the pan and keep it warm. Pour the sauce into the meat juices, add the peach halves, heat them through and add the Grand Marnier. Arrange the liver slices and peach halves on a warmed plate and coat them in the sauce.

Serve with tagliatelle and salad.

Season the meat with salt and pepper, brush it with the lemon juice and oil and roast it in the oven for 1½ hours at 200-225⁰ C (400-425⁰ F, Gas Mark 6-7). As soon as the meat starts to brown, add 125 ml (4 fl oz) hot water and the stock. Baste the meat occasionally and add water to the roasting tin as necessary.

Peel an onion and a carrot, dice them and add them to the roasting tin, with the bay leaves, about 20 minutes before the end of cooking time.

Take the meat out of the roasting tin and keep it warm. De-glaze the roasting tin with the white wine, strain the gravy and thicken it with the flour and crème fraîche. Adjust the seasoning as necessary. Serve with mashed potatoes.

Opposite:
Calf's liver
with peaches

VEAL ESCALOPES

Serves 4

4 veal escalopes	salt
50 g (2 oz) margarine	freshly ground pepper

Brown the escalopes in the margarine for 4-6 minutes each side and season with salt and pepper. Arrange them on a warm serving dish and pour the meat juices over them.

Serve with button mushrooms and boiled rice.

Below: *Veal escalopes*

CRISPY LOIN OF VEAL

Serves 6-8

1½ kg (3½ lb) loin of veal	3 bay leaves
juice of ½ lemon	125 ml (4 fl oz) white wine
3 tbsp oil	1 tbsp flour
250 ml (8 fl oz) chicken	150 g (5 oz) crème fraîche
stock	salt
1 onion	freshly ground pepper
1 carrot	

ESCALOPES CORDON BLEU

Serves 4

8 veal escalopes, each
weighing 75 g (3 oz)
4 thin slices of Gruyère
cheese, same size as the
escalopes
4 slices of boiled ham,

same size as the escalopes
2 eggs
60 g (2½ oz) breadcrumbs
60 g (2½ oz) margarine
salt
freshly ground pepper

Season the escalopes with salt and pepper. Place a slice of ham and a slice of cheese on top of 4 of them, then top each one with another escalope.

Beat the eggs, dip the escalopes in the beaten egg, then coat them in the breadcrumbs and brown them for 5 minutes on each side in the margarine.
Serve with jacket potatoes with crème fraîche and petit pois.

ROAST VEAL WITH GRAPES AND PEACHES

Serves 6-8

1 kg (2 lb) veal for roasting,
e.g. shoulder, loin, rump
knob of butter
vegetables for stewing, e.g.
carrot, leek turnip, onion
250 ml (8 fl oz) white wine
2 tbsp crème fraîche

2 peaches
100 g (3½ oz) black grapes
100 g (3½ oz) white grapes
salt
freshly ground pepper

Season the meat with salt and pepper, spread the butter over it and roast it in the oven with the prepared vegetables and a little water for 1-1½ hours at 200°C (400°F, Gas Mark 6). As soon as the meat starts to brown, add the white wine. Baste the meat occasionally with the juices and add more water to the roasting tin as necessary. Take the meat out of the roasting tin and keep it warm.

To make the gravy: De-glaze the roasting tin with a little water and strain it through a sieve. Stone the peaches and cut them in half, slice the grapes in half and remove the pips, then add the peaches and grapes to the gravy with the crème fraîche. Heat them through, season the gravy with salt and pepper and serve it separately. Accompany with a green salad.

SAUTÉED CALF'S LIVER WITH SAGE

Serves 4

800 g (1½ lb) calf's liver
500 g (1 lb) onions
100 g (3½ oz) butter
3-4 tbsp lemon juice
150 ml (5 fl oz) white wine
2 sprigs of fresh sage,

finely chopped
1-2 bunches fresh parsley,
chopped
salt
freshly ground pepper

Peel and dice the onions, brown them for about 10 minutes in half the butter, then reserve them. Cut the liver into thin strips, season it with salt and pepper and brown it on both sides for about 5 minutes in the remaining butter. Add the lemon juice to the liver, then reserve it.

De-glaze the pan with 100 ml (3½ fl oz) white wine and add the onions and the finely chopped sage. Reheat the onions for a minute or two, then add the liver, reheat it, and add the finely chopped parsley and remaining white wine. Serve immediately.

> **Suggestion:** You could use dried sage instead of fresh, but take care how much you use, because dried sage is very strongly flavoured.

Opposite: *Escalopes Cordon Bleu*
Right: *Sautéed calf's liver with sage*

ROAST PORK

Serves 6-8

1 kg (2 lb) pork for
roasting, e.g. shoulder,
middle loin, whole leg
5 tbsp olive oil

2 cloves of garlic
3 tbsp tomato purée
salt
freshly ground pepper

Season the meat with salt and pepper. Brown it all over
in the olive oil, then put it to one side. Peel the garlic,
brown it in the meat juices, then add the tomato purée
and ½ glass of water.
Add the meat, cover and braise for 1¼-1½ hours, turning
it occasionally. Slice the meat, arrange it on a warm
serving dish, adjust the seasoning in the gravy and serve
it with the meat.

Serve with petit pois, butter beans and dauphine
potatoes.

CASSOULET

Serves 6-8

500 g (1lb) pork shank
375 g (12 oz) neck end or
hand and spring of pork
150 g (5 oz) streaky bacon
100 g (3½ oz) garlic
sausage
1 piece of pork rind
500 g (1 lb) dried haricot
beans
3 onions

2 cloves
1 carrot
2 bay leaves
fresh thyme, chopped
5 cloves of garlic
3 tbsp tomato purée
2 tbsp breadcrumbs
salt
freshly ground pepper

Soak the beans in 1 litre (1¾ pints) of water for
12-24 hours. Bring them to the boil in a casserole dish.
Peel an onion and spike it with the cloves. Peel and

Opposite: *Roast pork*

Above: *Cassoulet*

SAUERKRAUT (PICKLED CABBAGE WITH PORK AND SAUSAGES)

Serves 6-8

300 g (10 oz) streaky bacon
375 g (12 oz) smoked shoulder of pork
500-750 g (1-1½ lb) salted belly pork (flank end)
1 pig's trotter, sliced
6-8 Frankfurters
2 coarse, meaty pork sausages
2 onions
2 cooking apples
2 tbsp lard
1½ kg (3½ lb) sauerkraut (pickled cabbage)
juniper berries
peppercorns
250 ml (8 fl oz) white wine
6-8 potatoes
salt
freshly ground pepper

Soak the salted belly pork in cold water for several hours to remove some of the salt. Put it into 1 litre (1¾ pints) boiling, salted water, bring it to the boil and simmer it for about 2 hours.

Peel and dice the onions. Peel the apples, cut them into quarters, then into slices. Rinse the pig's trotter under running water, drain it, then season it with salt and pepper.

Melt the lard in a large casserole dish and alternately layer the sauerkraut with the onions, sliced apples, sliced pig's trotter, juniper berries, peppercorns, streaky bacon and smoked pork shoulder, seasoning each layer with salt. Pour the wine and 250 ml (8 fl oz) water on top, and braise for 1½ hours. Add the two types of sausage and cook for a further 15 minutes.

Peel the potatoes. Cook them for 15 minutes in salted water. Take the meat out of the casserole dish, take it off the bone and slice it. Slice the sausages into chunks and arrange the sauerkraut on a serving dish. Arrange the meat, sausages and drained potatoes on top of the sauerkraut.

slice the carrot. Rinse the pork shank under running water and add it to the beans with the onion and sliced carrot. Add 100 g (3½ oz) streaky bacon, the pork rind and bay leaf. Season to taste with salt, pepper and thyme. Bring to the boil and simmer for 45 minutes. Rinse the neck end or hand and spring of pork under running water, drain it and cut it into pieces. Cut the remaining streaky bacon into slices. Peel the garlic and 2 onions and cut them into quarters. Fry the bacon to render the fat, then fry the meat, garlic and onions. Add the tomato purée and 250 ml (8 fl oz) water and simmer for 15 minutes.

Add the fried pork mixture to the beans and pork shank and braise for about 1½ hours, then take out the piece of streaky bacon, pork shank and pork rind. Slice the garlic sausage, piece of streaky bacon and pork shank thickly. Arrange the meat and beans in an oven-proof dish and season them with salt and pepper. Sprinkle the breadcrumbs on top and bake in the oven for 10 minutes at 225-250°C (425-475°F, Gas Mark 7-9).

BÄCKEROFEN

Serves 5-6

750 g (1½ lb) pork, beef or mutton, boned
4 carrots
1 leek
750 ml (1¼ pints) white wine
1 clove of garlic
10 black peppercorns
1 bay leaf
2 chilli seeds
250 g (8 oz) onions

750 g (1½ lb) potatoes
butter
½ tsp fresh thyme, chopped
1 tsp fresh basil, chopped
150-300g (5-10 oz) crème fraîche
2-3 tbsp breadcrumbs
salt
freshly ground pepper

Dice the meat. Chop the carrots and leek into small pieces and put them all in a large bowl. Pour the white wine over them.
Peel and crush the clove of garlic and add it to the bowl with the black peppercorns, bay leaf and chilli seeds, cover and leave to marinate for several hours (or overnight) in a cool place.

Peel and thinly slice the onions, peel and slice the potatoes into rounds. Butter an oven-proof dish generously and layer the onions, meat, vegetables and potatoes in it. Pour the marinade on top. Add a little more wine if necessary. Season with salt, pepper, thyme and basil.

Cover and braise in the oven for 2½-3 hours at 175-200°C (350-400°F, Gas Mark 4-6). After 2½ hours, try the meat and if it is cooked add the crème fraîche, sprinkle breadcrumbs on top, dot with butter and brown the dish in a very hot oven or under the grill. Serve straight from the oven.

CHUMP CHOPS WITH FRENCH BEAN PARCELS

Serves 4

250 g (8 oz) French beans
600 g (1¼ lb) pork chump chops or spare ribs
300 g (10 oz) potatoes

100 ml (3½ fl oz) water
salt
freshly ground pepper

Top, tail and wash the French beans. Season them with salt and place them on a big sheet of foil. Season the meat with salt and put it on top of the beans. Peel and dice the potatoes, season them with salt and add them to the meat and beans.

Add a drop of water to the meat and vegetables and fold the foil up to make a parcel, pierce it several times and cook the parcels in the oven for 1 hour and 10 minutes at 200°C (400°F, Gas Mark 6). Arrange the meat, beans and potatoes on a warm serving dish and serve.

Tip: You can make gravy using the cooking juices. Thicken them with flour and season with salt, pepper and brandy.

Left: *Bäckerofen*
Right: *Chump chops with French bean parcels*

PORK AND BEER STEW

Serves 4

600 g (1¼ lb) fillet of pork
2 onions
2 knobs of lard
paprika
250 ml (8 fl oz) beer
1 bay leaf
pinch of chilli

1 green pepper
1 tomato
2 gherkins
3-4 tbsp crème fraîche
salt
pepper

Cut the meat into thin slices. Peel and dice the onions, brown them in half of the lard, then reserve them. Brown the meat in the other half of the lard, add the onions, ½ teaspoon of paprika, beer, bay leaf and chilli. Season with salt and pepper and braise for 20-25 minutes.

Remove the stalk, core and seeds from the green pepper and cut it into thin strips. Blanch the tomato, then refresh it in cold water, skin it, cut it in half, de-seed it and cut it into slices.

Add the tomato, pepper and sliced gherkins to the meat. Cook them for a few minutes, then enrich the dish with crème fraîche and season it with paprika.
Serve with boiled potatoes or rice.

Below: *Pork and beer stew*

Above: *Neck end of pork, Chinese style*

NECK END OF PORK, CHINESE STYLE

Serves 2

350 g (11 oz) neck end of pork
2 tbsp soy sauce
3 tbsp sherry
2 cloves of garlic, finely chopped
1 tsp fresh ginger, chopped or pinch of ground ginger
1 tbsp cornflour

½ bottle tomato ketchup
4 tbsp pineapple juice
1-2 tbsp chilli
1 slice of pineapple, tinned in syrup
3 bunches of spring onions
30 g (1 oz) flaked almonds
2 tbsp oil
salt

Dice the meat. Blend together the soy sauce, sherry, finely chopped garlic, ginger and cornflour. Add the meat. Blend together the tomato ketchup, pineapple juice, chilli and drained, very finely chopped pineapple. Thinly slice the spring onions, including part of the green stalk. Toast the almonds in a dry frying pan until golden and put to one side.

Drain the meat. Heat a spoonful of oil in a frying pan and fry the meat for 2 minutes, stirring frequently. In another frying pan, brown the onions in the remaining oil for 1 minute, then season them with salt.
Pour the ketchup-based sauce over the meat, heat it through, then take the frying pan off the heat. Add the onions and stir thoroughly. Add the toasted almonds and serve immediately. Serve with boiled rice.

SMOKED GAMMON WITH CABBAGE

Serves 3

500 g (1 lb) smoked gammon
2 onions
2 cloves
chilli seeds
20 g (¾ oz) lard
600 g (1¼ lb) Savoy

cabbage
6 tbsp oil
2 tsp sugar
750 g (1½ lb) new potatoes
salt
freshly ground pepper

Peel the onions, spike them with the cloves and chilli seeds and cook them in 1 litre (1¾ pints) of boiling, salted water, with the meat, for 1½-1¾ hours. Take the meat out and strain the stock, reserving 500 ml (18 fl oz).

Put the meat, stock, cabbage sliced into ribbons and lard into a casserole dish, season with salt and pepper and braise for 30-45 minutes. Peel the potatoes, brown them on all sides in the oil and fry until crisp and golden. Take the meat out and slice it. Arrange it on a warm serving dish with the potatoes and cabbage.

CARBONNADE

IN A CHICKEN BRICK OR EARTHENWARE DISH
Serves 5

750 g (1½ lb) neck end or blade of pork
mustard
200 g (7 oz) onions
50 g (2 oz) butter

300 ml (10 fl oz) beer
1 bay leaf
salt
freshly ground pepper

Cut the meat into 4 slices. Season with salt and pepper and spread each slice with mustard. Melt the butter, brown the thinly sliced onions in it, and brown the meat on both sides.

Add the beer and the bay leaf, cover and simmer for about 1¾ hours.

Below: *Smoked gammon with cabbage*
Right: *Salted belly of pork*

PORK WITH RICE

Serves 3-4

500 g (1 lb) neck end or
blade of pork
500 g (1 lb) tomatoes
250 g (8 oz) onions
60 g (2½ oz) streaky bacon
knob of butter

cayenne pepper
1 stock cube
250 g (8 oz) rice
salt
freshly ground pepper

Cut the meat into small dice. Blanch the tomatoes then
refresh them in cold water, skin them and cut them into
quarters. Peel and thinly slice the onions. Dice the bacon
and fry it.
Add the butter and meat and brown it, stirring frequently,
so that it is sealed all over. Season with salt, pepper and
cayenne pepper and add the crumbled stock cube. Add
the onions and fry gently until caramelized.

Add the tomatoes and 750 ml (1¼ pints) water. After 25
minutes, add the rice. Simmer until the rice is cooked,
season with salt and pepper and add a little more
cayenne pepper to taste.

SALTED BELLY OF PORK

Serves 6-8

1 kg (2 lb) salted belly of
pork
1 bay leaf
6 peppercorns
5 chilli seeds
6 juniper berries
1 onion

800 g (1½ lb) sauerkraut
(pickled cabbage)
2 large apples
cayenne pepper

Put the meat into 1 litre (1¾ pints) boiling water with the
bay leaf, peppercorns, chilli seeds, juniper berries and
thinly sliced onion. Bring to the boil and simmer for 2¼-
2½ hours.
Take out the meat and strain the stock through a sieve,
reserving 500 ml (18 fl oz). Put the stock in a casserole
dish with the meat, sauerkraut, and peeled, cored and
diced apples. Cover, braise and add the cayenne pepper.
Serve with mushy peas.

PORK SPARERIBS WITH APRICOTS

Serves 6-8

1 kg (2 lb) pork spareribs
1-2 knobs of butter or
2 large onions
2-3 tbsp oil
4 tbsp brown sugar
1 tsp paprika
1 tbsp tomato ketchup
1 tbsp Worcester sauce

2 tbsp wine vinegar
4 tbsp lemon juice
500 g (1 lb) tinned
apricots, drained or 200 g
(7 oz) dried apricots
a few green olives
salt

Brown the spareribs on both sides in the oil or butter and put them in an oven-proof dish. Peel and thinly slice the onions and brown them gently in the meat juices.

Mix together the sugar, salt, paprika, tomato ketchup, Worcester sauce, vinegar, lemon juice and 250 ml (8 fl oz) water. Pour the mixture over the onions, bring to the boil and simmer for 3 minutes. Pour the sauce over the meat, then cover the dish with a lid or sheet of foil and braise in the oven for 55-60 minutes at 200-225°C (400-425°F, Gas Mark 6-7).

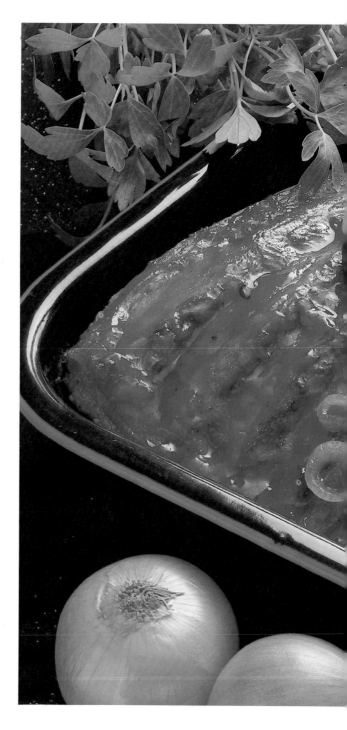

Ten minutes before the end of cooking time, add the apricots and green olives. Skim the fat from the sauce if preferred. Finish cooking the spareribs uncovered.

Serve with boiled rice or mashed potatoes.

Left: *Pork stew with olives*
Above: *Pork spareribs with apricots*

PORK STEW WITH OLIVES

Serves 5-6

750 g (1½ lb) pork for
roasting, e.g. middle loin,
whole leg etc.
1 small onion
4 tbsp oil
400 g (13 oz) button
mushrooms, thinly sliced

15 green olives, stuffed
75 g (3 oz) crème fraîche
1 tbsp cornflour
2 tbsp sherry
salt
freshly ground pepper

Peel and dice the onion and fry it in the oil. Sweat the mushrooms for 10 minutes with the onion. Cut the meat into small dice.

Add the meat and olives to the onion and mushroom mixture. Add 500 ml (18 fl oz) water, season with salt and pepper, cover and simmer for 30 minutes. Blend together the cornflour and crème fraîche and use it to thicken the gravy. Season to taste with sherry, salt and pepper.

Serve with boiled rice.

NECK END OF PORK WITH CELERY

Serves 4

600 g (1¼ lb) neck end of pork
600 g (1¼ lb) celery, approx. 5-6 sticks
4 tbsp oil

5 tbsp soy sauce
3 tbsp sherry
1 tbsp cornflour
salt

*C*ut the meat into thin slices, then into 1 cm (½ inch) wide ribbons. Wash the celery, cut off the root, cut in half lengthways, if necessary, and cut into 1 cm (½ inch) chunks.

Heat 2 spoonfuls of oil, fry the celery for 5 minutes, then reserve it and keep it warm. Carefully mix together 2 spoonfuls of soy sauce, 1 spoonful of sherry and the cornflour and dip the meat in the mixture. Heat 2 spoonfuls of oil, fry the meat, add the celery, 3 spoonfuls of soy sauce, 2 spoonfuls of sherry and 125 ml (4 fl oz) water. Stir carefully, cover and braise for 20 minutes. Season with salt if necessary. Serve with boiled rice.

FILLET OF PORK WITH ONIONS AND BUTTON MUSHROOMS

Serves 4

600 g (1¼ lb) fillet of pork
500 g (1 lb) baby onions or shallots
2 knobs of butter
500 ml (18 fl oz) tomato juice or purèed tomatoes
500 g (1 lb) baby button mushrooms

chilli powder
2 tbsp oil
bunch of fresh parsley, finely chopped
salt
freshly ground pepper

*P*eel the onions, sweat them in the butter, add the tomato juice and simmer them for 20 minutes. Wipe the mushrooms and add them to the onions. Season with salt, pepper and chilli powder, then cover and leave to simmer.

Season the meat with salt and pepper. Heat the oil, fry the meat to seal it all over, then add it to the vegetables and braise it for 10-15 minutes. Take the meat out, slice it and serve it with the vegetables. Sprinkle with finely chopped parsley.

Left: *Neck end of pork with celery*
Below: *Fillet of pork with onions and button mushrooms*

ROAST GAMMON JOINT

Serves 10-12

3 kg (7 lb) gammon joint
with rind
15 cloves
2-3 cloves of garlic
1-2 bay leaves
3 large onions

3 large tomatoes
sugar
flour
salt
freshly ground pepper

Ask your butcher to score the gammon rind in a
diamond pattern. Pierce the skin in several places and
insert the cloves. Peel and slice the garlic, break the bay
leaves into pieces and insert the garlic and bay leaves into
the incisions in the gammon rind. Cut the tomatoes and
onions into quarters or eighths and roast them in the
oven with the gammon for 2-2½ hours at 225-250°C
(425-475°F, Gas Mark 7-9).

Add hot water to the roasting tin and continue to top up
the water as it evaporates from the tin. If the gammon
browns too quickly, cover it with a sheet of foil. About 30
minutes before the end of cooking time, sprinkle sugar
over the gammon rind. The gammon can either be sliced
before serving, or presented whole. De-glaze the juices
from the roasting tin with water, strain them, thicken
them with flour and cold water blended together, season
with salt and pepper and serve separately.

Opposite: *Roast gammon joint*

PORK PLAITS WITH MADAGASCAR SAUCE

Serves 4

4 fillets of pork, flattened,
each weighing 200 g (7
oz)
paprika
2 knobs of butter
tomatoes
fresh parsley, chopped

150 g (5 oz) crème fraîche
3 tbsp tomato ketchup
1 tsp green peppercorns,
crushed
chilli powder
salt
freshly ground pepper

Cut the pork fillets in 3 lengthways, starting from the
thickest point, but do not cut all the way through. Make a
plait and secure it with a cocktail stick. Season with salt,
pepper and paprika and seal them in the butter, then fry
them on all sides for about 30 minutes. Leave them to
cool and serve them garnished with quartered tomatoes
and parsley. To make the sauce, mix together the crème
fraîche, tomato ketchup, green peppercorns, chilli
powder and salt.

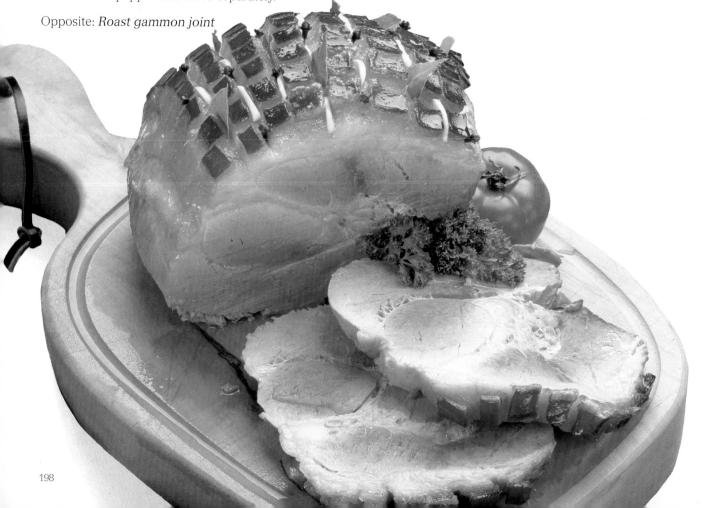

Above: *Pork plaits with Madagascan sauce*

ROAST PORK AU GRATIN

IN A CHICKEN BRICK OR EARTHENWARE DISH
Serves 6-8

1 kg (2 lb) pork for roasting	cheese, grated
sweet paprika	1 tsp cornflour
1 egg	salt
75 g (3 oz) Gruyère	freshly ground pepper

Season the pork with paprika, put it in a dampened chicken brick or unglazed earthenware dish, cover and roast in the oven for 2½ hours at 200-225°C (400-425°F, Gas Mark 6-7). Combine the egg and the grated Gruyère, spread the mixture over the roast pork after 2¼ hours and let the meat finish cooking without the lid. Slice the meat, arrange it on a serving dish and keep it warm.

To make the gravy: Make up the meat juices to 250 ml (8 fl oz) with water. Bring to the boil, thicken the gravy with cornflour slaked with cold water, and season it with salt, pepper and paprika. Serve with sautéed potatoes.

BROCHETTES OF LIVER

Serves 2-3

400 g (13 oz) pig's liver
8 medium-sized button
mushrooms
2 onions
1 apple
1 green pepper

knob of butter
12 stuffed green olives
4 tbsp oil
paprika
salt
pepper

Cut the meat into chunks. Peel the onions and apple and
cut them into eight pieces. Remove the stalk, core and
seeds from the green pepper and cut it into pieces.

Melt the butter, brown the liver in it for a few minutes,
then take it out of the pan and keep it warm. Quickly fry
the mushrooms, onions, apple and green pepper in the
meat juices. Alternating the vegetables, meat and olives,
spear them on skewers and fry them in the oil on all sides
for 5 minutes, then season to taste with salt, pepper and
paprika.

Serve with rice.

ROAST PORK WITH BACON

Serves 8-10

1½ kg (3½ lb) pork for
roasting
1 tsp crushed peppercorns
1 tsp paprika
4 big slices of smoked
bacon
2 tbsp oil

1 small green cabbage
1 onion
1 tbsp cornflour
150 g (5 oz) crème fraîche
ground cumin
fresh marjoram
bouquet garni
salt

Season the pork with the salt, peppercorns, paprika,
cumin and marjoram.

Separate the nicest cabbage leaves, blanch them, drain
them and wrap them around the pork. Then wrap a slice
of bacon around each parcel and secure them with cocktail
sticks. Brush the meat parcels with a spoonful of oil and
roast in the oven for 2 hours at 225°C (425°F, Gas Mark 7).
Peel and slice the onion thinly and add it to the meat.
As soon as the meat juices start to caramelize, add a little
water to the roasting tin and keep adding water as the
juices evaporate. Take the meat out and keep it warm.

Strain the meat juices, thicken them with a mixture of
cornflour and crème fraîche blended together and season
with salt and pepper.
Serve with dauphine potatoes and chanterelle mushrooms.

SAUSAGE KEBABS WITH VEGETABLES

IN A CHICKEN BRICK OR UNGLAZED EARTHENWARE DISH
Serves 2

250 g (8 oz) onions
250 g (8 oz) green peppers
250 g (8 oz) tomatoes
3 tbsp oil
4 Frankfurter sausages or chipolatas

4 slices streaky bacon, ½ cm (¼ inch) thick
2 or 3 gherkins
paprika
salt
freshly ground pepper

Peel the onions and slice them thinly. Remove the stalks, cores and seeds from the green peppers and cut them into strips. Reserve one tomato, blanch the others, plunge them into cold water, skin them and chop them into pieces.

Season the vegetables to taste with salt, pepper, paprika and 2 tbsp oil and put them in a chicken brick or unglazed earthenware dish dampened with water. Cut the sausages and bacon into 3 cm (1¼ inch) chunks, cut the gherkins into slices ½ cm (¼ inch) thick, and cut the reserved tomato into quarters. Alternating the meat with the tomato and gherkin, spear them on 6 skewers. Lay them on top of the vegetables and baste them with a mixture of 1 spoonful of oil and paprika to taste, cover the dish and roast the kebabs in the oven for 1 hour at 200-225⁰ C (400-425⁰ F, Gas Mark 6-7).

Left: *Brochettes of liver*
Below: *Sausage kebabs with vegetables.*

ROAST PORK STUFFED WITH CARROTS

Serves 6

1 kg (2 lb) pork for roasting	2 tbsp oil
250 g (8 oz) carrots	flour
paprika	salt
	freshly ground pepper

Peel the carrots and cook them for 10 minutes in salted water. Season the meat to taste with salt, pepper and paprika, make a cut in it and insert the cooked carrots. Baste the meat with oil, cover it with the remaining carrots, wrap it in a sheet of foil and roast it in the oven for 2 hours at 200°C (400°F, Gas Mark 6).

Slice the meat, bring the meat juices to the boil, thicken them with a little flour blended with cold water and season the gravy to taste with salt, pepper and paprika.

Below: *Roast pork stuffed with carrots*

SHOULDER OF PORK EN CROUTE

Serves 6-8

1½ kg (3½ lb) shoulder of pork	chopped
3 tbsp oil	1 tbsp fresh parsley, finely chopped
250 ml (8 fl oz) red wine	1 tbsp fresh dill, finely chopped
250 ml (8 fl oz) chicken stock	sprig of fresh rosemary
4 onions	1 tbsp breadcrumbs
2 carrots	150 g (5 oz) crème fraîche
1 clove of garlic	salt
3 knobs of butter	freshly ground pepper
2 tbsp fresh mint,	

Season the meat with salt and pepper. Put it into a roasting tin, add the oil and roast it for 2 hours at 200-225°C (400-425°F, Gas Mark 6-7). As soon as the juices start to caramelize, add some of the red wine and stock, and keep topping them up as the liquid evaporates during cooking, but reserving a little wine and stock for later.

Peel and quarter the onions, peel and slice the carrots, peel and crush the garlic and add these three ingredients to the meat 30 minutes before the end of cooking time. To make the crust, mix together the butter, mint, parsley, dill, rosemary and breadcrumbs and spread the resulting paste carefully over the meat 15 minutes before the end of cooking time.

Take the meat out of the roasting tin and keep it warm. De-glaze the pan with the reserved red wine and stock. Strain the gravy, bring it to the boil and add the crème fraîche, salt and pepper. Serve with dauphine potatoes.

SHOULDER OF PORK WITH CUMIN EN PAPILLOTE

Serves 6

1 kg (2 lb) neck end of pork	1 piece of celeriac
2 tsp cumin	flour
1 large onion	salt and freshly ground pepper

Season the meat with salt, pepper and cumin. Peel the onion and dice it roughly. Peel the piece of celeriac and cut it into quarters. Wrap the meat, onion and celeriac in a sheet of foil. Make sure the foil envelope is tightly closed, then roast the meat in the oven at 200°C (400°F, Gas Mark 6) for 1½-1¾ hours.

Slice the meat, thicken the gravy with a mixture of flour and cold water and add salt, pepper and a little cumin to taste.

Serve with dauphine or boiled potatoes.

Above: *Shoulder of pork with cumin en papillote*

FILLET OF PORK IN SPICY SAUCE

Serves 3-4

600 g (1¼ lb) fillet of pork
knob of butter
2-3 onions
1-2 gherkins
200 g (7 oz) button
mushrooms

250 ml (8 fl oz) whipping
cream
mustard
salt
freshly ground pepper

Cut the meat into 1 cm (½ inch) thick slices. Seal them on both sides in the butter, season them with salt and put them to one side. Peel and dice the onions finely, and sauté them in the meat juices. Slice the mushrooms thinly. Slice the gherkins and fry them with the mushrooms and onions.

Add the whipping cream, bring the sauce to the boil, simmer it for a few minutes, then season to taste with salt, pepper and mustard. Return the meat to the pan and leave it to braise. Serve with rice.

PIG'S TROTTERS

Serves 4

4 pig's trotters
3 onions

salt
freshly ground pepper

Season the pig's trotters with salt and pepper and roast them in the oven with a little water at 200-225°C (400-425°F, Gas Mark 6-7) for 1½ hours. As soon as the meat juices start to caramelize, add a little hot water and continue adding water throughout cooking, as the juices evaporate.

Peel and quarter the onions and add them to the meat 30 minutes before the end of cooking time. Take the meat out of the roasting tin and keep it warm. De-glaze the meat juices with a little water, strain if necessary, bring them to the boil and simmer for a few minutes, then serve the gravy with the meat.

Serve with mashed potato.

Below: *Fillet of pork in spicy sauce*
Left: *Pig's trotters*

PORK LOIN CHOPS STUFFED WITH PINEAPPLE

Serves 4

4 loin chops, each
weighing 250 g (8 oz)
4 slices of pineapple,
tinned in syrup

4 slices of raw ham
1-2 knobs of butter
fresh parsley

Cut a pocket in each of the chops. Drain the pineapple,
wrap a slice of ham around each slice of pineapple, insert
them in the pockets in the pork chops and secure them
with cocktail sticks. Melt the butter and fry the meat for
8-10 minutes on each side.
Serve garnished with parsley.

PORK LOIN CHOPS WITH CHANTERELLE MUSHROOMS

Serves 4

4 pork loin chops
2-3 knobs of butter
125 g (4 oz) chanterelle
mushrooms
1-2 tbsp fresh parsley,

chopped
3 tbsp crème fraîche
salt, paprika
crushed peppercorns
brandy

Season the pork chops to taste with salt, paprika and
crushed peppercorns, melt the butter and fry the meat for
8-10 minutes on each side. Add the previously sautéed
chanterelles, parsley, brandy and crème fraîche.

To make the sauce, peel and dice the onion and sauté it in the meat juices. Add the white wine, mustard, green peppercorns, stock cube made up with a little hot water and crème fraîche, bring it to the boil and simmer for a few minutes. Then season the sauce to taste with salt and pepper and serve it with the meat.

Serve with parsleyed potatoes or sautéed vegetables.

CURRIED PORK CHOPS EN PAPILLOTE

Serves 4

4 pork loin chops	fresh parsley
curry powder	salt
oil	freshly ground pepper
tomatoes	

*S*eason the pork chops with salt, pepper and curry powder, brush them with oil and wrap them in a sheet of foil. Roast them in the oven at 200°C (400°F, Gas Mark 6) for 30 minutes. Arrange the pork chops on a warm serving dish, garnish with tomato quarters and parsley and serve with the cooking juices.

Serve with tomato salad and sautéed potatoes.

Opposite:
Pork loin chops stuffed with pineapple

Below right:
Curried pork chops en papillote

PORK LOIN CHOPS IN PEPPER SAUCE

Serves 4

4 pork loin chops	1 tsp green peppercorns
2 tbsp oil	150 g (5 oz) crème fraîche
knob of butter	1 stock cube
1 onion	paprika
100 ml (3½ fl oz) white wine	salt
1 tsp mustard	freshly ground pepper

*S*eason the loin chops with salt, pepper and paprika, brown them in the oil and butter for 5 minutes on each side, then take them out of the pan and keep them warm.

PORK LOIN CHOPS WITH GREEN PEPPERCORNS

Serves 4

4 pork loin chops	bacon
1-2 tbsp preserved green	150 g (5 oz) onions
peppercorns	1-2 tbsp fresh parsley,
50 g (2 oz) butter	chopped
500 g (1 lb) chanterelle	salt
mushrooms	freshly ground pepper
100 g (3½ oz) streaky	

*D*rain the green peppercorns and crush them gently into the pork chops. Brown the chops in the butter for 5-7 minutes each side. Take the chops out of the pan and keep them warm. Wash the chanterelles and chop the biggest in half, or quarter them. Dice the bacon and fry it. Peel and dice the onions finely and sauté them with the bacon. Add the mushrooms and leave the mixture to sweat for 10-15 minutes. Season the mixture with salt and pepper and sprinkle with chopped parsley. Return the chops to the pan, heat through gently and serve.

LIVER PASTIES

Serves 4

300 g (10 oz) pig's liver	1 tbsp fresh parsley,
300 g (10 oz) frozen puff	chopped
pastry	1 tbsp brandy
3 eggs	fresh marjoram
2 heaped tbsp	fresh sage
breadcrumbs	salt
2 onions	freshly ground pepper
knob of butter	

*S*efrost the pastry at room temperature. To make the stuffing, mince the meat very finely. Add 2 eggs and the breadcrumbs. Peel and dice the onions. Melt the butter and fry the onions in it for 3 minutes. Bind together the onions and meat mixture, parsley, marjoram and sage to taste, the brandy, and season with salt and pepper.

Below: *Pork loin chops with green peppercorns*

Above: *Pork chops with mustard.*

Roll out the pastry into a rectangle 30 x 40 cm (12 x 16 inches) and cut out 6 circles 12 cm (4½ inches) in diameter and 6 more of 10 cm (4 inches) in diameter. Use the bigger circles to line buttered bun tins or individual tart moulds, press them down gently and prick them all over with a fork.

Put about 2 tablespoons of meat mixture into each mould. Beat the remaining egg, brush the edges of the pastry with it, cover the meat mixture with the remaining pastry circles and seal the edges of the pastry. Brush the pasties with egg wash and prick them with a fork. Bake them in the oven for about 25 minutes at 200-225°C (400-425°F, Gas Mark 6-7).

PORK CHOPS WITH MUSTARD

Serves 4

4 pork loin chops	mustard
3-4 onions	fresh parsley
2 cloves of garlic	curry powder
4 tbsp oil	salt
150 g (5 oz) crème fraîche	white pepper

Season the chops with salt and pepper and spread them with mustard. Peel and finely dice the garlic and onions, spread them over the chops and roast them in the oven for 30-35 minutes at 225-250°C (425-275°F, Gas Mark 7-9). Serve garnished with parsley.

To make the mustard dressing: Mix together the crème fraîche and 2 tsp mustard. Season the dressing with salt and curry powder to taste and serve it with the meat.

N.B.: Although the chops could be grilled, oven-cooking is especially recommended if you are cooking a large quantity.

MEATBALLS WITH CREAM CHEESE

Serves 4

200 g (7 oz) minced beef	2 eggs
200 g (7 oz) minced pork	40 g (1½ oz) breadcrumbs
2 onions	40 g (1½ oz) butter
200 g (7 oz) cream or curd	salt
cheese, drained	freshly ground pepper

Peel and dice the onions. Mix together the minced meats, onions, cream cheese and eggs. Season the mixture with salt and pepper. Dampen your hands and shape the mixture into 4 patties. Roll the meatballs in the breadcrumbs, then fry them in the butter for 5 minutes on each side.

Serve with carrots and mashed potatoes.

PORK CHOPS WITH APPLE SAUCE

Serves 4

4 pork loin chops, each	sauce or stewed apple
weighing 150 g (5 oz)	2 tsp veal stock
4 tbsp oil	salt
6 tbsp unsweetened apple	freshly ground pepper

Season the pork chops with pepper, brown them in the oil for 4-5 minutes on each side, then take them out of the pan and keep them hot. Add the apple sauce or stewed apple, 125 ml (4 fl oz) water and veal stock to the meat juices and stir them until combined. Simmer the sauce for a few minutes then season it with salt and pepper.

MEDALLIONS OF PORK WITH BACON

Serves 6

750 g (1½ lb) fillet of pork	40 g (1½ oz) margarine
8 thin slices of bacon	paprika
2 tsp mustard	marjoram
2 tsp tomato ketchup	salt
2 tsp breadcrumbs	freshly ground pepper

Cut the meat into 16 pieces. To make the stuffing, mix together the mustard, ketchup and breadcrumbs. Season the mixture with salt, pepper, paprika and marjoram to taste. Spread the mixture over one side of 8 of the pieces of pork, put another piece of meat on top, wrap a slice of bacon around each medallion and secure it with a cocktail stick.

Fry the meat in the margarine for 6 minutes on each side, basting frequently with the meat juices so that it stays moist and tender. You can add a few sprigs of thyme to the frying pan during cooking.

Left: *Medallions of pork with bacon*
Below: *Pork chops with apple sauce.*

CHINESE PORK

Serves 4

2 fillets of pork, each weighing 250 g (8 oz)	ground ginger
	2 tbsp honey
80 g (3 oz) baby onions	2 tbsp brown sugar
1 clove of garlic	2 tbsp oil
6 tbsp soy sauce	salt
4-5 tbsp sherry	

Peel and finely dice the onions and garlic and combine them with the soy sauce, 2 tablespoons of sherry, the ground ginger and salt. Add the meat, cover it and leave it to marinate overnight.

Melt the honey and the sugar over a gentle heat. Drain the meat and coat it in the melted honey mixture. Quickly brown the fillets on all sides in the oil, add the marinade and simmer for 20 minutes.

Whilst the pork is cooking, add 3-4 tablespoons of water if necessary. Take the meat out of the pan, de-glaze the juices with 2-3 tablespoons of sherry and pour the gravy over the pork fillets.

PORK CHOPS IN BREADCRUMBS

Serves 4

4 pork loin chops, each weighing 200 g (7 oz)	40 g (1½ oz) breadcrumbs
2 tbsp flour	50 g (2 oz) margarine
1 egg, beaten	salt and white pepper

Season the pork chops with salt and pepper, coat them in the flour, dip them in the beaten egg, then finally coat them in the breadcrumbs. Fry them in the margarine for 8 minutes on each side. Serve with parsleyed potatoes.

Variation: You could substitute veal cutlets (fry for 6 minutes each side) for pork chops.

NECK END OF PORK

Serves 6-8

1 kg (2 lb) neck end of pork	paprika
1 onion	salt
1 tomato	freshly ground pepper

Season the pork with salt and pepper, sprinkle with paprika and braise it in the oven with a little water for 1¾ hours at 200-225°C (400-425°F, Gas Mark 6-7). As soon as the meat juices start to caramelize, add a little hot water to the roasting tin, and continue adding water as necessary throughout the cooking time.

Peel the onion, wash the tomato, cut them both into quarters and add them to the meat 25 minutes before the end of cooking time. Slice the meat and arrange it on a warm serving dish. De-glaze the cooking juices with water, strain them and pour them over the meat.

PORK CHOPS WITH PICKLING ONIONS

Serves 4

4 pork loin chops, each weighing 200 g (7 oz)	4 tbsp white wine or water
4 cloves of garlic	2 tbsp crème fraîche
250 g (8 oz) pickling onions	paprika
2 knobs of butter	salt
	freshly ground pepper

Peel the garlic, crush it, spread it over both sides of the pork chops, cover them and leave them to macerate for about 30 minutes. Season the chops with salt, pepper and paprika. Peel the onions. Melt the butter and brown the meat and onions in it for 10 minutes, turning the meat halfway through. Take the chops out of the pan and keep them hot.

De-glaze the pan juices with the white wine or water, and incorporate the crème fraîche.

Leave the gravy to simmer for a few minutes, then add salt, pepper and paprika to taste and pour the gravy over the chops or serve it separately.

Serve with boiled potatoes and French beans.

Left: *Pork chops in breadcrumbs*
Right: *Pork chops with pickling onions.*

PORK FILLET WITH ARMAGNAC

Serves 4-5

2 fillets of pork, each
weighing 300-400 g (10-13
oz)
6 shallots
4 knobs of butter
6 tbsp Armagnac

200 ml (7 fl oz) whipping
cream
fresh thyme, chopped
salt
freshly ground pepper

Peel the shallots and dice them very finely, then brown them in 2 knobs of butter. Add a spoonful of Armagnac, fold in the whipping cream a little at a time, and simmer the sauce until smooth and creamy. Cover the sauce and reserve it. Season the meat with salt and pepper and seal it all over in the remaining butter. Add a little thyme, cover and sauté for 12 minutes, turning the meat halfway through cooking.

When the meat is cooked, wrap it in a sheet of foil. Separate the fat from the meat juices. De-glaze the pan with 3 spoonfuls of Armagnac, add the onion sauce, reheat it, adjust the seasoning and add a little more thyme.

Slice the meat and serve it on a warm serving dish with the sauce.

Below: *Pork fillet with Armagnac*

Above: *Stuffed fillet of pork*

STUFFED FILLET OF PORK

Serves 4

600 g (1¼ lb) fillet of pork
2-3 gherkins
5-6 sprigs of fresh parsley
100 g (3½ oz) Gruyère
cheese, in strips
3 tbsp oil
knob of butter

100 ml (3½ fl oz) white
wine
1 bay leaf
3 tbsp crème fraîche
mustard
salt

Cut a pocket lengthways in the meat. Fill it with mustard. Slice the gherkins and put them into the pocket with the parsley and cheese. Roll up the fillet and secure it with kitchen string. Brown the meat all over in the oil. Throw away the oil, add the butter to the pan and cook the meat for 25-30 minutes, then season it with salt, take it out of the pan and keep it warm.

De-glaze the pan juices with the white wine, add the bay leaf, fold in the crème fraîche, leave the sauce to simmer for a few minutes, then take out the bay leaf and serve the sauce with the meat.

PORK WITH BEANSPROUTS

Serves 4

500 g (1 lb) pork: neck end, blade or fillet
2 tbsp oil
250 g (8 oz) fresh beansprouts

50 g (2 oz) butter
2 tbsp white wine
2 tbsp whipping cream
4-5 tbsp soy sauce
4 slices stale bread

Cut the pork into thin slices, then into strips and sauté it in the oil. Add the washed and drained beansprouts and leave them to brown for 1 minute. Add the white wine, then the cream and soy sauce and leave to simmer. Fry the slices of stale bread on both sides in the butter until golden and serve them with the pork.

Serve with a green salad and tomato salad.

PORK CHOPS WITH PARMESAN

Serves 4

4 pork loin chops
1-2 knobs of butter
100 g (3½ oz) Parmesan, grated

200 g (7 oz) crème fraîche
salt
freshly ground pepper

Season the pork chops with salt and pepper and brown them in the butter for 3-5 minutes on each side. Mix together the grated Parmesan and crème fraîche, spread it over the chops and bake them in the oven for 10 minutes at 200°C (400°F, Gas Mark 6).

Serve with tagliatelle.

Left: *Pork with beansprouts*
Below: *Pork chops with Parmesan*

CRUSTED PORK

Serves 4

4 pork fillets, each
weighing 150 g (5 oz)
4 tbsp oil
pinch of white pepper

50 g (2 oz) butter
4 tsp fresh basil, chopped
2 tbsp breadcrumbs
1 tsp whipping cream

Mix together the oil, white pepper and 2 spoonfuls of basil. Marinate the chops in this mixture for 10 minutes. Melt the butter, fry the chops in it for 3-4 minutes on each side and season them with salt. Mix together the breadcrumbs, cream and 2 spoonfuls of basil. Spread the mixture over the chops and bake them in the oven at 225⁰ C (425⁰ F, Gas Mark 7) or under a hot grill for 5-10 minutes.

SHASHLIK

Serves 4

1 fillet of pork weighing
300 g (10 oz)
4 slices of liver (not too
thick), weighing 250 g (8
oz)
250 g (8 oz) tomatoes

1 large banana
1-2 onions
125 g (4 oz) streaky bacon
a few pickled gherkins
oil

*C*ut the pork, liver, bacon, tomatoes, banana, onion and gherkins into chunks or 3 cm (1¼ inch) slices and spear them alternately on skewers.

Brush them with oil and place them on a sheet of foil on a grill, then grill them, brushing them with oil again when turning them, for 6-8 minutes under an electric grill or 4-5 minutes under a gas grill.

Below: *Shashlik*
Left: *Crusted pork*

CYPRIOT STYLE PORK

Serves 4-6

800 g (1½ lb) fillet of pork
5 tbsp olive oil
5 tbsp lemon juice
1 tbsp juniper berries,
crushed

1 tbsp fresh oregano,
chopped
salt
freshly ground pepper

Cut the meat into 2 cm (¾ inch) thick slices. To make the marinade, combine the olive oil, lemon juice, juniper berries, oregano, salt and pepper and marinate the meat in it for 3 hours. Drain the pieces of meat, spear them on skewers and grill them on a barbecue for 8-10 minutes on each side.

GRILLED FILLET OF PORK

Serves 6-8

2 fillets of pork, each
weighing 500 g (1 lb)
1 tbsp oil

½ tsp paprika
mustard
salt

Spread the pork sparingly with mustard, put it under a preheated grill and grill it for 10 minutes on each side for an electric grill, and 10 minutes on one side and 7 minutes on the other for a gas grill. After the first minute, baste the pork frequently with a mixture of oil and paprika.

When the meat is cooked, season it with salt.

Below:
Cypriot-style pork

GRILLED PORK CHOPS

Serves 6

1 kg (2 lb) pork chops (loin or chump)	a few drops of Tabasco sauce
5 tbsp oil	salt
juice of 1 lemon	crushed black
2 cloves of garlic	peppercorns
Worcester sauce	

*T*o make the marinade, combine the oil, lemon juice, peeled and chopped garlic, peppercorns, Worcester sauce and Tabasco to taste. Marinate the chops in it for 30 minutes, stirring occasionally. Drain the meat and grill it for 10 minutes on each side. Season the chops with salt and pepper before serving them with mustard as an accompaniment.

PORK CHOPS WITH ORANGE

Serves 4

4 pork chops, boned	salt
1 onion	freshly ground pepper
3 tbsp orange juice	

*P*eel and thinly slice the onion, then mix it with the orange juice. Spread this mixture over the chops and season them with salt and pepper. Put the chops on a rack under a preheated grill and grill them for 6 minutes on each side.

Above: *Pork chops with orange*

PORK CHOPS WITH KOHL-RABI

Serves 4

4 pork chops (shoulder)
75 g (3 oz) thinly sliced
bacon
4 kohl-rabi
3 onions
knob of butter

100 ml (3½ fl oz) whipping
cream
125 g (4 oz) crème fraîche
salt
freshly ground pepper

Peel and wash the kohl-rabi. Cut them in half and then into slices. Peel the onions and dice them finely. Melt the butter and fry the chopped bacon in it, then add the onion and finally the kohl-rabi. Add the whipping cream and the crème fraîche, then season the mixture with salt and pepper.

Season the chops with pepper and grill them for 6-8 minutes on each side.

Serve the chops with the kohl-rabi mixture and boiled potatoes.

GRILLED NECK END OF PORK

Serves 4

4 shoulder chops
2 tbsp honey
3 tbsp soy sauce
4 tbsp oil
3 tbsp white wine

fresh thyme, chopped
fresh rosemary, chopped
salt
freshly ground pepper

Grill the chops under a preheated grill for 4 minutes on each side. Mix together the honey, soy sauce, oil, white wine, thyme, rosemary, salt and pepper. Baste the meat with this mixture and grill the chops for a further 3-4 minutes on each side.

GRILLED SAUSAGES

Serves 4

4 sausages   oil

Prick the sausages with a fork to prevent them bursting. Grill them for about 5 minutes on each side, basting them with oil during cooking.

Left: *Pork chops with kohl-rabi*

GRILLED BELLY OF PORK

Serves 4

8 thin slices of belly pork
3 tbsp mustard
1 tsp horseradish
juice of ½ lemon

2 tbsp oil
100 ml (3½ fl oz) beer
salt
freshly ground pepper

Combine the mustard, horseradish, lemon juice, oil, salt and pepper. Brush the slices of pork with this mixture, put the meat under a preheated grill and cook it for 5 minutes on each side. Then baste the slices of pork with beer and grill them for a further 3-4 minutes until crisp.

Below: *Grilled sausages*

STEWED SHOULDER OF LAMB WITH BUTTER SAUCE

Serves 4

4 slices of shoulder of lamb
1 litre (1 ¾ pints) chicken stock
250 ml (8 fl oz) white wine
1 large onion
500 g (1 lb) baby carrots
100 g (3½ oz) chilled butter, cubed
50 g (2 oz) capers

2 tsp zest of an unwaxed lemon
1 bunch of fresh parsley, finely chopped
1 bunch of fresh chives, finely chopped
2 sprigs of fresh tarragon, finel chopped
salt
freshly ground pepper

Bring the stock to the boil with the white wine and add the peeled and roughly chopped onion. Put the meat into the stock. Bring to the boil again and simmer for 15 minutes. Add the peeled carrots and cook for a further 15 minutes.

Strain off 250 ml (8 fl oz) stock and reheat it in a saucepan. Take it off the heat and immediately whisk in the chilled butter, a cube at a time, the capers, lemon zest, parsley, chives, and finely chopped tarragon. Season the sauce with salt and pepper. Arrange the meat and the carrots on a warm serving dish and serve with the sauce. Serve with potatoes.

Variation: You could also use leg of lamb instead of shoulder.

Below: *Stewed shoulder of lamb with butter sauce*

MUTTON STEW, ENGLISH STYLE
IN THE PRESSURE COOKER
Serves 4

800 g (1½ lb) mutton, shoulder or leg
2 cloves of garlic
2 knobs of butter
1 onion
1 carrot
½ leek
100 ml (3½ fl oz) chicken stock

100 ml (3½ fl oz) red wine
1 bay leaf
fresh basil, chopped
1 tbsp flour
1 tbsp fresh parsley, chopped
salt
freshly ground pepper

Peel the garlic and crush it with the salt. Rub the garlic into the mutton. Melt the butter in the pressure cooker and brown the mutton all over in it. Peel and roughly chop the onion, peel and slice the carrot and leek.

Add the vegetables to the meat. Add the stock and red wine, bay leaf and basil. Put the lid on the pressure cooker and steam for 45 minutes. Slice the mutton and keep it warm.

Blend together the flour and a little cold water, add it to the stock, bring the gravy to the boil, simmer it for 5 minutes, then strain it, season with salt and pepper and add the chopped parsley.

Serve with potatoes and French beans.

SADDLE OF MUTTON

Serves 6-8

1 kg (2 lb) saddle of mutton
herbes de Provence
1 onion
1 tomato

1 kg (2 lb) courgettes
salt
freshly ground pepper

Rub the herbes de Provence and some salt into the mutton and roast it with a little water for 1¼ hours at 225° C (425°F, Gas Mark 7). As soon as the juices start to caramelize, add a little hot water to the roasting tin and continue to add water occasionally as the liquid evaporates.

Peel the onion, skin the tomato and cut them both into quarters. Peel and slice the courgettes and add all the vegetables to the mutton 40 minutes before the end of cooking. Season with salt and pepper.

Slice the meat and serve it with the vegetables.

LEG OF LAMB WITH BEANS AND TOMATOES

Serves 4-6

1½ kg (3½ lb) leg of lamb
375 g (12 oz) haricot
beans
250 g (8 oz) onions
375 g (12 oz) French
beans
1 tsp fresh rosemary,
chopped
1 tsp fresh thyme,
chopped
4 tbsp olive oil
850 g (1 ¾ lb) tinned
tomatoes
2-3 cloves of garlic
salt
freshly ground pepper

Wash the haricot beans, put them in boiling water and simmer them for 5 minutes. Take them out of the pan and drain them. Peel the onions and cut them into quarters. Top, tail and wash the French beans.

Season the lamb with salt and pepper and rub the thyme and rosemary into it. Heat the oil, brown the lamb all over in it, add the vegetables, the tomatoes and their juice, bring to the boil and add the peeled and finely chopped (or crushed) garlic. Cover and simmer for 1-2½ hours.

Below: *Leg of lamb with beans and tomatoes*

BRAISED SHOULDER OF LAMB

Serves 4

750 g (1½ lb) shoulder of lamb, on the bone
1 clove of garlic
1 tsp salt
½ tsp coarsely ground pepper
3 tbsp oil
1 onion
½ bunch of spring onions
½ bunch of carrots
1 head of celery
2 tomatoes
100 ml (3½ fl oz) red wine
fresh parsley, chopped

Peel and finely chop the garlic and crush it with the salt. Rub the garlic into the lamb, season it with pepper, brown it all over in the oil in a roasting tin, then reserve it and keep it warm. Peel the onion and cut it into quarters. Clean the spring onions and slice them thinly. Peel the carrots and slice them. Wash and trim the celery and cut it into strips. Sauté the onions, carrots and celery in the meat juices for a few minutes. Blanch the tomatoes, refresh them in cold water, skin them, cut them into quarters, de-seed them and put them in a roasting tin with the lamb and other vegetables. Braise the meat in the oven for 40-45 minutes at 200-225°C (400-425°F, Gas Mark 6-7). After 20 minutes, add the red wine to the roasting tin.

Sprinkle fresh chopped parsley over the lamb and serve it with boiled potatoes.

Below: *Braised shoulder of lamb*

LEG OF LAMB WITH MUSHROOMS

Serves 6-8

1 kg (2 lb) leg of lamb	250 ml (8 fl oz) beef stock
3-4 cloves of garlic	250 ml (8 fl oz) red wine
3-4 knobs of butter	1 bay leaf
1 small onion	5 peppercorns
1 carrot	1 tsp tomato purèe
1 turnip	500 g (1 lb) mushrooms
1 stick of celery	salt
1 tbsp flour	black pepper

Peel the garlic, make several puncture holes in the lamb and insert the cloves of garlic. Season the meat with salt and pepper, brown it all over in the butter and put it to one side.

Peel and finely dice the onion. Peel or trim the other vegetables and make a julienne with them. Sauté the vegetables in the meat juices, with the onion. Sprinkle flour over the vegetables and cook it until it turns golden, stirring all the time. Add the red wine and stock, stir well and bring it to the boil. Add the bay leaf, peppercorns and tomato purée. Put the lamb in the pan, cover and simmer for 2 hours. Wipe the mushrooms, blanch them in boiling, salted water, refresh them in cold water, drain them and add them to the meat 30 minutes before the end of cooking.

Serve the mutton with dauphine potatoes.

Above: *Lamb cutlets with French beans*

LAMB CUTLETS WITH FRENCH BEANS

IN A CHICKEN BRICK OR EARTHENWARE DISH
Serves 6

1 kg (2 lb) mutton cutlets	milk
1 litre (1 ¾ pints) milk	fresh thyme, chopped
600 g (11/4 lb) French	flour
beans, fresh or frozen	salt
2 tbsp whipping cream or	freshly ground pepper
unsweetened condensed	

Marinate the mutton in the milk for 24 hours. Then drain it and remove the skin and all the fat except a thin layer. Season the mutton with salt, pepper and thyme.

Put the mutton and French beans in a dampened chicken brick, cover and bake in the oven for 1¾ hours at 200-225⁰ C (400-425⁰ F, Gas Mark 6-7). Then slice the meat, arrange it on a warm serving dish with the French beans and keep it hot. Thicken the cooking juices with flour and water blended together, stir in the whipping cream or condensed milk and season with salt.

Left: *Shoulder of lamb with vegetables*

SHOULDER OF LAMB WITH VEGETABLES

Serves 6

800 g (1½ lb) shoulder of lamb, boned	*3 cloves*
	10 peppercorns
2 carrot	*750 g (1½ lb) potatoes*
1 small stick of celery	*1 kg (2 lb) mixed*
1 onion	*vegetables*
1 bay leaf	*bunch of parsley*

Scrape the carrots, wash the parsley and carefully clean the celery. Wrap the lamb around the carrots, parsley and celery, secure with cocktail sticks and put the lamb into 1½ litres (2½ pints) boiling, salted water. Peel the onion, spike it with the cloves and bay leaf and add it to the lamb with the peppercorns. Simmer the lamb for 1½ hours, then drain it, slice it and keep it warm.

Strain off 500 ml (18 fl oz) stock, add the peeled potatoes and peeled and chopped vegetables to it and cook them for 20-25 minutes. Sprinkle chopped parsley over the vegetables and serve them with the lamb.

LAMB STEW WITH COURGETTES

Serves

800 g (1½ lb) leg of lamb	*4-6 baby courgettes*
7 tbsp olive oil	*fresh parsley, coarsely*
2 onions	*chopped*
4-6 tomatoes	*Gruyère cheese, grated*
2 cloves of garlic	*salt and freshly ground*
250 ml (8 fl oz) beef stock	*pepper*

Dice the lamb. Heat 4 spoonfuls of oil in a roasting tin or oven-proof casserole dish, and brown the lamb in it. Add the peeled and coarsely chopped onions. Blanch the tomatoes, then refresh them in cold water, skin them, cut them into small pieces and add them to the meat. Also add the roughly chopped parsley, pepper, peeled and crushed garlic, salt and stock and simmer the lamb for 1 hour.

Slice the courgettes and sauté them quickly in 3 spoonfuls of olive oil. Season them sparingly with salt, spread them over the lamb, top them with the grated cheese and bake them in the oven for 5-10 minutes at 225-250°C (425-475°F, Gas Mark 7-9).

Right: *Lamb stew with courgettes.*

SADDLE OF LAMB WITH ROSEMARY

Serves 6-8

1 saddle of lamb
3 cloves of garlic
3 tomatoes
2-3 onions
3 tbsp oil
3 tbsp fresh rosemary,
chopped

2-3 tbsp fresh parsley,
chopped
1 egg
2-3 slices toast
salt
freshly ground pepper

*S*eason the lamb with salt and pepper and rub it with the peeled and crushed garlic. Wash the tomatoes and cut them into pieces. Peel the onions and cut them into eight pieces. Brush a roasting tin or oven-proof dish with oil, spread a spoonful of rosemary over the base, put the meat, tomatoes and onions on top, sprinkle another spoonful of rosemary over the lamb and vegetables and roast the lamb in the oven for 1½ hours at 200-225°C (400-425°F, Gas Mark 6-7).

As soon as the juices start to caramelize, add a little hot water to the roasting tin. Baste the lamb occasionally and add more water from time to time as the liquid evaporates.

SADDLE OF LAMB WITH HERBS

Serves 6-8

1 saddle of lamb	marjoram, rosemary,
1-2 cloves of garlic	chopped
3-4 tbsp olive oil	2 tbsp cornflour
100 ml (3½ fl oz) white	1-2 tbsp crème fraîche
wine	salt
fresh mixed herbs, e.g.	freshly ground pepper
oregano, thyme,	

*T*o make the marinade, peel and crush the garlic and mix it with the olive oil, white wine, salt, pepper and herbs. Marinate the lamb in this mixture for 1-2 hours. Then roast the lamb in the oven for 40-45 minutes at 200-225⁰C (400-425⁰F, Gas Mark 6-7), basting it frequently with the marinade. Take the meat out of the oven, leave it to rest for 5 minutes, slice it and keep it warm.

De-glaze the meat juices with a little water, thicken them with a mixture of cornflour and water blended together, season the gravy with salt and pepper and add the crème fraîche.

Left: *Saddle of lamb with rosemary*
Below: *Saddle of lamb with herbs*

After 1¼ hours, mix together the chopped parsley, a spoonful of rosemary and the egg, season the mixture with salt and pepper and spread it over the meat. Cut the toast into small dice or process it in a mixer to make breadcrumbs, then sprinkle them over the meat and cook it for a further 15 minutes. Strain the meat juices through a sieve, season with salt and pepper and serve with the lamb.

Serve the lamb with sauté potatoes, grilled tomatoes, broccoli or jacket potatoes.

GRILLED LAMB

Serves 6

12 lamb cutlets
6 loin or chump chops
2 tbsp fresh parsley, finely chopped
250 ml (8 fl oz) olive oil
1 tsp fresh rosemary, chopped

1 tbsp fresh lovage, or 1 tbsp celery salt
½ tsp coarsely ground pepper
pinch of chilli powder
oil for grilling
salt

Combine the parsley, salt, olive oil, rosemary, lovage or celery salt, pepper and chilli powder.

Marinate the lamb in the flavoured oil for a few minutes. Brush the grill with oil and grill the lamb for 3-6 minutes on each side.

LAMB KEBABS

Serves 6

800 g (1½ lb) shoulder of lamb, boned
5 onions
1 clove of garlic
1 tsp salt
3 tbsp olive oil
1 tbsp curry powder

1 tsp ground ginger
2 tbsp lemon juice
2 red peppers
100 g (3½ oz) bacon
4 bay leaves
fresh thyme, optional
250 ml (8 fl oz) oil

Cut the meat into 4 cm (1½ inch) dice. Finely dice one onion. Crush the garlic with the salt. In a large bowl mix together the olive oil, onion, garlic, curry powder, ginger, and lemon juice. Add the lamb, cover and marinate for 4 hours.

Slice the red peppers in half. Remove the stalks, cores and seeds and cut the peppers into 4 cm (1½ inch) chunks. Chop the bacon. Peel 4 onions and cut them into quarters. Alternating these ingredients and the bay leaf, spear the lamb and vegetables on skewers and either fry them in the oil or grill them.

Serve the lamb kebabs with curried rice with raisins.

Below: *Grilled lamb*
Right: *Lamb kebabs*

LEG OF LAMB WITH ONION SAUCE

Serves 10-12

1½-2 kg (3½-4½ lb) leg of lamb
50 g (2 oz) streaky bacon
2-3 cloves of garlic
6 tbsp whipping cream
2 tbsp oil
2-3 carrots

11/4 kg (3 lb) onions
knob of butter
fresh thyme, chopped
cayenne pepper
salt
freshly ground pepper

Peel the garlic, pierce the lamb in several places and insert the cloves of garlic. Season the lamb with salt, pepper and thyme. Brown the meat all over in the oil. Peel 2 onions and cut them into quarters, peel and chop the carrots and add them to the lamb. Roast the meat in the oven for 2 hours at 225-250°C (425-475°F, Gas Mark 7-9).

As soon as the meat juices start to caramelize, add a little water to the roasting tin, then gradually add more water as the liquid evaporates, and turn the meat from time to time. Then take the meat out of the tin, cover it and leave it to rest for a few minutes, slice it and keep it warm.

To make the gravy, strain the meat juices, add water, bring the gravy to the boil and season it with salt and pepper.

To make the onion sauce: Peel and thinly slice the remaining onions. Slice the bacon and fry it in the butter, add the onions, season them with salt and add a little water. Cover and sweat for about 20 minutes, then take the bacon out, purée the onions in a food processor or with a hand-held mixer, then reheat them. Add the whipping cream, season the mixture with salt and cayenne pepper and serve the onion sauce with the lamb.

LAMB CUTLETS WITH PINEAPPLE

Serves 6

12 lamb cutlets, each weighing 60 g (2½ oz)
4 tbsp olive oil
2 tsp vinegar
½ tsp fresh rosemary, chopped
1-2 tsp fresh basil,

chopped
20 g (¾ oz) butter
4 pineapple rings, in syrup
3 tbsp sherry
fresh basil to garnish
salt

Combine 2 spoonfuls of olive oil, the vinegar, rosemary and basil. Marinate the chops in this mixture for 2 hours, then season them with salt. Fry the lamb in 2 spoonfuls of olive oil for 10 minutes on each side, then keep it hot.

Cut the pineapple rings in half, melt the butter and gently fry the pineapple in it. Add the sherry and simmer the pineapple for a minute. Arrange the lamb and pineapple on a warm serving dish and coat them in the sauce. Garnish the lamb with fresh basil leaves.

Serve with dauphine potatoes, rice or garlic bread and salad.

Above, left: Lamb cutlets with pineapple
Right: *Lamb chops with coriander sauce*

LAMB CHOPS WITH CORIANDER SAUCE

Serves 4

4 lamb chops
1 large onion
2 tbsp oil
3 tsp ground coriander
1 tsp ground ginger

1 tsp ground cumin
1 tub of natural yoghurt
fresh coriander, chopped
salt

To make the sauce, peel and finely chop the onion and fry it in a saucepan in a tablespoonful of oil. Add the ground coriander, ginger and cumin, then take the pan off the heat, fold in the yoghurt, season the sauce with salt and keep it warm.

Brush the lamb with 2 spoonfuls of oil, and sprinkle with fresh, chopped coriander. Grill the chops for 5-7 minutes on each side. Serve the chops with the sauce and accompany them with salad.

Variation: This sauce also goes well with lamb's or calf's liver drizzled with lemon juice, coated in flour and pan fried.

LAMB WITH GRILLED PINEAPPLE

Serves 6

1 joint of lamb for
roasting, e.g. loin, saddle,
chump
3 tbsp sherry
2 tbsp soy sauce
1 chicken stock cube
2 tsp hot mustard

1 tsp cornflour
1 pineapple
4 tbsp white wine
4 tbsp honey
250 ml (8 fl oz) whipping
cream

Blend together the sherry, soy sauce, chicken stock cube, mustard and two tablespoons of water, bring the mixture to the boil and thicken it with cornflour slaked with water, then cover it. Cut the lamb into 1 cm (½ inch) thick slices, brush them with the sauce and grill them for 10 minutes on each side. Peel a pineapple and spear it on a skewer.

Heat the white wine and stir the honey into it. Grill the pineapple for 8-10 minutes. During cooking, baste the pineapple with the wine and honey mixture. Then slice the grilled pineapple, whip the cream and serve them with the grilled lamb and boiled rice.

LAMB CHOPS WITH APPLES

Serves 4

4 lamb chops
1 onion
4 tbsp oil
ground ginger
4 knobs of butter

500 g(1 lb) apples
2 tbsp lemon juice
grated nutmeg
salt

Remove the fat from the chops and make incisions in the skin at 2 cm (¾ inch) intervals. Peel and chop the garlic, mix it with the oil and ginger. Put the lamb in the mixture, cover and marinate it for 1 hour. Then fry the meat in 2 knobs of butter for 5 minutes on each side, season it with salt and keep it warm.

To make the sauce, cut the apples into quarters, remove the pips and simmer them in water for 8-10 minutes. Sieve the stewed apple, add the lemon juice, 2 knobs of butter and grated nutmeg to it and serve it with the lamb.

SADDLE OF LAMB WITH HERBS AND PURÈED PINEAPPLE

Serves 8-10

1½ kg (3½ lb) saddle of
lamb
fresh, mixed herbs, e.g.
oregano, thyme,
marjoram, rosemary
½ tsp ground ginger
½ tsp dried sage
½ tsp black pepper

250 ml (8 fl oz) meat stock
340 g (11 oz) pineapple,
tinned in syrup
1 tbsp soy sauce
2 heaped tsp mustard
flour
salt

LAMB CHOPS WITH OLIVE COMPOTE

Serves 4

4 lamb chops	olives
2 tbsp oil	salt
150 g (5 oz) stuffed green	freshly ground pepper

Season the lamb with salt and pepper. Brown it for 5 minutes on each side in the oil, then take it out of the pan and keep it warm. Drain the olives, reserving 4 for garnish, put them into the pan with the meat juices, mash them roughly and leave them to simmer for a few minutes.

Spread the crushed olive sauce over the meat and garnish with the reserved whole olives.

Left: *Lamb with grilled pineapple*
Below: *Lamb chops with olive compote*

Chop the herbs finely, combine them with the ginger, sage, pepper and salt and baste the lamb with the mixture. Roll the meat up and tie it securely, then roast it in the oven with a little water for 1½ hours at 200-225⁰C (400-425⁰F, Gas Mark 6-7). As soon as the meat juices start to caramelize, add a little stock to the roasting tin, baste the lamb occasionally with the juices, and add more stock to the tin as the liquid evaporates.

Purée the pineapple in a food processor or with a hand-held mixer and fold in the soy sauce and mustard. Thirty minutes before the end of cooking time, baste the lamb with 3 tablespoons of pineapple purée, then take it out of the oven and keep it warm.

De-glaze the meat juices with a little water, season the gravy with salt and pepper, thicken it with flour and water blended together and bring the gravy to the boil.

CARP IN BEER

Serves 5-6

1½ kg (3½ lb) carp, cleaned
1 large onion
1 carrot
2 knobs of butter
1 tbsp flour
500 ml (18 fl oz) beer
1 bay leaf
2 cloves

5 slices of lemon
100 g (3½ oz) gingerbread
1 tbsp raisins
1 tbsp flaked almonds
lemon juice
salt
pepper

Rinse the carp thoroughly in cold water, pat it dry and cut it into thick steaks. Peel and dice the onion, peel the carrot and cut it into matchsticks. Brown the vegetables in 1 knob of butter, stirring frequently, then take them out of the pan and keep them warm.

To make the sauce: Melt the butter, add the flour and cook it until it is golden and a roux forms, then add the beer. Whisk the sauce to prevent lumps forming, bring it to the boil, add the onion, carrot, bay leaf, cloves and lemon slices, season it with salt and pepper and simmer it for 30 minutes.

Strain the sauce through a chinois or sieve, reserving the vegetables, and pour it into a big frying pan or casserole dish (it should be big enough to put the fish steaks into it without them overlapping). Keep the reserved vegetables warm. Crumble the gingerbread and add it to the sauce with the raisins and almonds.

Bring the sauce to the boil, adjust the seasoning and add lemon juice to taste. Put the carp steaks in the sauce and simmer them over a low heat for 20-35 minutes. If the sauce reduces too much, add more beer.
Serve the carp on a warmed serving dish surrounded by the vegetables and accompanied by boiled potatoes.

MULLET WITH BACON AND VEGETABLES

Serves 4

2 mullet, each weighing approx. 1 kg (2 lb)
lemon juice
125 g (4 oz) thinly sliced bacon
6 tomatoes, skinned
2 aubergines, each weighing 250 g (8 oz)

1 leek
2 onions
50 g (2 oz) butter
1 tbsp flour
250 ml (8 fl oz) double cream
paprika
salt and pepper

Scale the mullet, gut them and cut off the fins and tails. Rinse them under cold, running water, pat them dry, sprinkle with lemon juice and leave them to macerate for 15 minutes, then season them with salt and pepper.

Lard the mullet with the slices of bacon, arranging any remaining bacon on the base of an oven-proof dish. Slice the tomatoes and aubergines. Carefully wash the leek, slice it into rings and drain them. Peel and thinly slice the onions, then spread the vegetables over the bacon in the base of the dish and put the mullet on top. Dot the fish with several knobs of butter and grill it at 200-225ßC (400-425ßF, Gas Mark 6-7) for 35-40 minutes.

To make the sauce: Blend together the flour and double cream, add the cooking juices from the fish and season it to taste with paprika.

Serve with steamed potatoes and salad.

Left: *Carp in beer*
Right: *Mullet with bacon and vegetables*

STEAMED FILLET OF COLEY

IN THE PRESSURE COOKER
Serves 4

4 fillets of coley
1 tbsp lemon juice
1 knob of butter
800 g (1½ lb) vegetables,
e.g. cabbage, carrots,
celery, leek

2 tomatoes
100 g (3½ oz) button
mushrooms
fresh parsley, chopped
salt

*P*our 250 ml (8 fl oz) water into the pressure cooker. Sprinkle lemon juice over the coley fillets and season them with salt. Wash and peel the vegetables and cut them into very thin strips. Blanch the tomatoes in boiling water. Refresh them in cold water, skin and slice them.

Wipe the mushrooms and slice them thinly. Put the vegetables in the inner pan, put the fish on top and drizzle a little melted butter over. Seal the pressure cooker and steam the fish for 8-10 minutes. Arrange the

fish on a serving dish, smother it in vegetables and garnish with fresh, chopped parsley.

Right: *Halibut jardinière*
Below: *Steamed fillet of coley*

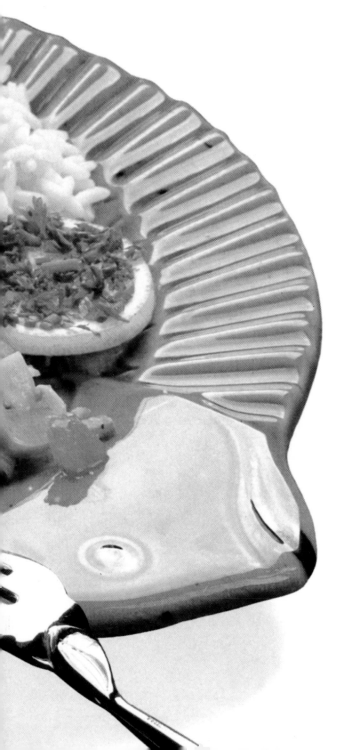

HALIBUT JARDINIÈRE

Serves 4

4 halibut steaks, weighing 800 g (1½ lb) in total	200 g (7 oz) tin button mushrooms
250 g (8 oz) tin mixed petit pois and carrots	1 tbsp flour
250 g (8 oz) tin asparagus tips	lemon juice
	paprika
3 knobs of butter, melted	butter
1 small onion	salt
	pepper

Rinse the halibut steaks in cold water, pat them dry, sprinkle them with lemon juice and leave them to marinate for about 15 minutes. Wipe them dry and season them with salt, pepper and paprika. Arrange the halibut steaks in the centre of a buttered oven-proof dish.

Drain the carrots, peas and asparagus, arrange the vegetables around the halibut, season them with salt, melt 2 knobs of butter and drizzle it on top, cover the dish with foil and bake the steaks in the oven at 200-225°C (400-425°F, Gas Mark 6-7) for about 25 minutes.

To make the mushroom sauce: Peel and slice the onion thinly. Drain the mushrooms, reserving 250 ml (8 fl oz) of the liquor. Melt a knob of butter and fry the onions in it. Add the mushrooms, then add the flour and stir it until cooked. Add the liquor from the mushrooms and whisk the sauce to prevent lumps forming. Bring the sauce to the boil, simmer it gently for about 10 minutes, then season it with salt and pepper.

Serve the halibut and mushroom sauce with boiled potatoes.

PROVENÇALE FISH STEW

Serves 4

800 g (1½ lb) hake or coley	chopped
2-3 spring onions	pinch of fresh sage, chopped
1 leek	1 bay leaf
400 g (13 oz) red and green peppers	125 ml (4 fl oz) white wine
3 plum tomatoes	150 g (5 oz) crème fraîche
2 cloves of garlic	½ vegetable stock cube
30 g (1 oz) butter or	cayenne pepper
2 tbsp oil	salt
pinch of fresh thyme,	pepper
	lemon juice

Peel the whites of the spring onions and chop them finely. Wash the leek, cut it in half lengthways, then into 1 cm (½ inch) pieces and drain them.

Cut the peppers in half, remove the cores and seeds, wash them and cut them into strips. Blanch the plum tomatoes in boiling water, refresh them in cold water, skin, de-seed and dice them. Peel and crush the garlic. Melt the butter or oil in a frying pan and fry the vegetables with the thyme, sage and bay leaf. Add the wine, then leave the sauce on a low heat for 8-10 minutes to reduce. Wash the fish in cold water, pat it dry and chop it into large dice.

Stir the crème fraîche and ½ stock cube into the vegetables, add the diced fish, season to taste with cayenne pepper, salt, pepper and lemon juice. Simmer for 10-15 minutes.

Serve with rice or boiled potatoes.

PIKE ON A BED OF VEGETABLES

Serves 4-6

1 pike, weighing about 1½ kg (3½ lb), dressed	250 g (8 oz) button mushrooms
150 g (5 oz) bacon	250 g (8 oz) red cabbage
lemon juice	melted butter
250 g (8 oz) carrots	salt
250 g (8 oz) celery	pepper
250 g (8 oz) leeks	

Wash the pike in cold water and pat it dry. Sprinkle lemon juice over it and leave it to marinate for 15 minutes, then wipe it, season with salt inside and out and put it in a large, buttered dish.

Wash and peel the carrots and celery, carefully clean the leeks, mushrooms and red cabbage. Cut the vegetables into very thin strips and arrange them around the fish. Season the vegetables with salt and pepper and drizzle melted butter over them.

Cover the dish with foil and bake the pike in the oven at 200-225⁰ C (400-425⁰ F, Gas Mark 6-7) for about 35 minutes.

Left: *Provençale fish stew*
Right: *Pike on a bed of vegetables*

FISH STEAKS IN BEER

Serves 4

4 monkfish or cod steaks,
each weighing 200 g
(7 oz)
250 g (8 oz) leeks
250 g (8 oz) carrots
250 g (8 oz) celery
1 sprig of fresh parsley
3 knobs of butter

250 ml (8 fl oz) lager-style
beer
250 ml (8 fl oz) mild beer
1 meat stock cube
4 cayenne peppercorns
zest of an unwaxed lemon
lemon juice
salt and pepper

Rinse the fish in cold water, pat it dry, sprinkle it with lemon juice and leave to marinate for about 15 minutes, then season it with salt. Carefully wash and peel the leeks, carrots and celery, then cut the vegetables into very thin strips. Wash and finely chop the sprig of parsley. Melt a knob of butter in a frying pan and sweat the vegetables and parsley in it.

Add both types of beer to the vegetables, stir well, then add the stock cube, cayenne pepper, pepper and lemon zest. Cover and leave to simmer on a gentle heat for 20 minutes.

Add the fish to the sauce, and simmer until the fish is cooked (about 15 minutes). Arrange the fish on a warm serving dish. Blend the flour with 2 knobs of melted butter and stir the roux into the sauce, simmer it for 2-3 minutes, then adjust the seasoning to taste.

Serve the fish coated in the sauce, with rice or boiled potatoes.

HALIBUT WITH VEGETABLES

Serves 4

4 halibut steaks, each
weighing 200 g (7 oz)
juice of 1 lemon
1 carrot
3 spring onions
2 courgettes
100 ml (3½ fl oz) dry
white wine
1 knob of butter

100 ml (3½ fl oz) crab
bisque, tinned
400 g (13 oz) cream
cheese
fresh mixed herbs, finely
chopped
grated horseradish
salt
pepper

Left: *Fish steaks in beer*
Below: *Halibut with vegetables*

Rinse the halibut steaks in cold water, pat them dry, drizzle with lemon juice, leave them to marinate for 15 minutes, then wipe them. Peel and slice the carrot. Prepare the spring onions, retaining the green parts, and chop them roughly. Wash the courgettes and slice them thinly.

Place the vegetables in a casserole dish or saucepan with the white wine, butter and crab bisque, then bring the pan to the boil, cover and simmer for 15 minutes.

Put the halibut steaks on top of the vegetables, season them with salt and pepper, cover and simmer over a gentle heat for a further 10 minutes.

Carefully combine the cream cheese, chopped herbs and grated horseradish in a bain-marie or basin over a saucepan of boiling water, until heated through.

Top each halibut steak with 2-3 tablespoons of this sauce, then serve the remainder separately.

Accompany the halibut steaks with parsleyed potatoes.

COD CREOLE

Serves 4

800 g (1½ lb) cod fillets	1 knob of butter
1-2 tbsp lemon juice	fresh parsley, chopped
250 g (8 oz) sweetcorn, tinned	salt
	pepper
75 g (3 oz) streaky bacon	

Rinse the cod fillets in cold water, pat them dry and cut them into 2 cm (¾ inch) cubes, then drizzle them with lemon juice, leave them to marinate for 15 minutes, then pat them dry and season them with salt.

Drain the sweetcorn, dice the bacon. Sauté the sweetcorn in the melted butter and season with salt. Butter an oven-proof dish, put the cod fillets in the middle, arrange the sweetcorn around the fish and cover the dish with foil.

Bake the fish in the oven at 225-250°C (425-475°F, Gas Mark 7-9) for 25-30 minutes. Garnish with chopped parsley and serve with sautéed or boiled potatoes.

Below: *Hake with onions and green peppercorns*

HAKE IN WHITE WINE

Serves 2-3

400 g (13 oz) hake fillets	3-4 tbsp tomato ketchup
1 onion	1 tbsp fresh parsley, chopped
2 knobs of butter	
100 ml (3½ fl oz) white wine	lemon juice
	salt
150 g (5 oz) crème fraîche	pepper

Rinse the hake fillets in cold water, pat them dry, drizzle them with lemon juice, leave them to marinate for 15 minutes, then wipe them and season them with salt. Peel and slice the onion thinly. Melt the butter in a frying pan and sweat the onion over a low heat until it is translucent. Add the hake fillets and white wine. Simmer the hake over a gentle heat for about 10 minutes. Arrange the hake and onions on a serving dish and keep them warm.

To make the sauce: Blend together the tomato ketchup and crème fraîche, add them to the juices from the frying pan, bring the sauce to the boil, season it with salt and pepper, then coat the fish in the sauce and garnish with chopped parsley.

Serve with boiled potatoes or rice.

HAKE WITH ONIONS AND GREEN PEPPERCORNS

Serves 4

4 hake fillets, each weighing 200 g (7 oz)	250 ml (8 fl oz) beer
juice of 1 lemon	100 g (3½ oz) crème fraîche
250 g (8 oz) onions	green peppercorns
2 knobs of butter	salt
1 tsp fresh tarragon, chopped	pepper

Rinse the hake in cold water and pat it dry. Drizzle it with the lemon juice, leave it to marinate for 15 minutes, then wipe it and season it with salt. Peel and thinly slice the onions and sweat them in the butter. Season the onions with salt, pepper and tarragon and put the hake fillets on top.
Cover and sauté over a low heat for 10-15 minutes. Arrange the hake fillets on a warm plate and keep them warm. Add the beer and crème fraîche to the pan, stir and bring to the boil. Add the green peppercorns, pour the sauce over the fish and serve with boiled potatoes.

PRAWNS IN SPICES AND GARLIC BUTTER

Serves 2

400 g (13 oz) prawns,
frozen
2-3 cloves of garlic
2 knobs of butter
2-3 tbsp sherry

fresh dill, chopped
1 lemon
salt
freshly ground pepper

Defrost the prawns at room temperature. Peel and finely chop the garlic. Melt the butter in a cast-iron frying pan, add the garlic, then the prawns and cook them for 5 minutes, stirring them frequently. Season them with salt and pepper and add the sherry and chopped dill to taste.

Serve the prawns on a warm serving dish, garnished with slices of lemon and sprigs of dill.

Below: *Prawns in spices and garlic butter*

STEAMED COD

Serves 4

1.2 kg (3 lb) cod, cleaned
and gutted
2 tbsp lemon juice
1 bouquet garni
1 bay leaf
10 peppercorns

3 cloves
5 dried chillies
1 onion
1 tbsp vinegar
salt and pepper

Rinse the cod in cold water, pat it dry, drizzle it with lemon juice, leave it to marinate for 15 minutes, then wipe it and season it with salt. Pour 250 ml (8 fl oz) water into a casserole dish or fish kettle, season it with salt and add the bouquet garni, bay leaf, pepper, chilli, cloves, the peeled and diced onion and vinegar.

Put the fish on a rack in the water, or in the fish kettle basket, cover and steam for about 20 minutes.

Serve the fish on a warm serving dish with melted butter and boiled potatoes.

Variation: This method of cooking is also suitable for other types of fish. The cooking time differs depending on type: haddock - 20 minutes; coley - 20 minutes; hake - 20 minutes; ling - 30 minutes; zander (scale, gut, cut off fins, leave head) - about 30 minutes; pike (scale, gut, cut off fins, leave head) - about 30 minutes; eel (gut, remove the skin and head, chop into 5 cm (2 inch) chunks) - 20 minutes.

STEAMED HALIBUT

Serves 4

4 halibut steaks, each
weighing 200 g (7 oz)
2 tbsp lemon juice
1 small onion
1-2 knobs of butter
1 bay leaf
10 peppercorns

1 clove
2 dried chillies
1 leek
fresh parsley, chopped
salt
pepper

Rinse the halibut steaks in cold water, pat them dry, drizzle them with lemon juice, leave them to marinate for 15 minutes, then wipe them and season them with salt

and pepper. Peel and thinly slice the onion. Melt the butter in a frying pan and sweat the onion in it until translucent. Add the fish and spices and sauté over a low heat for 8-10 minutes.

Arrange the halibut steaks on a warm serving dish and garnish with rings of leek and chopped parsley.

Serve with boiled, parsleyed potatoes and hollandaise sauce (see page 93).

TUNA STEAKS ALHAMBRA

Serves 4

4 tuna steaks, each
weighing 150 g (5 oz)
juice of 1 lemon
60 g (2½ oz) flour
1 clove of garlic
2 knobs of butter
1 large onion

4 tomatoes, skinned
125 ml (4 fl oz) white wine
fresh oregano, chopped
salt
pepper

Rinse the tuna steaks in cold water, pat them dry, drizzle them with lemon juice, leave them to marinate for 15 minutes, then wipe them and season them with salt. Coat the tuna steaks in the flour.

Rub a frying pan or casserole dish with the peeled garlic. Melt the butter in the pan, then sauté the tuna steaks on each side. Peel and thinly slice the onion and add it to the pan. Finely dice the tomatoes and add them to the pan, then season with salt and oregano to taste. Pour the wine over the tuna steaks. Cover the pan and poach the tuna for 20 minutes. Serve piping hot.

Left: *Steamed cod*
Right: *Tuna steaks Alhambra*

PAUPIETTES OF COLEY WITH TOMATO SAUCE

Serves 4

750 g (1½ lb) coley fillets
4 tbsp lemon juice
1 tbsp mustard
1 small onion
350 g (11 oz) tomatoes
30 g (1 oz) butter
30 g (1 oz) flour

250 ml (8 fl oz) white wine
2 tbsp tomato purée
paprika
Tabasco sauce
salt
celery salt

Rinse the coley fillets in cold water, pat them dry, drizzle them with 2 tablespoons of lemon juice, leave them to marinate for 15 minutes, then wipe them and season them with salt and celery salt. Spread a thin layer of mustard over the coley fillets, roll them up and secure them with cocktail sticks.

To make the tomato sauce: Peel and thinly slice the onion, wash and chop the tomatoes and sweat them both in the butter. Turn the heat up, add the flour, stir it in well, add the white wine and whisk the sauce to prevent lumps forming. Bring the sauce to the boil and strain it through a chinois or sieve. Adjust the seasoning with celery salt and paprika, season with salt, the tomato purée, remaining lemon juice and Tabasco sauce. Poach the fish fillets in the sauce for about 20 minutes.

Tip: The paupiettes can also be garnished with thin strips of sweet and sour pickled gherkins.

DAB ROLLS WITH WHITE WINE

Serves 4

750 g (1½ lb) dab or sole
fillets
30 g (1 oz) butter
30 g (1 oz) flour
250 ml (8 fl oz) white wine

5 tbsp cream
lemon juice
butter
salt and pepper

Rinse the dab fillets in cold water, pat them dry, drizzle them with lemon juice, leave them to marinate for 30 minutes, then wipe them and season them with salt. Roll up the fillets and arrange them in an oven-proof dish.

To make the sauce: Melt the butter, add the flour and cook it, stirring constantly, but do not let it brown, then add the wine and bring the sauce to the boil, whisking it all the time. Add the cream, with salt and lemon juice to taste. Pour the sauce over the fish rolls. Bake the fish in the oven at 175-200⁰ C (350-400⁰ F, Gas Mark 4-6) for 25-35 minutes.

Below:
Paupiettes of coley with tomato sauce

MACKEREL WITH GRUYÈRE

Serves 4

4 dressed mackerel each weighing about 250 g (8 oz)	chopped
	4 tbsp vinegar
	30 g (1 oz) butter
1 bay leaf	30 g (1 oz) flour
6 juniper berries	50 g (2 oz) Gruyère, grated
a few mustard seeds	
1 onion	4 tbsp crème fraîche
2 sprigs fresh parsley,	salt and pepper

Rinse the mackerel in cold water. Make a court-bouillon with 750 ml (1¼ pints) water, salt, pepper, the vinegar, bay leaf, peeled and sliced onion, juniper berries, mustard seeds and parsley. Bring it to the boil and simmer for 5 minutes. Add the fish to the court-bouillon, bring to the boil again and cook over a low heat for 10 minutes. Take out the fish and keep them warm.

To make the sauce: Strain the fish stock through a chinois or sieve, retaining 400 ml (14 fl oz). Melt the butter in a saucepan and add the flour, stirring all the time. Add the fish stock and bring the sauce to the boil, whisking constantly to prevent lumps forming, then reduce the heat and simmer the sauce for 3 minutes, still whisking. Add the grated Gruyère and cream. Adjust the seasoning and pour the sauce over the mackerel.

EEL IN PARSLEY SAUCE

Serves 4

1 kg (2 lb) dressed eel	1 knob of butter
1 cup of fresh parsley, chopped	1 tbsp flour
	1 egg yolk
1 sage leaf, chopped	4 tbsp double cream
8 tarragon leaves, chopped	1 tbsp lemon juice
	1 tbsp fresh dill, chopped
250 ml (8 fl oz) white wine	salt and pepper

Rinse the eels in cold water, dry them, remove the fins and cut them into 5 cm (2 inch) chunks. In a saucepan, heat the white wine with half of the parsley, the sage and tarragon. Bring to the boil and add the chopped eel, season with salt, cover and simmer it for 15 minutes. Take the eel out of the stock and keep it warm.

To make the sauce: Melt the butter and add the flour, stirring all the time. Gradually add the fish stock, whisking all the time to prevent lumps forming. Bring the sauce to the boil, reduce the heat and continue cooking, whisking constantly.

Add the egg yolk, cream, lemon juice, remaining parsley and dill to the sauce, then season it with salt and pepper to taste. Pour the sauce over the pieces of eel.

Serve with steamed potatoes.

Below: *Eel in parsley sauce*

PIKE IN WHITE SAUCE

Serves 4

1 pike, weighing 1½ kg (3½ lb)	1 tbsp capers
50 g (2 oz) butter	2 anchovy fillets, chopped
35 g (generous 1 oz) flour	1 egg yolk
500 ml (18 fl oz) meat stock	2 tbsp cream
150 g (5 oz) button mushrooms	vinegar
	white wine
	salt and pepper

Scale and gut the fish, rinse it in cold water and pat it dry. Cut it into chunks and drizzle them with vinegar, leave them to marinate for 30 minutes, then season them with salt. Seal the chunks of pike in 2 knobs of butter and fry them over a gentle heat for about 20 minutes.

To make the sauce: Sauté the mushrooms in a frying pan, in a little butter. Melt 30 g (1 oz) butter in a saucepan, add the flour, stir, add the meat stock and bring the sauce to the boil, whisking all the time to prevent lumps. Simmer the sauce for 5 minutes, stirring all the time. Add the mushrooms, capers, and chopped anchovy fillets and simmer for several minutes. Fold in the egg yolk and cream, season with salt, adjust the seasoning with pepper and white wine. Pour the sauce over the fish.

Below: *Pike in white sauce*
Right: *Fish Stroganoff*

MOULES MARINIÈRE

Serves 2

1 kg (2 lb) mussels	400 ml (14 fl oz) white wine
2 small onions	1 clove of garlic
50 g (2 oz) butter	salt
1 bouquet garni	pepper
1 tbsp fresh parsley, chopped	

Rinse the mussels in cold water, scrub them and remove the beards. Rinse them until the water is clear and throw away any which are open. Peel and thinly slice the onions. Melt the butter in a saucepan and brown the onions in it. Add the white wine, parsley, bouquet garni, salt and pepper. Leave to simmer for a few minutes.

Add the mussels to the stock and simmer them for 10 minutes, stirring constantly, until they open. Throw away any mussels which stay closed. Strain the mussels and put them in a deep dish. Adjust the seasoning in the stock and pour it over the mussels.

FISH STROGANOFF

Serves 2

400 g (13 oz) cod or haddock fillets	gherkins
	lemon juice
1 large onion	mustard
1 tbsp capers	tomato purée
250 ml (8 fl oz) meat stock	paprika
1 tbsp cornflour	fresh parsley, chopped
1 tbsp crème fraîche	salt
2 sweet and sour pickled	pepper

Rinse the fish fillets in cold water, pat them dry, drizzle them with lemon juice and leave them to marinate for 15 minutes. Peel and thinly slice the onion. Bring the meat stock to the boil with the onion and capers, simmer it for 5 minutes. Thicken the stock with the cornflour and add the tomato purée, thinned down with water, the mustard, paprika and gherkins cut into thin strips. Season the sauce with salt, pepper and lemon juice, bring it to the boil and add the cream.

Chop the fish fillets into large dice and cook them in the sauce over a low heat for 10-15 minutes.

Serve the fish stew in a warmed , deep dish, and garnish with chopped parsley.

BLANQUETTE DE POISSON

Serves 4

750 g (1½ lb) cod or	celery salt
haddock fillets	paprika
30 g (1 oz) butter	2 egg yolks
30 g (1 oz) flour	2 tbsp crème fraîche
500 ml (18 fl oz) meat stock	slices of lemon
1 tbsp capers	fresh parsley, chopped
lemon juice	tomatoes
white wine	salt

Rinse the fish fillets in cold water, pat them dry, drizzle them with lemon juice, leave them to marinate for 15 minutes, then season them with salt. Cut the fish into large dice.

To make the sauce: Melt the butter and add the flour, stirring all the time. Add the stock and bring the sauce to the boil, whisking to prevent lumps forming. Put the fish fillets into the sauce. Season the sauce with salt, then add the capers. Add the white wine, lemon juice, celery salt and paprika to taste. Poach the fish for 10-15 minutes on a low heat. Take the fish out of the sauce. Enrich the sauce with the beaten egg yolks and cream, then adjust the seasoning.

Serve the blanquette of poisson in a ring of herb-flavoured rice and garnish with lemon slices, quartered tomatoes and chopped parsley.

FILLETS OF SOLE IN MUSTARD SAUCE

Serves 2-4

12 fillets of sole, weighing	150 ml (5 fl oz) meat stock
about 600 g (1¼ lb) in total	2 tbsp mustard
125 ml (4 fl oz) white wine	100 g (3½ oz) cream
6 peppercorns	juice of 1 lemon
a few mustard seeds	salt
1 slice of lemon	pepper
25 g (1 oz) butter	
25 g (1 oz) flour	
150 ml (5 fl oz) milk	

Rinse the fillets of sole in cold water, pat them dry, then roll them up and secure them with cocktail sticks. Add the water, peppercorns, mustard seeds, lemon and salt to the white wine. Bring the stock to the boil. Add the fillets of sole and cook them over a gentle heat for 10 minutes. Take the fillets out of the stock and put them on a warm serving dish.

Opposite: Blanquette de poisson

To make the sauce: Melt the butter and add the flour, stirring all the time. Then add the milk and stock and bring the sauce to the boil, whisking it to prevent lumps forming. Simmer the sauce for 5 minutes over a gentle heat, stirring constantly. Add the mustard, cream and lemon juice, then season the sauce with salt and pepper. Pour some of the sauce over the fish and serve the rest separately. Serve the sole with curried rice or petit pois.

Below: Fish rolls

FISH ROLLS

IN THE PRESSURE COOKER
Serves 4

4 hake fillets, weighing	1-2 tbsp flour
about 750 g (1½ lb) in total	100 g (3½ oz) cream
juice of ½ lemon	mustard
8 slices of streaky bacon	salt
750 g (1½ lb) leeks	pepper
2 knobs of butter	

Rinse the hake fillets in cold water, pat them dry, drizzle them with lemon juice, leave them to marinate for 15 minutes, then season them with salt. Spread each fillet with a thin layer of mustard, then roll each one up between 2 slices of bacon.

Wash the leeks and cut them into 2 cm (¾ inch) pieces. Melt the butter in the pressure cooker and add the leeks. Season the leeks with salt and pepper, add 125 ml (4 fl oz) water and leave the leeks to simmer over a low heat.

Arrange the fish rolls on top of the leeks, put the lid on the pressure cooker and cook the hake for about 8 minutes. Before serving, thicken the leeks with the flour and cream and adjust the seasoning. Serve the hake fillets with parsleyed potatoes and tomato salad.

HAKE IN TOMATO SAUCE

IN THE PRESSURE COOKER
Serves 4

4 hake fillets, each
weighing 200 g (7 oz)
1 tbsp lemon juice
750 g (1½ lb) plum
tomatoes
1 medium onion
2 cloves of garlic
2 tbsp olive oil
50 g (2 oz) streaky bacon

70 g (3 oz) tomato purée
1 tsp green peppercorns,
crushed
2 tbsp cream
1-2 tbsp fresh basil,
chopped
salt
pepper

Rinse the fish fillets in cold water, pat them dry, drizzle
them with lemon juice, leave them to marinate for
15 minutes, then season them with salt. Blanch the
tomatoes in boiling water, then refresh them in cold
water. Skin them and cut them into small dice. Peel and
thinly slice the onion and garlic. Heat the oil in the
pressure cooker, add the onions, garlic and tomatoes and
season with salt and pepper.

To make the sauce: Dice the bacon and add it to the
tomatoes with the tomato purée, thinned down with
water, the green peppercorns, cream and basil. Wipe the
fish thoroughly, add it to the sauce and season it with salt
and pepper. Put the lid on the pressure cooker and cook
the hake for 3 minutes. Let the steam escape slowly, take
the lid off the pan and arrange the hake on a warm
serving dish.
Strain the sauce and thicken it with a little butter and
flour, kneaded together, if it is too watery.

Serve the hake in its sauce with steamed potatoes.

Below: *Hake in tomato sauce*

PAN-FRIED HAKE FILLETS

Serves 4

750 g (1½ lb) hake fillets
2 tbsp lemon juice
1 egg

75 g (3 oz) breadcrumbs
80 g (3 oz) butter
flour
salt and pepper

Rinse the fish fillets in cold water, pat them dry and cut
them into portions. Drizzle them with lemon juice and
leave them to marinate for 15 minutes, then season them
with salt and pepper.
Beat an egg, dip the hake fillets in the egg wash, then

coat each side of the fillets in flour, and then in breadcrumbs. Heat the butter and fry the hake fillets in it for 5-6 minutes on each side until golden brown.

Above: *Pan-fried hake fillets*

STEAMED HADDOCK

Serves 4

1½ kg (3½ lb) dressed haddock	butter
lemon juice	lemon slices
	fresh parsley
	salt

Rinse the fish in cold water, pat it dry, drizzle it with lemon juice, season it with salt and pepper and dot with knobs of butter. Put the haddock in an oven-proof dish, cover with an upturned plate or foil and bake in the oven at 175-200°C (350-400°F, Gas Mark 4-6) for 40 minutes.

Garnish with parsley and lemon slices. Serve with steamed potatoes and a mixed salad.
This recipe is also suitable for other types of fish: coley, cod, ling - 10-12 minutes; sole fillets - 15 minutes.

COLEY WITH ALMONDS

Serves 2

2 coley fillets, each weighing about 200 g (7 oz)
2 tbsp flour
1 egg, beaten
4 tbsp breadcrumbs
1 tbsp oil
200 g (7 oz) cream cheese

fresh, mixed herbs, chopped
1 knob of butter
4 tbsp flaked almonds
lemon juice
parsley
slices of unwaxed lemon
salt and pepper

Rinse the coley fillets in cold water, pat them dry, drizzle them with lemon juice, leave them to marinate for 15 minutes, then season them with salt and pepper. Coat the coley in the flour, then in the beaten egg and finally in the breadcrumbs.

Heat the oil in a frying pan and fry the coley for about 10 minutes on each side until golden. Arrange the coley fillets on a warm serving dish. Beat the cream cheese, add the fresh, mixed herbs and spread the mixture over the fish. Toast the almonds and divide them amongst the fish fillets. Garnish with parsley and slices of lemon.

Serve with boiled potatoes.

FILLETS OF SOLE IN BREADCRUMBS

Serves 4

8 fillets of sole	2 knobs of butter
lemon juice	flaked almonds, toasted
melted butter	salt and pepper
breadcrumbs	

Rinse the fillets of sole in cold water, pat them dry, drizzle them with lemon juice, leave them to marinate for 30 minutes, then season them with salt and pepper. Dip the fillets in melted butter and coat them in the breadcrumbs. Heat 2 knobs of the butter in a frying pan and fry the fillets of sole for 5-10 minutes on each side until golden brown. Garnish with the toasted, flaked almonds and serve immediately.

STUFFED ZANDER

Serves 3-4

1 zander, weighing about 1 kg (2 lb), dressed	lemon juice
1 slice of stale bread	fresh mixed herbs, chopped
1 onion	salt and pepper
250 g (8 oz) minced beef	
1 egg	
1 tsp mustard	
3 thin slices streaky bacon	
250 g (8 oz) tin button mushrooms	
100 g (3½ oz) crème fraîche	
2 tsp cornflour	

Rinse the fish in cold water, pat it dry, drizzle it with lemon juice and leave it to marinate for 15 minutes.

To make the stuffing: Soak the bread in water to soften it, then squeeze it out well. Peel the onion and slice it thinly, mix the minced beef with the bread and onion. Add the egg, mustard, salt, pepper and half the fresh, mixed herbs.

Season the zander inside and out with salt and pepper, stuff it and place it in an oven-proof dish. Cut the slices of bacon in half and arrange them on top of the zander. Bake at 200⁰ (400⁰ F, Gas Mark 6), uncovered, for 1 hour. Drain the mushrooms, reserving the liquor, and cut them in half. Add them to the fish 20 minutes before the end of cooking time. Put 250 ml (8 fl oz) of liquor from the mushrooms into a saucepan, add the cream, cornflour and remaining mixed herbs. Bring the sauce to the boil, season it with salt and pepper and serve it with the fish.

Left: *Coley with almonds*
Below: *Stuffed zander*

261

TROUT MEUNIÈRE

Serves 4

4 dressed trout, each
weighing 150-300 g
(5-10 oz)
lemon juice
flour
4 tbsp oil

50 g (2 oz) butter
Worcester sauce
fresh parsley, chopped
1 lemon, sliced
salt

Rinse the trout in cold water, wipe them well, drizzle them with lemon juice, then season them with salt and coat them in the flour. Heat the oil and cook the trout on both sides for about 10 minutes. Tip the oil out of the pan. Melt the butter in the frying pan until it foams and turns brown, then turn the trout in this beurre noisette. Take the trout out of the pan and keep them warm. De-glaze the butter with the lemon juice and Worcester sauce, and pour the beurre noisette over the trout. Garnish the trout with chopped parsley and accompany with buttered potatoes and a green salad.

Rinse the herrings in cold water, dry them well and drizzle them with lemon juice, leave them to marinate for 15 minutes, then season them inside with salt and pepper. Brown the diced bacon and reserve it.

Fry the herring in the bacon fat. Peel and thinly slice the onions, scatter them around the herrings and sweat them over a gentle heat for 10 minutes. Arrange the herrings on a warm serving dish. Return the bacon to the pan to finish cooking. Garnish the fish with bacon, onions, dill, parsley and lemon slices.

Serve with jacket potatoes and a green salad.

COLEY FISHCAKES

Serves 4

500 g (1 lb) coley fillets	1 egg
1 slice of stale bread	1 tbsp fresh parsley,
juice of 2 lemons	chopped
1 medium onion	breadcrumbs
1 tbsp oil	salt
60 g (2½ oz) butter	pepper
1 tbsp mustard	

Soften the bread in cold water. Rinse the coley fillets in cold water, dry them, then drizzle them with the juice of one lemon. Leave them to marinate for 30 minutes, then mince them together with the bread. Peel and finely chop the onion and sweat it in the oil. Add the egg, parsley, onion, juice of 1 lemon and mustard to the minced fish and bread mixture, combine them thoroughly and season with salt and pepper. Shape the mixture into fillets or fishcakes and coat them in the breadcrumbs. Heat the butter in a frying pan and fry the fishcakes on both sides for about 10 minutes.

Serve with potato salad and remoulade dressing (see page 126).

Facing page: *Trout meunière*
Below: *Pan-fried herrings with bacon*

PAN-FRIED HERRINGS WITH BACON

Serves 4

8 small, fresh herrings, dressed	2 small onions or shallots
juice of 1 lemon	fresh dill and parsley, chopped
150 g (5 oz) smoked bacon, diced	a few slices of lemon
1 slice of bacon	salt and pepper

PAN-FRIED DAB

Serves 4

4 dressed dab, each	80 g (3 oz) butter
weighing 300 g (10 oz)	flour
2 tbsp lemon juice	salt and pepper

Rinse the dab in cold water, pat them dry, drizzle them with lemon juice and leave them to marinate for 30 minutes. Season them inside and out with salt, then toss them in the flour. Heat the butter in a frying pan and fry the fish on both sides for 6-8 minutes, until golden. Serve with potato salad or rice flavoured with fresh, mixed herbs. This recipe is also suitable for other types of fish, but the cooking times will differ: trout (300 g/10 oz), 8-10 minutes; sole (250 g/8 oz), 5-7 minutes.

DAB WITH BACON

Serves 4

4 dressed dab, each	lemon juice
weighing 300 g (10 oz)	flour
2 tbsp oil	a few slices of lemon
200 g (7 oz) streaky bacon,	salt and pepper
sliced	

Rinse the dab in cold water and pat them dry, then drizzle them with lemon juice. Leave them to marinate for 30 minutes, then season with salt and pepper. Toss the dab in the flour. Heat the oil and fry the bacon in it. Add the fish and fry them on each side, for 15-20 minutes, until golden. Arrange the dab on a warm serving dish. Garnish with the bacon and decorate with slices of lemon.

Below:
Pan-fried dab

Above: Curried fish

CURRIED FISH

Serves 2-3

400 g (13 oz) fish fillets	1 tbsp white wine
lemon juice	1 tsp sugar
2 knobs of butter	1 tsp curry powder
1 apple	1 tbsp mango chutney
150 g (5 oz) crème fraîche	salt and pepper

Rinse the fish fillets in cold water, pat them dry, drizzle them with lemon juice and leave them to marinate for 15 minutes, then season them with salt and pepper.

Melt the butter in an oven-proof dish, and arrange the fillets in it. Peel the apple, remove the core and seeds and dice it finely. Blend together the crème fraîche, white wine, sugar, curry powder and mango chutney, season the mixture with salt and pepper, then add the diced apple. Spread this mixture over the fish fillets. Bake the fish in the oven for 30 minutes at 175-200⁰C (350-400⁰F, Gas Mark 4-6). Serve with rice.

COLEY WITH SPINACH

Serves 4

750 g (1½ lb) coley, hake	2 knobs of butter
or cod fillets	150 g (5 oz) crème fraîche
2 tbsp lemon juice	1 tbsp Parmesan, grated
450 g (15 oz) creamed	salt
spinach, frozen	pepper

Rinse the fish fillets in cold water, pat them dry, drizzle them with lemon juice and leave them to marinate for 30 minutes, then season them with salt and pepper.

Defrost the spinach according to the instructions on the packet. Butter an oven-proof dish and arrange half the fish fillets in it. Spread the spinach over the fish and cover it with the remaining fillets. Mix together the crème fraîche and Parmesan and spread it over the fish. Bake the fish in the oven at 200-225⁰C (400-425⁰F, Gas Mark 6-7) for 35-40 minutes.

TROUT À LA FLORENTINE

Serves 4

4 dressed trout, each
weighing 200 g (7 oz)
600 g (1¼ lb) leaf spinach,
frozen
80 g (3 oz) streaky bacon
1 onion
3-4 tbsp flour

60 g (2½ oz) butter
lemon juice
2-3 tbsp white wine
150 g (5 oz) crème fraîche
salt
pepper

Defrost the spinach at room temperature. Cut the bacon
into small dice, fry it in a frying pan to render the fat, add
the spinach and cook over a low heat for a few minutes,
then season with salt and pepper. Butter an oven-proof
dish and spread the spinach and bacon over the base.

Rinse the trout in cold water, pat them dry, drizzle them
with lemon juice inside and out and leave them to
marinate for 15 minutes, then season them with salt and
pepper and toss them in the flour. Melt the butter in a
frying pan and fry the trout on both sides.

Arrange the trout on top of the spinach. Blend together
the crème fraîche and Parmesan and spread it over the
trout. Bake the fish in the oven at 200°C (400°F, Gas Mark
6) for 20-25 minutes. De-glaze the cooking juices with the
white wine, strain them, stir in the crème fraîche and coat
the trout with this sauce when cooked.

Below: *Trout à la Florentine*

COD STUFFED WITH PARSLEY

Serves 4

1 dressed cod, weighing
1½ kg (3½ lb)
lemon juice
bunch of spring onions
50 g (2 oz) butter
2-3 tbsp fresh flat leaf
parsley, chopped

2-3 tbsp fresh curly
parsley, chopped
2 tomatoes
Worcester sauce
salt
pepper

Rinse the cod in cold water, pat it dry, drizzle it with
lemon juice and leave it to marinate for 30 minutes, then
season it inside and out with salt and pepper.

Above: *Cod stuffed with parsley*

STUFFED PIKE AU GRATIN

Serves 4

1 dressed pike, weighing
1½ kg (3½ lb)
juice of 1 lemon
1 slice of stale bread
1 small onion
60 g (2½ oz) sliced button
mushrooms, tinned
250 g (8 oz) minced beef
1 egg
1 tbsp fresh parsley,
chopped
1 tbsp mustard
100 g (3½ oz) fatty bacon
4 slices of Gruyère cheese
1 level tbsp cornflour
2 tbsp tomato ketchup
tomatoes
salt
pepper

Rinse the pike in cold water, pat it dry, drizzle it with lemon juice inside and out, leave it to marinate for 15 minutes, then season it with salt and pepper.

To make the stuffing: Soften the bread in cold water. Peel and slice the onion thinly. Drain the mushrooms, reserving the liquor. Add these ingredients to the minced meat and combine thoroughly with the egg, parsley and mustard. Stuff the pike with this mixture.

Place the bacon in the centre of a sheet of foil and put the pike on top. Fold the foil to make a tightly-sealed parcel. Bake the pike in the oven at 225-250°C (425-475°F, Gas Mark 7-9). After 50 minutes in the oven, open the parcel and collect the cooking juices. Make 8 incisions in the side of the pike and insert the slices of Gruyère. Return the pike to the oven and cook for a further 5-10 minutes.

To make the sauce: Mix together the reserved fish juices and liquor from the mushrooms to make 250 ml (8 fl oz). Thicken the sauce with cornflour, bring it to the boil, add the tomato ketchup and season it with salt and pepper. Garnish the pike with sliced tomato and parsley. Serve the sauce separately.

Accompany the fish with steamed or sautéed potatoes and a green salad.

To make the stuffing: Peel the spring onions and cut them into rolls. Melt the butter and fry the onions over a low heat, then add the chopped parsley. Season the mixture with salt and pepper and cook it over a low heat, then season to taste with Worcester sauce.

Spread a sheet of foil over a baking sheet. Stuff the cod's belly cavity with the parsley mixture. Wash the tomatoes, slice them and arrange them on top of the fish, then season with salt and pepper. Fold the foil to make a parcel, and bake the cod in the oven at 200°C (400°F, Gas Mark 6) for 45 minutes.

Serve with sautéed potatoes and a green salad.

TROUT EN CHEMISE

Serves 4

4 dressed trout, each
weighing 200 g (7 oz)
1 cayenne pepper pod
sweet paprika
2 knobs of butter

12 thin slices of streaky
bacon
200 g (7 oz) cream
salt and pepper

Rinse the trout in cold water, pat them dry, then season inside and out with salt and pepper . Butter an oven-proof dish. Wrap the trout in the bacon and put them in the dish. Bake them in the oven at 200-225⁰C (400-425⁰F, Gas Mark 6-7) for 20 minutes. Season the cream with salt and pepper, add the cayenne pepper and paprika and pour the sauce over the trout 5 minutes before the end of cooking time.

Serve with parsleyed potatoes and chicory, lettuce or tomato salad.

Opposite: *Trout en chemise*
Below: *Paupiettes of coley in piquant sauce*

PAUPIETTES OF COLEY IN PIQUANT SAUCE

Serves 4

750 g (1½ lb) coley flllets
2 tbsp lemon juice
1 onion
50 g (2 oz) streaky bacon
2 gherkins, pickled in
vinegar
2 tsp mustard

150 g (5 oz) crème fraîche
2 tbsp Madeira
30 g (1 oz) of Gruyère,
grated
5 knobs of butter
salt and pepper

Rinse the coley fillets in cold water and pat them dry, then drizzle them with lemon juice. Leave them to marinate for 30 minutes, then season them with salt and pepper. Cut the fillets into medium-sized pieces, roll them up and secure them with a cocktail stick. Butter an oven-proof dish and arrange the fish rolls in it.

To make the sauce: Peel the onion and slice it thinly, cut the bacon into small dice. Render the bacon in a frying pan and fry the onion with it. Put the bacon and onion to one side. Dice the gherkins, add them to the bacon and onion mixture with the mustard and crème fraîche, season the sauce with salt and pepper, then add the Madeira. Pour the sauce over the coley fillets, top with grated Gruyère and dot with butter, and bake the coley in the oven at 200-225° C (400-425° F, Gas Mark 6-7 for 25-35 minutes.

COD FILLETS AU GRATIN

Serves 4

400 g (13 oz) cod fillets
4 slices of boiled ham
juice of 1 lemon
2 onions
5 tomatoes
150 g (5 oz) sliced button
mushrooms, tinned
2 pots of natural yoghurt
1 bunch of fresh chives,
chopped
1 bunch of fresh dill,
chopped
1 bunch of fresh parsley,
chopped
sweet paprika
2 knobs of butter
2 tbsp breadcrumbs
150 g (5 oz) Gruyère,
grated
salt
pepper

Rinse the fish fillets in cold water, pat them dry, drizzle them with lemon juice and leave them to marinate for 15 minutes, then season them with salt and pepper. Peel the onions and slice them thinly. Cut the ham into small dice and fry it in a frying pan with the onions. Wash and slice the tomatoes. Drain the mushrooms. Mix together the yoghurt, chives, dill, parsley and paprika and season with salt and pepper. Butter an oval, oven-proof dish, put the fish fillets in it, together with the onions, ham, mushrooms and tomatoes. Cover all these ingredients with yoghurt dressing. Sprinkle the breadcrumbs and grated Gruyère on top, and dot with butter. Bake in the oven at 200-225°C (400-425°F, Gas Mark 6-7) for 20 minutes. Serve with curried rice.

Opposite: *Cod fillets au gratin*

TUNA IN TOMATO SAUCE

Serves 4

4 tuna steaks, each
weighing 200 g (7 oz)
2 red peppers
3-4 tomatoes
1 green chilli
2 bunches of flat leaf
parsley
3 cloves of garlic
300 g (10 oz) onions
4 tbsp oil
1 tbsp paprika
1 meat stock cube
250 g (8 oz) button
mushrooms
4 tbsp oil
salt
pepper

Cut the peppers in half, remove the core and seeds and cut them into thin slices.

To make the sauce: Blanch the tomatoes in boiling water, refresh them in cold water, skin and de-seed them and chop them finely. De-seed the chilli and chop it. Wash and drain the parsley and chop it finely.
Peel and thinly slice the garlic and onions. Heat the oil in a frying pan and sweat the onions and garlic in it. Add the peppers, tomatoes, chilli and parsley and sweat over a

Top left: *Cod fillet au gratin*

OYSTERS AU GRATIN

Serves 4

2 dozen oysters	fresh dill, chopped
50-75 g (2-3 oz) butter	mustard
1 tbsp fresh parsley,	garlic
chopped	breadcrumbs
50 g (2 oz) Gruyère,	a few slices of lemon
grated	salt and pepper

Wash the oysters carefully, then open them, strain off the liquor and remove the beards. Take them out of the shells and wash them again.

Melt the butter and add the parsley, dill, mustard and garlic, and stir well. Adjust the seasoning then leave the mixture to go cold. Fill the oyster shells with the herb butter and put the oysters on top. Sprinkle grated Gruyère and breadcrumbs on top.

Dot each oyster shell with a knob of butter and bake them in the oven at 200°C (400°F, Gas Mark 6) for 5 minutes. Garnish with lemon slices.

low heat for 10 minutes, stirring constantly. Season with salt, pepper and paprika and add the stock cube, dissolved in a glass of water. Rinse the tuna steaks in cold water, pat them dry and add them to the tomato sauce. Cover the pan and simmer over a low heat for 30 minutes.

Slice the mushrooms thinly, spread them over the fish and cook for a few minutes more. Serve the tuna with boiled potatoes or rice.

Bottom right: *Oysters au gratin*

PAN-FRIED FILLETS OF PIKE

Serves 4

4 fillets of pike
50 g (2 oz) fatty bacon
1 tbsp oil

lemon juice
fresh parsley, chopped
salt

Rinse the pike fillets in cold water, then pat them dry. Drizzle them with lemon juice and leave them to marinate for 30 minutes, then season them with salt.

Dice the bacon finely and fry it in the oil. Add the pike fillets and fry them on both sides until golden. Cook them for 10 minutes.

Serve on a warm serving dish garnished with chopped parsley.

Below: *Grilled dab*

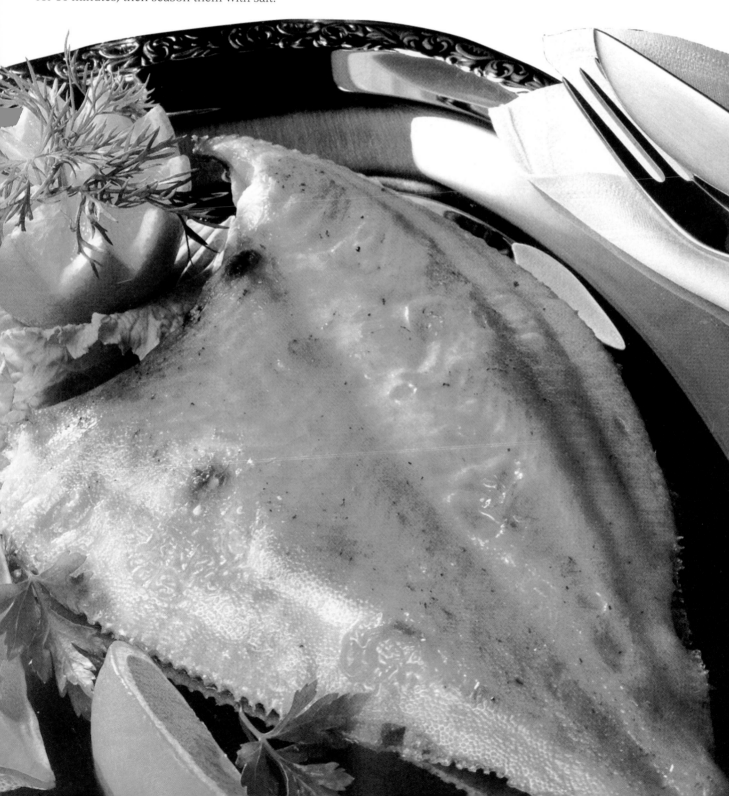

GRILLED DAB

Serves 4

4 dressed dab each weighing 300 g (10 oz)	juice of 1 lemon salt

Rinse the dab in cold water, pat them dry, drizzle them with lemon juice and leave them to marinate for 15 minutes.

Grill them for 4-6 minutes on each side, then season them with salt.

MACKEREL WITH CABBAGE

Serves 4-6

2 dressed mackerel, each weighing 1.2 kg (3 lb)	5 juniper berries
1 small white cabbage, weighing about 750 g (1½ lb)	1 bay leaf
	2 cooking apples
	vinegar
8-10 onions	lemon juice
50 g (2 oz) lard	salt and pepper

Cut the cabbage into 8 pieces, then slice them thinly. Peel and quarter the onions. Melt the lard in a frying pan, brown the onions in it, then continue cooking them on a low heat. Add the cabbage, juniper berries, bay leaf, 1 glass of water, and season with salt and pepper.

Below: Mackerel with cabbage

Cover the pan and steam the cabbage for 5 minutes. Peel, core and slice the apples. Add them to the cabbage, season with salt and pepper again and stew for 10 minutes. Season the cabbage to taste with vinegar and keep it hot. Rinse the mackerel in cold water, pat them dry, sprinkle them with lemon juice, leave them to marinate for 15 minutes, then season them with salt and pepper. Grill them for 7 minutes on each side. Serve the grilled mackerel on a bed of cabbage.

PAN-FRIED PERCH

Serves 4

2-3 dressed perch, weighing about 1½ kg (3½ lb)	2 egg yolks
	50 g (2 oz) butter
	breadcrumbs
juice of 1 lemon	salt
2-3 tbsp fresh, mixed herbs, chopped	pepper

Rinse the fish in cold water and pat them dry. Make a marinade using the lemon juice, salt, pepper and mixed herbs and marinate the perch in it for 2-3 hours. Take the perch out of the marinade and pat them dry. Strain the marinade and whisk a knob of melted butter and 2 egg yolks into it.

Dip the fish in the marinade and then coat them in breadcrumbs. Melt the butter and fry the perch in it for 20-25 minutes.

Serve on a warm serving dish with parsley potatoes and chicory salad.

TROUT WITH ALMONDS

Serves 4

4 small trout, dressed	flour
2 tbsp lemon juice	oil
1 egg, beaten	sprigs of fresh dill
50 g (2 oz) flaked almonds	salt
1 lemon, sliced	pepper

Rinse the trout in cold water, pat them dry, drizzle them with lemon juice and leave them to marinate for 15 minutes, then season them inside and out with salt and pepper. Toss the fish in the flour, then in the beaten egg and finally in the flaked almonds, pressing them in well so that they stick.

Heat the oil to 170°C (325-350°F) and deep-fry the trout, two at a time, until they are nice and golden brown (5-7 minutes). Put the trout on kitchen paper to drain,

garnish with slices of lemon and sprigs of dill and serve on a warm dish.
Serve with petit pois, herbed mashed potato and a green salad.

DEEP-FRIED FISH IN BATTER

Serves 4-5

750 g (1½ lb) fish fillets: haddock, cod or coley
100 g (3½ oz) flour
1 egg

125 ml (4 fl oz) milk
1 tbsp oil or melted butter
lemon juice or vinegar
oil for frying
salt

Rinse the fish fillets in cold water, pat them dry, drizzle them with lemon juice or vinegar and leave them to marinate for 30 minutes, then season them with salt and cut them into portions.

To make the batter: Put the flour in a large bowl and make a well in the centre. Beat the egg with the milk, season with salt, then gradually pour the egg and milk mixture into the flour, stirring all the time. Add the oil or melted butter and continue stirring until there are no lumps.

Dip the fish portions in the batter, then fry them in bubbling oil until crisp and well-browned (about 10 minutes). Drain them on kitchen paper. Serve with potato salad.

GREEN EEL WITH THYME

Serves 6

1 kg (2 lb) green eels, dressed
oil

sprigs of thyme
salt
pepper

Rinse the eels in cold water, pat them dry, cut them into chunks and season them with salt and pepper.

Put the sprigs of thyme on an oiled grill, then put the chunks of eel on top. Grill them for 15 minutes on each side. The eel can either be cooked on a barbecue or under a conventional grill.

Serve with a mixed salad and crusty bread.

Left: *Trout with almonds*
Right: *Deep-fried seafood*

DEEP-FRIED SEAFOOD

Serves 2

4 uncooked prawns
200 g (7 oz) ready-to-cook squid or cuttlefish
6-8 baby carrots
500 g (1 lb) fennel
8 sprigs of fresh parsley

250 g (8 oz) flour
250 ml (8 fl oz) beer
1 egg
lemon juice
oil for frying
salt and pepper

Wash and trim the carrots, cut the fennel into quarters, rinse the sprigs of parsley. Remove the heads and entrails from the prawns and wash them in cold water. Wash the squid in cold water and cut them into rings. Drizzle them with lemon juice and leave them to marinate for 15 minutes.

To make the batter: Sieve the flour into a large bowl, make a well in the centre and pour a little beer into the well. Add the egg and stir, working from the middle and gradually adding the remaining beer. Stir until all the lumps have disappeared, then season with salt and pepper.

Heat the oil to 180⁰ C (350⁰ F). Dip the vegetables, parsley and seafood in the batter, then put them in the hot oil. Fry the vegetables for 10-12 minutes and the seafood for 3-5 minutes. Drain the deep-fried vegetables and seafood on kitchen paper, season with salt, garnish with lemon slices and serve immediately.

MEDALLIONS OF VENISON WITH CHANTERELLE MUSHROOMS

Serves 4

4 slices of venison fillet, each weighing 150 g (5 oz) and about 2 cm (¾ inch) thick
400 g (13 oz) chanterelle mushrooms
3 knobs of butter

1 tbsp lard
125 ml (4 fl oz) meat stock
125 ml (4 fl oz) red wine
150 g (5 oz) crème fraîche
2 tbsp redcurrant jelly
salt
pepper

Cash the chanterelle mushrooms, drain them and cut the largest in half. Sweat them in the melted butter for about 15 minutes, season them with salt and pepper, reserve them and keep them warm. Melt the lard and seal the venison in it for 3 minutes on each side, season it with salt and pepper and keep it hot.

De-glaze the frying pan with the meat stock and red wine and boil the resulting gravy until reduced by half. Thicken the gravy with the crème fraîche and redcurrant jelly. Heat it through, then season it with salt and pepper. Arrange the venison medallions and mushrooms on a warm serving dish and pour the sauce over them. Serve with French beans with lardons.

MEDALLIONS OF VENISON WITH ARTICHOKES

Serves 4

4 medallions of venison
250 ml (8 fl oz) red wine
8 juniper berries
250 g (8 oz) onions
100 g (3½ oz) parsley butter

1 tin of artichoke hearts
4 vol-au-vent cases
4 tbsp crème fraîche
salt
pepper

Marinate the venison medallions in the red wine and juniper berries for 1 hour. Strain the marinade. Peel the onions and slice them thinly. Heat 40 g (1½ oz) parsley butter and sweat the onions in it, add half of the marinade and simmer it over a low heat for about 10 minutes.

Drain the artichoke hearts and add them to the onions. Leave them to braise for 3 minutes, then take the mixture out of the pan and keep it warm. Reheat the vol-au-vent cases in the oven and keep them warm. Melt the remaining parsley butter in a frying pan and brown the venison medallions in it for 3-4 minutes on each side. Arrange the meat on a warm serving dish and keep it hot. De-glaze the pan with the remaining marinade, thicken

Below: *Medallions of venison with chanterelle mushrooms*

the resulting gravy with the crème fraîche and season it with salt and pepper. Fill the vol-au-vent cases with the artichoke mixture and arrange them on the serving dish. Serve the gravy separately.
Serve the venison with boiled potatoes or spétzle.

Above: *Medallions of venison with artichokes*

MEDALLIONS OF VENISON WITH MORELLO CHERRIES

Serves 4

4 slices of haunch of
venison, each weighing
150 g (5 oz) and 2 cm
(¾ inch) thick
50 g (2 oz) bacon
2 onions
1 tbsp flour
250 ml (8 fl oz) soured
cream or crème fraîche

2 tbsp lard
4 slices bread
6 juniper berries, crushed
200 g (7 oz) tinned
Morello cherries, pitted
1 tbsp redcurrant jelly
8 orange segments
butter
salt

Cut the bacon into small dice. Peel the onions and slice them thinly. Fry the bacon in a small saucepan to render the fat, then fry the onions in the bacon fat. Add the flour and cream and stir well. Bring the sauce to the boil and simmer it for about 10 minutes, then season it with salt. Shape the slices of venison into medallions and fry them in the lard for 4 minutes on each side, basting them frequently with the meat juices. Season the venison with salt and keep it warm.

Fry the slices of bread in the melted butter until crisp and golden, then arrange them on a warm serving dish. Arrange the medallions on top of the fried bread and divide the crushed juniper berries amongst the venison medallions. De-glaze the pan juices with water, add the previously made sauce and reheat gently without boiling, then pour the finished sauce over the venison. Combine a few cherries with the redcurrant jelly and garnish the venison medallions with them. Arrange the remaining cherries on slices of orange.

Below: *Medallions of venison with Morello cherries*

HUNGARIAN VENISON STEW

Serves 4

400 g (13 oz) saddle or fillet of venison	cooked
1 red pepper	1 sweet and sour pickled gherkin
1 green pepper	1 heaped tsp cornflour
2 onions	4 tbsp soured cream or crème fraîche
50 g (2 oz) butter or margarine	1 tbsp fresh parsley, chopped
sweet paprika	salt
250 ml (8 fl oz) meat stock	pepper
250 g (8 oz) beetroot,	

Cut the peppers in half, remove the cores and seeds, then cut them into thin strips. Peel the onions and slice them thinly. Slice the venison thinly. Melt the butter in a frying pan and fry the sliced venison in it for 6 minutes, stirring so that the meat is sealed all over, then take it out of the pan and keep it warm. Fry the onions in the meat juices until golden, then add the peppers, sweat them for a few minutes, season them with salt and pepper and sprinkle with paprika. Add the meat stock and braise the vegetables for 30 minutes.

Cut the beetroot and gherkin into thin strips. Add them to the vegetables with the venison. Bring the stew to the boil and simmer for 5-10 minutes. Blend together the cornflour and cream and use it to thicken the stew. Garnish with chopped parsley.

Serve with parsleyed potatoes or gnocchi.

MEDALLIONS OF VENISON WITH PINEAPPLE AND BÊARNAISE SAUCE

Serves 4

600 g (1¼ lb) fillet of venison, boned	2 egg yolks
100 g (3½ oz) butter	4 slices of tinned pineapple
1 shallot	3 tbsp oil
1 tsp wine vinegar	sugar
2 tbsp white wine	mustard
fresh tarragon, chopped	salt
fresh basil, chopped	pepper
black peppercorns, crushed	a few basil leaves

Peel the shallot and slice it thinly. Put the wine vinegar and white wine into a saucepan, add the shallot, tarragon and basil. Season with the black pepper and bring to the boil, simmer for 5 minutes, then allow to go cold. Heat this base for béarnaise sauce in a bain-marie or double saucepan and add the egg yolks, whisking constantly, until a smooth, creamy sauce forms, then add 80 g (3 oz) butter, whisking all the time. Season with salt, pepper and a little sugar. Keep the sauce hot in the bain-marie.

Drain the pineapple. Cut the fillet of venison into medallions 3 cm (1¼ inches) thick. Spread a little mustard on both sides. Heat the oil in a frying pan and fry the medallions for 6 minutes on each side, season with salt and pepper, then keep them hot. Melt the remaining butter and sauté the slices of pineapple.

Arrange the pineapple slices on a warm serving dish, then lay the venison on top of the pineapple, pour the béarnaise sauce over and garnish with basil leaves.

Below: *Hungarian venison stew*

MEDALLIONS OF VENISON WITH BLACKBERRIES

Serves 4

8 medallions of venison, each weighing 70 g (3 oz)	8 slices of bacon
250 g (8 oz) blackberries	chilli powder
100 ml (3½ fl oz) red wine, Burgundy if possible	brandy
1 tbsp sugar	angostura bitters
½ tsp mustard	lard
grated zest of ¼ of an unwaxed orange	salt
	pepper

Pick over the blackberries, wash them and cook them for a few minutes in a little water, then purée them through a sieve or chinois to obtain a coulis. Thin down the coulis with the wine, add a little sugar, the mustard, orange zest and chilli. Mix thoroughly and heat through but do not allow to boil. Flavour the sauce to taste with the brandy and angostura bitters.

Wrap a slice of bacon around each medallion, secure it with kitchen string, then season with salt and pepper. Melt the lard in a frying pan and fry the medallions for 2 minutes on each side. Take off the string. Pour some of the sauce over the medallions, then serve the rest separately.

Right: *Haunch of venison with almonds*
Below: *Haunch of venison with button mushrooms*

VENISON STEW WITH OYSTER MUSHROOMS

Serves 4

500 g (1 lb) haunch of venison	1 tbsp flour
3-4 tbsp lard	500 ml (18 fl oz) meat stock
1 onion	300 g (10 oz) oyster mushrooms
1 tsp fresh thyme, chopped	1 tbsp flour or cornflour
1 tsp fresh marjoram, chopped	2-3 tbsp red wine
	salt and pepper

Cut the meat into large cubes. Melt the lard in a casserole dish and seal the meat on all sides, then season with salt and pepper. Peel and slice the onion thinly, then fry it with the meat. Add the thyme and marjoram. Sprinkle the meat with flour, and cook until it turns golden, stirring all the time. Add the meat stock and stir well. Put the lid on the casserole dish and simmer for an hour. Wipe the oyster mushrooms and blanch them in boiling, salted water. Refresh them, drain them and add them to the meat. Simmer for a further 25 minutes. Blend the flour and red wine together, add it to the gravy to thicken it, then adjust the seasoning.

Serve with gnocchi or spètzle.

HAUNCH OF VENISON WITH BUTTON MUSHROOMS

Serves 4

4 slices of haunch of venison, each weighing 150 g (5 oz)	40 g (1½ oz) butter or margarine
250 g (8 oz) button mushrooms	fresh parsley, chopped
	olive oil
	salt and pepper

Wipe the mushrooms and slice them. Melt the butter and sweat the mushrooms in it. Season them with salt and pepper, then add the parsley and keep them warm.

Brush the venison with olive oil. Cook under a preheated grill for 3-6 minutes on each side, then season with salt and pepper. Garnish with the mushrooms.

Serve with sautéed potatoes.

HAUNCH OF VENISON WITH ALMONDS

Serves 4

4 slices of haunch of
venison, each weighing
150 g (5 oz)
grated nutmeg
2 tbsp flour

1 egg, beaten
80 g (3 oz) flaked almonds
50 g (2 oz) butter
salt

Sprinkle the slices of venison with salt and nutmeg.
Dip them alternately in the beaten egg, flour and flaked
almonds, crushing the almonds down onto the meat.
Melt the butter and fry the meat in it for 3-6 minutes on
each side (take care that the almonds don't burn).
Arrange the venison on a warm serving dish.
De-glaze the pan juices with a little water, and pour the
juices over the meat.

Serve with potato croquettes, slices of pineapple and
cranberries.

Above: *Haunch of venison with cream*

HAUNCH OF VENISON WITH CREAM

Serves 4

4 slices of haunch of venison, each weighing 125 g (4 oz)	40 g (1½ oz) lard 75 g (3 oz) almonds,	skinned and toasted 150 g (5 oz) crème fraîche grated nutmeg	salt pepper

reduces. Season with salt and pepper and pour the sauce over the venison.

Serve with potato croquettes, slices of pineapple and cranberry jelly.

MEDALLIONS OF WILD BOAR WITH CRANBERRIES

Serves 4

8 medallions of wild boar	fresh thyme, chopped
3 onions	fresh marjoram, chopped
250 ml (8 fl oz) red wine	fresh rosemary, chopped
300 g (10 oz) crème fraîche	fresh sage, chopped
	lard
4 tbsp cranberry jelly	salt
cranberries	pepper

Roll the medallions of wild boar in a mixture of cranberries, thyme, marjoram, rosemary and sage. Melt the lard and brown the medallions for 4 minutes on each side, arrange them on a warm serving dish and keep them warm.

To make the sauce: Peel the onions, slice them and sauté them in the meat juices. Add the wine, bring to the boil, season with salt and pepper, then add the cream and cranberry jelly. Pour some of the sauce over the medallions and serve the rest separately.

Serve with orange segments and potato croquettes.

Below: *Medallions of wild boar with cranberries*

Sprinkle the slices of venison with salt and nutmeg. Melt the lard in a frying pan and brown the slices of venison in it for 2-4 minutes on each side. Arrange them on a warm serving dish and garnish with the almonds. Keep them warm.

De-glaze the pan juices with the crème fraîche, bring the sauce to the boil and continue simmering until the sauce

WILD BOAR CHOPS, ITALIAN STYLE

Serves 4

4 wild boar chops,
weighing about 600 g
(1¼ lb)
fresh rosemary, chopped
8 juniper berries, crushed
2 tbsp olive oil
2 onions

250 g (8 oz) courgettes
2 plum tomatoes
1 tbsp fresh basil, chopped
pinch of dried oregano
1 tbsp wine vinegar
salt and pepper

Season the chops with salt and sprinkle them with pepper, rosemary and the crushed juniper berries. Heat the olive oil in a frying pan. Brown the chops for 5 minutes on each side (they should still be pink in the middle), then leave them to cool. Peel the onions, slice them and sweat them in the meat juices. Wash and slice the courgettes. Add them to the pan with the onions. Blanch the tomatoes, refresh them in cold water, skin, de-seed and dice them. Stir the diced tomatoes into the courgette and onion mixture, seal them quickly over a high heat for a few minutes (the vegetables should still be quite crisp).

Add the basil, oregano and vinegar, season with salt and pepper, then cook for a further 7 minutes. Arrange the chops on a serving dish on a bed of vegetables, garnish with tomatoes and fresh, mixed herbs. Serve with garlic bread.

ash the orange and pare off the zest, avoiding any of the white pith. Cut the zest into very thin strips. Simmer it with the red wine for 10 minutes, then leave it to cool. Whisk together the redcurrant jelly, orange zest and mustard, thin the sauce down with a little wine if necessary. Season the Cumberland sauce with salt and lemon juice.

Cut the venison, bacon and gherkin into 2 cm (¾ inch) dice and thread them alternately onto skewers. Heat the oil in a frying pan and fry the kebabs on all sides for 10 minutes, then season them with salt and pepper.

Arrange the kebabs on a serving dish and serve the Cumberland sauce separately.

Serve with mashed potato or potato croquettes and a mixed salad.

Left: *Italian-style wild boar chops*
Below: *Forester's kebabs with Cumberland sauce*

FORESTER'S KEBABS WITH CUMBERLAND SAUCE

Serves 4

500 g (1 lb) saddle of
venison, boned
1 unwaxed orange
3 tbsp red wine
250 g (8 oz) redcurrant jelly
2 tsp mustard
lemon juice

100 g (3½ oz) streaky
bacon
1 sweet and sour pickled
gherkin
4 tbsp olive oil
salt
freshly ground pepper

BRAISED THIGH OF WILD RABBIT

Serves 4

4 rabbit thighs, each
weighing 200 g (7 oz)
500 ml (18 fl oz) red wine
2 bay leaves
2 cloves of garlic, crushed
½ tsp dried thyme
1 clove
1 large onion
½ tsp dried marjoram

100 g (3½ oz) smoked
bacon
1 shallot
a little flour
1 tsp tomato purèe
1-2 tbsp orange flavoured
liqueur e.g. Cointreau,
Grand Marnier
salt and black pepper

Pour the wine into a large bowl and add the bay leaves, garlic, thyme and clove. Peel and thinly slice the onion and add it to the marinade. Remove the skin and layer of fat from the rabbit thighs. Leave them to marinate for 6-8 hours in the marinade, turning them occasionally. Take the meat out of the marinade, drain it, season it with salt and pepper and sprinkle it with marjoram. Cut the bacon into small dice and render them in a casserole dish. Add the rabbit thighs and seal them all over. Peel and dice the shallot. Peel and thinly slice the vegetables. Add the shallot and vegetables to the meat. Sprinkle flour over the meat and vegetables.

Strain the marinade and add some of it to the casserole with the meat and vegetables. Cover and braise for 1 hour. Turn the rabbit thighs from time to time and top up the marinade frequently.

Arrange the rabbit thighs on a warm serving dish. Pass the gravy through a sieve or chinois, add the tomato purée, stir well, and bring to the boil. Flavour with the orange liqueur. Pour the gravy over the meat. Serve with potato croquettes.

Above right: *Hare thighs*
Below: *Braised thigh of wild rabbit*

HOT GAME PIES

Serves 4

200 g (7 oz) game (hare, venison)
60 g (2½ oz) bacon
1 onion
2 tbsp fresh parsley, chopped
a little fresh thyme, chopped
2 tbsp cream
1 tbsp port
300 g (10 oz) frozen flaky pastry
1 egg, separated
butter
salt and pepper

Mince the meat and bacon. Peel and slice the onion thinly, and add it to the meat with the chopped parsley, thyme, cream and port. Combine well to make a stuffing mix and adjust the seasoning.

Defrost the pastry at room temperature. Roll it out until big enough to form 12 squares 10 x 10 cm (4 x 4 inches). Divide the meat mixture amongst 6 of the squares.

Whisk the egg white and spread it over the other 6 pastry squares. Put these squares, moistened side down, on top of those covered with stuffing and secure them with cocktail sticks. Beat the egg yolk and brush the pastry cases with it. Butter a baking sheet, transfer the pies to it and bake them in the oven at 200-225° C (400-425° F, Gas Mark 6-7) for 15 minutes.

Serve with Cumberland sauce (see page 287) or cranberry jelly.

HARE THIGHS

Serves 4

4 hare thighs, weighing 1½ kg (3½ lb)
10 juniper berries, crushed
50 g (2 oz) lard
3 medium onions
1 bay leaf
6 small chillies
500 ml (18 fl oz) red wine
flour or cornflour
salt and pepper

Take the skin off the hare thighs, sprinkle them with salt, pepper and juniper berries. Melt the lard in a casserole dish and brown the meat on all sides. Peel and thinly slice the onions and add them to the casserole dish with the bay leaf and chillies. Add the red wine, cover and braise for 1½ hours. Turn the meat from time to time and add water as necessary to prevent the thighs sticking to the bottom of the dish.

Arrange the thighs on a warm serving dish. Strain the gravy through a sieve or chinois and thicken it with a little flour or cornflour, reheat gently, then season it with

salt and pepper. Pour the gravy over the thighs. Serve with red cabbage and potato gnocchi.

HARE STEW WITH CHANTERELLE MUSHROOMS

Serves 4

2 feet and 2 thighs from a young hare
50 g (2 oz) lard
1 onion
2 cloves of garlic
8 black peppercorns
1 tsp dried thyme
1 bay leaf
1 tbsp flour
250 ml (8 fl oz) red wine
250 ml (8 fl oz) meat stock
300 g (10 oz) chanterelle mushrooms
salt

Cut the meat into pieces. Melt the lard in a cast-iron casserole dish and brown the pieces of meat in it.

Peel and finely dice the onion and brown it with the meat. Peel the garlic and crush it in a mortar with peppercorns, thyme and bay leaf. Sprinkle the seasonings over the meat and season it with salt. Sprinkle flour over the hare, stir it well to ensure it is sealed on all sides, then add the wine and stock. Cover and simmer for 1-1½ hours.

Wipe the mushrooms, slice them and add them to the stew 15 minutes before the end of cooking time, then adjust the seasoning.

Serve the hare stew with spétzle.

GAME GOULASH WITH MUSHROOMS

Serves 4

500 g (1 lb) game (venison, wild boar)

1 sachet freeze- dried ceps

1 tbsp oil

60 g (2½ oz) streaky bacon

2 onions

1 clove of garlic

½ tsp dried thyme

250 ml (8 fl oz) meat stock

250 ml (8 fl oz) mild beer

1 bunch of fresh parsley

1 bay leaf

250 g (8 oz) button mushrooms

250 g (8 oz) tomatoes

2 tbsp crème fraîche

salt

pepper

Reconstitute the ceps in water. Dice the game and bacon. Heat the oil in a casserole dish, fry the diced bacon and seal the meat on all sides.

Peel the onions and garlic, slice them thinly and fry them with the game. Season them with salt and pepper, sprinkle with thyme and add the stock and mild beer. Rinse the ceps, add them to the stew with the parsley and bay leaf and simmer for 1½ hours.

Wipe the button mushrooms, slice them thinly and add them to the goulash 15 minutes before the end of cooking time. Blanch the tomatoes, refresh them in cold water and skin them. De-seed them and cut them into quarters and add them to the goulash 5 minutes before the end of cooking. Take out the parsley and bay leaf. Stir the crème fraîche into the gravy, bring it to the boil and season it with salt and pepper.

Serve with dumplings or potatoes and a green salad.

VENISON STEW WITH CHANTERELLE MUSHROOMS

Serves 4

600 g (1¼ lb) haunch of venison, boned	500 ml (18 fl oz) boiling water
150 g (5 oz) streaky bacon	300 g (10 oz) chanterelle mushrooms
2 knobs of lard	3 level tbsp flour or cornflour
4 medium onions	4 tbsp red wine
10 juniper berries	redcurrant jelly
5 chillies	salt and freshly ground pepper
1 clove	
1 bay leaf	
1 tbsp fresh thyme, chopped	

Dice the meat and chop the bacon into pieces. Melt the lard in a casserole dish and fry the meat and bacon until brown all over.

Peel the onions, slice them thinly and fry them with the meat. Season the venison with salt and pepper, add the juniper berries, chillies, clove, bay leaf and thyme, then the hot water. Cover and simmer for 2 hours. Add more water occasionally to prevent the meat sticking to the dish. Rinse the mushrooms, drain them and add them to the stew 15 minutes before the end of cooking time. Blend together the flour and red wine, add it to the stew to thicken it, season it with salt and pepper and add the redcurrant jelly to taste.

Serve with potato croquettes and Brussels sprouts.

VENISON GOULASH

Serves 4-6

500-700 g (1-1½ lb) venison	50 g (2 oz) pumpernickel or other dark bread
50 g (2 oz) bacon	1 tsp cornflour
2 onions	1-2 tbsp redcurrant jelly
2 tbsp olive oil	salt
1 bay leaf	pepper
3 cloves	paprika
5 juniper berries, crushed	
250 ml (8 fl oz) meat stock	
250 ml (8 fl oz) red wine	

Cut the meat into chunks. Soak the meat in cold water for 3 hours, or until the meat turns paler in colour (change the water occasionally). Drain the meat and pat it dry.

Dice the bacon, then peel the onions and slice them thinly. Heat the oil in a casserole dish and fry the venison, bacon and onions in it, then add the bay leaf, cloves, juniper berries, stock and half the wine, stirring all the time. Simmer the goulash for 1-1½ hours. Crumble the bread into the remaining wine, wait until it swells, then stir it into the goulash. Blend the cornflour with a little water, thicken the goulash and add the redcurrant jelly, stirring all the time. Season the dish to taste with salt, pepper and paprika.

Serve with dumplings or buttered pasta or potatoes.

Left: *Game goulash with mushrooms*
Below: *Venison stew with chanterelle mushrooms*

SADDLE OF VENISON

Serves 6

1½ kg (3½ lb) saddle of venison
40 g (1½ oz) butter
100 g (3½ oz) bacon, sliced

125 ml (4 fl oz) soured cream or crème fraîche
cornflour
salt
pepper

Rub the venison with salt and brush it with melted butter. Arrange half the slices of bacon over the base of a roasting tin, put the venison on top, then cover it with the remaining bacon. Roast the venison in the oven at 225⁰C (425 ⁰, Gas Mark 7) for 1-1½ hours. As soon as the meat juices start to caramelize, add a little hot water and baste the meat frequently to prevent it drying out.

Ten minutes before the end of cooking time, pour the cream over the meat, take the meat off the bone, slice it, arrange the slices on a warm serving dish, then keep it warm. De-glaze the pan juices with water, bring them to the boil and thicken the resulting gravy with a little cornflour, then adjust the seasoning.

Serve with pears and cranberry jelly and red cabbage.

SADDLE OF VENISON WITH MANDARIN ORANGES

Serves 6

1½ kg (3½ lb) saddle of venison
40 g (1½ oz) butter
100 g (3½ oz) bacon
2 juniper berries, crushed
1 onion
6 pears
250 ml (8 fl oz) white wine
2 tbsp sugar
1 sachet powdered gelatine or 2 leaves of gelatine
3 tbsp white wine
200 g (7 oz) mandarin

segments
1 heaped tsp cornflour
250 ml (8 fl oz) mandarin or orange juice
2-3 tbsp cranberry sauce
zest of 1 unwaxed orange, grated
cinnamon
mustard
lemon juice
fresh parsley, chopped
salt
pepper

Below: *Saddle of venison*

Above: *Saddle of venison with mandarin oranges*

Rub the saddle of venison with the salt and brush it with melted butter. Slice the bacon and spread half of the slices over the base of a roasting tin, put the saddle of venison on top and cover it with the remaining bacon. Roast in the oven for 35-50 minutes. As soon as the meat juices start to caramelize, add the juniper berries and peeled, sliced onion, then add a little hot water. Baste the meat frequently with the juices to prevent it drying out.

Take the meat off the bone, leave it to cool, cut it up, then return it to the oven. Peel and core the pears. Heat the wine and sugar, add cinnamon to taste and poach the pears in the syrup for 5 minutes (they should still be firm). Leave them to cool in the syrup.

Blend the gelatine into 3 tbsp white wine and leave it to soak for 10 minutes. Then heat the gelatine, stirring all the time, until it has dissolved completely. Drain the pears, stir the syrup into the gelatine and refrigerate. Put the saddle of venison on a rack, garnish it with mandarin segments. As soon as the gelatine solution thickens, spread some of it over the pears, then baste the saddle of venison with the rest. Put the venison in the refrigerator.

To make the mandarin sauce: Slake the cornflour with the mandarin or orange juice, bring it to the boil and leave it to cool. Purée the cranberries through a sieve and add them to the orange sauce with the grated orange zest. Season the sauce with salt, pepper, mustard and lemon juice to taste.

Arrange the saddle of venison on a large platter and garnish it with sprigs of parsley. Stuff the pears with the cranberries and arrange them around the venison. Garnish them with parsley and serve the mandarin sauce separately.

Accompany the saddle of venison with a salad of lamb's lettuce.

SADDLE OF VENISON WITH PRUNES IN ARMAGNAC

Serves 6

1 kg (2 lb) saddle of
venison
50 g (2 oz) blanched
almonds
500 g (1 lb) prunes, pitted
125 ml (4 fl oz) Armagnac
2 sprigs of fresh thyme
100 g (3½ oz) piece of
bacon, thinly sliced

2 spring onions
250 g (8 oz) game bones
½ bottle red wine
250 ml (8 fl oz) water
400 g (13 oz) shallots
15 g (½ oz) diced bacon
2 slices of bacon
salt and pepper

*T*oast the almonds for a few minutes in a dry frying pan. Soak the prunes in water, bring them to the boil, drain them, then put them in a large bowl with the Armagnac and leave them to soak.

Remove the small fillets from the back of the saddle of venison and reserve them. Rub the saddle of venison with salt and pepper. Wash the thyme, pat it dry and put it on top of the meat, pressing it down gently. Cover the venison with the sliced piece of bacon.

Put the meat in a roasting tin. Peel the onions, chop them roughly and scatter them around the venison with the bones. Add the red wine to the tin and roast in a hot oven at 225⁰C (425⁰F, Gas Mark 7) for 30-35 minutes. As soon as the meat juices start to caramelize, add some water to the roasting tin. Baste the meat frequently. Peel the shallots and cut them into quarters. Fry the diced bacon to render the fat, then add the shallots. As soon as the venison is cooked, take it out of the oven and wrap it in foil to keep it hot. Bring the gravy to the boil, strain it through a chinois or sieve, add the prunes and Armagnac and season with salt and pepper.

Fry the 2 slices of bacon to render the fat, season the reserved venison fillets with salt and pepper and fry them with the bacon for 5 minutes.

Take the meat off the bone, slice it, then arrange it on a warm serving dish and garnish with the prunes, almonds and onions.

Serve the gravy separately and accompany the venison with pilau rice.

HAUNCH OF VENISON SAINT HUBERT

Serves 2-3

500 g (1 lb) haunch of
venison
2 onions
1 knob of lard
100 ml (3½ fl oz) red wine
2 tbsp cranberry jelly
150 g (5 oz) crème fraîche
juniper berries, crushed

fresh thyme
fresh marjoram
fresh rosemary
fresh sage
salt
pepper

*R*ub the haunch of venison with the salt, juniper berries and herbs. Peel and dice the onions. Melt the lard in an oven-proof casserole dish and brown the haunch of venison on all sides, then add the onions. Cover the casserole dish and braise the venison for 30 minutes.

Take the cooked meat out of the casserole dish and keep it hot. De-glaze the juices with the red wine, strain them, add the cranberry jelly and crème fraîche and bring the sauce to the boil. Season it to taste with salt and pepper.

Slice the meat and serve the sauce separately. Serve with potato croquettes and braised fennel.

Right: *Haunch of venison Saint Hubert*
Left: *Saddle of venison with prunes in Armagnac*

SADDLE OF WILD BOAR

Serves 8

2 kg (4½ lb) saddle of wild boar, with the fillet
1 tub of low fat natural yoghurt
1 bunch of fresh parsley
100 g (3½ oz) celery
10 juniper berries, crushed
10 peppercorns, crushed
½ bottle red wine
500 ml (18 fl oz) water
250 ml (8 fl oz) cream
50 g (2 oz) lard
sherry vinegar
salt and pepper

Remove from the saddle the two small fillets located above the chops and those along the spinal column. Reserve the fat. Brush the meat with low fat yoghurt and leave to macerate for 24 hours. Chop the bones and brown them in a roasting tin with the fat from the boar. Wash the parsley and celery, chop them roughly and add them to the bones, then put the roasting tin in a hot oven for 30 minutes.

Transfer the bones and vegetables to a casserole dish, add the pepper, juniper berries, wine and water, bring to the boil and simmer for 30 minutes. Strain the gravy through a chinois or sieve and skim off the fat. Add the cream and continue cooking until the gravy thickens and reduces, then season it to taste with salt, pepper and sherry vinegar.

Melt the lard, wipe the yoghurt off the fillets, dry them, sprinkle them with salt and firstly fry the fillets in the lard for 10 minutes, then take them out of the pan and wrap them in foil. Seal the small fillets in the lard for 3-4 minutes, wrap them in foil and keep them warm. Leave them to rest for 10 minutes so that the juices are released. Slice the meat into 1 cm (½ inch) thick slices and arrange them on a warm serving dish with the fillet.

Serve the gravy separately and accompany the wild boar with caramelized shallots, cabbage and potato dumplings.

WILD BOAR WITH SAUERKRAUT

Serves 6

1.2 kg (3 lb) shoulder of wild boar, boned
1 tbsp butter
½ tsp salt
½ tsp pepper
2 juniper berries, crushed
1 knob of lard
750 g (1½ lb) sauerkraut or pickled cabbage
1 cooking apple
1 bay leaf
250 ml (8 fl oz) white wine
4 slices streaky bacon, each weighing 150 g (5 oz)
4 Toulouse or other meaty sausages

Melt the butter in a roasting tin, seal the meat all over, add ½ teaspoon of salt, ½ teaspoon of pepper and the juniper berries. Melt the lard in a casserole dish or saucepan, add the sauerkraut and leave it to cook for a few minutes.

Peel the apple, grate it and add it to the sauerkraut with the bay leaf. Then add the white wine, cover and braise for about 1¼ hours. After 1 hour, fry the bacon and sausages in a frying pan and put them on top of the sauerkraut, then continue cooking.

Take the meat out of the pan, slice it and keep the slices warm. Adjust the seasoning in the sauerkraut, arrange it on a serving dish and arrange the meat on top.

Serve with potatoes.

Left: *Saddle of wild boar*
Right: *Wild boar with sauerkraut*

SADDLE OF HARE WITH MORELLO CHERRIES

Serves 4-5

1 saddle of hare weighing 700 g (1½ lb)	125 ml (4 fl oz) red wine
500 g (1 lb) Morello cherries, tinned	2 tsp cornflour
	fresh parsley
	salt and pepper

Drain the cherries, reserving the syrup or juice and pour one eighth of it into a warmed chicken brick or earthenware casserole dish. Add most of the cherries and all the wine and season with salt.

Season the saddle of hare with salt and pepper and put it in amongst the cherries. Cover and braise in a hot oven at 200-225°C (400-425°F, Gas Mark 6-7) for 1 hour. Garnish the hare with the remaining cherries and parsley. Make up the sauce with water, bring it to the boil and thicken it with cornflour. Pour the cherry sauce over the hare.

YOUNG PARTRIDGE WITH LENTILS

Serves 4

4 oven-ready baby partridge, each weighing 250 g (8 oz)	margarine
	2 litres of meat stock
300 g (10 oz) lentils	2 cloves
2 carrots	100 g (3½ oz) bacon
2 leeks	250 ml (8 fl oz) soured cream or crème fraîche
3 onions	port
¼ celeriac	salt
50 g (2 oz) butter or	pepper

Wash the lentils, soak them for 12-24 hours in cold water, then drain them. Wash or peel the carrots, leeks, celeriac and 2 onions and cut them into very thin strips, to make a julienne. Melt the butter in a casserole dish and sweat the vegetables in it, add the lentils and meat stock, then bring to the boil. Season the partridge inside and out with salt.

Peel the remaining onion, spike it with the cloves and add it to the stock with the partridge, then bring to the boil. Cover and simmer for 1 hour.

Take the cooked partridge out of the casserole, take the meat off the bone and dice it. Dice the bacon and fry it in a frying pan with the pieces of partridge meat. Stir the

meat and bacon into the lentils, add the cream, bring to the boil quickly, adjust the seasoning and finish with a drop of port.

RABBIT WITH TARRAGON

Serves 6-8

1 oven-ready rabbit, weighing 2.5 kg (5½ lb)	water
	8-10 slices streaky bacon
1 bunch of fresh tarragon	1 tsp sugar
100 g (3½ oz) mustard	150 g (5 oz) crème fraîche
50 g (2 oz) butter	fresh savory
200 ml (7 fl oz) white wine	Worcester sauce
200 ml (7 fl oz) meat stock	salt
500 g (1 lb) French beans	pepper
125 ml (4 fl oz) boiling	

Joint the rabbit and cut the saddle into 3 pieces. Wash the tarragon, chop it finely and blend it into the mustard. Heat the butter in a casserole dish and fry the meat in it. Add the white wine and stock, then simmer for about 1¼ hours.

Top and tail the French beans, put them in boiling, salted water with the savory and blanch them for 3 minutes. Drain them and season them with salt and pepper.

Make little bundles of 8-10 beans, wrap a slice of bacon around each until the bacon is used up, then put them around the rabbit about 30 minutes before the end of cooking time. Arrange the rabbit and beans on a warm serving dish and keep them hot.

Strain the gravy through a chinois or sieve and let it reduce by half, then add the tarragon mustard, sugar and crème fraîche. Season to taste with Worcester sauce. Pour some of the gravy over the rabbit, serve the rest separately and accompany the rabbit with potato croquettes.

Left: *Saddle of hare with Morello cherries*
Below: *Rabbit with tarragon*

SADDLE OF HARE À LA CRÈME

Serves 4

1 saddle of hare weighing	1 tbsp cornflour
600 g (1¼ lb)	grated nutmeg
1-2 knobs of butter	sugar
75 g (3 oz) streaky bacon	lemon juice
2 juniper berries, crushed	white wine
2 onions	salt
250 ml (8 fl oz) crème	pepper
fraâche or soured cream	

*T*ake the fillets off the hare, season with salt and pepper, sprinkle with nutmeg and brush with melted butter. Spread the slices of bacon over the base of a roasting tin, put the hare on top and cover it with the remaining bacon. Leave to roast for half an hour.

As soon as the meat juices start to caramelize, add the juniper berries and the peeled onions, cut into quarters. Add hot water and top up regularly so that the stock does not dry up. Add the hare fillets 5 minutes before the end of cooking time. Arrange the meat on a warm serving dish.

To make the sauce: Pour the meat juices into a saucepan and add the cream. Bring the gravy to the boil, thicken it with cornflour, and season to taste with salt, nutmeg, sugar, lemon juice and white wine.
Serve with cranberry jelly, potato gnocchi or mashed potato.

ROAST HARE

Serves 6

1 oven-ready hare,	5 chillies
weighing 2 kg (4½ lb)	150 g (5 oz) soured crèam
50 g (2 oz) butter, melted	or crème fraîche
125 g (4 oz) bacon, sliced	5 tbsp unsweetened
1 medium onion	condensed milk
1 medium carrot	fresh rosemary, chopped
1 bay leaf	cornflour
10 juniper berries,	salt
crushed	pepper

*C*ut the hare into joints, season with salt and pepper, sprinkle with rosemary and brush with melted butter. Arrange half the slices of bacon in the bottom of a roasting tin, put the hare joints on top and cover them with the remaining bacon (reserving some for the saddle).

Peel the onion and carrot, cut them into small dice and add them to the meat with the bay leaf, juniper berries and chillies. Put the roasting tin in a hot oven, but don't add the saddle for the first 15 minutes. As soon as the meat juices start to caramelize, add hot water to the roasting tin, then baste the meat frequently. Cook for 1-1½ hours at 200-225°C (400-425°F, Gas Mark 6-7). Combine the cream and condensed milk and baste the hare with it 10 minutes before the end of cooking time.

Arrange the meat on a warm serving dish and keep it warm. De-glaze the roasting tin with water, strain the gravy through a chinois or sieve and thicken it with cornflour. Adjust the seasoning.

Left: *Saddle of hare á la cräme*

Above: *Roast hare*

PHEASANT

Serves 6

1 oven-ready pheasant,
with giblets, weighing 1
kg (2 lb)
50 g (2 oz) thinly sliced
bacon
250 ml (8 fl oz) soured

cream or crème fraîche
30 g (1 oz) butter
flour
lemon juice
salt and pepper

Season the pheasant inside and out with salt. Rinse the giblets, chop them finely and season them with salt. Stuff the pheasant with this mixture, then sew up the cavity with kitchen thread. Wrap the slices of bacon around the pheasant. Melt 2 knobs of butter and brown the pheasant all over. Put the pheasant in a roasting tin and cook it in the oven at 225-250⁰ C (425-475⁰ F, Gas Mark 7-9) for 45-60 minutes.

As soon as the meat juices start to caramelize, add hot water to the roasting tin and baste the pheasant frequently with the liquid so that the meat doesn't dry out. Add the cream 10 minutes before the end of cooking time. Take the pheasant out of the oven and put it on a warm serving dish, remove the kitchen thread and take out the stuffing. Keep the bird hot.

De-glaze the meat juices with water, and bring the resulting gravy to the boil. Thicken the sauce with equal quantities of butter and flour kneaded together, then season with salt and lemon juice.

PHEASANT IN ASPIC

Serves 4

1 oven-ready pheasant, weighing 1 kg (2 lb)
2 bananas
1 tbsp lemon juice
1 tbsp shredded coconut
40 g (1½ oz) bacon, thinly sliced

30 g (1 oz) lard
1 onion
1 carrot
1 clove
3 chillies
3 peppercorns
250 ml (8 fl oz) meat stock

4 tbsp pineapple juice
2 tbsp powdered gelatine or 2 leaves of gelatine
3 tbsp Madeira
pineapple chunks in syrup, tinned

ground ginger
toasted almonds
slices of orange
cherries
salt
pepper

Drain the pineapple, peel one banana and finely dice both it and the pineapple. Add the lemon juice, coconut and ginger. Stuff the pheasant with this mixture. Sew up the cavity with kitchen thread. Sprinkle the pheasant with ginger and season it with salt and pepper. Cover the pheasant with the slices of bacon, then truss it tightly with string.

Melt the lard in a casserole dish and brown the pheasant all over. Peel the onion and carrot and dice them finely. Add the vegetables to the pheasant with the spices, cover and cook for 45-60 minutes. As soon as the meat juices start to caramelize, add the stock and baste the pheasant frequently so that it does not dry out. A little before the end of cooking time, baste the pheasant with the pineapple juice. Take the pheasant out of the oven and leave it to go cold, then remove the string and bacon.

Dissolve the gelatine in the Madeira and leave it to swell for 10 minutes. De-glaze the meat juices with the remaining stock, strain the resulting gravy through a chinois or sieve, leave it to cool and skim off the fat. Make up the gravy with water to obtain 250 ml (8 fl oz), bring it to the boil and season it to taste with salt, pepper and ginger. Take it off the heat and add the gelatine, stirring until the gelatine has dissolved completely.

Leave the aspic to cool then brush the pheasant with it, building it up layer by layer until the whole pheasant is coated with it. Refrigerate the remaining jelly until it sets completely, then cut it into dice. Garnish the pheasant with toasted almonds and cover the feet with paper sleeves. Arrange the pheasant on a serving dish, surrounded by diced aspic, cherries, pineapple chunks, sliced banana and orange.

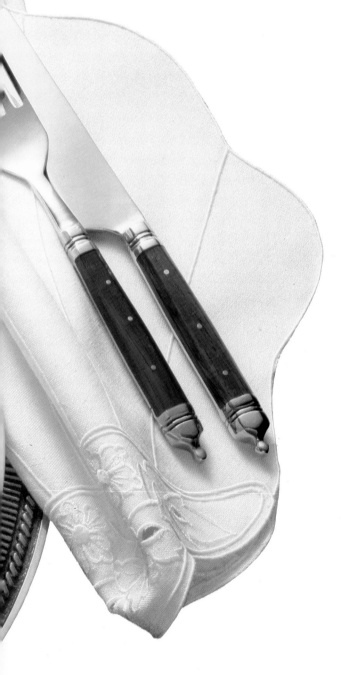

Left: *Pheasant*
Right: *Pheasant in aspic*

PHEASANT ON A BED OF CABBAGE

Serves 6

3 oven-ready pheasant,
each weighing 750 g
(1½ lb)
750 g (1½ lb) new
potatoes
1½ kg (3½ lb) white
cabbage
250 g (8 oz) onions
1 bay leaf
2 cloves
250 g (8 oz) baby carrots

100 g (3½ oz) goose fat
250 g (8 oz) piece of
streaky bacon
125 ml (4 fl oz) meat stock
1 bunch of fresh thyme
100 g (3½ oz) fatty bacon,
thinly sliced
800 g (1½ lb) cervelat, or
other salami-type sausage
salt and pepper

Wash the potatoes and boil them, then skin them. Take off the outer cabbage leaves, then cut it into 8 pieces, remove the hard stalks, wash it and cut it into ribbons.

Peel the onions, spike one with the bay leaf and cloves and chop the rest. Cut one of the pheasants into joints. Peel the carrots. Melt the goose fat in a casserole dish and sweat the chopped onions in it, add the piece of bacon, the jointed pheasant, the cabbage and carrots and brown them, stirring frequently.

Add the spiked onion, stock and thyme and braise for 45 minutes, adding more stock if necessary. Season the remaining pheasants inside and out with salt and pepper. Lard them with the sliced bacon and put them in a roasting tin.

Below: *Pheasant on a bed of cabbage*

Roast the pheasants in the oven for 45-60 minutes at 225-250° C (425-475°F, Gas Mark 7-9). Add the potatoes 20 minutes before the end of cooking time and roast them in the meat juices.

Put the cervelat or sausage in with the braised cabbage about 15 minutes before the end of cooking time. Arrange the cabbage and carrots on a large platter. Slice the piece of bacon and the cervelat and arrange them next to the cabbage with the braised pheasant joints. Arrange the two roast pheasant on top of the bed of cabbage.

PHEASANT STUFFED WITH ALMONDS

Serves 4

1 oven-ready pheasant,
weighing 1 kg (2 lb)
2 knobs of butter
1 egg, separated
3 tbsp breadcrumbs
2 tbsp flaked almonds
6 tbsp crème fraâche
pinch of grated nutmeg
2 tbsp lard

50 g (2 oz) shallots
500 ml (18 fl oz) meat
stock
1 tbsp flour or cornflour
a few thin slices of bacon
fresh tarragon, chopped
salt
pepper

Cream the egg yolk and butter together until light and fluffy, then add the breadcrumbs, almonds and 3 tablespoons of cream, season with salt and grated nutmeg. Whisk the egg white until stiff and fold it carefully into the almond mixture. Stuff the pheasant with this mixture and sew up the cavity. Season the pheasant with salt and pepper and sprinkle with tarragon. Wrap the slices of bacon around the pheasant and truss it.

Melt the lard in a casserole dish and brown the pheasant all over. Peel the shallots and add them to the meat with the stock, braise for 1 hour, adding more water to the gravy if necessary. Cut the cooked pheasant into joints and slice the stuffing.

Arrange the pheasant and stuffing on a warm serving dish and keep them warm under a sheet of foil. Make up the cooking juices with water, add the remaining cream and bring to the boil, stirring all the time. Thicken the gravy with the cornflour and season to taste with salt and pepper.
To serve, accompany the pheasant with potato croquettes or potato dumplings, Brussels sprouts or broccoli.

Below: *Pheasant stuffed with almonds*

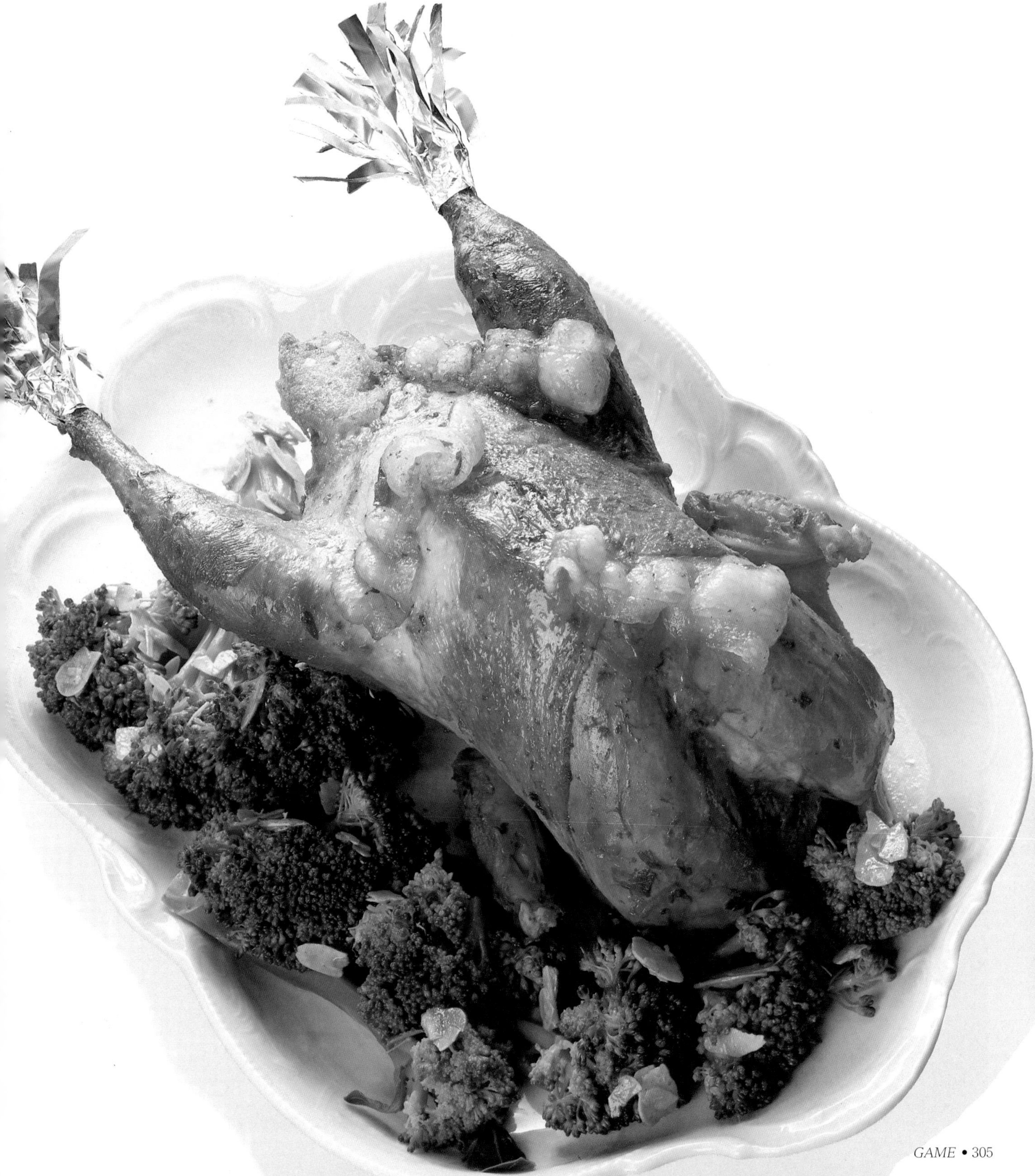

TURKEY LEG JOINTS IN SPICY SAUCE

Serves 4-6

2 turkey leg joints
4 tbsp oil
2 onions
1 clove of garlic
250 ml (8 fl oz) meat stock
500 ml (18 fl oz) beer
2 cloves
1 tsp ground cinnamon
pinch of Cayenne pepper

2 tbsp tomato purée
50 g (2 oz) raisins
1 apple
1 orange
1-2 tsp cornflour
2 knobs of butter
sugar
salt and pepper

Heat the oil in a casserole dish and brown the joints all over. Peel the onions and garlic, chop them finely, then brown them with the turkey. Add the stock and half the beer, then add the cloves, cinnamon, cayenne pepper and tomato purée. Stir and bring to the boil, then cover and simmer over a low heat for 1½ hours. Turn the turkey joints occasionally and add more beer if necessary. Peel and core the apple, grate it and add it to the casserole dish with the raisins 10 minutes before the end of cooking time.

Arrange the turkey joints on a warm serving dish and keep them warm. Thicken the sauce with the butter and cornflour, season with salt and pepper, and add sugar and cayenne pepper to taste to give a sweet and spicy flavour. Garnish the joints with slices of orange and onions.

Serve with rice and a chicory or lamb's lettuce salad.

Above: *Turkey leg joints in spicy sauce*

TURKEY LEG JOINT WITH CHIVES

Serves 4

1 turkey leg joint, on the bone, weighing about 1 kg (2 lb)	500 g (1 lb)
1 bunch of fresh parsley	3 hard-boiled eggs
6 peppercorns	2 tsp hot mustard
300 g (10 oz) carrots	125 ml (4 fl oz) oil
2-3 sticks of celery	1 bunch of fresh chives, chopped
2 medium leeks	vinegar
1 cauliflower, weighing	salt and pepper

Wash the parsley. Bring 1½ litres (2½ pints) salted water to the boil, add the turkey joint and parsley and season with pepper, then simmer gently. Peel the carrots and cut them into 3 cm (1¼ inch) sticks. Clean the celery, retaining the leaves and cut it into 4 cm (1½ inch) chunks. Add the carrots and celery to the stock after 50 minutes. Carefully wash the leeks and cut them into 4 cm (1½ inch) chunks. Cut the cauliflower into florets, wash them and add them to the stock, with the leek, after 1 hour. Cook for a further 15 minutes, then leave the meat and vegetables to go cold in the stock.

To make the dressing: Mash the hard-boiled eggs, mix them with the mustard and gradually add the oil in a trickle, whisking all the time (the dressing should thicken), then season with salt, pepper, vinegar and the chopped chives.

Take the turkey joint and vegetables out of the stock. Drain them, arrange the vegetables on a serving dish and pour the dressing over them. Take the turkey meat off the bone, slice it and arrange the slices on top of the vegetables. Garnish with fresh chives.

Below: *Turkey leg joint with chives*

TURKEY LEG JOINTS A LA CRÈME

Serves 4-6

2 turkey leg joints	125 ml (4 fl oz) meat stock
50 g (2 oz) bacon	125 g (4 oz) chanterelle
3 tbsp oil	mushrooms, tinned
1 onion	100 g (3½ oz) cream
6 tbsp sherry	salt and pepper

Dice the bacon. Heat the oil in a frying pan and fry the bacon in it, then brown the turkey joints all over.

Peel and thinly slice the onion and add it to the turkey, then add the sherry and stock, cover and braise over a low heat for 20-30 minutes. Drain the mushrooms, chop them finely and add them to the turkey joints. Enrich the gravy with the cream and season it with salt and pepper.

Serve with risotto or pasta and a salad.

STUFFED TURKEY LEG JOINTS

IN A CHICKEN BRICK OR EARTHENWARE CASSEROLE DISH
Serves 4-6

1-2 turkey leg joints,	chopped
boned, weighing 750 g	2 tsp cornflour
(1½ lb)	2 knobs of butter
400 g (13 oz) sausage	salt
meat	pepper
1 tbsp fresh parsley,	

Season the turkey joints inside and out. Combine the sausage meat and chopped parsley and stuff the joints with it, sew up the cavities, and season them with salt and pepper.

Pour a little water into the bottom of a casserole dish, put the meat on top, cover and braise in a hot oven at 200-225 °C (400-425 °F, Gas Mark 6-7) for 1½ hours. When the meat is cooked, slice it and arrange it on a warm serving dish, then keep it warm. Add 250 ml (8 fl oz) water to the meat juices, bring the gravy to the boil, thicken it with butter and cornflour and adjust the seasoning.

BRAISED GOOSE THIGHS IN A SALT CRUST

Serves 4-6

4 goose thighs, weighing	2 carrots
1½ kg (3½ lb)	1 leek
4 tbsp sea salt	1 cooking apple
8 juniper berries	2-3 tbsp cornflour
2 bay leaves	salt and pepper
1 onion	

Roll the goose thighs in the salt. Crush the juniper berries and chop the bay leaves. Put the goose thighs, juniper berries and bay leaves in a dish and leave them to macerate in a cool place for 3-4 days. Turn the thighs every day.

TURKEY KEBABS

Serves 4

750 g (1½ lb) turkey escalopes	2 onions
5 tbsp white wine	250 g (8 oz) tomatoes
3 tbsp soy sauce	200 g (7 oz) streaky bacon
2 tbsp oil	2 tbsp oil
1 green pepper	paprika
	salt and pepper

*B*lend together the white wine, soy sauce, oil, paprika, salt and pepper to make the marinade. Cut the meat into 4 cm (1½ inch) dice and marinate them in the marinade for 1 hour. Take the meat out of the marinade and pat it dry.

Remove the core and seeds from the pepper and cut it into chunks. Peel the onions, wash the tomatoes and cut the vegetables into quarters. Cut the bacon into cubes. Thread the pieces of turkey, pepper, tomatoes, onions and bacon onto skewers.

Cover the grill pan with a sheet of foil and heat the grill to a heat suitable for cooking the kebabs. Grill the kebabs for 6-8 minutes on each side, basting them occasionally with the marinade.

Left: *Turkey leg joints á la crème*
Below: *Turkey kebabs*

Wash the goose thighs in cold water, pat them dry and put them in a roasting tin. Peel the onions and carrots and wash the leek, then cut them into very thin strips to make a julienne. Peel and core the apple and cut it into quarters. Arrange the vegetables and apple around the thighs and put the roasting tin into a hot oven at 200-225⁰C (400-425⁰F, Gas Mark 6-7) for 1 hour. As soon as the meat juices start to caramelize, add 250 ml (8 fl oz) hot water. Skim off the fat frequently and baste the meat with the juices. Arrange the thighs on a serving dish and keep them warm.

To make the gravy: Strain the meat juices through a chinois or sieve, and skim off the fat. Thicken the gravy with the cornflour, bring it to the boil and simmer it over a low heat for 5 minutes, then adjust the seasoning.

Serve with potato gnocchi, red cabbage and unsweetened apple sauce.

TURKEY ESCALOPES

Serves 4

4 turkey escalopes	75 g (3 oz) butter
50 g (2 oz) flour	slices of lemon
1 egg, beaten	salt
50 g (2 oz) breadcrumbs	pepper

Sprinkle the escalopes with salt, then coat them in the flour, then in beaten egg, and finally in breadcrumbs.

Heat the butter in a frying pan and fry the escalopes on both sides, for about 12 minutes, until golden brown. Arrange them on a warm serving dish and garnish with slices of lemon.

Serve with mashed potato and a mixed salad.

Below: *Turkey escalopes*

Above: *Stuffed turkey*

STUFFED TURKEY

Serves 6

1½ kg (3½ lb) turkey breast
40 g (1½ oz) butter
200 g (7 oz) bacon
1 small onion
50 g (2 oz) turkey liver
4-5 tbsp brandy
1 egg

2 tbsp breadcrumbs
2-3 tbsp oil
300 ml (10 fl oz) white wine
4 tbsp crème fraîche
crushed peppercorns
salt
pepper

Cut the meat in half widthways to form a pocket. Melt the butter, add the pepper and brush it over the turkey breast, inside and out. Cut 6 strips of bacon and dice the rest. Peel and slice the onion and fry it with the diced bacon. Wash the turkey liver in cold water, pat it dry and cut it into thin strips. Fry the liver with the onions and bacon, then add the brandy. Combine the egg, breadcrumbs, onion, liver and bacon to make the stuffing and fill the pocket in the turkey with this mixture, then sew it up with kitchen thread or secure it with cocktail sticks.

Heat the oil in a frying pan and brown the meat all over in it. Arrange the slices of bacon on the base of a roasting tin, put the meat on top, add 250 ml (8 fl oz) white wine and braise in a hot oven at 200-225 °C (400-425 °F, Gas Mark 6-7) for 1 hour. Baste the meat occasionally with the juices and add water if necessary to prevent the meat drying out.
Arrange the meat on a warm serving dish and keep it warm. De-glaze the meat juices with the remaining white wine, bring to the boil and strain. Enrich the gravy with the crème fraîche and adjust the seasoning.

CURRIED CHICKEN LEG JOINTS

Serves 4

4 chicken leg joints
20 g (¼ oz) lard
2 onions
4 apples
2 slices of pineapple,

tinned in syrup
1 tbsp curry powder
250 ml (8 fl oz) pineapple
juice
salt and pepper

Season the chicken joints with salt and pepper. Heat the lard in a casserole dish. Brown the meat all over, then reserve. Peel the onions and apples and cut them into quarters. Drain 2 slices of pineapple and reserve 250 ml (8 fl oz) juice. Dice the pineapple and brown it in the casserole dish with the onions and apples. Add the curry powder, 250 ml (8 fl oz) hot water and the pineapple juice and season with salt.

Put the chicken joints in the casserole dish and simmer them over a low heat for 25-30 minutes. Take the chicken joints out of the casserole dish, and brown them under a hot grill, if liked. Add more curry powder to taste to the sauce. Serve piping hot.

Below: *Curried chicken leg joints*

Above: *Fried chicken*

CHICKEN GOULASH

Serves 4

4 chicken breasts,
weighing about 500 g (1 lb)
300 g (10 oz) onions
50 g (2 oz) butter
2 tbsp paprika
300 g (10 oz) red peppers
400 g (13 oz) tomatoes,
tinned

1 meat stock cube
2 bay leaves
1 bunch of fresh parsley
2 sweet and sour pickled
gherkins
2 hard-boiled eggs
cumin
salt

Peel the onions, slice them and brown them in the melted butter in a casserole dish. Sprinkle the paprika on top and allow to reduce. Cut the chicken breasts into 3 cm (1¼ inch) dice. Cut the peppers in half, remove the cores and seeds, wash them and cut them into 2 cm (¾ inch) chunks. Drain and chop the tomatoes, reserving the juice. Put the meat, peppers, tomatoes and tomato juice into the casserole dish.

Add the stock, cumin and bay leaves and season with salt. Put the lid on the dish and simmer the goulash for 20 minutes. Wash, drain and chop the parsley. Dice the gherkins finely and add them to the goulash with the parsley. Pour the goulash into a deep serving dish. Chop the hard-boiled eggs and use them to garnish the goulash. Serve with pasta or mashed potatoes.

FRIED CHICKEN

Serves 4

1 oven-ready chicken
1 egg
paprika
breadcrumbs
oil for frying

tomatoes
slices of lemon
fresh parsley, chopped
salt
pepper

Joint the chicken. Beat the egg with some paprika, salt and pepper. Brush the chicken joints all over with the egg wash, then coat them in breadcrumbs. Heat the oil in a chip pan or deep fat fryer to 180-190 °C (350 °F) and cook the chicken joints for about 10 minutes or until they are a deep golden brown, then drain them.
Serve garnished with tomato quarters, slices of lemon and fresh parsley.

CHICKEN LEG JOINTS WITH SHERRY

Serves 4

4 chicken leg joints	250 ml (8 fl oz) meat stock
knob of butter	250 ml (8 fl oz) crème
1 onion	fraîche
2 tbsp flour	150 ml (5 fl oz) sherry
2 tsp curry powder	salt and pepper

Season the chicken joints with salt and pepper. Heat the butter in a frying pan and brown the chicken joints all over, then fry them for 25-30 minutes. Remove the chicken from the pan and keep it warm.

Peel the onion, slice it thinly and brown it in the juices from the chicken. Sprinkle the flour over the onions, stir until the flour is cooked, then add the curry powder and stock and bring the sauce to the boil, whisking all the time to prevent lumps forming, then simmer it for 5 minutes.

Add the crème fraîche, stirring all the time, then finish the sauce with the sherry. Pour some of the sauce over the chicken and serve the rest separately.

Serve with buttered rice, spring vegetables and salad.

Below: *Chicken leg joints with sherry*

Above: *Shepherd's chicken leg joints*

SHEPHERD'S CHICKEN LEG JOINTS

Serves 2

1 chicken leg joint
½ tsp marjoram
½ tsp thyme
½ tsp rosemary

juice of 1 lemon
1 tbsp oil
salt and pepper

Stir the dried herbs into the oil. Season the chicken with salt and pepper. Brush the leg joint with the herb oil and place it under a hot grill at 200-225 °C (400-425 °F, Gas Mark 6-7) for 20 minutes, brushing it frequently with the herb oil.

Serve with a salad of French beans.

CHICKEN KEBABS

Serves 3-4

500 g (1 lb) chicken breast meat
100 g (3½ oz) streaky bacon
2-3 slices pineapple in

syrup
3 knobs of butter
salt
freshly ground pepper

Cut the chicken and bacon into 3 cm (1¼ inch) cubes, then season them with salt and pepper. Drain the pineapple chunks. Thread the pieces of pineapple and meat alternately onto skewers.

Melt the butter in a frying pan and fry the kebabs all over, for about 8 minutes or until golden brown. Arrange on a warm serving dish.

CHICKEN BREASTS IN MARSALA

Serves 2-3

2-3 chicken breasts	150 g (5 oz) crème fraîche
2-3 thin slices uncooked	fresh sage, chopped
ham	salt
2 tbsp lard	pepper
3-4 tbsp Marsala	

Season the chicken breasts with pepper and sprinkle them with sage. Wrap a slice of ham around each breast and secure with a cocktail stick. Melt the lard and fry the meat in it for 10 minutes. Take the meat out of the frying pan and keep it warm. De-glaze the juices with the Marsala, then add the crème fraîche and stir well. Bring the sauce to the boil and adjust the seasoning. Remove the cocktail sticks and put the chicken breasts into the sauce. Cook for a further 2 minutes over a low heat. Serve with risotto and a salad of lamb's lettuce.

CHICKEN BREASTS WITH AVOCADO AND MIXED HERBS

Serves 4-6

6 chicken breasts	1 bunch of fresh flat leaf
zest of 1 unwaxed lime,	parsley
grated	1 bunch of fresh tarragon
juice of 1 unwaxed lime	3 ripe avocados
juice of 1 unwaxed lemon	cress
30 g (1 oz) butter	slices of lemon
2 egg yolks	salt
250 ml (8 fl oz) oil	pepper

Put the chicken breasts in a bowl with the salt, pepper and grated lime zest. Cover the bowl, turn the meat after ½ hour and leave to marinate for an hour. Melt the butter and fry the chicken breasts in it for 5 minutes on each side, then leave them to cool.

Above: *Chicken breasts with avocado and mixed herbs*
Left: *Chicken breasts in Marsala*

To make the mayonnaise: Beat the egg yolks with a little lime juice, season with salt, then gradually add the oil in a thin trickle, whisking all the time, until the mayonnaise thickens. Adjust the seasoning. Wash the parsley and tarragon, remove the stalks, chop them finely and add them to the mayonnaise, reserving a few sprigs for garnish.

Cut the avocados in half, remove the stones, peel them and cut each avocado into slices 1 cm (½ inch) thick.

Arrange them in a fan shape on a serving dish, sprinkle them with lemon juice and garnish with cress. Cut the chicken breasts into thin slices and arrange them on the bed of avocado. Pour the herb mayonnaise over them. Garnish with slices of lemon, tarragon leaves or cress.

Variation: You could use a bunch of fresh basil in the mayonnaise instead of tarragon and parsley.

CHICKEN STEW

Serves 4-6

600 g (1¼ lb) chicken
breasts
1 small onion
1 tbsp olive oil
1 small tin chanterelle
mushrooms

pinch of dried thyme
250 ml (8 fl oz) meat stock
150 g (5 oz) crème fraîche
fresh parsley, chopped
salt
freshly ground pepper

Slice the chicken breasts thinly. Peel and dice the onion. Heat the oil in a frying pan and brown the onion in it, then add the chicken, and fry until golden.

Drain the chanterelle mushrooms, add them to the meat, season it with salt, pepper and dried thyme, add the stock and simmer over a low heat for about 5 minutes. Add the cream, bring the gravy to the boil, adjust the seasoning and garnish with chopped parsley.

GOOSE LEGS WITH BRAISED CABBAGE

Serves 4

2 goose legs	30 g (1 oz) lard
1 white cabbage,	salt
weighing 2 kg (4½ lb)	pepper
2 large onions	

Take the outer leaves off the cabbage, then cut it into quarters. Remove the thick stalks and slice the cabbage into ribbons. Peel and dice the onions. Melt the lard in a casserole dish and brown the goose legs all over, then add the onions and brown them. Add 250 ml (8 fl oz) water and the cabbage to the meat and onions, season it with salt and pepper and cover and simmer for 1½ hours. Take the meat off the bone and arrange it in a warmed, deep serving dish. Adjust the cabbage's seasoning, and serve it with the goose legs, accompanied by boiled potatoes.

Above: *Tongan chicken curry*
Left: *Chicken stew*

TONGAN CHICKEN CURRY

Serves 2-3

2-3 chicken breasts	ginger
2 knobs of butter	150 g (5 oz) crème fraîche
100 g (3½ oz) mandarin	1 tbsp mandarin juice
segments	1 tbsp pineapple syrup
100 g (3½ oz) pineapple	curry powder
chunks in syrup	lemon juice
1 piece of preserved	salt and pepper

Melt 1 knob of butter in a frying pan, slice the chicken breasts thinly and fry the slices in the butter until sealed all over. Season them with salt and pepper, sprinkle with curry powder, then take them out of the pan and keep them warm. Add a knob of butter and curry powder to taste to the frying pan, then add the mandarin segments, pineapple chunks and finely chopped stem ginger and simmer over a low heat. Add the crème fraîche, mandarin juice and pineapple syrup, bring the sauce to the boil, season it with salt, pepper and lemon juice, then add the meat to the sauce and heat it through.

CURRIED CHICKEN

Serves 4

1 oven-ready chicken	40 g (1½ oz) butter
1 fresh bouquet garni	2 tbsp curry powder
2 carrots	3 slices pineapple in syrup
1 stick of celery	1 banana
1 leek	1 apple
1 onion	salt

Wash the herbs for the bouquet garni, leek and celery, then put the chicken in 2 litres (3½ pints) of boiling, salted water with the bouquet garni and simmer it for 1 hour. Take the chicken meat off the bone and slice it thinly. Strain the stock and reserve 500 ml (18 fl oz). Peel the carrots and onions, then cut the vegetables into very thin matchsticks, to make a julienne.

Melt the butter and sweat the vegetables in it for 10 minutes, then add the curry powder and sliced chicken, sauté it for a few minutes, then add the reserved chicken stock and bring to the boil.

Drain the pineapple, peel the banana, peel and core the apple, and dice the fruit. Add the fruit to the curry, simmer for 3-5 minutes, then adjust the seasoning.

Serve with rice and green salad.

Below: *Curried chicken*

CHICKEN FRICASSÉE

Serves 4

1 oven-ready chicken	200 g (7 oz) asparagus
1 pack of vegetables for	spears, tinned
stews, e.g. carrot, leek,	150 g (5 oz) peas, frozen
turnip	2 tbsp crème fraîche
2 onions	1 egg yolk
1 bay leaf	2 tbsp cold milk
6 peppercorns	1 tbsp fresh parsley,
30 g (1 oz) butter	chopped
250 g (8 oz) button	salt
mushrooms	pepper
40 g (1½ oz) flour	

Put the chicken into enough boiling, salted water to cover it, bring to the boil and skim off the fat. Peel one onion and the vegetables, chop them and add them to the stock with the bay leaf and peppercorns. Simmer the chicken for 1¼ hours. The meat should be covered by the stock all the time, so add more water if necessary. Take the chicken out of the stock, strain it and reserve 750 ml (1¼ pints). Take the meat off the bone, remove the skin and dice it roughly.

To make the sauce: Peel the other onion and slice it thinly, then melt the butter and sweat the onion in it. Wipe the mushrooms, slice them and sweat them in the butter with the onion. Add the flour, stirring all the time until the flour is cooked, then add the stock. Whisk the sauce to prevent lumps forming, bring it to the boil and simmer it for 5 minutes, stirring constantly.

Drain the asparagus, and add it to the sauce with the peas, then bring the sauce to the boil again. Simmer over a low heat for 3-5 minutes, then season to taste with salt and pepper. Beat together the egg yolk and milk and whisk it into the sauce to thicken and enrich it. Reheat the meat in the sauce. Garnish the fricassée with diced carrot and chopped parsley. Serve with rice.

Right: *Chicken fricassée*

CHICKEN STEW A LA CRÈME

Serves 4

500 g (1 lb) chicken breasts
30 g (1 oz) butter
30 g (1 oz) flour
150 g (5 oz) button
mushrooms, tinned

150 g (5 oz) crème fraîche
paprika
salt
pepper

Slice the chicken breast thinly, season with salt and pepper and sprinkle it with paprika. Melt the butter and fry the chicken in it for about 7 minutes, then sprinkle the chicken with the flour, stir well and leave to cook on a low heat for 1-2 minutes.

Drain the mushrooms and reserve the brine, adding enough water to make it up to
250 ml (8 fl oz) liquid. Add this to the chicken, and bring the sauce to the boil, stirring all the time. Slice the mushrooms thinly and add them to the meat with the cream, bring the stew to the boil again and simmer it for 5 minutes. Season with salt, pepper and more paprika to taste.

Below: *Chicken leg joints with braised carrots*

CHICKEN LEG JOINTS WITH BRAISED CARROTS

Serves 4

4 chicken leg joints
750 g (1½ lb) carrots
50 g (2 oz) butter
3 onions
1 tsp cornflour

paprika
fresh thyme, chopped
fresh parsley, chopped
salt and pepper

Peel the carrots, wash them and cut them into matchsticks ½ centimetre (¼ inch) thick. Season the chicken joints with salt and pepper and sprinkle them with paprika. Heat 3 knobs of butter in a casserole dish and brown the meat all over. Peel the onions, slice them and brown them with the chicken. Add the carrots and thyme, season with salt and pepper and add enough water to cover the chicken and vegetables. Cover and simmer for 25-30 minutes, stirring occasionally.

Arrange the chicken joints on a warm serving dish and keep them warm. Add ½ a glass of water to the vegetables, and bring them to the boil. Knead together the remaining butter and cornflour and stir it into the vegetables to thicken them. Season with salt and pepper to taste and serve the vegetables with the chicken legs, garnished with chopped parsley.

STUFFED CHICKEN LEG JOINTS

Serves 4

4 chicken leg joints
100 g (3½ oz) Gruyère
cheese, in a piece
4 slices uncooked ham
4 slices pineapple, tinned
in syrup

oil
paprika
parsley
salt
pepper

Bone out the chicken joints. Cut the cheese in 4 length-ways, wrap a slice of ham around each piece of cheese and insert the rolls of ham into the chicken joints, then truss the cavity with kitchen thread. Put the chicken joints on a rack in a grill pan.

Arrange the slices of pineapple beside the chicken, and grill both for 15 minutes on each side. Stir a little paprika into some oil and brush the chicken joints and pineapple with it during cooking. Arrange on a warm serving dish and garnish with parsley.

Right:: *Chicken stew á la crème*

CHICKEN LIVER STEW

Serves 4

500 g (1 lb) chicken livers
750 g (1½ lb) new
potatoes
60 g (2½ oz) butter
2 tbsp oil
250 g (8 oz) baby onions
or shallots
500 g (1 lb) carrots

2 bay leaves
250 g (8 oz) leeks
1 tsp dried thyme
1 bunch of fresh flat leaf
parsley
salt
pepper

Peel, wash and dry the potatoes. Heat the oil and half the butter in a casserole dish and sauté the potatoes in it for about 20 minutes, stirring them frequently, then season them with salt and pepper. Peel the onions and carrots, slice them and add them to the potatoes with the bay leaves and sweat them for 20 minutes.

Wash the leek, slice it into rings, rinse them and add them to the vegetables. Season them with salt and pepper, sprinkle with thyme and leave to sweat for a further 10 minutes. Wash the chicken livers in cold water and take out the gristle and white cores. Heat the remaining butter in a frying pan and fry the livers in it for 8-10 minutes, then add them to the vegetables. Wash and dry the parsley. Strip off the leaves and chop them finely, and use to garnish the chicken liver stew.

CHICKEN LIVERS WITH APPLES

Serves 4

500 g (1 lb) chicken livers
500 g (1 lb) cooking
apples
500 g (1 lb) onions
130 g (5 oz) butter

4 tbsp flour
4 slices wholemeal bread
fresh marjoram
salt
pepper

Wash the livers in cold water, wipe them dry and remove any gristle and the white cores. Peel the apples, core them and cut them into thin slices. Peel the onions

Below: *Chicken liver stew*
Right:: *Chicken livers with apples*

and slice them thinly. Melt 50 g (2 oz) butter in a frying pan and fry the onions until golden, then season them with salt. Reserve the onions and keep them warm. Add 30 g (1 oz) butter to the frying pan and seal the apples in it.

Take the apples out of the pan as soon as they have turned a nice golden-brown and keep them warm.

Season the chicken livers with pepper and toss them in the flour. Heat 50 g (2 oz) butter in a frying pan and fry the chicken livers for 8-10 minutes, turning them frequently.

Toast the 4 slices of wholemeal bread and arrange them on warmed plates. Arrange the chicken livers on top of the bread, season, and garnish with the onions and sliced apples. Decorate with fresh marjoram.

BRAISED BREAST OF GOOSE

Serves 4

750 g (1½ lb) breast of goose, on the bone	fat
2 bunches of vegetables for stews, e.g. carrots, leeks, turnips	100 g (3½ oz) bacon, sliced
1 onion	250 ml (8 fl oz) white wine
40-50 g (1½-2 oz) goose	salt
	pepper

Season the goose breast with salt. Prepare the vegetables and cut them into thin matchsticks to make a julienne. Peel the onion and slice it thinly. Heat the goose fat in a casserole dish and brown the vegetables in it. Add the goose breast such that the bones are on the base of the casserole dish, cover the breast with the slices of bacon and add the white wine. Put the lid on the casserole dish and braise for 1½ -1¼ hours, adding more white wine occasionally.

As soon as the goose breast is cooked, slice it and arrange it on a warm serving dish. Strain the gravy through a chinois or sieve and pour the gravy over the slices of meat.

Left: *Braised breast of goose*
Below: *Goose legs with peppers*

GOOSE LEGS WITH PEPPERS

Serves 4

2 goose legs, weighing about 1 kg (2 lb)	peppers
	500 g (1 lb) tomatoes
1 tbsp lard	paprika
3 onions	fresh parsley, chopped
500 g (1 lb) red and green	salt
	pepper

Season the goose legs with salt and sprinkle them with paprika. Heat the lard in a casserole dish and brown the meat all over. Throw away half the fat which has been used for cooking. Peel the onions, cut them into quarters and fry them with the goose legs until golden. Add a glass of water, cover and braise. Turn the goose legs frequently and baste them with the cooking juices. Slice the peppers in half, core and de-seed them, wash them and slice them thinly. Blanch the tomatoes in boiling water, then refresh them in cold water, skin and chop them. Add the vegetables to the meat after an hour, season with salt and pepper and simmer for 45 minutes. Take the meat off the bone, slice it and keep it warm. Adjust the seasoning of the vegetables and add paprika to taste.

Serve the vegetables in a warmed, deep serving dish, arrange the sliced meat on top, garnish with chopped parsley and accompany with gnocchi.

CHICKEN CHASSEUR

Serves 4

1 oven-ready chicken	2 tbsp brandy
3 tbsp olive oil	125 ml (4 fl oz) meat stock
60 g (2½ oz) butter	100 g (3½ oz) tomatoes
250 g (8 oz) button mushrooms	3-4 tbsp fresh parsley, chopped
½ onion	salt
100 g (3½ oz) flour	pepper
125 ml (4 fl oz) white wine	

Cut the chicken into joints and season them with salt and pepper. Heat the olive oil and butter in a casserole dish and brown the chicken joints all over. Take them out of the casserole dish and keep them warm. Wipe the mushrooms and slice them thinly. Slice the half onion and fry it in the casserole dish with the mushrooms. Add the flour and cook it for a few minutes, stirring all the time, then add the white wine, brandy and stock.

Blanch the tomatoes in boiling water, refresh them in cold water, then skin them, chop them and add them to the mushrooms. Bring the sauce to the boil, put the lid on the casserole dish and simmer the mushrooms and tomatoes for 8 minutes. Add the chicken joints, cover the dish again and simmer over a low heat for 30 minutes.

Arrange the chicken joints on a warm serving dish and keep them warm. Reduce the sauce, add the chopped parsley, then pour the sauce over the chicken.

Left: *Chicken chasseur*
Below: *Chicken Marengo*

CHICKEN MARENGO

Serves 4

1 oven-ready chicken	10 green olives, pitted
1 clove of garlic	10 g (¼-½ oz) black truffles, preserved
2 tbsp oil	
500 g (1 lb) tomatoes	4 cooked crayfish
250 ml (8 fl oz) white wine	salt
250 g (8 oz) baby button mushrooms	pepper

Cut the chicken into quarters. Peel and crush the garlic. Season the chicken with salt and pepper and rub it with the garlic. Heat the oil in a casserole dish and brown the chicken quarters all over. Blanch the tomatoes in boiling water, refresh them in cold water, skin them and cut them into quarters, de-seed them and add them to the meat.

Add the white wine, put the lid on the casserole dish and simmer for 45 minutes. Turn the chicken joints occasionally and add more white wine as necessary. Wipe the mushrooms, drain the olives and add them to the casserole dish after 30 minutes. Cover the dish again and continue to simmer on a low heat.

Arrange the chicken joints on a serving dish and keep them warm. Season the sauce with salt and pepper and pour it over the chicken. Garnish with thin slices of truffle and crayfish.

chicken quarters. Peel the onion and garlic and slice them thinly, then add them to the meat. Add 250 ml (8 fl oz) water, put the lid on the casserole dish and braise for 45 minutes. Turn the chicken occasionally during cooking. Arrange the meat on a warm serving dish and keep it hot. Add some water to the sauce to make it up to 400 ml (14 fl oz). Add the tomato purée, remaining paprika, cayenne pepper and marjoram and bring the sauce to the boil. Enrich and thicken it with the cream and cornflour, adjust the seasoning, then return the meat to the casserole dish and heat it through in the sauce. Serve with pasta or rice.

BRAISED CHICKEN

Serves 4-6

1 oven-ready chicken	1 tbsp cayenne pepper
2-3 tbsp paprika	70 g (3 oz) tomato purée
3 tbsp oil	3 tbsp cream
1 onion	1 tsp cornflour
1 clove of garlic	salt
1 tsp dried marjoram	pepper

Cut the chicken into quarters and season them with salt. Sprinkle them with half of the paprika. Heat the oil in a casserole dish and brown the

Above:
Braised chicken

CHICKEN WITH ONIONS

Serves 4-6

1 oven-ready chicken, weighing about 1½ kg (3½ lb)	1 tbsp fresh thyme, chopped
2 tbsp oil	2 bay leaves
500 g (1 lb) baby onions or shallots	100 g (3½ oz) crème fraîche
250 g (8 oz) carrots	salt
3 knobs of butter	pepper

Cut the chicken into 8 joints. Heat the oil in a casserole dish and brown the chicken pieces in it. Take them out of the casserole dish and season them with salt and pepper. Peel the onions and cut them into quarters. Peel and slice the carrots.

Melt the butter in the casserole dish, fry the onions and carrots in it and season them with salt, pepper and thyme. Put the chicken back in the casserole dish with the bay leaves, put the lid on the dish and cook for 20 minutes.

Add the crème fraîche at the last minute and stir it in well. Serve the chicken with boiled potatoes.

Below: *Chicken with onions*

COQ AU VIN

IN THE PRESSURE COOKER
Serves 4-6

1 oven-ready chicken	250 ml (8 fl oz) meat stock
80 g (3 oz) streaky bacon	1 bay leaf
50 g (2 oz) butter	4 cloves
1 onion	2 tbsp cornflour
200 g (7 oz) button	fresh rosemary
mushrooms	salt and pepper
300 ml (10 fl oz) red wine	

Cut the chicken into 6 or 8 joints and season them with salt and pepper. Dice the bacon and brown it in the pressure cooker. Add the butter and brown the chicken joints all over.

Peel and dice the onion. Wipe the mushrooms, cut them into quarters and brown them with the meat for a few minutes. Add 250 ml (8 fl oz) wine and the stock, then the bay leaf, cloves and rosemary. Put the lid on the pressure cooker and steam the chicken gently for 15 minutes.

Arrange the meat on a warm serving dish and keep it hot. Slake the cornflour with the remaining wine and use it to thicken the sauce. Bring to the boil and simmer for 5 minutes, stirring all the time, then season with salt and pepper.

Serve with mashed potatoes or pasta and chicory salad.

Left: *Coq au vin*
Below: *Chicken with leeks*

CHICKEN WITH LEEKS

Serves 4-6

1 oven-ready chicken,	125 ml (4 fl oz) white wine
weighing 1½ kg (3½ lb)	150 g (5 oz) crème fraîche
1 tbsp paprika	salt
2 knobs of butter	pepper
750 g (1½ lb) leeks	

Cut the chicken into joints, season them with salt and sprinkle them with the paprika. Melt the butter and fry the chicken joints in it.

Carefully clean the leek, cut it into rings, rinse and drain them. Sweat the leeks in the butter, then add the white wine. Spread the leeks over the base of an oven-proof dish and put the chicken joints on top. Bake in the oven at 200 ⁰C (400 ⁰F, Gas Mark 6) for 40 minutes.

Arrange the meat on a warm serving dish and keep it hot. Spread the crème fraîche over the leeks and adjust the seasoning to taste.

CURRIED CHICKEN AND BANANA

BAKED EN PAPILLOTE
Serves 4

1 oven-ready chicken	oil
1 apple	1½ tbsp honey
3 bananas	knob of butter
1½ tsp curry powder	salt and pepper

To make the stuffing, peel the apple and a banana and cut them into thin slices. Stir 1 spoonful of curry powder into the fruit and season with salt.

Season the chicken inside and out with salt and pepper. Stuff it with the sliced fruit and truss it with kitchen string. Brush a sheet of foil with oil and wrap it around the chicken. Put the chicken parcel on the oven shelf at 250-275 °C (475 °F, Gas Mark 9) for 1 hour. Open up the parcel and turn back the foil 15 minutes before the end of cooking time. Blend the honey and remaining curry powder together and brush the chicken with it, then turn the chicken and baste the other side. Take the cooked chicken out of the foil, reserving the juices, remove the kitchen thread, take out the stuffing and joint the chicken.

Arrange the chicken joints on a warm serving dish with the stuffing. Cut the 2 remaining bananas in half lengthways. Heat the butter and fry the banana halves on both sides. Pour the meat juices from the foil parcel over the bananas, then arrange the bananas around the chicken joints.

Serve with curried rice and salad.

LEMON CHICKEN

Serves 4-6

1 large chicken	1 unwaxed lemon
8 cloves of garlic	1 bunch of fresh parsley
juice of 1 lemon	100 ml (3½ fl oz) crème
1 tsp salt	fraîche
4 tbsp oil	1 tsp fresh rosemary
2 cooking apples	salt

Peel the garlic, crush it in the lemon juice, add the oil and season with salt. Brush the chicken with the garlic, oil and lemon mixture inside and out and wrap it in a sheet of foil. Leave it to marinate for 30 minutes.

Peel, core and quarter the apples, remove the lemon zest, wash the parsley. Stuff the chicken with the quartered apples, lemon zest and sprigs of parsley, then truss it with kitchen thread. Skewer the chicken on the spit and spit-roast it under the grill for 30-35 minutes. Blend together the cream and rosemary, baste the chicken with this mixture and roast for a further 5 minutes. Then baste the chicken again with more of the mixture and roast again for 5 minutes. Continue thus until the skin is crisp and golden.

Take the chicken off the spit and cut it in half. Take out the stuffing and arrange the chicken and stuffing on a warm serving dish.

Serve with chips and a mixed salad.

Right:: *Lemon chicken*
Left: *Curried chicken and banana.*

CHICKEN WITH MARJORAM AND PEPPERS

Serves 4-6

1 oven-ready chicken,
weighing 1½ kg (3½ lb)
2 cloves of garlic
50 g (2 oz) butter
3 fresh marjoram leaves,
chopped
2 tbsp fresh marjoram,

chopped
250 ml (8 fl oz) white wine
1-2 green peppers
1-2 red or yellow peppers
500 g (1 lb) plum tomatoes
salt
freshly ground pepper

Cut the chicken into quarters and season them with salt and pepper. Peel and finely chop the garlic. Blend together the garlic and butter and spread this mixture over the chicken portions. Arrange the pieces of chicken in an oven-proof dish and sprinkle them with marjoram leaves. Roast the chicken pieces in the oven at 225 °C (425 °F, Gas Mark 7) for about 1 hour.

Add the white wine after 20 minutes, then baste the chicken frequently to prevent it drying out. Slice the peppers in half, core and de-seed them, then wash them and cut them into thin strips. Blanch the tomatoes, refresh them in cold water, skin them and cut them into quarters.

After 40 minutes add the peppers to the chicken, then add the tomatoes 5 minutes later, stirring to combine them. Leave them to braise for 10 minutes. Garnish with chopped marjoram.

STUFFED DUCK

Serves 4

1 oven-ready duck
2-3 cooking apples

50 g (2 oz) raisins
salt and pepper

Season the duck inside and out with salt and pepper. Peel, quarter and core the apples. Stuff the duck with the raisins and apple quarters, then season with salt and pepper.

Put the duck in an oven-proof casserole dish, with a little water, put the lid on the dish and roast in the oven at 200-225 °C (400-425 °F, Gas Mark 6-7) for 1½ hours.

Cut the duck into joints, and arrange them on a warm serving dish. Pour the cooking juices into a gravy boat, adjust the seasoning and pour some of the juices over the meat.

Left: *Chicken with marjoram and peppers*
Below: *Stuffed duck*

DUCK WITH THYME

Serves 4-6

1 oven-ready duck,	chopped
weighing about 2 kg	1 tsp fresh rosemary
(4½ lb)	1 tbsp olive oil
1 kg (2 lb) potatoes	2 onions
3 tbsp fresh thyme,	salt and pepper

Wash the potatoes. Put them in a saucepan with enough water to cover, add salt and bring to the boil. Simmer them for 15-20 minutes. Drain them, leave them to cool a little, then peel them. Season them with salt, sprinkle them with thyme and rosemary and drizzle them with oil.

Season the duck with salt inside and out. Stuff the duck with some of the herbed potatoes. Put the duck on its back in a roasting tin, with a little cold water and roast it in the oven at 225 °C (425 °F, Gas Mark 7) for 1½ hours.

Peel the onions, cut them into quarters and add them to the duck after 15 minutes' cooking time. Pierce the duck under the wings and in the thighs to release the fat. After 30 minutes skim off the fat. As soon as the duck juices start to caramelize, add a little hot water to the roasting tin and baste the duck frequently. Add the remaining potatoes to the roasting tin 15 minutes before the end of cooking time and roast until golden.

Joint the duck and serve it on a warm serving dish with the roast potatoes, garnished with sprigs of thyme and rosemary. Serve the juices separately.

ROAST DUCK WITH RICE

Serves 4-6

1 oven-ready duck	1 bunch of fresh parsley
1 packet easy-cook long	1 tsp fresh sage
grain rice	fresh marjoram
3 onions	1 egg, beaten
2 carrots	1 tbsp honey
1 apple	2 tbsp cornflour
30 g (1 oz) butter	salt and pepper
duck giblets, cooked	

Below: *Duck with thyme*

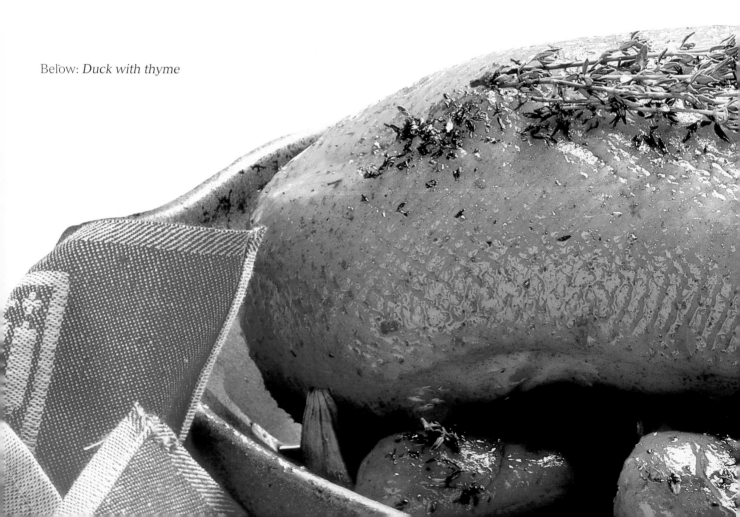

Cook the rice for 10-12 minutes until the grains are fluffy and separate, then drain it. Peel the onion and slice it thinly. Peel and slice the carrots. Peel, core and dice the apple. Melt the butter and sauté the onion, carrots and apple, then leave them to cool.

Slice the giblets thinly. Wash the parsley and chop it finely. Mix together the rice, parsley and giblets, then add the sage, some marjoram, the beaten egg and vegetables. Season the stuffing with salt and pepper to taste. Sprinkle the duck inside and out with salt, pepper and marjoram. Stuff the duck with the rice mixture.

Pour a little cold water into a roasting tin and put the duck in the tin on its back, then roast it on the bottom shelf of the oven at 200 °C (400 °F, Gas Mark 6) for 2 hours. Pierce the duck under the wings and in the thighs occasionally to the release the fat. Baste it with the juices during cooking.

Dissolve the honey in a little hot water and baste the duck with the honey mixture 30 minutes before the end of cooking time.

Above: *Roast duck with rice*

Cut the duck into joints, arrange them on a warm serving dish and keep them warm. De-glaze the roasting tin with water, bring the resulting gravy to the boil, strain it and skim off the fat. Thicken the gravy with a little cornflour, and adjust the seasoning to taste.

DUCK WITH SPRING ONIONS

Serves 4-6

1 oven-ready duck, with giblets	3 tbsp sherry
2-3 bunches spring onions	½ tsp root ginger, grated
40 g (1½ oz) butter	100 g (3½ oz) crème fraîche
30 g (1 oz) sugar	1 slice of fresh root ginger
4 tbsp soy sauce	salt and pepper

Prepare the onions, retaining 15 cm (6 inches) of green. Melt the butter and fry the onions in it, sprinkle them with sugar, stir gently and leave them to sweat. Add half the soy sauce, season the onions with salt and leave them to cool. Season the duck inside and out with salt, then stuff it with the spring onions. Close the cavity by folding over the flap of skin and trussing the bird. Baste the duck with the butter in which the onions were cooked, put it on its back in a roasting tin and add the giblets.

Roast the duck in the oven at 200 °C (400 °F, Gas Mark 6) for 2 hours. Add hot water to the roasting tin after 15 minutes. Blend together the remaining soy sauce, the sherry and grated ginger and pour it over the duck after half an hour, then continue roasting.

Arrange the duck on a warm serving dish and keep it warm. De-glaze the juices with hot water, bring the resulting gravy to the boil, strain it and skim off the fat. Thicken the gravy with the crème fraîche, season it with salt and pepper and adjust the seasoning with more soy sauce or sherry. Peel the piece of root ginger, slice it thinly and add it to the gravy.

Serve the gravy separately. Accompany the duck with rice and mushrooms.

SWEET AND SOUR DUCK

Serves 4-6

1 oven-ready duck	paprika
250 g (8 oz) pears in syrup	1 tbsp cornflour
250 g (8 oz) apricots in syrup	knob of butter
fresh thyme	wine vinegar
	salt and pepper

Season the duck inside and out with salt. Drain the pears and apricots and stuff the duck with them. Truss the duck, season with salt and pepper and sprinkle with thyme. Pour a little water into the bottom of an oven-proof casserole dish or lidded roasting tin and put the duck in it. Cover and roast in the oven at 200-225 °C (400-425 °F, Gas Mark 6-7) for 1 hour and 10 minutes. Joint the duck, arrange the joints on a serving dish and keep them warm. Skim the fat off the gravy, add some water and bring the gravy to the boil. Thicken the gravy with the butter and cornflour, then season it to taste with salt, pepper and vinegar.

Above: *Sweet and sour duck*
Right:: *Duck with spring onions*

ROAST DUCK WITH GARLIC

Serves 4-6

1 oven-ready duck	4 tbsp soy sauce
2 slices fresh root ginger	1 tsp ground cinnamon
2 cloves of garlic	125 ml (4 fl oz) chicken
2 shallots	stock
5 tbsp runny honey	1 tbsp vinegar
zest of ½ unwaxed	salt
orange, grated	pepper

Season the duck inside and out with salt. Wash the ginger and chop it finely. Peel and finely chop the garlic and shallots. Combine the garlic and shallots with 2 tablespoons of honey and 2 tablespoons of soy sauce, the grated orange zest, cinnamon and chicken stock.

Bring this mixture to the boil, then leave it to cool for 3 minutes. Sew up the cavity in the belly of the duck with kitchen thread. Put the duck in a roasting tin, pour the hot marinade into the duck through the neck cavity, then sew it up. Put the duck on its back and roast it in the oven at 200 °C (400 °F, Gas Mark 6) for 30 minutes. Pierce the duck under the wings and in the drumsticks to release the fat.

As soon as the duck juices start to caramelize, add a little hot water, then baste the duck frequently. Cook it for a further 1½ hours at 175 °C (350 °F, Gas Mark 4). Blend together the remaining honey and soy sauce, season the mixture with salt and pepper, add the vinegar, stir well and baste the duck with this mixture during cooking. Take the bird out of the oven, remove the kitchen thread, drain off the liquid inside the duck and serve it separately. Skim the fat off the juices in the roasting tin, strain them, pour them over the duck and serve it immediately.

Tip: Add 250 g (8 oz) peeled shallots after the duck has been in the oven for 30 minutes.

DUCK WITH APPLES

Serves 4-6

1 oven-ready duck	1 clove of garlic
weighing 2½ kg (5½ lb),	1 head of Chinese leaf
with giblets	75 g (3 oz) streaky bacon
fresh oregano	4 large cooking apples
250 g (8 oz) shallots	salt and pepper
1 onion	

Season the duck inside and out with salt and pepper, then sprinkle it with oregano. Put the duck and giblets in a roasting tin and roast them at 250 °C (475 °F, Gas Mark 9) for 45 minutes. Pierce the duck under the wings and in the drumsticks to release the fat. Take the duck out of the oven, arrange it on a warm serving dish and keep it warm.

Peel the shallots, onion and garlic and slice them thinly. Wash the Chinese leaves and cut them into strips. Skim some of the fat from the duck juices. Heat the duck fat in a saucepan, brown the shallots, garlic and onion in it, then add the Chinese leaf and stir well.

Put the Chinese leaf mixture in the roasting tin and put it in the oven. Dice the bacon and add it to the Chinese leaf. Put the duck in the roasting tin on top of the Chinese leaf and roast it for a further 45 minutes. Stir the vegetables occasionally. Peel and core the apples and slice them thinly. Add them to the duck after 30 minutes.

Left: *Roast duck with garlic*
Right:: *Duck with apples*

ROAST PIGEONS

Serves 4

4 oven-ready pigeons	1 tbsp cornflour
knob of butter	salt
3 tbsp cream	pepper

Make an incision in the belly of each pigeon and season inside with salt. Fold the neck flap outwards and hold it in place with the wings. Season the giblets with salt and pepper. Insert the giblets into the pigeons with the butter and stick the feet in the stomach opening.

Pour a little water into a roasting tin and put the pigeons in it. Roast them at 200-225 °C (400-425 °F, Gas Mark 6-7) for 40-60 minutes. As soon as the pigeon juices start to caramelize, add a little hot water, then baste the pigeons frequently. Arrange the pigeons on a warm serving dish and keep them warm. De-glaze the roasting tin with water, add the cream, make up the gravy with water and bring it to the boil in a saucepan.
Thicken the gravy with the cornflour and adjust the seasoning.

Variation: Mince the giblets, mix them with some breadcrumbs, an egg, salt, a pinch of grated nutmeg and chopped parsley, stuff the pigeons with it and truss them with string.

GUINEA FOWL WITH TUNA

Serves 4

1 oven-ready guinea fowl	100 ml (3½ fl oz) olive oil
1 packet of vegetables for stew	2 hard-boiled eggs
1 bunch of fresh parsley	1 tbsp capers
1 bunch of fresh basil	juice of 1 lemon
1 egg yolk	white wine
1 tsp mustard	tomatoes, quartered
2 tsp vinegar	slices of lemon
150 g (5 oz) tuna in brine	salt and pepper

Put the guinea fowl in a saucepan with enough water to cover, season with salt, bring to the boil and skim it. Prepare the vegetables, parsley and half the basil, add them to the guinea fowl and season with pepper. Bring to the boil and simmer for 45-50 minutes. Leave the guinea fowl to go cold in the stock, then drain it and joint it. Take off the skin and arrange the joints on a serving dish, with a few basil leaves around the meat. Blend together the egg yolk, mustard and vinegar, season with

salt and pepper, then whisk the dressing. Gradually add the oil to the dressing, whisking all the time. Drain the tuna. Shell the hard-boiled eggs, chop them finely and combine them with the tuna. Mix together the tuna and chopped egg, the mayonnaise dressing and capers. Adjust the seasoning with lemon juice and white wine. Pour the dressing over the guinea fowl. Garnish with tomato quarters and slices of lemon.

PARTRIDGES IN WINE

Serves 4

4 oven-ready partridge	125 ml (4 fl oz) red wine
60 g (2½ oz) bacon, sliced	1 tbsp cornflour
40 g (1½ oz) butter	4 tbsp cream
1 onion	fresh sage
5 juniper berries	salt and pepper

PARTRIDGE DOLMA

Serves 4

4 oven-ready partridges	40 g (1½ oz) butter
fresh oregano	125 ml (4 fl oz) red wine
stuffed vine leaves, tinned	250 ml (8 fl oz) cream
marinated vine leaves	zest of ½ an unwaxed
(available from	lemon
delicatessens)	salt and freshly ground
8 slices smoked bacon	pepper

Season the partridges inside and out with salt and pepper, then sprinkle them with oregano. Stuff the partridges with the stuffed vine leaves, then wrap a marinated vine leaf around each partridge, followed by a slice of bacon around each one and truss them.
Pour a little cold water into the bottom of a roasting tin. Put the partridges in the roasting tin and roast them in a hot oven for 45 minutes. As soon as the juices start to caramelize, add the red wine, then baste the partridges frequently, adding more wine as necessary.

Take the partridges out of the oven, arrange them on a warm serving dish, and keep them warm. De-glaze the juices with the cream, add the lemon zest, bring the gravy to the boil and adjust the seasoning. Serve with potato croquettes.

Season the partridges inside and out with salt and pepper, then wrap the slices of bacon around them. Melt the butter in a casserole dish and brown the partridges all over. Peel the onion, cut it into quarters and brown it with the partridges, then add the juniper berries, sage and red wine. Braise the partridges for 45-60 minutes, basting them from time to time and adding wine or water to the juices as necessary.
Cut the partridges in half, arrange them on a warm serving dish, and keep them warm. De-glaze the juices with water, strain the resulting gravy and bring it to the boil. Blend together the cornflour and cream and use to thicken the gravy. Adjust the seasoning with more wine, salt and pepper.

Serve the partridges with potato croquettes or Brussels sprouts.

Above: *Roast pigeons*
Right: *Partridge Dolma*

CHINESE LEAF STEW

Serves 5-6

250 g (8 oz) beef	2 onions
250 g (8 oz) mutton	1 kg (2 lb) Chinese leaf
250 g (8 oz) pork	2 tomatoes
2-3 tbsp oil	125 ml (4 fl oz) white wine
1 clove of garlic	salt and pepper

Dice the meat, heat the oil in a casserole dish and seal the diced meat in it, then season with salt and pepper. Peel and crush the garlic. Peel and slice the onions. Add the garlic and onions to the meat and brown them on a high heat. Add 250 ml (8 fl oz) water and simmer for
45 minutes.

Trim away any damaged or wilted leaves from the Chinese leaves. Cut the remaining leaves in half, then into strips, wash and drain them. Blanch the tomatoes in boiling water, refresh in cold water, skin them and cut them in half. Add the Chinese leaves and tomatoes to the meat, and another 250 ml (8 fl oz) water. Bring the stew to the boil, season it with salt and pepper, put the lid on the casserole dish and simmer on a low heat for 30 minutes, stirring occasionally. Add the white wine and bring to the boil again before serving. Serve with rice or potatoes.

SALSIFY STEW

500 g (1 lb) pork	40 g (1½ oz) butter
750 g (1½ lb) salsify, cleaned	fresh thyme and sage
750 g (1½ lb) potatoes	salt and pepper

Serves 4

Dice the meat. Wash the salsify and chop it finely. Peel and chop the potatoes. Melt the butter and brown the meat in it, then season with salt.

Add 250 ml (8 fl oz) water to the meat, together with the salsify, potatoes and herbs. Simmer the stew over a low heat for 1¾ hours, then adjust the seasoning.

STEWED VEAL WITH RICE

500 g (1 lb) shoulder of veal, boned	1 yellow pepper
4 tbsp oil	1 red pepper
1 onion	1 large courgette
1 clove of garlic	2 knobs of butter
200 g (7 oz) rice	20 stuffed green olives
1 litre (13/4 pints) meat stock	paprika
	fresh basil and thyme
	salt and pepper

Serves 4

Dice the meat. Heat the oil in a casserole dish and brown the meat for 10 minutes. Peel the onion and garlic, slice them thinly and sweat them with the meat. Add the rice and stock, bring to the boil and simmer for 20 minutes, stirring from time to time.

Cut the peppers in half, core and de-seed them, then cut them into strips. Wipe and slice the courgette. Melt the butter in a frying pan, sweat the vegetables for 15 minutes, then season them with salt and pepper. Slice the olives into rings and add them to the vegetables. As soon as the rice is cooked, add the vegetables to the rice, season with salt and pepper, sprinkle with paprika, basil and thyme and serve immediately.

Left: *Chinese leaf stew*

VEGETABLE STEW WITH MEATBALLS

Serves 6

500 g (1 lb) bones	1 egg
350 g (12 oz) potatoes	1 tbsp fresh parsley,
1 kg (2 lb) mixed	chopped
vegetables, frozen	fresh savory
200 g (7 oz) minced beef	fresh thyme
200 g (7 oz) minced pork	fresh marjoram
1 slice of stale bread	mustard
1 onion	salt and pepper

Wash the bones in cold water and wipe them dry. Bring some salted water to the boil, add the bones, skim and

Above: *Vegetable stew with meatballs*
Opposite: *Provenáale pea soup*

simmer for 1½ hours. Peel and dice the potatoes. Take the bones out of the stock and strain it. Add the potatoes and vegetables to the stock and season with salt and pepper. Add the herbs to taste and simmer on a low heat for about 15 minutes.

Soften the bread in cold water, then squeeze it out. Peel and finely chop the onion. Combine the minced meats, onion, egg, bread and mustard, season with salt, then shape the mixture into little balls. Turn the heat under the stew to the lowest setting and simmer the meatballs in the stock for 5-10 minutes. Garnish the stew with chopped parsley.

Tip: Add a little broccoli.

PROVENÇALE PEA SOUP

Serves 3-4

450 g (15 oz) frozen leeks
500 g (1 lb) tomatoes, tinned
300 g (10 oz) peas, frozen
125 ml (4 fl oz) meat stock
1 clove of garlic
1 tbsp olive oil
1-2 tbsp vinegar

3-4 eggs
3-4 slices bread for toasting
rosemary
cayenne pepper
salt
pepper

Peel and crush the garlic. Heat the oil in a saucepan and brown the garlic, add the leeks and roughly chopped tinned tomatoes, then season to taste with rosemary, cayenne pepper, salt and pepper.

Bring to the boil, stirring occasionally, cover and simmer for 15 minutes. Add the peas and cook them for 5 minutes. Then add the meat stock, 1 litre (1¾ pints) water and the vinegar and bring the soup to the boil.

Poach each egg separately in the soup. Take them out carefully and drain them.
Toast the bread, arrange an egg on top of each slice of toast in a soup bowl, then pour the soup over the egg and toast.

MUSHROOM AND BEEF STEW

Serves 4

500 g (1 lb) forerib or backrib of beef
100 g (3½ oz) streaky bacon
1 bottle of white wine
250 g (8 oz) baby onions or shallots
500 g (1 lb) new potatoes
knob of lard

250 g (8 oz) button mushrooms
4-5 tbsp brandy
1 meat stock cube
1 bunch of fresh parsley
herbes de Provence, dried
salt
pepper

Cut the meat into chunks. Dice the bacon and render it in a casserole dish. Add the meat to the bacon, seal it all over, then season with salt, pepper and herbes de Provence. Add 250 ml (8 fl oz) white wine. Put the lid on the casserole dish and simmer the stew for 1 hour.

Melt the butter in a frying pan and brown the onions and potatoes in it, stirring all the time. Wipe the mushrooms, cut them into quarters and sweat them with the onions and potatoes.

Add the vegetables to the meat with the brandy and remaining white wine, adjust the seasoning and simmer for 25-35 minutes. Garnish with chopped parsley.

DRIED PEA SOUP WITH SALTED BELLY PORK

Serves 4

400 g (13 oz) dried peas
2 litres (3½ pints) meat
stock
1 kg (2 lb) salted belly pork
500 g (1 lb) potatoes

1 pack of stew vegetables
4 coarse, meaty sausages
marjoram
salt and pepper

Soak the peas in cold water for 12-24 hours. Pour the peas and soaking liquid into a stock pot or large saucepan, add the pork and bring the meat and peas to the boil. Simmer them on a low heat until they are almost tender (1-1½ hours).

Slice the potatoes. Clean and peel the stew vegetables, cut them into thin strips to make a julienne, then add them with the potatoes and sausages to the soup, season with salt and pepper and simmer for a further 30 minutes to 1 hour. Adjust the seasoning, garnish with marjoram and serve with croutons.

Variation: You can use a piece of streaky bacon instead of the salted belly pork.

BEEF STEW WITH VEGETABLES

Serves 5

750 g (1½ lb) forerib or
back rib of beef
1 kg (2 lb) Chinese leaf
4 carrots
2 leeks
1 celeriac
500 g (1 lb) potatoes

2 tbsp tomato purée
1 bunch of fresh parsley,
chopped
1 bunch of fresh dill,
chopped
fresh thyme
salt
pepper

Dice the meat, add it to 1 litre (1¾ pints) boiling water, skim and simmer for 1 hour. Remove any damaged leaves from the Chinese leaf, cut off the thick spines and cut the leaves in half lengthways, slice them into ribbons, wash and drain them.

Peel the carrots, celeriac and potatoes and clean the leeks. Wash the vegetables, cut them into very thin strips to make a julienne and add them to the meat with the Chinese leaf. Season the stew with salt, pepper and thyme to taste and simmer for 45 minutes. Take the meat out of the stew and dice it, then return it to the pan, add the tomato purée and stir well. Garnish with chopped dill and parsley.

BEAN STEW WITH KASSELER
(SMOKED NECK END OF PORK)
Serves 5

750 g (1½ lb) smoked neck
end of pork or belly pork
or smoked gammon
125 g (4 oz) onions
3 tbsp oil
800 g (1½ lb) haricot
beans, tinned
425 g (14 oz) kidney beans,

tinned
125 ml (4 fl oz) meat stock
1 bunch of fresh flat leaf
parsley
1 bunch of fresh chives
cayenne pepper
salt and pepper

CABBAGE AND TOMATO SOUP

Serves 6

125 g (4 oz) minced beef	slice of stale bread
125 g (4 oz) minced pork	1 small onion
1 kg (2 lb) cabbage	1 tbsp mustard
750 g (1½ lb) potatoes	1 egg
500 g (1 lb) tomatoes	salt and pepper
60 g (2½ oz) butter	

Wash the cabbage and cut it into thin strips. Peel and wash the potatoes, then dice them. Blanch the tomatoes in boiling water, refresh them in cold water, skin and chop them.

Melt the butter in a frying pan, add the cabbage and potatoes, stirring all the time. Add 1 litre (1¾ pints) water, season with salt and pepper, bring to the boil, cover and simmer for 40 minutes. Soak the bread in cold water, then squeeze it out. Peel and finely chop the onion. Combine the meat, onion, egg, bread and mustard, season with salt and pepper and shape into about 20 little meatballs. Add the meatballs and tomatoes to the soup and simmer for a further 20 minutes. Season with salt and pepper to taste.

Above: *Dried pea soup with salted belly pork*
Right: *Bean stew with Kasseler*

Take the meat off the bone and cut it into pieces. Peel the onions and slice them thinly. Heat the oil in a casserole dish and brown the meat all over, then add the onions. As soon as the onions have browned, add the haricot and kidney beans.

Add the meat stock to the casserole dish, cover, bring to the boil and simmer over a low heat for 10 minutes, then season with salt and pepper. Adjust the seasoning with cayenne pepper. Garnish with chopped parsley and chives.

BROAD BEANS WITH MUTTON

Serves 4

400 g (13 oz) mutton	40 g (1½ oz) butter
750 g (1½ lb) potatoes	savory
750 g (1½ lb) broad beans,	salt
shelled or 3 kg (7 lb)	pepper
unshelled	

Cut the meat into pieces. Peel and dice the potatoes. Top, tail and wash the beans. Melt the butter in a casserole dish and brown the meat all over, then season it with salt and pepper.

Add the potatoes, beans and savory, then add 400 ml (14 fl oz) water. Put the lid on the casserole dish and simmer on a low heat for 1-1¼ hours. Adjust the seasoning.

CHICKEN CASSEROLE

Serves 4

1 kg (2 lb) chicken wings and carcass	2-3 carrots
	2 leeks
500 g (1 lb) chicken breasts	1 bouquet garni
	3 tbsp fresh parsley,
2 onions	chopped
1 pack vegetables for stew plus	salt
	pepper
1 kg (2 lb) potatoes and	

Put the chicken carcass and wings in cold, salted water, add the bouquet garni and bring to the boil. Add the chicken breasts, bring to the boil again and skim. Peel the onions and cut them into quarters. Wash the vegetables from the stew pack and cut them into thin strips to make a julienne. Add them to the chicken with the onions, bring to the boil, then reduce the heat and simmer for 1 hour. Take the meat out of the stock and reserve it.

Peel and dice the potatoes. Add them to the stock, bring to the boil and simmer for 5 minutes. Peel the carrots and cut them into matchsticks. Add them to the stock, bring to the boil and simmer for 7 minutes. Wash and trim the leeks, retaining 10 cm (4 inches) of green. Slice them and add them to the other ingredients in the stock.
Bring the stock to the boil again, simmer for 3-5 minutes, then return the meat to the casserole dish, heat it through and adjust the seasoning. Serve garnished with chopped parsley.

BRAISED FRENCH BEANS WITH TOMATOES

Serves 4

400 g (13 oz) mutton	2 onions
250 g (8 oz) tomatoes	1 clove of garlic
750 g (1½ lb) French beans	herbes de Provence, dried
	fresh parsley, chopped
500 g (1 lb) potatoes	salt and pepper
40 g (1½ oz) butter	

Cut the meat into small pieces. Blanch the tomatoes in boiling water, refresh them in cold water, skin and chop them. Top and tail the beans. Peel and dice the potatoes.

Melt the butter in a casserole dish and brown the meat all over. Peel the onions and garlic and slice them thinly. Add the meat, together with the tomatoes, turn the heat up high, season with salt, pepper and herbes de Provence. Add 1 litre (1¾ pints) water, then add the beans and potatoes. Put the lid on the casserole dish and simmer for 1-1¼ hours on a low heat. Adjust the seasoning and garnish with chopped parsley.

LEEKS AND SAUSAGE STEW

Serves 4

75 g (3 oz) streaky bacon
4 coarse, meaty sausages
1 kg (2 lb) leeks
750 g (1½ lb) floury
potatoes
2 carrots
1 celeriac

1 onion
1 tbsp oil
1 litre (1¾ pints) meat
stock
1-2 tbsp fresh parsley,
chopped
salt and pepper

Left: *Braised French beans with tomatoes*
Below: *Leeks and sausage stew*

Wash and trim the leeks, retaining 10 cm (4 inches) of green, cut them in half lengthways, then cut them into 1 cm (½ inch) pieces, rinse them carefully and drain them. Peel the carrots and celeriac and cut them into very thin strips to make a julienne. Peel and dice the potatoes and onion. Dice the bacon.

Heat the oil in a casserole dish, fry the diced bacon to render it, then add the vegetables, except for the leeks, and brown them, stirring occasionally. Add the stock and sausages. Bring to the boil, simmer for 10 minutes, then add the leeks and season with salt and pepper.

Bring to the boil again and simmer for 15-20 minutes. Adjust the seasoning and serve garnished with chopped parsley.

the rest. Melt the butter in a casserole dish and fry the diced pig's cheek. Add the turnips and onions, stirring constantly, then season with salt, pepper and thyme. Cook for a few minutes, then add 500 ml (18 fl oz) water and lay the slices of meat on top of the vegetables.

Put the lid on the casserole dish and simmer on a low heat for 25 minutes. Peel the potatoes, dice them and cook them with the vegetables for 15 minutes, then season with salt and pepper to taste.

FISH STEW

Serves 4

500 g (1 lb) cod fillets	125 ml (4 fl oz) white wine
250 g (8 oz) button	1 bouquet garni
mushrooms	2 tbsp fresh parsley,
250 g (8 oz) French beans	chopped
400 g (13 oz) potatoes	lemon juice
1 large onion	salt
50 g (2 oz) butter	pepper

Rinse the fish fillets in cold water and pat them dry, then sprinkle them with lemon juice and leave them to marinate for a few minutes. Season them with salt and chop them into medium-sized pieces. Wipe the

PARSNIP STEW

Serves 4-5

600 g (1¼ lb) breast of	500 g (1 lb) potatoes
lamb or forerib of beef	750 g (1½ lb) parsnips
1 bouquet garni	1 tbsp fresh dill, chopped
1 bay leaf	fresh parsley, chopped
4 small chillies or 1 tbsp	salt and pepper
chilli paste	

Put the meat into boiling, salted water, add the bay leaf, bouquet garni and chilli. Bring to the boil and simmer for 1¼ hours. Peel and dice the potatoes and add them to the stew, then simmer them for 5 minutes. Peel the parsnips, dice them, season them with pepper and simmer them for 10 minutes with the potatoes.

Serve the stew garnished with chopped dill and parsley.

RAGOUT OF BABY TURNIPS

Serves 5-6

1½ kg (3½ lb) baby	knob of butter
turnips	750 g (1½ lb) potatoes
350 g (12 oz) onions	fresh thyme
1 kg (2 lb) smoked pig's	salt
cheek	pepper

Peel the turnips and onions, then dice them. Dice one quarter of the pig's cheek, removing the rind, and slice mushrooms, peel the onion and cut them into thin slices. Top and tail the beans. Peel and dice the potatoes.

Melt the butter, sweat the onions until translucent, then add the mushrooms, beans and potatoes. Season with salt and pepper and brown for a few minutes on a high heat. Add 1 litre (1¾ pints) water and the bouquet garni, cover and simmer for 25 minutes. Add the fish and white wine, season with salt and pepper and simmer on a low heat for 10-15 minutes. Garnish with chopped parsley.

Below: *Ragout of baby turnips (right) and Parsnip stew (left)*
Left-hand page: *Fish stew*

BRAISED LEEKS

Serves 4-5

150 g (5 oz) streaky bacon	4 tomatoes, skinned
1 large onion	500 g (1 lb) cervelat or
knob of butter	salami
500 g (1 lb) potatoes	curry powder
1 kg (2 lb) leeks	paprika
500 ml (18 fl oz) meat	salt and pepper
stock	

Dice the bacon. Peel the onion and slice it thinly. Melt the butter in a casserole dish and brown the bacon and onion in it. Peel and dice the potatoes. Wash the leeks, cut them into 5 cm (2 inch) chunks, rinse and drain them. Brown them in the casserole dish with the potatoes. Add the stock, bring to the boil and simmer for about 15 minutes. Cut the tomatoes into quarters, slice the cervelat and add it to the leeks with the tomatoes. Sprinkle with curry powder, paprika and salt and simmer for 5-10 minutes.

POTATO SOUP WITH PEPPERS

Serves 4

500 g (1 lb) forerib of beef
2-3 marrow bones
1 pack of vegetables for
stew
1 kg (2 lb) potatoes
2-5 green peppers
150 g (5 oz) streaky bacon

4 onions
1 bouquet garni
4 Frankfurter sausages
peppercorns
paprika
salt and pepper

Put the meat and marrow bones into cold, salted water
with the peppercorns and bouquet garni, bring to the
boil and skim. Peel and slice the pack of stew vegetables
thinly, add them to the stock, bring to the boil and
simmer for 1½-2 hours. Strain the stock, take the meat off
the bone, dice it and reserve it. Peel the potatoes and
chop them. Cut the peppers in half, core and de-seed
them and cut them into thin strips.

Dice the bacon, then peel the onions and slice them
thinly. Fry the bacon to render the fat, add the onions
and fry them for a few minutes, then add the bacon,
onions and potatoes to the stock. Add the peppers, bring
to the boil, then simmer on a low heat for 10 minutes.
Season with salt, pepper and paprika. Slice the
Frankfurters and poach them for 5 minutes in the soup.

POTATO SOUP WITH EGGS

Serves 4-5

2 eggs
125 ml (4 fl oz) cold milk
grated nutmeg
25 g (1 oz) streaky bacon
2 knobs of butter
1 pack of vegetables for
stew
1½ litres (2½ pints) meat

stock
1 kg (2 lb) potatoes
1 egg yolk
250 ml (8 fl oz) double
cream
cress
salt
freshly ground pepper

Above: *Five types of hearty stews and their basic*
ingredients: *potatoes, onions, parsley and chives.*

Beat the eggs with the milk and season with salt and
nutmeg. Butter a ramekin, pour the beaten egg into it,
then put the ramekin in a roasting tin filled with water,
and put the tin in the oven. As soon as the water starts to
boil, turn off the heat - the water should not boil any
more. Leave the eggs to set (about 30 minutes) then turn
them out and dice them.

Dice the bacon, then melt the remaining butter in a
casserole dish and fry the bacon in it. Slice the
vegetables thinly and fry them with the bacon. Add the

stock and bring to the boil. Peel the potatoes and chop
them. Add them to the stock and simmer for
20-25 minutes. Purée the soup in a food processor or
with a hand mixer. Beat together the egg yolk and cream
and use it to thicken and enrich the soup, then season
with salt and pepper. Carefully fold in the diced egg and
garnish with cress.

POTATO AND TOMATO SOUP

Serves 4

1 kg (2 lb) potatoes
1 pack of vegetables for
stew
400 g (13 oz) tomatoes
2 onions
2 knobs of butter
1½ litres (2½ pints) meat

stock
1 kg (2 lb) potatoes
150 g (5 oz) crème fraîche
1 tbsp fresh basil, chopped
1 tbsp fresh chives,
chopped
salt and pepper

Peel the onions, slice them thinly and dice the vegetables for stew. Melt the butter in a casserole dish and sauté the vegetables. Add the stock and bring to the boil.

Peel the potatoes, chop them, add them to the stock and simmer them for 12-15 minutes. Purée the soup in a food processor or with a hand blender. Add the cream, basil and chives and stir well. Blanch the tomatoes in boiling water, refresh them in cold water, skin and dice them and add them to the soup. Bring the soup to the boil and season it with salt and pepper.
Serve with diced, smoked ham.

VEGETARIAN SOUP

Serves 6-7

250 g (8 oz) carrots	50 g (2 oz) butter
500 g (1 lb) potatoes	2 litres (3½ pints)
250 g (8 oz) French beans	vegetable stock
250 g (8 oz) tomatoes	2 tbsp fresh parsley,
250 g (8 oz) cauliflower	chopped
250 g (8 oz) Brussels	salt
sprouts	pepper
2 onions	

Peel the carrots and potatoes, top and tail the beans and chop them. Blanch the tomatoes in boiling water, refresh them in cold water, skin them and cut them into quarters. Wash the cauliflower and separate the florets. Wash the Brussels sprouts, remove any damaged leaves and score a cross in the base of each sprout. Peel and dice the onions.

Melt the butter in a casserole dish and fry the onions, potatoes, carrots and Brussels sprouts for 5 minutes. Add the stock, cover and simmer for 10 minutes. Add the French beans, cauliflower and tomatoes and simmer on a low heat for 20 minutes, then season with salt and pepper and serve garnished with chopped parsley.

BEEF WITH WHITE CABBAGE

Serves 4

500 g (1 lb) beef	2 onions
1 white cabbage	1 bouquet garni
500 g (1 lb) potatoes	1 tsp cumin
250 g (8 oz) carrots	salt
40 g (1½ oz) butter	pepper

Cut the meat into chunks. Wash the cabbage and cut it into thin strips. Peel the carrots and potatoes and cut them into very thin matchsticks. Melt the butter in a casserole dish and seal the meat all over.

Peel the onions, slice them thinly and brown them for a few moments with the meat. Season the beef with salt, pepper and cumin, add 500 ml (18 fl oz) water and the bouquet garni and simmer on a low heat for 45 minutes. Add the vegetables and simmer for a further 20 minutes. Season with salt and pepper.

DRIED PEA SOUP WITH NECK END OF PORK
Serves 4-5

400 g (13 oz) dried peas	stew
2 litres (3½ pints) meat	2 onions
stock	75 g (3 oz) streaky bacon
400 g (13 oz) neck end of	fresh marjoram
pork	salt
500 g (1 lb) potatoes	pepper
1 pack of vegetables for	

Soak the peas for 12-24 hours. Pour the water from the peas into a stock pot or large saucepan and bring it to the boil with the peas and meat, then simmer.
Peel the potatoes and vegetables for stew and cut them into very thin matchsticks. Add them to the peas and meat with the marjoram, season with salt and pepper and simmer on a low heat for 2 hours. Take the cooked meat out of the stock, dice it, then return it to the soup.

Peel the onions, then dice them with the bacon. Render the bacon in a frying pan and fry the onions until golden, then add the onions and bacon to the soup.

Left: *Vegetarian soup*

Above: *Vegetable soup with carrots*

VEGETABLE SOUP WITH CARROTS

Serves 4-5

*100 g (3½ oz) haricot
beans
250 g (8 oz) belly of pork,
boned
500 g (1 lb) forerib
1 kg (2 lb) carrots
500 g (1 lb) potatoes
100 g (3½ oz) celeriac
250 g (8 oz) apples*

*2 knobs of butter
2 onions
750 ml (1¼ pints) water
from soaking the beans
2 tbsp fresh, mixed herbs,
chopped: flat leaf parsley
and chervil
salt and pepper*

Wash the beans and soak them for 12-24 hours. Cut the belly of pork into pieces. Peel the carrots, potatoes and celeriac, and cut them into very thin matchsticks. Peel the apples, core and slice them. Melt the butter in a casserole dish and seal the meat all over.

Slice the onion thinly. Add it to the meat when the meat begins to brown, season with salt and pepper.
Add some of the water in which the beans were soaked, then add the beans. Bring to the boil, simmer for 30 minutes then add the vegetables. Bring to the boil again, then add the apples after a further 15 minutes' simmering.

Cook the apples for 10 minutes. Take out the foreribs, take the meat off the bone, dice it and return it to the pan. Heat it through with the vegetables, then adjust the seasoning.

Garnish with chopped parsley and chervil.

RABBIT WITH LENTILS AND CHANTERELLE MUSHROOMS

Serves 6

1 saddle of rabbit, weighing 600 g (1¼ lb)	250 g (8 oz) lentils
6 rabbit's thighs	1 litre (1¾ pints) meat stock
200 g (7 oz) bacon, diced	250 g (8 oz) chanterelle mushrooms
50 g (2 oz) butter	2 cloves of garlic
1 tbsp fresh thyme, chopped	1 tbsp sherry vinegar
40 ml (1½ fl oz) Calvados or brandy	125 ml (4 fl oz) red wine
	salt and pepper

Cut the saddle of rabbit into 4 pieces and season it with salt and pepper. Heat 30 g (1 oz) butter in a casserole dish, fry the diced bacon and reserve it. Seal the pieces of rabbit all over, sprinkle them with the thyme and add the Calvados or brandy.

Stirring all the time, add the lentils and then add the meat stock. Bring to the boil, cover and simmer on a low heat for 1 hour, stirring occasionally. Wash, chop and drain the mushrooms.

Melt 20 g (¾ oz) butter in a frying pan, and sweat the mushrooms with the peeled and chopped garlic. Season with salt and pepper, then add the vinegar and red wine. Add the fried bacon and mushrooms to the lentils 15 minutes before the end of cooking time. Adjust the seasoning with salt, pepper and more thyme.

Tip: Wine vinegar and a drop of sherry can be substituted for the sherry vinegar.

SWEDE STEW

Serves 4

400 g (13 oz) belly of pork, boned	2 onions
1 kg (2 lb) swede	1 bouquet garni
750 g (1½ lb) potatoes	1 tbsp fresh parsley, chopped
40 g (1½ oz) butter	salt and pepper

Cut the meat into small pieces. Peel the swede and potatoes and cut them into very thin matchsticks to make a julienne. Melt the butter in a casserole dish and seal the pork in it. Peel and slice the onions thinly and fry them with the meat. Season with salt and pepper, add the

bouquet garni, potatoes and swede, stirring all the time, then add 1 litre (1¾ pints) water. Simmer on a low heat. Adjust the seasoning and garnish with chopped parsley.

POTATO SOUP WITH SAUSAGES

Serves 6

500 g (1 lb) coarse, meaty sausages	stock
2 onions	1½ kg (3½ lb) potatoes
2 packs of vegetables for stew	fresh thyme, lovage and parsley, chopped
80 g (3 oz) butter	salt
1½ litres (2½ pints) meat	pepper

Peel the onions and slice them. Wash and peel the stew vegetables and cut them into thin matchsticks, to make a julienne. Melt the butter in a casserole dish and brown the onions and vegetables.

Add the stock to the casserole dish, then peel the potatoes and chop them into pieces. Add the sausages, potatoes, thyme and lovage to the stock, season with salt and pepper, bring to the boil and simmer gently for 30 minutes. Adjust the seasoning and garnish with chopped parsley.

Left: *Rabbit with lentils and chanterelle mushrooms*
Below: *Potato soup with sausages*

Dice the beef, top and tail the beans, peel and dice the potatoes. Melt the butter in a casserole dish and brown the meat all over. Peel the vegetables for stew and the onion and slice them thinly.

Fry the onion with the meat, then add the stew vegetables and season with salt, pepper and savory. Add 500 ml (18 fl oz) water, and then add the potatoes and beans. Simmer gently for 1 hour.

Variation: Brown 250 g (8 oz) tomatoes with the meat and onions, but reduce the volume of liquid to 250 ml (8 fl oz).

PEA AND HAM SOUP

Serves 4

500 g (1 lb) sparerib or	200 g (7 oz) dry cured ham
belly of pork	2 eggs, beaten
1 bouquet garni	6 slices French toast
1 pack of vegetables for	fresh thyme, chopped
stew	salt
1 kg (2 lb) peas, shelled	pepper

Put the meat into 1½ litres (2½ pints) cold, salted water with the bouquet garni and bring to the boil, then simmer for 20 minutes.

Peel the vegetables for stew and cut them into thin strips to make a julienne. Add the vegetables and peas to the stock, bring to the boil and simmer for 20 minutes. Season with salt, pepper and thyme.

To make the ham meatballs: Cut the ham into small dice. Crush the French toast in a tea towel or plastic bag with a rolling pin. Combine the resulting crumbs with the diced ham and beaten eggs. Using your hands, shape the mixture into little balls, add them to the soup and simmer them for 10 minutes.

BRAISED SAVOY CABBAGE WITH BACON

Serves 6

1 Savoy cabbage	and clod of beef
2-3 onions	fresh thyme, chopped
150 g (5 oz) streaky bacon,	1 bay leaf
sliced	salt and pepper
500 g (1 lb) forerib or neck	

Remove any damaged leaves from the cabbage and cut it into 8 pieces. Cut away the thick spines, then wash the leaves and slice them into ribbons. Peel and slice the onions. Place the slices of bacon in the bottom of a casserole dish and layer the sliced onions on top. Cover and sweat for them 10 minutes.

Cut the meat into chunks, add it to the casserole dish, then add the cabbage, bay leaf and thyme. Season with salt and pepper, add 125 ml (4 fl oz) water, cover and simmer for 1½ hours.

BROAD BEANS WITH CARROTS

Serves 4-5

500 g (1 lb) broad beans,	2 knobs of butter
shelled or 2 kg (4½ lb) with	75 g (3 oz) streaky bacon,
pods	diced
400 g (13 oz) baby carrots	4 tbsp crème fraîche
400 g (13 oz) potatoes	salt
1 onion	pepper
12 fresh sage leaves	

BEEF WITH FRENCH BEANS

Serves 4-6

400 g (13 oz) beef	stew
1 kg (2 lb) French beans	1 onion
750 g (1½ lb) potatoes	fresh savory, chopped
40 g (1½ oz) butter	salt
1 pack of vegetables for	pepper

Above: *Broad beans with carrots*
Left: *Pea and ham soup*

Wash the broad beans, peel and slice the carrots. Peel, wash and dice the potatoes. Peel the onion and slice it thinly. Rinse the sage leaves carefully, reserve 4 or 5 for a garnish and chop the rest.

Melt the butter in a casserole dish and fry the diced bacon and onions. Add the broad beans, carrots, potatoes and the chopped sage, season with salt and pepper, and sweat the ingredients for a few minutes.

Add 125 ml (4 fl oz) of water, cover and simmer the vegetables for 20-30 minutes. Enrich the vegetables with the crème fraîche and garnish with sage leaves.

Serve with grilled sausages or pork chops.

Above: *Vegetable casserole with cream cheese*

VEGETABLE CASSEROLE WITH CREAM CHEESE

Serves 4

1 large onion
4 courgettes
1 red pepper
1 green pepper
2 large tomatoes
6 tbsp vinegar, fruit
vinegar if possible e.g.
raspberry

herbes de Provence
5 tbsp olive oil
200 g (7 oz) cream cheese
1 clove of garlic
2 eggs
2 tbsp fresh parsley,
chopped
salt and pepper

Peel and slice the onion, wipe the courgettes and slice them. Cut the peppers in half, core and de-seed them and cut them into thin strips. Wash and chop the tomatoes. Layer the vegetables in a large casserole dish, seasoning each layer with salt, pepper and herbes de Provence, add the vinegar and olive oil, cover and sweat them for 40 minutes, without stirring.

Blend together the cheese, the peeled and crushed garlic and the eggs, and season the mixture with salt and pepper. Pour the cheese mixture over the vegetables 5 minutes before the end of cooking time, cover, reduce the heat and leave the cheese and egg mixture to set. Garnish with chopped parsley.

SAVOY CABBAGE SOUP

Serves 6-7

100 g (3½ oz) haricot
beans
500 g (1 lb) streaky bacon
1 Savoy cabbage
3 onions
3-4 cloves of garlic
2 carrots
2 pieces of Hamburg
parsley (or 5 sprigs of
fresh parsley)
2 leeks

2 sprigs of fresh thyme
2 sprigs of fresh
marjoram
2-3 sprigs of fresh parsley
2-3 celery leaves
2-3 bay leaves
500 g (1 lb) potatoes
500 g (1 lb) garlic sausage
salt
freshly ground pepper

Wash the beans and soak them in cold water for
12-24 hours. Fill a stock pot with 1 litre (1¾ pints) water,
add the bacon, bring to the boil and simmer for 1 hour.
Remove any damaged cabbage leaves, cut it into
quarters, cut off the thick spines, wash it and cut it into
ribbons.

Peel and slice the onions, peel and crush the garlic. Peel
the carrots and Hamburg parsley, trim the leek, reserving
10 cm (4 inches) of green, and cut the vegetables into
rounds. Add the beans and their liquor to the stock, then
add the vegetables. Bring to the boil and simmer for 20-
25 minutes.

Carefully wash the herbs and add them to the vegetables.
Peel and dice the potatoes. Prick the garlic sausage with
a fork and add it to the soup with the potatoes. Bring the
soup to the boil again and simmer it for 15-20 minutes.
Take the bacon and sausage out of the stock pot, slice
them and return them to the soup. Adjust the seasoning
to taste.

HARICOT BEAN AND
MUTTON STEW

Serves 5-6

250 g (8 oz) haricot beans
750 g (1½ lb) mutton
250 g (8 oz) onions
1 tsp fresh thyme
fresh rosemary
4 tbsp oil

3 cloves of garlic
500 g (1 lb) tinned
tomatoes
cayenne pepper
salt and pepper

Soak the beans in 1 litre (1¾ pints) of cold water for
12-24 hours. Bring them to the boil in the soaking liquor,
skim, cover and simmer gently for 35 minutes.

Take the meat off the bone and cut it into chunks. Peel
the onions and chop them roughly. Crush the thyme and
rosemary in a mortar. Heat the oil in a casserole dish and
brown the pieces of mutton all over. Add the onions and
herbs, season with salt and pepper and gradually add the
hot liquor from the beans.

Cover the casserole dish and simmer the contents for
15 minutes. Add the drained beans and roughly chopped
tomatoes and juice. Season to taste with cayenne pepper,
cover and simmer for 1 hour. Peel and crush a clove of
garlic, add it to the beans and season with salt and
pepper.

Serve the stew with a green salad.

Below: *Haricot bean and mutton stew*

BREAST OF VEAL WITH BABY CARROTS AND SPINACH

Serves 7-8

1½ kg (3½ lb) breast of
veal, salted
1 bouquet garni
750 g (1½ lb) carrots
750 g (1½ lb) turnips
400 g (13 oz) onions
1 kg (2 lb) waxy potatoes
250 g (8 oz) leaf spinach,
frozen

1 bunch of fresh flat leaf
parsley, washed and
leaves stripped off
1-2 tsp mustard powder
200 g (7 oz) crème fraîche
2 tbsp horseradish, grated
salt and white pepper

Put the veal into salted water with the bouquet garni,
bring it to the boil and simmer it for an hour, uncovered,
turning the meat after 30 minutes.

Peel the carrots and turnips, cut the carrots into sticks
and slice the turnip. Peel the onions and slice them
thinly, then add the carrots, turnip and onion to the meat.
Simmer for a further 30 minutes. Take the meat out of the
stock, take it off the bone and dice it. Peel the potatoes

and grate them coarsely. Cook the grated potato in the stock with the spinach and parsley leaves, season with salt, pepper and mustard powder, stirring to prevent the mustard from forming lumps. Return the diced veal to the vegetables, and simmer gently for a further 30 minutes. Whip the cream until it forms soft peaks, fold in the grated horseradish and serve separately.

FRENCH BEAN STEW WITH LEG OF LAMB

Serves 7-8

1½ kg (3½ lb) leg of lamb
2-3 knobs of lard
300 g (10 oz) baby onions
or shallots
2 cloves of garlic
750 g (1½ lb) French
beans

500 g (1 lb) potatoes
2 large green peppers
2-3 sprigs of savory
fresh parsley, chopped
salt and pepper

Cut the meat into chunks. Melt the lard in a casserole dish and brown the meat all over, then season it with salt and pepper. Peel the onions and cut them in half. Peel the garlic, chop it and fry the garlic and onions with the meat. Add 500 ml (18 fl oz) water and simmer gently for 30 minutes.

Top and tail the beans, peel the potatoes and chop them. Cut the peppers in half, core and de-seed them and cut them into thin strips. Add the vegetables and savory to the meat. Add another 500 ml (18 fl oz) water to the stock, bring to the boil, cover and simmer for 30-45 minutes. Adjust the seasoning and garnish with chopped parsley.

Left: Breast of veal with baby carrots and spinach
Below: French bean stew with leg of lamb

SAVOY CABBAGE WITH HAM SAUSAGE

Serves 6

750 g (1½ lb) Savoy
cabbage
400 g (13 oz) potatoes
1 onion
50 g (2 oz) lard

600 g (1¼ lb) continental
ham sausage
salt
freshly ground white
pepper

Wash the cabbage and slice it thinly. Peel the potatoes
and onion and dice them. Melt the lard in a casserole
dish and brown the onions in it. Add the cabbage,
season with salt and pepper, then add the potatoes.

Bury the sausage in the vegetables, add 250 ml (8 fl oz)
water and simmer, then adjust the seasoning. Slice the
sausage and serve it with the cabbage.

BEEF STEW WITH PUMPKIN

Serves 6

500 g (1 lb) beef
1 pack of vegetables for
stew
1 kg (2 lb) pumpkin
3 onions
3 tbsp oil

500 g (1 lb) tomatoes
2 tbsp fresh basil,
chopped
vinegar or lemon juice
salt
freshly ground pepper

Peel or trim the vegetables for stew and put them in
salted water with the beef. Bring to the boil, skim, then
simmer gently for 1 hour. Take out the meat and cut it
into chunks. Strain the stock, reserving 1 litre (1¾ pints).
Peel the pumpkin, de-seed it and dice the flesh. Peel the
onions and slice them thinly.

Heat the oil in a frying pan and fry the onions and
pumpkin for 5 minutes. Blanch the tomatoes in boiling
water, refresh them in cold water, skin them and chop
them roughly. Put them in a pan with the reserved stock,
meat, basil, pumpkin and onions. Simmer for 5 minutes.
Season with salt, pepper and lemon juice or vinegar to
taste.

SUMMER CASSEROLE WITH ONIONS

Serves 4

500 g (1 lb) onions
500 g (1 lb) carrots
500 g (1 lb) potatoes
200 g (7 oz) minced beef
200 g (7 oz) minced pork

500 ml (18 fl oz) meat
stock
dried herbes de Provence
fresh parsley, chopped
salt and pepper

Peel the onions, carrots and potatoes and slice them.
Season the minced meat with salt and pepper and layer
the meat and vegetables in an earthenware casserole
dish, add more salt and pepper, sprinkle with herbes de
Provence and pour the meat stock over.

Cover the casserole dish and bake in the oven at
200-225°C (400-425°F, Gas Mark
6-7) for 1¾ hours. Garnish with chopped parsley.

Left: *Savoy cabbage with ham sausage*
Right: *Summer casserole with onions*

SAVOY CABBAGE WITH SMOKED NECK END OF PORK

Serves 4-5

1½ kg (3½ lb) Savoy cabbage
500 g (1 lb) smoked neck end of pork, boned, or smoked gammon

250 g (8 oz) smoked pig's cheek
1 onion
2 coarse, meaty sausages
salt and pepper

*P*repare the cabbage by removing any damaged leaves and the stems and wash it carefully. Blanch it in boiling water for 1-2 minutes, drain it and chop it roughly.

Put the smoked neck end of pork or gammon in a large casserole dish with the pig's cheek, the peeled and sliced onion and the cabbage. Add the sausages and some water and season with salt and pepper. Bring to the boil, cover and simmer for 1 hour. Take out all the meat and slice it all except the sausages. Arrange it on a warm serving dish with the whole sausages, adjust the cabbage seasoning and serve it with the meat, accompanied by sautéed potatoes.

FRENCH BEAN AND SAVORY STEW

Serves 4-5

250 g (8 oz) stewing beef
250 g (8 oz) stewing pork
3 tbsp oil
2 large onions
500 g (1 lb) potatoes
500 g (1 lb) French beans
1 small red pepper
3-4 sprigs savory

250 g (8 oz) button mushrooms
250 g (8 oz) tomatoes
2 tbsp fresh parsley, chopped
paprika
salt
pepper

Cut the meat into 1½ cm (⅝ inch) dice. Heat the oil in a casserole dish and brown the meat all over. Peel the onions, slice them thinly and add them to the meat. Season with salt, pepper and paprika. Add 750 ml (1¼ pints) water and bring to the boil.

Peel and chop the potatoes, top and tail the French beans and chop them. Cut the peppers in half, core and de-seed them, then slice them thinly. Wash the savory carefully. Wipe the mushrooms and slice them thinly. After 30 minutes add the potatoes to the meat. Bring to the boil, simmer for 5 minutes, then add the beans, red pepper and savory. Simmer for a further 10 minutes, then add the mushrooms. Bring to the boil again and cook on a high heat for 3-5 minutes.

Blanch the tomatoes in boiling water, refresh them in cold water, skin them and cut them into quarters. Add them to the meat and vegetables and adjust the seasoning. Garnish the stew with chopped parsley.

Left: *Savoy cabbage with smoked neck end of pork*
Below: *French bean and savory stew*

HESSE STEW

Serves 2-3

300 g (10 oz) beef	savory
2 tbsp oil	250 g (8 oz) tomatoes, ski-
150 g (5 oz) leeks	nned
1 clove of garlic	1 tbsp fresh parsley,
300 g (10 oz) French	chopped
beans	salt and pepper

Slice the meat thinly. Heat the oil in a casserole dish and seal the meat on a high heat. Wash the leeks, slice them into rings and add them to the meat with the peeled and sliced garlic. Sweat them on a low heat, season with salt and pepper, then add 500 ml (18 fl oz) water and cook for a further 35 minutes.

Top and tail the beans. Add them to the stew with the savory and cook for a further 20 minutes. Add the tomatoes and cook them for 5 minutes. Adjust the seasoning and sprinkle with chopped parsley. Serve with pasta.

LABSKAUS

TRADITIONAL MEAT AND MASHED POTATO HASH FROM HAMBURG

Serves 4-5

600 g (1¼ lb) salted beef	6 tbsp vinegar from
1 bouquet garni	pickled gherkins
5 large onions	400 ml (14 fl oz) beef stock
75 g (3 oz) butter	nutmeg
1 kg (2 lb) potatoes, boiled	salt
and kept hot	

Bring 500 ml (18 fl oz) salted water to the boil with the bouquet garni. Add the meat and simmer it for 2 hours. Take the meat out of the stock, straining off 400 ml (14 fl oz) stock. Peel the onions, then mince the cooked meat and onions.

Melt the butter in a casserole dish and fry the minced meat and onions in it for 5 minutes, stirring all the time. Mash the boiled potatoes with the gherkin vinegar.

Add the stock to the meat, stir well, then add the mashed potato. Stir well again to combine the meat and potato, then season to taste with salt, pepper and nutmeg.

Left: *Hesse stew*
Right: *Bremen eel soup*

BREMEN EEL SOUP

Serves 6

750 g (1½ lb) mixed	6-7 tbsp meat stock
vegetables e.g. carrots,	250 g (8 oz) flour plus 3
leeks, turnips, beans and	tbsp flour
cauliflower	1 bouquet garni
400 g (13 oz) eel, skinned	fresh parsley, chopped
1 onion	salt
9 tbsp oil	pepper

Peel the onion and slice it thinly, sauté it in 3 tablespoons of oil. Wash or peel the vegetables, cut them into thin matchsticks or separate into florets and sauté them with the onion. Add 1 litre (1¾ pints) water and the stock and bouquet garni, bring to the boil and simmer for 5 minutes.

Sift 250 g (8 oz) of flour into a bowl with a pinch of salt. Bring 250 ml (8 fl oz) water to the boil with 3 tablespoons of oil, pour the mixture into the flour and beat it until air bubbles form in the thick batter. Shape the batter into little dumplings using a teaspoon.

Heat 3 tablespoons of oil in a saucepan, then add the 3 tablespoons of flour and cook until the flour is golden. Add the soup, stirring constantly to prevent lumps forming. Wash the eels, bone them and cut the flesh into chunks. Add the eel to the soup together with the dumplings, bring to the boil and simmer for 20 minutes. Adjust the seasoning and garnish with chopped parsley.

MOCK TURTLE SOUP

Serves 4

500 g (1 lb) bones
500 g (1 lb) calf's head
500 ml (18 fl oz) vinegar
1 onion
60 g (2½ oz) streaky bacon
1 bay leaf
5 juniper berries
5 chillies
5 peppercorns
1 pack of vegetables for
stew
125 ml (4 fl oz) Madeira

50 g (2 oz) butter
60 g (2½ oz) flour
200 g (7 oz) button
mushrooms
125 ml (4 fl oz) red wine
fresh marjoram, thyme,
basil and sage
hot paprika
cayenne pepper
salt and pepper

Wash the bones and calf's head in cold water. Bring
500 ml (18 fl oz) and the vinegar to the boil in a stock pot.
Blanch the meat and bones in it, then drain them. Peel
the onion and slice it thinly, dice the bacon. Sauté the
bacon, onion, meat and bones in a casserole dish. Add
2 litres (3½ pints) water, the bay leaf, juniper berries,
chillies and peppercorns and season with salt. Simmer
gently for 1½ hours. Peel and wash the vegetables for
stew and cut them into thin matchsticks, to make a
julienne. Add them to the casserole dish and simmer for
30 minutes. Take the meat and bones out of the soup.
Slice the meat thinly. Put it in a deep dish, pour the
Madeira over, cover and leave it to marinate. Strain the
stock, reserving 1¼ litres (2¼ pints).

Mash the vegetables. Melt the butter and cook the flour
in it to form a roux, then add the stock, stirring
constantly. Add the marjoram, thyme, basil, sage and
paprika and bring to the boil. Wipe the mushrooms, slice
them in quarters and add them to the soup with the red

wine. Season with salt and cayenne pepper. Simmer
gently for a further 10 minutes, then serve immediately.

RHINELAND SOUP WITH HULLED BARLEY AND PRUNES

Serves 4

250 g (8 oz) prunes
2 meat stock cubes
100 g (3½ oz) hulled barley
30 g (1 oz) butter

1 egg yolk
salt
pepper

Soak the prunes in water for 12-24 hours. Bring 1¼ litres
(2¼ pints) water to the boil, add the stock cubes, then the

Above: *Nordic pea soup*
Left: *Rhineland soup with hulled barley and prunes*

hulled barley and butter, bring to the boil again and simmer gently for 1 hour. Season to taste with salt and pepper. Beat the egg yolk with 2 tablespoons of water and add it to the soup to thicken it.

NORDIC PEA SOUP

Serves 4-6

500 g (1 lb) peas, tinned	500 ml (18 fl oz) meat stock
500 g (1 lb) potatoes	2-4 coarse, meaty sausages
1 pack of vegetables for stew	4 Frankfurters
1 onion	fresh parsley, chopped
2 tbsp lard	salt
	pepper

*P*eel the onion and potatoes, wash and peel the vegetables for stew and cut them into thin matchsticks, to make a julienne. Melt the lard and fry the chopped onion, then add the diced potatoes and stew vegetables. Sweat the vegetables for a few minutes, then add the meat stock.

Add all the sausages to the stock, bring to the boil and simmer for 10 minutes, then add the tinned peas and their liquor to the soup, bring to the boil again and simmer for 5 minutes. Season to taste with salt and pepper and garnish with chopped parsley.

BEEF STEW PROVENÇALE

Serves 6

1 kg (2 lb) beef
2 bay leaves
4 cloves of garlic
500 ml (18 fl oz) white wine
2 tbsp brandy
3 tbsp olive oil
125 g (4 oz) bacon
250 g (8 oz) belly of pork
4 carrots
2 onions

250 g (8 oz) tomatoes
100 g (3½ oz) black olives
1 tbsp fresh chives, chopped
1 tbsp fresh parsley, chopped
fresh thyme
fresh rosemary
fresh marjoram
salt and pepper

Cut the beef into 5-6 cm (2-2½ inch) cubes. Pour the wine, brandy and olive oil into a bowl, add the bay leaf and crushed garlic and mix well. Leave the meat to marinate in this mixture for 12 hours in a cool place.

Slice the bacon and belly pork. Peel the carrots and onions. Blanch the tomatoes in boiling water, refresh them in cold water and skin them. Slice the vegetables into rings. Pit the olives. Take the meat out of the marinade.

Layer the vegetables and meat in an oven-proof dish, sprinkling each layer with salt, pepper, parsley, chives, thyme, rosemary and marjoram. Pour the marinade over the layers, cover and braise for 2½ hours at 175-200° C (355-400° F, Gas Mark 4-6). Garnish with chopped parsley and serve with steamed potatoes or pasta.

AMERICAN MUSSEL SOUP

Serves 2

20 mussels	1 meat stock cube
250 g (8 oz) potatoes	1 bay leaf
1 bouquet garni	3-4 tbsp white wine
2-3 tbsp lemon juice	celery leaves
1 piece of celeriac	fresh thyme
2 tomatoes, skinned	fresh marjoram
1 green pepper	cayenne pepper
1 onion	fresh parsley, chopped
75 g (3 oz) streaky bacon	salt
3-4 tbsp oil	pepper

Wash the mussels in several times in cold water, using fresh water each time. Scrub the shells carefully, remove the beards and rinse until the water runs clear. Throw away any open mussels as they are not safe to eat. Bring 1 litre (1¾ pints) of water to the boil with the lemon juice and bouquet garni and add the mussels. Cook them until they open - usually for about 5 minutes. Throw away any mussels which do not open. Strain the mussel stock through a chinois or sieve and make up to 1 litre (1¾ pints) with water. Take the mussels out of their shells.

Peel the celeriac, wash it, then dice it with the tomatoes. Cut the pepper in half, core and de-seed it, then slice it thinly. Peel, wash and dice the potatoes. Peel the onion and slice it thinly. Fry the bacon in the oil, then add the onion. Add the mussel stock, meat stock cube, bay leaf, celery leaves, thyme, marjoram, cayenne pepper and vegetables, bring to the boil and simmer for 40 minutes, then add the mussels. Season to taste with white wine, salt and pepper and garnish with chopped parsley.

Left: *Beef stew provenáale*
Below: *American mussel soup*

TRANSYLVANIAN PEPPER SOUP

Serves 6

300 g (10 oz) streaky bacon
6 green peppers
2 large onions
500 g (1 lb) potatoes
1 litre (1¾ pints) meat
stock
300 g (10 oz) tomatoes,
skinned

250 ml (8 fl oz) double
cream
2 tbsp fresh parsley,
chopped
paprika
celery salt
salt

Dice the bacon and render it. Core and de-seed the peppers, cut them into 1 cm (½ inch) thick strips and wash them. Peel and dice the onions. Brown the onions and peppers in the bacon fat. Peel and finely dice the potatoes and add them to the vegetables.

Add the meat stock to the pan, season with salt, paprika and celery salt. Cover and simmer for 25 minutes. Chop the tomatoes roughly and add them to the soup. Leaving the pan uncovered, simmer the tomatoes for 2 minutes, then fold in the double cream and garnish with chopped parsley.

SPANISH PEASANT SOUP

Serves 6-8

250 g (8 oz) beef
250 g (8 oz) mutton
3-4 tbsp oil
1 onion
2½ litres (4½ pints) meat
stock
200 g (7 oz) potatoes
200 g (7 oz) carrots
2 leeks
300 g (10 oz) peas, frozen

1 chorizo, or other spicy
sausage
100 g (3½ oz) uncooked
ham
dried thyme and basil
garlic granules
fresh parsley, chopped
salt
pepper

Dice the meat, then heat the oil and brown the meat in it. Add the peeled and thinly sliced onion to the meat, then season with salt, pepper, thyme, basil and garlic. Add the meat stock, bring to the boil and simmer gently for 45 minutes.

Peel the potatoes and carrots and wash the leeks. Cut them into thin matchsticks, to make a julienne, and add them to the soup. Bring to the boil again and simmer for a further 5 minutes. Add the peas and simmer for a further 10 minutes, then slice the sausage and ham and add them to the soup a few minutes before the end of cooking time. Serve garnished with chopped parsley.

FRENCH BEAN SOUP WITH CHIPOLATA SAUSAGES

Serves 4

1 kg (2 lb) French beans
1 pack of vegetables for
stew
2 knobs of butter
750 ml (1¼ pints) meat
stock
500 g (1 lb) potatoes

savory
250 g (8 oz) chipolata
sausages with herbs
fresh mixed herbs,
chopped
salt

Top and tail the beans. Peel and wash the vegetables for stew and cut them into thin matchsticks to make a julienne. Melt the butter and sauté the vegetables in it, then add the stock and season with salt. Bring to the boil, then reduce the heat. Peel and dice the potatoes and add them to the soup with the savory. Bring to the boil again and simmer for 15 minutes. Cut the sausages into 4 cm (1½ inch) chunks and poach them with the vegetables for 7 minutes. Serve garnished with fresh, chopped mixed herbs.

Left: *Spanish peasant soup*
Right: *French bean soup with chipolata sausages*

CATALONIAN STYLE VEGETABLES

Serves 6-7

4 large onions
60 g (2½ oz) lard
2 green peppers
200 g (7 oz) carrots
250 g (8 oz) potatoes
300 g (10 oz) peas, frozen
1¼ litres (2¼ pints) meat
stock

200 g (7 oz) uncooked ham
or bacon
2 hard-boiledeggs
2 tbsp fresh parsley,
chopped
fresh rosemary
salt and pepper

Peel the onions and slice them thinly. Melt the lard in a casserole dish and sweat the onions in it. Cut the peppers in half, core and de-seed them and cut them into thin strips. Brown the peppers with the onions. Peel the carrots and potatoes, cut them into thin matchsticks to make a julienne and add them to the pan with the peas, then add the stock. Season to taste with salt, pepper and rosemary.
Cover and simmer for 15-20 minutes. Cut the ham into thin strips. Shell the eggs and slice them. Arrange the ham and eggs on top of the vegetables and garnish with chopped parsley.

ANDALUSIAN CREAM OF TOMATO SOUP

Serves 4

2 small onions
80 g (3 oz) bacon, diced
2 tbsp oil
1 tbsp flour
1 kg (2 lb) tomatoes,
skinned
500 ml (18 fl oz) meat stock
100 g (3½ oz) button
mushrooms, tinned

100 g (3½ oz) peas, tinned
2 egg yolks
100 g (3½ oz) crème
fraîche
4 tbsp sherry
fresh parsley, chopped
salt
pepper

Peel and slice the onions thinly and fry them in a casserole dish with the bacon. Sprinkle the flour on top, and stir for 1-2 minutes until cooked. Roughly chop the tomatoes, add them to the pan and sweat them until reduced. Add the meat stock, bring to the boil and season with salt and pepper, then simmer gently for 10 minutes. Pass the soup through a sieve, puréeing the tomatoes.

Drain the mushrooms and peas and add them to the soup. Beat together the egg yolks and cream and add them to the soup to thicken and enrich it, then add the sherry. Garnish with chopped parsley.

FISH SOUP Á LA HOLLANDAISE

Serves 4

750 g (1½ lb) hake	stew
2 meat stock cubes	3-4 tbsp oil
6 peppercorns	1 egg yolk
1 bay leaf	3-4 tbsp crème fraîche
3 cloves	lemon juice
zest of 1 unwaxed lemon	fresh parsley, chopped
1 pack of vegetables for	salt

Skin and bone the fish, cut it into chunks and drizzle it with lemon juice. Bring 1 litre (1¾ pints) of water to the boil, dissolve the stock cubes in it and add 3 peppercorns, the bay leaf, cloves and lemon zest to make a court bouillon. Wash and peel the vegetables for stew, cut them into very thin matchsticks to make a julienne and add them to the stock with the fish skin and bones. Simmer for 40 minutes.

Strain the stock. Heat the oil, seal the chunks of fish in it, then add them to the stock and adjust the seasoning to taste with salt and the remaining peppercorns, crushed. Simmer for 5-10 minutes. Beat together the egg yolk and cream and use it to thicken and enrich the soup. Garnish the soup with chopped parsley and serve with garlic bread.

Left: *Catalonian style vegetables*
Below: *Fish soup á la hollandaise*

Heat the oil in a casserole dish and fry the minced meat until sealed, taking care to break up any large lumps. Peel the onions and slice them thinly. Add them to the meat and sweat them in the juices. Season the meat with salt, pepper, paprika and basil. Add the rice and stock, cover the casserole dish and simmer for 20-25 minutes.

Add the peas to the cooked rice, heat them through and adjust the seasoning.

BORSCHT

Serves 6

1 kg (2 lb) beetroot	2-3 tbsp vinegar
500 g (1 lb) beef	150 g (5 oz) crème fraîche
250 g (8 oz) streaky bacon	fresh chervil
100 g (3 ½ oz) onions	monosodium glutamate
250 g (8 oz) carrots	Worcester sauce
250 g (8 oz) celeriac	fresh parsley, chopped
250 g (8 oz) cabbage	salt and pepper
1 leek	

Peel and dice the beetroot, sprinkle them with salt and reserve them. Put the meat and bacon into 2 litres (3½ pints) boiling, salted water and simmer it for 1½ hours. Peel the onions, potatoes and celeriac and cut them into thin matchsticks to make a julienne. Take the outer leaves off the cabbage, slice it thinly, wash and drain it. Wash the leek thoroughly and cut it into matchsticks.

Take the meat out of the stock and dice it. Add the vegetables, diced meat and chervil to the stock and season it with salt and pepper. Bring to the boil again and simmer for 1 hour. Season to taste with monosodium glutamate, vinegar and Worcester sauce. Fold in the cream and garnish the borscht with chopped parsley.

SPANISH STEW

Serves 5-6

250 g (8 oz) pork	½ tsp cumin
250 g (8 oz) beef	2 tbsp crème fraîche
250 g (8 oz) veal	2 tbsp fresh parsley,
3 large onions	chopped
1½ kg (3½ lb) potatoes	paprika
40 g (1½ oz) butter	salt and pepper

Dice the meat. Peel the onions and slice them thinly. Peel and dice the potatoes. Melt the butter in a casserole dish, brown the meat all over, then brown the onions and finally the potatoes. Season with salt, pepper, paprika and cumin then add 400 ml
(14 fl oz) water and simmer for 1¼ hours, stirring occasionally. Blend together the crème fraîche and cornflour and thicken the stew 10 minutes before the end of cooking time.

Garnish with chopped parsley.

BOLOGNESE RICE

Serves 4

200 g (7 oz) minced beef	stock
200 g (7 oz) minced pork	300 g (10 oz) peas, tinned
2 tbsp oil	paprika
4-5 onions	fresh basil
250 g (8 oz) long grain	salt
rice	pepper
800 ml (1¼ pints) meat	

HUNGARIAN FISH SOUP

Serves 5

750 g (1½ lb) fish fillets:	skinned
cod, hake, coley, fresh or	2-3 tbsp flour
frozen	1 sachet of court bouillon
250 g (8 oz) onions	or carton of chilled,
2-3 tbsp oil	ready-made stock
1 green pepper	lemon juice
1 red pepper	salt
250 g (8 oz) tomatoes,	

Cut the fish into chunks, sprinkle them with lemon juice and salt. Peel the onions and slice them thinly. Heat the oil in a casserole dish and sauté the onions in it.
Cut the peppers in half, core and de-seed them, then cut them into thin strips. Roughly chop the tomatoes, then add the vegetables to the onions. Sweat them over a low heat, then sprinkle on the flour, stirring all the time, to bind the vegetables. Add the court bouillon made up with 1 litre (1¾ pints) of water, or 1 litre (1¾ pints) of ready-made stock. Bring to the boil and simmer for 15 minutes. Add the fish and simmer gently for a further 10-15 minutes.

Left: *Spanish stew*
Below: *Borscht*

INDIAN SOUP WITH RICE

Serves 2

1 small onion	50 g (2 oz) rice
2-3 tbsp oil	2-3 tbsp sherry
2-3 tbsp flour	1 egg yolk
1 tsp curry powder	3-4 tbsp crème fraîche
2 meat stock cubes	

Peel the onion and slice it thinly. Heat the oil in a saucepan and brown the onion, then add the flour and curry powder, stirring all the time. Dissolve the stock cubes in 1 litre (1¾ pints) water and add it to the saucepan.

Add the rice, bring to the boil and simmer for 20 minutes. Add the sherry, then beat together the egg yolk and crème fraîche and add the mixture to the soup to enrich and thicken it.

IRISH STEW

Serves 4

1 kg (2 lb) white cabbage	3 knobs of butter
200 g (7 oz) potatoes	250 ml (8 fl oz) meat stock
3 onions	cumin
1 carrot	salt
500 g (1 lb) mutton	pepper

Cut the cabbage into 4 pieces and slice it thinly. Peel the potatoes, onions and carrot and cut them into thin matchsticks to make a julienne. Dice the meat.

Melt the butter in a casserole dish and seal the meat all over. Add the onions, sweat them in the meat juices for a few minutes, then add the cabbage, potatoes and carrot. Add the hot stock and season with pepper and cumin. Cover the casserole dish and braise for 45 minutes to 1 hour. Adjust the seasoning before serving.

Below: *Indian soup with rice*

Above: *Irish stew*

BOUILLABAISSE

Serves 5-6

750 g (1½ lb) fish: cod,
monkfish, eel, sole and
dab
juice of 1 lemon
1 onion
3-4 tbsp olive oil
1 leek
1 head of fennel
2 tomatoes, skinned
1 clove of garlic, sliced
3 meat stock cubes
1 bay leaf
1 bouquet garni

5 peppercorns
2 cloves
250 g (8 oz) mussels,
cooked
100 g (3½ oz) prawn tails
or crayfish, fresh or
frozen
saffron
garlic croutons
rouille (mayonnaise with
garlic, saffron and olive
oil)
salt and pepper

Cut the fish into chunks and sprinkle them with lemon juice. Peel the onion and slice it into rings. Heat the oil in a casserole dish and brown the onion. Slice the leek into rings. Clean the fennel, cut it into small pieces, and chop the tomatoes more roughly. Add the garlic and vegetables to the onions, sweat them on a low heat, then dissolve the stock cubes in 1½ litres (2½ pints) water and add it to the casserole dish. Season with the bay leaf, peppercorns, cloves, bouquet garni, saffron and salt.

Bring to the boil and simmer gently for 15 minutes. Then add the pieces of fish to the soup and simmer them for a further 15 minutes. Add the mussels and prawns or crayfish a few minutes before the end of cooking time.

Place a garlic crouton in each soup bowl, pour the soup over the top and accompany with rouille served separately.

RUSSIAN KIDNEYS

Serves 2

300 g (10 oz) calf's kidneys
2 onions
3-4 tbsp oil
2 meat stock cubes
1 large gherkin, pickled in vinegar
1 sweet and sour pickled

gherkin
100 g (3½ oz) button mushrooms, tinned
1 egg yolk
2-3 tbsp cream
fresh parsley, chopped
pepper

Slice open the kidneys and remove the cores. Blanch them by pouring boiling water over them. Set the kidneys aside in the water for about 1 hour, then drain and slice them. Peel the onions and slice them thinly. Heat the oil in a casserole dish and sauté the onions. Dissolve the stock cubes in 1 litre (1¾ pints) of water and add it to the onions.

Dice the gherkins, and add them to the stock with the kidneys. Bring to the boil and simmer for 20 minutes. Drain the mushrooms and slice them in half. Cook them with the kidneys for about 10 minutes, then season with pepper.

Beat together the egg yolk and cream and use to thicken and enrich the sauce. Garnish with chopped parsley.

CHINESE CHICKEN SOUP

Serves 6-8

1 chicken
30 g (1 oz) Chinese mushrooms
6 tbsp instant chicken stock
1 pack of vegetables for stew, e.g. carrot, leek,

celery
50 g (2 oz) Chinese rice noodles
340 g (11 oz) bamboo shoots, tinned
soy sauce
chilli powder

Soak the mushrooms in cold water for a few hours, then drain them and cut them into thin strips. Bring 2½ litres (4½ pints) water to the boil and add the chicken stock. Wash and peel the vegetables for stew and cut them into thin matchsticks to make a julienne. Put the chicken and stew vegetables into the boiling stock, bring to the boil again and simmer gently for 1 hour.

Take the chicken out of the stock, bone it and dice the meat. Add the noodles and mushrooms to the stock and simmer them for 20 minutes. Return the meat and mushrooms to the soup, add the soy sauce and bring to the boil again. Season to taste with soy sauce and chilli powder.

SERBIAN BEANS

Serves 4

400 g (13 oz) forerib or backrib of beef
175 g (6 oz) onions
2 cloves of garlic
1 red pepper
1 green pepper
1 leek
125 g (4 oz) celeriac
3 tbsp oil

500 g (1 lb) tomatoes, tinned
500 g (1 lb) haricot beans, tinned
cayenne pepper
hot paprika
fresh savory, chopped
salt and pepper

Stew the meat in 125 ml (4 fl oz) water for 1 hour. Take the meat out of the pan, reserve it and strain the stock. Peel the onions and garlic and slice them thinly. Cut the peppers in half, core and de-seed them, then cut them into thin strips. Carefully wash the leek and cut it into rings. Peel and dice the celeriac.

Right: *Serbian beans*
Left: *Russian kidneys*

Heat the oil in a casserole dish, sweat the vegetables in it and add the meat stock. Roughly chop the tomatoes and add them to the stock with the beans and the liquor from both. Season to taste with salt, pepper, cayenne pepper and paprika and simmer for 12-15 minutes. Dice the meat, return it to the casserole dish and heat it through with the beans. Garnish with chopped savory.

ORIENTAL RAGOUT

Serves 5

750 g (1½ lb) shin of beef
30 g (1 oz) butter
3 onions
1 clove of garlic
1 carrot
200 g (7 oz) long grain rice
500 g (1 lb) cabbage

50 g (2 oz) cashew nuts
50 g (2 oz) raisins
1 tbsp mango chutney
750 ml (1¼ pints) chicken stock
curry powder
salt
pepper

Slice the meat thinly. Melt the butter in a cast-iron dish and brown the sliced meat in it. Peel and chop the onions and garlic. Peel and dice the carrot. Add the onions, garlic and carrot to the meat. Add the rice and seal it for a few minutes, stirring constantly.

Wash the cabbage and cut it into thin strips. Add it to the meat with the cashew nuts and raisins. Season with salt, pepper and a generous sprinkling of curry powder. Stir in the mango chutney and add the stock.
Mix the ingredients thoroughly then put the dish in the oven at 200°C (400°F, Gas Mark 6) for 1 hour, stirring occasionally.

Soak the kidney beans in cold water in a covered bowl for 12-24 hours. Dice the meat. Heat the lard in a frying pan and seal the meat all over. Put the kidney beans and the soaking water in a large saucepan with the meat stock and diced beef. Bring to the boil and simmer for 1¼ hours.

Cut the peppers in half, core and de-seed them, peel the onions and dice both the peppers and onions. Sauté them for 5-6 minutes in the meat juices in the frying pan, together with the tomato purée, chilli powder and paprika. Add the vegetables to the beans, bring to the boil, and simmer for 30 minutes.

Blanch the tomatoes in boiling water, refresh them in cold water, skin them and cut them into quarters. Add them to the chilli con carne 10 minutes before the end of cooking time. Season to taste with basil, peeled and sliced garlic and red wine.

Opposite: *Oriental ragout*
Below: *Chilli con carne*

CHILLI CON CARNE

Serves 6

750 g (1½ lb) dried red kidney beans
1 kg (2 lb) lean beef
50 g (2 oz) lard
1½ litres (2½ pints) meat stock
4 onions
1 green pepper

1 red pepper
4 tbsp tomato purée
2 tsp chilli powder
3 tbsp paprika
5 tomatoes
1-2 cloves of garlic
1 tbsp fresh basil, chopped
red wine

CAULIFLOWER AU GRATIN

Serves 6

1 medium cauliflower, weighing about 1½ kg (3½ lb)	pickled in vinegar
	125g (4 oz) raw ham
	50 g (2 oz) butter
200 g (7 oz) boiled ham	20 g (¾ oz) flour
200 ml (7 fl oz) crème fraîche	100 ml (3½ fl oz) milk
4 eggs	50 g (2 oz) Parmesan, grated
1 tsp green peppercorns,	salt

Remove the leaves and stalk from the cauliflower. Separate the florets, wash them carefully and put them into boiling, salted water. Cook them for 12 minutes and drain them. Mince the boiled ham.

Carefully combine the cream, 1 egg, the minced ham and green peppercorns. Dice the raw ham finely and add it to the mixture. Pour half of this mixture into a buttered gratin dish, then add half of the cauliflower, then another layer of cream and ham mixture and a final layer of cauliflower.

To make the sauce: Melt the butter and add the flour and cook, stirring all the time, until the flour colours slightly. Add the milk, whisking all the time to prevent lumps forming. Bring the sauce to the boil and simmer for 5 minutes. Separate the 3 remaining eggs, beat the eggs yolks and add them to the sauce with the grated Parmesan. Whisk the egg whites until stiff, then fold them into the sauce and pour it over the cauliflower. Cook the cauliflower in an oven preheated to 200ºC (400ºF, Gas Mark 6).

Above: *Cauliflower au gratin*
Left: *Celery au gratin*

CELERY AU GRATIN

Serves 4-6

1 kg (2 lb) celery
750 g (1½ lb) turkey breast
100 g (3½ oz) sandwich
bread
100 ml (3½ fl oz) chicken
stock
1 egg
3 tbsp white wine
3 tbsp cream
1 tsp lemon juice
zest of ½ an unwaxed
lemon

1 tsp Dijon mustard
1 box of cress
80 g (3 oz) butter
40 g (1½ oz) flour
500 ml (18 fl oz) milk
100 g (3½ oz) Gorgonzola
cheese
whole nutmeg or pinch of
grated nutmeg
salt and freshly ground
pepper

Cut the turkey breast into small cubes. Soak the bread in the stock. Squeeze it out and process it in a food mixer with the turkey, egg, wine, cream, lemon juice and zest, mustard and cress.

Melt 40 g (1½ oz) butter and fold it into the turkey mixture, then season with salt and pepper. Prepare the celery by removing any string, then wash the stalks and cut them in half. Butter a gratin dish and put half the celery in it with the concave side uppermost. Cover the celery with the meat mixture, then top with the remaining celery, this time with the concave side down.

To make the sauce: Melt 40 g (1½ oz) butter, add the flour and cook, stirring all the time, until the flour colours slightly. Bring the milk to the boil and add it to the roux, whisking all the time to prevent lumps forming.
Bring the sauce to the boil and simmer for 5 minutes, then add the Gorgonzola and stir until it is completely melted. Season with salt and pepper.

Pour the sauce over the celery and grate a little nutmeg on top, or sprinkle with the pinch of grated nutmeg. Bake the celery in the oven at 200ºC (400ºF, Gas Mark 6) for about 1 hour. If the top of the gratin browns too quickly, cover it with a sheet of foil. Serve with a green salad.

POTATO AND HAM AU GRATIN

Serves 5-6

1 kg (2 lb) potatoes
75 g (3 oz) raw ham
75 g (3 oz) boiled ham
30 g (1 oz) margarine
35 g (generous 1 oz) butter

250 ml (8 fl oz) meat stock
250 ml (8 fl oz) milk
2 tbsp breadcrumbs
knobs of butter
salt

Wash the potatoes and cook them in boiling water for about 20 minutes. Drain and peel them. Leave them to cool, then slice them into rounds. Dice both the boiled and raw ham finely. Butter a gratin dish and alternately layer the potatoes and ham, finishing with a layer of potato.

To make the sauce: Melt the butter, add the breadcrumbs and stir until they turn a light golden brown. Add the hot stock and the milk and whisk the sauce to prevent lumps forming. Bring the sauce to the boil, simmer it for 5 minutes, then season it with salt.

Pour the sauce over the potatoes and sprinkle with the breadcrumbs, then dot with butter. Bake in a preheated oven at 200-225°C (400-425°F, Gas Mark 6-7) for 30-40 minutes.

Variation: You can vary the sauce by beating together 250 ml (8 fl oz) cream, 250 ml (8 fl oz) meat stock, 1 tbsp cornflour and 2 eggs. You can also substitute grated cheese for the breadcrumbs.

AUBERGINES AU GRATIN

Serves 4-6

500 g (1 lb) tomatoes
500 g (1 lb) aubergines
1 tbsp oil
2 onions
500 g (1 lb) minced veal
150 g (5 oz) natural
yoghurt

3 eggs
1 tbsp flour
sweet paprika
fresh thyme
fresh rosemary
salt
freshly ground pepper

Blanch the tomatoes in boiling water, then refresh them in cold water, remove the stalks and slice them. Top and tail the aubergines and wash them, then cut them into ½ cm (¼ inch) thick slices. Sprinkle the aubergines with salt and leave them to drain for 30 minutes, then pat them dry with a tea towel or kitchen paper. Heat the oil and fry the aubergine slices on each side until brown, then take them out of the pan and reserve them.

Peel and finely chop the onions and brown them in the oil. Add the minced veal and brown it, breaking down any large lumps. Season to taste with salt, pepper, paprika, thyme and rosemary.

Layer the aubergines, tomatoes and meat alternately in a buttered gratin dish, seasoning each layer with the paprika, thyme, rosemary, salt and pepper. Bake the gratin for 30 minutes at 250ºC (475ºF, Gas Mark 9). Beat together the yoghurt, eggs and breadcrumbs and season with salt. Pour this mixture over the gratin and put it back in the the oven for a further 15 minutes.

Left: *Potato and ham au gratin*
Below: *Aubergines au gratin*

PASTA AND TOMATO BAKE

Serves 4

200 g (7 oz) pasta	chopped
750 g (1½ lb) tomatoes	2 tbsp fresh chives, finely
150 g (5 oz) raw ham	chopped
3 eggs	2 tbsp Parmesan, grated
100 ml (3½ fl oz) milk	2 tbsp breadcrumbs
2 tbsp fresh parsley,	salt and pepper

Cook the pasta in 1½ litres (2½ pints) boiling, salted water for 8 minutes, stirring from time to time, then rinse in cold water and leave it to drain.

Blanch the tomatoes in boiling water for a few seconds, then refresh them in cold water and skin them. Remove the stalks and slice them into rounds. Dice the ham. Butter a gratin dish and alternately layer tomatoes, ham and pasta. Beat together the eggs, milk, parsley and chives, season with salt and pepper, then pour this mixture over the pasta.

Combine the breadcrumbs and Parmesan and sprinkle over the top of the bake, then bake it for 30 minutes at 200ºC (400ºF, Gas Mark 6). If necessary, cover the bake with a sheet of foil to stop it browning too quickly.

KOHL-RABI AND HAM BAKE

Serves 6

1 kg (2 lb) kohl-rabi,	200 g (7 oz) ham
weighed without leaves	3-4 eggs
1 tbsp flour	grated nutmeg
knob of butter	salt
1 tbsp crème fraîche	pepper

Peel the kohl-rabi, reserving the leaves, wash it and cut it into ½ cm (¼ inch) thick strips. Put them in 250 ml (8 fl oz) salted water, bring to the boil and simmer for 10-15 minutes (the kohl-rabi should retain some bite). Drain the kohl-rabi, reserving the cooking liquid.

Melt the butter and stir in the flour. Add the cooking liquid from the kohl rabi and bring to the boil, stirring all the time. Whisk the sauce to prevent lumps forming and simmer for 5 minutes.

Add the cream, then add the chopped kohl-rabi leaves and cooked kohl-rabi, and season with salt and pepper. Dice the ham. Layer the kohl-rabi and ham alternately in a buttered gratin dish. Beat the eggs, add a little grated nutmeg, and season with salt and pepper. Pour this mixture over the kohl-rabi and ham, cover the dish and bake in the oven at 225-250ºC (425-475ºF, Gas Mark 7-9) for 30 minutes.

POTATO AND SAUSAGE BAKE

Serves 6

1 kg (2 lb) potatoes
4 hard-boiled eggs
2 small smoked
Continental-style sausages
300 g (10 oz) crème

fraîche
3 tbsp breadcrumbs
a few knobs of butter
salt

Wash the potatoes and cook them in boiling water for 20-30 minutes. Leave them to cool a little, peel them, then leave them to cool completely. Slice them into rounds. Shell the hard-boiled eggs and slice the eggs and sausages into rounds.

Layer these three ingredients alternately in a buttered gratin dish, seasoning each layer of potato and egg with salt, and finishing with a layer of potato. Pour the cream over the potatoes and top with breadcrumbs. Dot with a few knobs of butter and bake in a preheated oven at 225-250ºC (425-475ºF, Gas Mark 7-9) for 30 minutes.

Above: *Potato and sausage bake*
Below: *Pasta and tomato bake*

MEXICAN CORN AU GRATIN

Serves 6

250 g (8 oz) minced beef
250 g (8 oz) minced pork
1 onion
1 clove of garlic
1 tbsp oil
300 g (10 oz) sweetcorn,
tinned
150 g (5 oz) salami
500 g (1 lb) tomatoes

200 g (7 oz) Gruyère
cheese
2 tbsp breadcrumbs
a few knobs of butter
chilli powder
ground cinnamon
fresh oregano, chopped
salt
pepper

Peel the onion and garlic and chop them finely, then sauté them in the oil. Add the minced meat and brown it, breaking down any large lumps, then season to taste with salt, pepper, chilli and cinnamon. Transfer the meat to a buttered gratin dish and level it out.

Drain the corn and spread it over the meat. Cut the slices of salami into strips and arrange them on top of the corn. Blanch the tomatoes in boiling water, then refresh them in cold water and skin them. Remove the stalks and cut the tomatoes into quarters, then into thin slices. Arrange them on top of the salami, then season with pepper and oregano.

Grate the Gruyère and stir it into the breadcrumbs, then sprinkle over the tomatoes. Dot with a few knobs of butter then bake the gratin in a preheated oven at 200°C (400°F, Gas Mark 6) for 30 minutes.

FARMHOUSE BAKE WITH CREAM CHEESE

Serves 4

150 g (5 oz) egg pasta
150 g (5 oz) pasta verde
750 g (1½ lb) tomatoes
250 g (8 oz) boiled ham
3 eggs
200 ml (7 fl oz) cream

1 bunch of fresh chives
½ bunch of fresh parsley
400 g (13 oz) cream
cheese
salt and pepper

Cook the pasta in 1½ litres (2½ pints) boiling, salted water for 8 minutes, stirring occasionally. Rinse it in cold water and leave to drain.

Blanch the tomatoes quickly in boiling water, refresh them in cold water, then skin them. Remove the stalks and slice the tomatoes into rounds. Dice the ham.

Beat together the eggs and cream and season with salt and pepper. Wash the herbs, pat them dry in a tea towel, then chop them.

Butter a gratin dish, cover the base with a layer of tomato, season it with salt, pepper, chives and parsley, then add the ham and pasta and sprinkle with herbs. Pour the egg and cream mixture over the pasta. Bake in a preheated oven at 200°C (400°F, Gas Mark 6) for about 40 minutes. Beat the cream cheese and pour it over the pasta 10 minutes before the end of cooking time.

Right: *Farmhouse bake with cream cheese*
Left: *Mexican corn au gratin*

PASTA AND CREAM CHEESE BAKE

Serves 4

200 g (7 oz) spaghetti
1 tbsp oil
250 g (8 oz) cream cheese
150 g (5 oz) crème fraîche
3 eggs
1 tsp ground cumin
2 tbsp fresh chives, finely

chopped
2 Continental-style
smoked sausages
50 g (2 oz) streaky bacon
salt
pepper

Cook the spaghetti in 2½ litres (4½ pints) boiling, salted water with the oil for about 10 minutes or until the pasta is cooked but still al dente. Rinse the pasta in cold water and leave it to drain. Beat together the cream cheese, cream, eggs, cumin and chives and season with salt and pepper. Slice the sausages and mix them into the spaghetti with the cream mixture. Transfer the pasta to a buttered gratin dish. Slice the bacon thinly and arrange it on top of the pasta. Bake the pasta in a preheated oven at 200-225°C (400-425°F, Gas Mark 6-7) for about 50 minutes.

MINNA'S BAKE WITH SAUERKRAUT

Serves 4-5

200 g (7 oz) carrots
1 slice of stale bread
1 small onion
125 g (4 oz) minced beef
125 g (4 oz) minced pork

1 egg
700 g (1½ lb) sauerkraut
or pickled cabbage
2-3 Frankfurters
salt and pepper

COURGETTES AU GRATIN

Serves 3-4

500 g (1 lb) courgettes	2 tbsp oil
100 g (3½ oz) boiled ham	100 g (3½ oz) Gruyère,
2 onions	grated
2 tbsp flour	grated nutmeg
2 eggs	saltand pepper

Chop the courgettes roughly, throw away the tops and tails, wash the remaining chunks and pat them dry. Season the pieces of courgette with salt, then press them in a tea towel. Dice the ham, peel and dice the onions. Beat together the flour and eggs, then add this batter to the courgettes with the ham and onions. Season with pepper and grated nutmeg. Brush a gratin dish with oil and transfer the courgette mixture to the dish. Bake the courgettes in the oven at 225ºC (425ºF, Gas Mark 7) for 30 minutes, then sprinkle the dish with grated Gruyère and return it to the oven for a few minutes until the cheese bubbles and turns golden brown.

Scrape the carrots, wash them and cook them in 150 ml (5 fl oz) water for about 20 minutes. Soak the bread in some water, then squeeze it out. Peel the onion, dice it and combine it with the bread, minced meat and egg, then season with salt and pepper. Butter a gratin dish.

Slice the carrots and arrange them in a ring around the base of the dish. Then arrange the meat in a circle inside the carrots and finally put half the sauerkraut in the centre.

Slice the sausages and arrange the slices on top of the sauerkraut, then cover them with the remaining sauerkraut. Cover the dish and bake the meat and vegetables in a preheated oven at 200-225ºC (400-425ºF, Gas Mark 6-7) for 1-1½ hours. Leave the bake to rest for a few minutes before turning it out onto a plate.

Above: *Pasta and cream cheese bake*
Richt: *Courgettes au gratin*

POTATOES AU GRATIN WITH SPINACH

Serves 6

750 g (1½ lb) floury
potatoes
250 ml (8 fl oz) milk
150 g (5 oz) streaky bacon
150 g (5 oz) cheese,
grated

750 g (1½ lb) spinach
1 onion
1 clove of garlic
knob of butter
salt and pepper

Peel the potatoes and wash them, then slice them into
rounds. Bring the milk to the boil and add the potatoes.
Simmer them gently for 10 minutes in a lidded pan.

Dice the bacon and add it to the potatoes with 50 g (2 oz)
of the cheese, then season with salt and pepper. Arrange
the potatoes in the middle of a buttered gratin dish. Pick
over and carefully wash the spinach, do not drain it, but
put it in a saucepan and sweat it in the lidded pan until
the leaves are starting to break down, then drain it. Peel

the onion and garlic and chop them finely. Fry the onion
and garlic in the butter , then add the spinach and sauté it
quickly, then arrange it around the potatoes. Sprinkle the
potatoes and spinach with the remaining cheese. Bake in
a preheated oven for 5-10 minutes.

FRENCH TOAST AU GRATIN

Serves 3

5 slices of stale bread
4-6 knobs of herb butter
250 g (8 oz) baby button
mushrooms
80 g (3 oz) salami
125 g (4 oz) ham
2 onions

1-2 tbsp oil
3-4 tbsp fresh mixed
herbs, chopped
3 eggs
200 g (7 oz) cream cheese
salt
pepper

Dice the bread. Melt the butter and fry the diced bread
in it. Peel and wipe the mushrooms, cutting any large
ones in half. Dice the salami and ham. Peel the onions
and chop them finely. Heat the oil and fry the onions in

it, then add the ham, salami and mushrooms and season the mixture with salt and pepper. Add the fried bread, reserving a few pieces, and the mixed herbs. Transfer the mixture to a buttered gratin dish.

Beat together the eggs and cream cheese. Pour the mixture over the bread and ham, and top with the reserved fried bread. Bake in the oven at 200-225°C (400-425°F, Gas Mark 6-7) for 30 minutes.

SPINACH AU GRATIN

Serves 6-8

1½ kg (3½ lb) spinach	12 sage leaves
750 g (1½ lb) onions	500 g (1 lb) Gruyère
4 tbsp oil	250 g (8 oz) cream cheese
1 clove of garlic	250 ml (8 fl oz) cream
12 slices of sandwich	4 eggs
bread	salt and pepper
375 g (12 oz) boiled ham	

Peel the onions and slice them thinly. Heat the oil and fry the onions in it for about 20 minutes, then season with salt and pepper. Carefully pick over and wash the spinach. Do not drain it, but put it into a saucepan, cover and sweat until the leaves are just starting to break down, then drain the spinach and chop it roughly.

Peel and crush the garlic. Rub a 4 litre (7 pint) casserole dish with the crushed garlic. Toast 6 slices of bread and line the base of the dish with them, then cover the bread with half of the ham. Rinse the sage leaves and place 6 of them on top of the ham. Grate half of the Gruyère and sprinkle it over the ham.

Then add the spinach and onions to the dish, layering them alternately. Blend together the cream cheese, cream and eggs and pour this mixture over the spinach. Top the spinach with the remaining slices of bread, then the rest of the ham and sage leaves. Arrange slices of Gruyère on top. Bake the spinach in the oven at 200°C (400°F, Gas Mark 6) for 50 minutes.

Below: *French toast au gratin*

Left: *Potatoes au gratin with spinach*

MACARONI AND HAM BAKE

Serves 2

150 g (5 oz) macaroni
200 g (7 oz) boiled ham
60 g (2½ oz) Gruyère
2 eggs
250 ml (8 fl oz) milk

grated nutmeg
2 tbsp breadcrumbs
a few knobs of butter
salt and pepper

Cook the macaroni in 1½ litres (2½ pints) boiling, salted water. When cooked, pour it into a colander, rinse it in cold water and leave it to drain. Dice the ham and grate the cheese. Butter a gratin dish and alternately layer the macaroni, ham and cheese, finishing with a layer of macaroni.

Beat together the eggs and milk and season with salt, pepper and grated nutmeg. Pour this mixture over the macaroni, then sprinkle with breadcrumbs. Dot the breadcrumbs with butter and bake in the oven at 225-250°C (425-475°F, Gas Mark 7-9) for about 30 minutes.

BAKED FISH WITH DILL SAUCE

Serves 6

750 g (1½ lb) fish fillets
500 g (1 lb) potatoes
250 g (8 oz) carrots
80 g (3 oz) butter
juice of 2 lemons
60 g (2½ oz) flour
500 ml (18 fl oz) milk

4 bunches of fresh dill
4 eggs
100 g (3½ oz) Gruyère,
grated
300 g (10 oz) peas, frozen
salt and pepper

Peel the potatoes, scrape the carrots, wash them both and cut them into thin rounds. Put the sliced potatoes into salted water and bring them to the boil, cook them for 5 minutes, then drain them. Arrange them in a buttered gratin dish.

Melt 20 g (½ oz) butter, brown the carrots in it and season them with salt and pepper. Add 2 tablespoons of water, cover and braise the carrots for 10 minutes. Then pour the carrots over the potatoes. Rinse the fish fillets in cold water and pat them dry. Slice them in half lengthways. Sprinkle them with 2 tablespoons of lemon juice and leave them to marinate for 30 minutes. Pat them dry and season them with salt.

To make the sauce: Melt 60 g (2½ oz) butter, add the flour and cook, stirring all the time, until the flour colours slightly. Add the milk and whisk the sauce to prevent lumps forming, then bring to the boil and simmer for 10 minutes. Season with salt, pepper and the remaining lemon juice. Take the sauce off the heat. Rinse the dill and chop it finely, then fold the dill, beaten eggs and grated Gruyère into the sauce.

Pour half of the sauce over the vegetables, then cover this with a layer of peas, then add the fish fillets. Pour the remaining sauce over the top. Bake the fish in a preheated oven at 180°C (350°F, Gas Mark 4) for 30 minutes, then increase the heat to 225°C (425°F, Gas Mark 7) and bake for a further 20 minutes.

N.B.: The bake may seem very runny, but once the crust has been pierced the liquid will be absorbed by the vegetables, which will then be very juicy.

Left: *Macaroni and ham bake*

Above: *Savoy cabbage au gratin*

SAVOY CABBAGE AU GRATIN

Serves 6

1 kg (2 lb) Savoy cabbage
1 onion
1 clove of garlic
200 g (7 oz) stale bread
250 g (8 oz) cheese

1 meat stock cube
250 ml (8 fl oz) white wine
butter
salt

Remove the damaged outer leaves from the cabbage, then cut the cabbage into eight pieces and cut away the stalk. Wash the cabbage and cut it into ribbons. Peel the onion and garlic and cook them with the cabbage in 300 ml (10 fl oz) salted water for about 15 minutes, then drain the vegetables in a colander and reserve the cooking liquid.

Cut the bread into thin strips and dice the cheese. Butter a gratin dish and alternately layer the cabbage, bread and cheese, finishing with a layer of cheese.

Dissolve the stock cube in 750 ml (1¼ pints) of the reserved cabbage water and add the white wine. Pour the stock over the cabbage. Bake in a preheated oven at 225ºC (425ºF, Gas Mark 7) for 25-30 minutes.

HUNGARIAN PICKLED CABBAGE BAKE

Serves 6

750 g (1½ lb) sauerkraut
or pickled cabbage
70 g (3 oz) lard
2 bay leaves
125 g (4 oz) long grain
rice
1 onion

175 g (6 oz) minced beef
175 g (6 oz) minced pork
2 small Continental-style
smoked sausages
400 ml (14 fl oz) cream
salt and pepper

Melt 50 g (2 oz) of lard. Fork through the pickled cabbage and fry it in the lard. Add 250 ml (8 fl oz) water, the bay leaves, salt and pepper and cook the pickled cabbage for about 50 minutes until all the juices have been boiled off. Adjust the seasoning.

Bring 1 litre (1¾ pints) of salted water to the boil, add the rice and boil for 12-15 minutes. Transfer the rice to a sieve or colander and rinse it in cold water. Peel and dice the onion and cook it with 5 tablespoons of water until all the liquid has evaporated.

Season the meat with salt and pepper, add 20 g (1 oz) of lard to the onions and fry the meat with them. Then add the rice. Slice the sausages. Butter a gratin dish and alternately layer the pickled cabbage, meat mixture and sausage, finishing with a layer of pickled cabbage garnished with a few slices of sausage. Pour the cream over the top. Bake in a preheated oven at 225-250°C (425-475°F, Gas Mark 7-9) for about 30 minutes.

VEGETABLES AU GRATIN

Serves 6-8

500 g (1 lb) potatoes
400 g (13 oz) carrots
350 g (11 oz) courgettes
250 g (8 oz) tomatoes
2 onions
1 clove of garlic
1 tbsp oil
500 g (1 lb) minced beef

500 g (1 lb) minced pork
8 sage leaves
200 g (7 oz) Gruyère
3 tbsp breadcrumbs
butter
salt
pepper

Peel the potatoes and wash them, then slice them into rounds. Blanch them in boiling, salted water for 5 minutes, then lift them out with a slotted spoon and drain them. Layer them in a buttered gratin dish.

Peel the onions and garlic and chop them finely. Brown them in the oil, then add the meat and fry it, breaking up any large lumps, and season it with salt and pepper. Rinse 4 of the sage leaves in cold water, pat them dry in a tea towel, chop them and add them to the meat. Arrange one third of the meat on top of the potatoes.

Scrape the carrots and cut them into rounds. Blanch them for 3 minutes in boiling, salted water, then lift them out with a slotted spoon and drain them. Put the carrots on top of the layer of meat, then put half the remaining meat on top of the carrots.

Top and tail the courgettes, wash them and slice them into rounds. Blanch then in boiling water for 3 minutes, then take them out with a slotted spoon and drain them. Arrange them on top of the layer of meat, then pour the remaining meat over the courgettes.

Blanch the tomatoes in boiling water, refresh them in cold water, then remove the stalks, skin them and slice them. Arrange them on top of the meat and season them with salt and pepper. Rinse the remaining sage leaves in cold water, pat them dry with a tea towel, chop them and sprinkle them over the tomatoes.

Grate the Gruyère cheese. Stir it into the breadcrumbs and sprinkle the mixture over the tomatoes. Dot with butter and bake in a preheated oven at 200°C (400°F, Gas Mark 6) for about 30 minutes.

Variation: This recipe can also be prepared using minced lamb and fresh thyme.

Above: *Vegetables au gratin*
Left: *Hungarian pickled cabbage bake*

SAVOY CABBAGE BAKE

Serves 8

1½ kg (3½ lb) Savoy cabbage	500 g (1 lb) potatoes
3 onions	500 g (1 lb) cooking apples
60 g (2½ oz) lard or goose fat	80 g (3 oz) breadcrumbs
250 g (8 oz) spicy sausage	salt
	pepper

Prepare the cabbage, wash it and chop it roughly. Peel 2 onions and chop them finely. Melt 20 g (scant 1 oz) lard, sauté the onions in it, then add the cabbage and 250 ml (8 fl oz) water and season with salt and pepper. Cover and simmer for 1 hour. Slice the sausage.
Peel the potatoes, wash them and slice them into rounds. Cook them in salted water for about 7 minutes, then drain them. Peel the apples, cut them into quarters, core and de-seed them and cut them again into large pieces. In a buttered gratin dish layer one quarter of the cabbage, then the sausage, potatoes and apples, finishing with the remaining cabbage.

Peel the remaining onion and slice it into rings. Melt the remaining lard and fry the onion rings in it, then add the breadcrumbs and fry them on a high heat. Spread the onion and breadcrumb mixture over the cabbage, then bake in a preheated oven at 200°C (400°F, Gas Mark 6) for 30 minutes.

CHICKEN PIE

Serves 4-6

500 g (1 lb) chicken breast	200 g (7 oz) sweated chanterelle mushrooms
2 rolls of frozen flaky pastry	3 tbsp cream
2 tbsp oil	1 bunch of fresh chives
250 g (8 oz) sweated button mushrooms	1 egg yolk
150 ml (5 fl oz) white wine	salt
	pepper

Defrost the pastry at room temperature. Dice the chicken. Heat the oil and fry the pieces of chicken, then season them with salt and pepper. Add the button mushrooms, white wine, chanterelle mushrooms and cream and stir well.

Left: *Savoy cabbage bake*
Right: *Chicken pie*

Butter a gratin dish or pie dish well and line it with a sheet of pastry, leaving a pastry border all round. Transfer the chicken mixture to the pie dish. Rinse the chives in cold water, drain them and pat them dry in a tea towel, then chop them and scatter them over the meat.

Trim the pastry case and crimp the edges, reserving the trimmings for garnish. Take the other sheet of pastry and use it to cover the meat. Seal the edges of the pastry and make a little cross in the centre to allow the steam to evaporate.

Garnish with decorations cut from the pastry trimmings, beat the egg yolk and brush the pastry with the egg wash. Bake in a preheated oven at 200°C (400°F, Gas Mark 6) for 35-40 minutes.

DESSERTS

CINNAMON PUDDING

IN THE PRESSURE COOKER
Serves 6-8

500 ml (18 fl oz) milk
pinch of salt
125 g (4 oz) semolina
100 g (3½ oz) butter
100 g (3½ oz) sugar
1 sachet vanilla sugar
3 eggs

1 sachet vanilla custard
mix
1 tsp ground cinnamon
50 g (2 oz) raisins
25 g (1 oz) ground
almonds

*B*ring 375 ml (12 fl oz) salted milk to the boil and take it off the heat. Sprinkle the semolina into the milk, stirring all the time, then leave it to swell, stirring occasionally. Cream the butter until light and fluffy, then gradually beat in the sugar, vanilla sugar, eggs and hot semolina mixture.

Slake the custard mix with 4-5 tablespoons of cold milk, then add the semolina mixture, cinnamon, raisins and almonds. Pour the pudding mix into a well-buttered 500 ml (18 fl oz) mould, such as a savarin mould. The mould should be no more than two-thirds full. Cover the mould and put it into a pressure cooker with enough water to come one-third of the way up the sides of the

STEAMED BREAD PUDDING

Serves 6-7

250 g (8 oz) stale bread	almonds
375 ml (12 fl oz) hot milk	50 g (2 oz) raisins
100 g (3½ oz) butter	zest of 1 unwaxed lemon,
100 g (3½ oz) sugar	grated
2 eggs, separated	salt
50 g (2 oz) ground	

Cut the bread into small cubes and pour the hot milk over it, then leave it to soak, stirring occasionally. Cream the butter until light and fluffy, then gradually beat in the sugar and egg yolks, then the bread, almonds, raisins, salt and grated lemon zest.

Whisk the egg whites until stiff, then fold them carefully into the mixture. Pour the mixture into a well-buttered pudding basin or mould. Cover the mould and put it in a pan of boiling water (the water should come no higher than 2 cm (¾ inch) below the lid of the mould), and steam for 1 hour. Turn the pudding out of the mould.

Serve it hot or cold with custard (see page 422).

Variation: You could substitute stale Danish pastries or cake for some of the bread, and use a little less sugar.

mould. Close the pressure cooker and steam for 45 minutes.

Serve with stewed fruit or custard (see page 422).

Above: *Cinnamon pudding*
Right: *Steamed bread pudding*

STEAMED FRUIT PUDDING

IN THE PRESSURE COOKER
Serves 6-8

200 g (7 oz) dried pears
200 g (7 oz) prunes, pitted
200 g (7 oz) dried apricots
200 g (7 oz) flour
1 sachet dried yeast
30 g (1 oz) sugar
1 sachet of vanilla sugar
pinch of ground ginger

pinch of ground cloves
1 tsp ground cinnamon
1 tbsp kirsch
65 g (2½ oz) hazelnuts,
roughly chopped
65 g (2½ oz) candied
lemon peel, finely diced
100 g (3½ oz) raisins

Soak the dried fruits in 375 ml (12 fl oz) water for several hours, cook the reconstituted fruit in the soaking liquid for about 2 minutes, then drain, reserving the juice. When the fruit has cooled, chop it finely. Sift the flour and yeast into a large bowl and make a well in the centre. Add the sugar, vanilla sugar, ginger, cloves and cinnamon, kirsch and 150 ml (5 fl oz) of cold fruit syrup (or water if preferred). Cream all the ingredients together to form a smooth mixture, then fold in the chopped fruit, nuts, candied lemon peel and raisins.

Transfer the mixture to a well-buttered 500 ml (18 fl oz) pudding basin or mould. Cover the mould, put it in a pressure cooker with enough water to come one-third of the way up the mould, then put the lid on the pressure cooker and steam for about 1 hour. Turn the pudding out of the mould.

Serve with custard (see page 422) or stewed fruit.

Variation: You could use other dried fruit such as dates, figs, apples or peaches.

Right: *Peach savarin*
Below: *Steamed fruit pudding*

PEACH SAVARIN

Serves 6

500 g (1 lb) peaches
175 g (6 oz) sugar
1 sachet of vanilla sugar
375 ml (12 fl oz) white
wine or cider

65 g (2½ oz) cornflour
3 eggs, separated
oil
whipped cream

Blanch the peaches and skin them. Slice them in half and stone them. Cook them in 375 ml (12 fl oz) water with the sugar and vanilla sugar until they are soft. Drain them, reserving the syrup, adding some water, if necessary, to make the syrup up to 250 ml (8 fl oz), and keep it hot. Add the white wine or cider and bring the juice to the boil.

Blend the cornflour with the egg yolks and 6 tablespoons of cold water, then add the hot fruit syrup, return the custard to the pan and bring to the boil again.   Whisk the egg whites until stiff and fold them into the custard.

Brush the inside of a savarin mould with oil, arrange the peach halves in the mould, then pour the custard on top and chill.

Turn the peach savarin out onto a round serving dish and decorate with whipped cream.

Variation: You could use plums, pears or apricots instead of peaches.

PRALINE CROWN

Serves 4

2 knobs of butter	1 litre (1¾ pints) milk
140 g (5 oz) sugar	250 g (8 oz) apricots in
100 g (3½ oz) chopped	syrup
almonds	whipped cream
2 sachets vanilla custard	½ orange
mix	1-2 tbsp Grand Marnier

*M*elt the butter and 60 g (2½ oz) sugar to make a caramel sauce, then add the almonds and cook until the caramel turns golden. Pour the caramel mixture onto an oiled baking sheet or marble board and leave it to go cold, then break up the praline and crush it into small pieces.

Make up the custard mix according to the instructions on the packet, using 1 litre (1¾ pints) milk. Rinse a savarin or ring mould with cold water, pour the custard into the mould and refrigerate until set. Turn the custard out onto a serving dish and sprinkle all over with praline. Drain the apricots, reserving 250 ml (8 fl oz) of syrup. Arrange the apricots in the centre of the custard and decorate them with whipped cream.

To make the sauce: Wash and dry the half orange, remove the zest and cut it into very thin strips. Bring them quickly to the boil with the reserved apricot syrup. Add the Grand Marnier and leave to cool.
Serve the orange syrup with the praline crown.

CRÈME CARAMEL

Serves 4

knob of butter	boiled
175 g (6½ oz) sugar	1 sachet vanilla sugar
4 eggs	salt
500 ml (18 fl oz) milk,	

*M*ake a caramel sauce by melting together 100 g (3½ oz) sugar and the butter, and cooking it until the sugar turns golden. Pour the caramel into 4 ramekins. Beat the eggs, add the remaining 75 g (3 oz) sugar and gradually whisk in the hot milk. Then stir in the vanilla sugar and a pinch of salt.

Pour the custard into the ramekins, then stand them in a roasting tin filled with boiling water. The water should come only halfway up the sides of the ramekins.
Bake the custards at 180°C (350°F, Gas Mark 4) for 20-25 minutes.

BAKED CUSTARD

Serves 3-4

3 eggs	1 sachet of vanilla sugar
500 ml (18 fl oz) milk	salt
80 g (3 oz) butter	

*B*ring the milk to the boil with the sugar and a pinch of salt. Preheat the oven to 180°C (350°F, Gas Mark 4). Beat the eggs in a large bowl, then gradually add the boiling milk, whisking all the time. Pour the custard into a pudding basin or mould and put the mould into a roasting tin filled with hot water.
Bake the custard for 20 minutes. Leave the custard to go cold before turning it out and garnishing with fresh fruit.

Left: *Praline crown*
Below: *Baked custard*

CUSTARD

Serves 4

500 ml (18 fl oz) milk	1 vanilla pod
4 egg yolks	
100 g (3½ oz) caster sugar	

Put the egg yolks and sugar in a large bowl and whisk them until light and foaming. Bring the milk to the boil with the vanilla. Pour the boiling milk on to the egg mixture, whisking all the time, then return the custard to the saucepan. Heat the custard gently, whisking all the time, until it thickens enough to coat the back of a spoon. The custard should not be allowed to boil.

Tip: Put a metal plate or heat diffuser between the saucepan and heat to obtain a more even distribution of heat.

CHOCOLATE AND CHESTNUT CHARLOTTE

Serves 6

20-25 ratafia biscuits, or	80 g (3 oz) butter
sponge fingers	200 g (7 oz) chestnut
150 ml (5 fl oz) dark rum	purée, unsweetened
200 g (7 oz) good quality	4 eggs, separated
cooking chocolate	salt

Soak the biscuits in the rum for a few minutes. Reserve 10 of them and arrange the rest around the sides and base of a charlotte mould. Melt the butter and chocolate together over a gentle heat until smooth, then add the chestnut purée, stirring well. Take the mixture off the heat and beat in the egg yolks, then leave it to cool.

Whisk the egg whites until stiff, then fold them carefully into the cool custard mixture. Pour half of the mixture into the prepared mould, cover with 5 biscuits, then add the remaining custard and finish with the last 5 biscuits. Shake the mould gently to allow the custard to settle. Refrigerate the charlotte for several hours, or overnight if possible and turn out before serving.

STEAMED ALMOND OR HAZELNUT PUDDING

Serves 6

100 g (3½ oz) butter	almonds or hazelnuts
100 g (3½ oz) sugar	150 g (5 oz) flour
1 sachet of vanilla sugar	50 g (2 oz) cornflour
3 eggs	½ sachet dried yeast
a few drops of almond	3 tbsp milk
essence	salt
50 g (2 oz) ground	

Cream the butter until light and fluffy, then gradually fold in the sugar, vanilla sugar, eggs, a pinch of salt, a few drops of almond essence and the ground almonds or hazelnuts. Sift together the flour, cornflour and yeast, then gradually add the milk. Pour the mixture into a buttered pudding basin or mould. Bake in the oven at 200-225°C (400-425°F, Gas Mark 6-7) for 30-40 minutes.

Serve with chocolate sauce or custard.

SEMOLINA PUDDING

Serves 4

600 ml (1 pint) milk
1 sachet vanilla custard mix
30 g (1 oz) semolina

50 g (2 oz) sugar
2 eggs, separated

Bring 500 ml (18 fl oz) milk to the boil. Mix together the custard powder, semolina, sugar and egg yolks, and slake with 6 tablespoons of cold milk. Take the milk off the heat, pour the custard mixture into the hot milk, stirring all the time, then return the pan to the heat and bring to the boil quickly.

Allow the custard to cool, then whisk the egg whites until stiff and fold them carefully into the custard mixture. Pour the mixture into a glass serving dish or soufflé dish rinsed out with cold water and refrigerate. Turn out the pudding and serve decorated with whipped cream.

STEAMED SEMOLINA AND VANILLA PUDDING

Serves 4

400 ml (14 fl oz) milk
100 g (3½ oz) semolina
75 g (3 oz) butter
60 g (2½ oz) sugar
1 sachet vanilla sugar
3 eggs
4 drops of lemon oil

1 sachet of vanilla custard mix
3 tbsp milk
1 tsp dried yeast
1-2 tbsp raisins

Bring the milk to the boil with a pinch of salt, then take it off the heat. Sprinkle the semolina onto the hot milk, stirring constantly, then leave it to swell. Cream the butter until light and fluffy, then fold in the sugar, vanilla sugar, eggs, lemon oil and semolina. Blend the custard mix with 3 tablespoons of cold milk and add it to the semolina mixture. Finally fold in the yeast and raisins. Pour the mixture into a pudding basin or mould and put it into a roasting tin with a little water in the base and bake at 180-200°C (350-400°F, Gas Mark 4-6) for 1 hour.

Below: *Semolina pudding*
Left: *Steamed almond or hazelnut pudding*

RED WINE MOUSSE

Serves 4

1 packet of raspberry jelly
125 g (4 oz) sugar
250 ml (8 fl oz) red wine

250 ml (8 fl oz) double
cream

Bring 250 ml (8 fl oz) water to the boil and take it off the heat. Dissolve the jelly in the hot water, dissolve the sugar in the red wine and add it to the jelly. Bring the jelly to the boil again, then leave it to cool, stirring occasionally, but do not let it set. Whip the double cream until it forms soft peaks and fold it into the jelly. Spoon the dessert into individual dishes or a large glass bowl and refrigerate until it sets.
Serve with plain shortcake or similar biscuits.

WALNUT AND ORANGE MOUSSE

Serves 2

4 leaves of gelatine	orange liqueur (Grand
2 eggs, separated	Marnier or Cointreau)
75 g (3 oz) sugar	250 ml (8 fl oz) double
250 ml (8 fl oz) orange juice	cream
125 ml (4 fl oz) milk	75 g (3 oz) walnuts, shelled

Soften the gelatine in cold water, leave it to reconstitute for 10 minutes, then dissolve it in a saucepan with a drop of water, stirring until it is completely dissolved. Whisk the egg yolks and sugar until pale and foamy, then whisk in the orange juice, milk, 2 tablespoons of orange liqueur and the warm gelatine and refrigerate.

Whisk the egg whites until stiff. Whip the cream until it forms soft peaks. As soon as the orange mixture starts to set, fold in the egg whites and whipped cream (reserving a little cream for decoration). Chop the walnuts finely, reserving a few for decoration, and fold them into the cream, then add more of your preferred liqueur to taste. Transfer the mousse to a large glass dish or individual sundae dishes and refrigerate. Decorate the mousse with the remaining whipped cream and chopped nuts.

BANANA MOUSSE

Serves 3

3 bananas	3 eggs, separated
75 g (3 oz) sugar	salt

Peel the bananas and purée them in a blender or food processor with the sugar and egg yolks. Transfer the banana mixture to a saucepan and cook it over a low heat for 3 minutes, until it thickens, then leave it to cool completely.

Whisk the egg whites with a pinch of salt until stiff, then fold them carefully into the banana mixture.

Serve well chilled.

Below: *Walnut and orange mousse*
Left: *Red wine mousse*

WHITE WINE MOUSSE

Serves 2

100 ml (3½ fl oz) white
wine
1 egg white

1 sachet lemon dessert mix
150 ml (5 fl oz) double
cream

Make up the lemon dessert mix with the white wine, 100 ml (3½ fl oz) water and the egg white, according to the instructions on the packet, but do not let it boil. Whip the double cream until it forms soft peaks, then fold it into the lemon mixture. Transfer the dessert to individual sundae dishes and refrigerate it for 30 minutes.

RUM MOUSSE

Serves 4

4 egg yolks
65 g (2½ oz) sugar
1 sachet vanilla sugar
zest of ½ unwaxed lemon,
grated
6 tbsp rum

1 tsp powdered gelatine or
2 leaves of gelatine
350 ml (11 fl oz) double
cream
grated chocolate
salt

Whisk the egg yolks, sugar and vanilla sugar until the mixture is pale and foamy, then add a pinch of salt, the lemon zest and rum. Soften the gelatine in 3 tablespoons of cold water and fold it into the egg mixture.
Heat the mixture in a saucepan until the gelatine dissolves completely, stirring all the time, then allow to cool and refrigerate. As soon as the mousse starts to set,

below: *Rum mousse*

whip the double cream until it forms soft peaks and fold it into the rum mixture. Decorate with grated chocolate.

PARADISE CREAM

Serves 4

1 sachet of vanilla dessert
mix (Angel Delight or
similar)

300 ml (10 fl oz) milk
500 g (1 lb) stewed fruit, to
taste

Make up the dessert mix with the cold milk, according to the instructions on the packet. Divide the stewed fruit between individual dishes and top with the dessert mix.

VANILLA AND ORANGE CREAM

Serves 4

250 ml (8 fl oz) freshly
squeezed orange juice
(about 5 oranges)
1 sachet vanilla dessert mix

250 ml (8 fl oz) double
cream
slices of orange

Pour the orange juice and 6 tablespoons of water into a large bowl. Add the contents of the packet dessert mix. Whisk briskly to obtain a smooth mix, then whip the double cream and fold it into the orange mixture. Leave to set for about 20 minutes, then garnish with slices of orange.

CREAMED SEMOLINA

Serves 4

2 egg yolks
150 g (5 oz) crème fraîche
500 ml (18 fl oz) milk

½ vanilla pod
2 tablespoons sugar
50 g (2 oz) semolina

Whisk the egg yolks with 1 tablespoon of cream. Split the vanilla pod and scrape out the essence. Add the remaining cream to the milk, with the vanilla pod, vanilla essence and sugar, bring to the boil and simmer for 5-10 minutes. Sprinkle the semolina onto the hot milk, stirring constantly, leave to swell, then take the pan off the heat and fold in the beaten egg.

The semolina can be served hot or cold.

Opposite, *from left to right: Vanilla and orange cream, white wine mousse, paradise cream.*

ORANGE BAVAROIS

Serves 6

1 sachet of powdered
gelatine or 4 leaves of
gelatine
8 egg yolks
70 g (3 oz) sugar
1 sachet of vanilla sugar
125 ml (4 fl oz) orange
liqueur, e.g. Grand

Marnier or Cointreau
1-2 tbsp lemon juice
500 ml (18 fl oz) double
cream
3 oranges
500 g (1 lb) strawberries
25 g (1 oz) pistachio nuts,
shelled and chopped

*B*lend the gelatine with 3 tablespoons of cold water and
leave it to soften for 10 minutes. Whisk together the egg
yolks, 50 g (2 oz) sugar, the vanilla sugar, orange liqueur
and lemon juice in a double saucepan, or a bowl over a
pan of boiling water, until a thick custard forms. Fold in
the gelatine. Stand the bowl in cold water and whisk the
mixture until it begins to thicken.

Whip the double cream until it forms soft peaks then fold
it into the custard and refrigerate it. Peel and segment
the oranges. Slice the strawberries in half. Sprinkle the
fruit with the remaining sugar and arrange them on
plates.
Serve the fruit with the bavarois, sprinkled with chopped
pistachio nuts and accompanied by shortbread biscuits.

Above: Crème diplomate
Left: Orange bavarois

CRÈME DIPLOMATE

Serves 4

1 sachet vanilla dessert mix
50 g (2 oz) sugar
500 ml (18 fl oz) milk
40 g (1½ oz) candied lemon peel
125 g (4 oz) raisins
1 tsp sugar
250 ml (8 fl oz) double cream

1 sachet of vanilla sugar
100-125 g (3½-4 oz) sponge fingers or ratafia biscuits
2-3 tbsp rum
50 g (2 oz) bitter chocolate, grated
salt

*M*ake up the dessert mix according to the instructions on the packet. Refrigerate it, and stir it occasionally. Dice the candied lemon peel finely, then heat it in 4 tablespoons of water with the raisins and sugar until the water has evaporated completely. Leave to cool, then refrigerate.

Whip the double cream and vanilla sugar until it forms soft peaks, then fold it into the chilled dessert mix. Soak the sponge fingers or biscuits in the rum. Transfer the cream mixture to a large glass dish or individual sundae dishes.

Serve with mini chocolate rolls.

FLOATING ISLANDS

Serves 4

4 eggs, separated
500 ml (18 fl oz) milk
100 g (3½ oz) caster sugar
1 sachet of vanilla sugar
salt

Bring the milk to the boil with a pinch of salt and the vanilla sugar. Beat together the egg yolks and caster sugar until the mixture is pale and foamy. Gradually stir in the boiling milk. Return the custard to the pan and cook on a low heat, stirring constantly, until the custard thickens enough to coat the back of a spoon. Take the custard off the heat to prevent it boiling.

Whisk the egg whites until very stiff. Heat 2-3 litres (3½-5½ pints) of water. When the water starts to simmer, drop heaped tablespoons of egg white into it. Leave them to cook for a few moments, then turn them. Drain them on kitchen paper. Continue cooking the egg white in this way until it is all used up. Arrange the floating islands on top of the cooled custard.

PARADISE GRAPEFRUIT

Serves 4

2 grapefruit
1 sachet of lemon dessert mix
250 ml (8 fl oz) milk
slices of lemon

Slice the grapefruit in half. Carefully scoop out the flesh, remove the pith and membranes, chop the flesh and drain it.

Make up the lemon dessert mix according to the instructions on the packet, but use only 250 ml (8 fl oz) milk. Fold in the chopped grapefruit. Transfer the mixture to the grapefruit shells and garnish with slices of lemon.

Above: *Paradise grapefruit*
Opposite: *Bananas with ginger*

BANANAS WITH GINGER

Serves 6

3 bananas
3 red plums
½ tsp ground ginger
3-4 tbsp orange juice
6 tbsp Cointreau
1 tsp powdered gelatine
or 1 leaf of gelatine
125 ml (4 fl oz) milk

½ vanilla pod
2 egg yolks
1 tbsp sugar
250 ml (8 fl oz) double
cream
plain chocolate, grated or
chocolate sprinkles

Peel and slice the bananas. Dice the plums finely and combine them with the sliced bananas, orange juice, ginger and 3 tablespoons of Cointreau, then leave them to marinate.

To make the Cointreau sauce: Blend the gelatine with 2 tablespoons of cold water and leave it to soften for 10 minutes. Bring the milk to the boil, split the vanilla pod, scrape out the essence, add the pod and essence to the milk, bring to the boil again and allow to cool a little.

Whisk together the egg yolks and sugar. Add the milk, then transfer the mixture to a double saucepan, or a basin over a saucepan of boiling water, and heat the custard until it thickens (about 6-7 minutes). Fold in the gelatine and stir until dissolved.

Stand the pan in cold water, and stir the custard occasionally. Add the remaining 3 tablespoons of Cointreau as soon as the mixture starts to thicken. Whip the double cream until it forms soft peaks and fold it into the custard.

Arrange the gingered bananas in dessert dishes, spread the custard over the top and refrigerate. Garnish with the grated chocolate.

APRICOT BAVAROIS

Serves 6

1 kg (2 lb) apricots
150 g (5 oz) sugar
zest of 1 unwaxed lemon, grated
3 tbsp lemon juice
6 tbsp eau-de-vie or schnapps

2 vanilla pods
6 egg yolks
1 sachet powdered gelatine
500 ml (18 fl oz) double cream

Wash and chop the apricots. Cook them in a lidded saucepan for 10-15 minutes in a little water with 100 g (3½ oz) sugar and the lemon zest and juice. Add the eau-de-vie to the apricots and strain them, reserving the syrup (about 125 ml (4 fl oz)). Arrange the apricots in individual dishes and refrigerate them. Split the vanilla pods in half lengthways, scrape out the essence and blend it with 3 tablespoons of apricot syrup, the egg yolks and remaining sugar. Whisk the mixture until a thick cream forms. Blend the gelatine with 3 tablespoons of cold water, then leave it to soften for 10 minutes. Once the gelatine has softened, heat it with the apricot syrup until it dissolves, then gradually whisk the apricot syrup into the egg mixture.

Whip the double cream until it forms very stiff peaks. As soon as the custard starts to thicken, fold the cream into it. Cover the apricots with the bavarois and refrigerate.

CHERRY BOMBE

Serves 10-12

1½ kg (3½ lb) Morello cherries, stewed
6 tbsp cherry or pear schnapps
7 tbsp caster sugar
1 sachet powdered

gelatine
1 litre (1¾ pints) double cream
2 sachets vanilla sugar
cherries for decoration

Above: *Apricot bavarois*
Left: *Cherry bombe*

Drain the cherries, reserving the syrup and marinate them for at least 1 hour in the schnapps with 3 tablespoons of caster sugar. Blend the gelatine with 5 tablespoons of cold water, leave it to soften for 10 minutes, then heat it, stirring all the time, until it dissolves.

Add 4 tablespoons of caster sugar and the vanilla sugar to the double cream and whip it until it forms soft peaks. Fold in 1 tablespoon of melted gelatine. Carefully fold the remaining gelatine into the cream, then add the cherries and alcohol. Pour the mixture into a mould, tapping the mould from time to time to make sure the mixture settles.

Cover the mould and refrigerate it for several hours and preferably overnight. Quickly dip the mould into hot water just before serving and turn the bombe out onto a serving dish.

Serve immediately, garnished with cherries.

CARAMEL CREAM

Serves 4-6

150 g (5 oz) sugar	8 egg yolks
500 ml (18 fl oz) double cream	3 tbsp powdered gelatine

Heat the sugar in a frying pan until it starts to caramelize. Add the double cream, stir well, bring to the boil, take the pan off the heat and whisk in the egg yolks one by one.

Blend the gelatine with 3 tablespoons of cold water and leave it to soften for 10 minutes, then add it to the cream mixture, stirring all the time. Heat the cream mixture in a double saucepan, or a bowl over a saucepan of boiling water, stirring constantly, until the mixture thickens. Pour the mixture into individual dessert dishes and refrigerate.

CHARLOTTE RUSSE

Serves 6-7

200 g (7 oz) dried fruit
8 tbsp maraschino
1 vanilla pod
250 ml (8 fl oz) milk
4 egg yolks
1 whole egg
50 g (2 oz) sugar

1 sachet vanilla sugar
1 sachet powdered
gelatine
500 ml (18 fl oz) double
cream
28 sponge fingers

Reserve a few pieces of dried fruit for decoration, then chop the rest and soak them in the maraschino. Cover them and leave them to macerate overnight. Split the vanilla pod in half lengthways, add it to the milk and bring to the boil. Whisk the egg yolks, the whole egg, sugar and vanilla sugar until the mixture is pale yellow. Gradually add the milk, then return the custard to the pan and heat it gently, stirring constantly until the custard thickens. Blend the gelatine with 3 tablespoons of cold water, leave it to soften for 10 minutes, then heat it, stirring all the time, until completely dissolved. Let the gelatine cool a little before folding it into the custard. Stand the pan of custard in cold water and whisk it until it cools. Whip the double cream until it forms soft peaks, then fold 3 tablespoons into the macerated fruits. Reserve a little whipped cream for decoration and fold

Above: *Cranberry pudding*
Left: *Charlotte russe*

the rest into the custard. Cut the sponge fingers in half and use them to line the sides of a sandwich tin.

Transfer the custard to the tin, level it off and refrigerate it. Before serving, turn the charlotte out. Put the reserved whipped cream in a piping bag and pipe rosettes of cream around the charlotte. Garnish with the reserved dried fruit.

CRANBERRY PUDDING

Serves 4

1 tsp powdered gelatine
125 ml (4 fl oz) port
1 tbsp sugar
zest of ½ an unwaxed
lemon, grated
1 tbsp lemon juice

250 g (8 oz) cranberry
preserve
250 ml (8 fl oz) double
cream
cranberries for garnish

Blend the gelatine with 2 tablespoons of cold water, leave it to soften for 10 minutes, then heat it, stirring all the time, until dissolved. Combine the port, sugar, cranberry preserve, lemon zest and juice, fold in the warm gelatine and refrigerate.

Before the cranberry mixture sets, whip the double cream until it forms soft peaks and fold two-thirds of it into the cranberries. Decorate the pudding with the remaining cream and garnish with cranberries.

Above: *Orange mousse*
Left: *Sherry mousse*

SHERRY MOUSSE

Serves 4

2 tsp powdered gelatine
16 sponge fingers
8 tbsp sherry
3 egg yolks
125g (4 oz) sugar

1 sachet of vanilla sugar
1 tbsp orange juice
750 ml (1¼ pints) double cream
4 maraschino cherries

Blend the gelatine with 3 tablespoons of cold water in a small saucepan, leave to soften for 10 minutes, then heat through, stirring constantly, until the gelatine dissolves. Put the sponge fingers on a plate and drizzle them with 4 tablespoons of sherry. Put the egg yolks, sugar, vanilla sugar and orange juice in a double saucepan, or a bowl over a pan of boiling water, and whisk until the mixture is creamy. Separate the double boiler, or take the bowl out of the pan, and continue whisking until the mixture is cool. Whip the double cream until it forms soft peaks, reserving some for decoration. Fold the cream into the egg mixture with the remaining sherry and the gelatine. Leave the mousse to cool. Arrange 4 sponge fingers in an individual sundae dish and fill the dish with mousse. Decorate with the reserved whipped cream and garnish with the maraschino cherries.

ORANGE MOUSSE

Serves 4

2 large oranges
1 sachet of powdered gelatine
3 eggs, separated
100 g (3½ oz) sugar

1 tbsp lemon juice
150 ml (5 fl oz) double cream
flaked almonds

Slice the oranges in half and squeeze the juice, avoiding damaging the skins. Reserve 10 tablespoons of juice. Scoop out the flesh and put the orange shells in the freezer. Blend the gelatine with 6 tablespoons of cold water and leave it to soften for 10 minutes, then heat it through, stirring constantly, until dissolved. Whisk the egg yolks with two-thirds of the sugar until a creamy mixture forms. Fold in the reserved orange juice and warm gelatine, then refrigerate the mixture. Whisk the egg whites until stiff, then incorporate the remaining sugar, whisking all the time. Whip the cream until it forms soft peaks.
Fold the egg whites and whipped cream into the orange mixture. Pipe the orange mousse into the frozen orange shells and decorate with flaked almonds or a coating of melted chocolate.

MACAROONS WITH RED FRUIT

Serves

500 g (1 lb) strawberries	250 ml (8 fl oz) double
250 g (8 oz) raspberries	cream
juice of 1 lime	200 g (7 oz) small almond
180 g (6½ oz) sugar	macaroons
3 egg yolks	4 tbsp port
1½ tsp powdered gelatine	
1½ tbsp orange liqueur	

Wash the strawberries, drain them, hull them and cut them into halves or quarters. Drizzle them with the lime juice, sprinkle them with 30 g (1 oz) sugar and leave them to marinate. Cook the raspberries in 2 tablespoons of water with 50 g (2 oz) sugar until soft, then purée them through a sieve. Whisk together the egg yolks and 100 g (3½ oz) sugar, then gradually fold in the raspberry purée.

Blend the gelatine with 2 tablespoons of cold water, leave it to soften for 10 minutes, then heat it through, stirring constantly, until dissolved. Add the orange liqueur and fold the gelatine into the raspberry mousse. When the mousse starts to thicken whip the cream until it forms soft peaks and fold half of it into the raspberry mixture and refrigerate the mousse.

Below: *Macaroons with red fruit*

Divide three quarters of the macaroons between individual dessert dishes and drizzle them with the port. Add the strawberries, then the raspberry mousse and garnish with the remaining macaroons. Decorate the mousse with the reserved whipped cream and sprinkle with grated lime zest.

CLAFOUTIS

(FRUIT BAKED IN A BATTER PUDDING)
Serves 6

500 g (1 lb) cherries or	125 g (4 oz) caster sugar
greengages, pears or	300 ml (10 fl oz) milk
plums	knob of butter
60 g (2½ oz) flour	salt
3 eggs	

Wash the cherries and remove the stalks. Sift together the flour, sugar and a pinch of salt. Beat the whole eggs and milk into the flour.

Butter a gratin dish, arrange the cherries in it and pour the batter over them. Bake the clafoutis in the oven at 200-225ºC (400-425ºF, Gas Mark 6-7) for 45 minutes. Dredge with caster sugar before serving.

APPLE AND GINGER MOUSSE

Serves 4

2 large cooking apples	grated
250 ml (8 fl oz) white wine	100 g (3½ oz) preserved
1 sachet powdered	ginger
gelatine or 4 leaves of	250 ml (8 fl oz) double
gelatine	cream
2 egg yolks	1 dessert apple, for
100 g (3½ oz) sugar	decoration
zest of 1 unwaxed lemon,	

Peel and core the cooking apples, cut them into 8 pieces and cook them in the white wine until soft, then purée them. Blend the gelatine with 3 tablespoons of cold water, leave to soften for 10 minutes, then heat it through, stirring constantly, until the gelatine has dissolved. Stir it into the apple purée.

Whisk together the egg yolks and sugar and stir in the lemon zest. Add the apple purée, stir, then refrigerate the mixture for 45 minutes. Finely chop the ginger, reserving a little for decoration. Whip the cream until it forms soft peaks and fold the cream and ginger into the apple purée,

constantly, until dissolved, then fold it into the custard and refrigerate. Fold half of the apricot slices into the mousse when it has started to thicken but is not yet set.

Whip the cream until it forms soft peaks and fold it in to the apricot mousse, then refrigerate it. Push the raspberries through a sieve and stir 25 g (1 oz) of sugar and the raspberry liqueur into the purée. Decorate the bavarois with the raspberry sauce and remaining slices of apricot.

Above left: *Apple and ginger mousse*
Below: *Apricot bavarois with raspberry sauce*

then transfer it to individual sundae dishes. Wash the remaining apple, dry it and slice it very thinly into rounds. Decorate the mousse with the reserved ginger and slices of apple.

APRICOT BAVAROIS WITH RASPBERRY SAUCE

Serves 6-8

750 g (1½ lb) ripe apricots	gelatine or 4 leaves of
6 egg yolks	gelatine
125 g (4½ oz) sugar	250 ml (8 fl oz) double
1 vanilla pod	cream
1 tbsp lemon juice	250 g (8 oz) raspberries
2 tbsp eau-de-vie or	1-2 tbsp raspberry liqueur
schnapps	
1 sachet powdered	

Cut the apricots in half and stone them. Purée two-thirds of the apricots and slice the rest. Whisk the egg yolks with 100 g (3½ oz) sugar until the mixture turns pale and foamy.
Split the vanilla pod in half lengthways, scrape out the essence and fold it into the egg mixture, then add the apricot purée, lemon juice and eau-de-vie. Blend the gelatine with 3 tablespoons of cold water and leave it to soften for 10 minutes, then heat it through, stirring

PEACH PUDDING WITH CHOCOLATE SAUCE

Serves 4

4 ripe peaches
100 g (3½ oz) sugar
1 sachet vanilla custard
mix
500 ml (18 fl oz) cold milk

250 ml (8 fl oz) double
cream
100 g (3½ oz) bitter
chocolate

Blanch the peaches in hot, but not boiling water, refresh them in cold water, skin them, slice them in half and stone them. Bring 125 ml (4 fl oz) water to the boil with 100 g (3½ oz) sugar and cook the peaches in the syrup for 5 minutes. Drain them and leave them to cool. Make up the custard according to the instructions on the packet, pour into individual dessert bowls or a large dish, and refrigerate it. Cut the peach halves into 4 slices and arrange them in a fan shape on top of the custard. Whip half of the cream until it forms soft peaks and use it to decorate the custard.

To make the chocolate sauce: Break the chocolate up into squares, put them in a double saucepan, or a bowl over a pan of boiling water, and stir until the chocolate softens, then stir in the remaining double cream. Pour this chocolate sauce, or ganache, over the custard and peaches.

MACAROONS WITH WINE MOUSSE

Serves 4-6

4 egg yolks	gelatine or 4 leaves of
125-150 g (4-5 oz) caster	gelatine
sugar	350 ml (11 fl oz) double
125 ml (4 fl oz) red wine	cream
brandy or rum	250 g (8 oz) black grapes
1 sachet of powdered	100 g (3½ oz) macaroons

Whisk together the egg yolks and caster sugar until the mixture turns pale, then add the wine. Blend the gelatine with 3 tablespoons of cold water, leave it to soften for 10 minutes, then heat it through stirring constantly, until the gelatine has dissolved, then stir it into the egg mixture and refrigerate it.

When the custard starts to set, whip the cream until it forms soft peaks and fold it into the mousse. Wash and dry the grapes, reserving a few for decoration. Slice the other grapes in half and de-seed them. Soak the macaroons in brandy or rum.

Alternately layer the mousse, the halved grapes and macaroons in a large glass dish, finishing with a layer of mousse. Garnish with the reserved grapes and whipped cream.

Left: *Peach pudding with chocolate sauce*
Above right: *Macaroons with wine mousse*

CHOCOLATE MOUSSE

Serves 4

1 tsp powdered gelatine	250 ml (8 fl oz) double
or 1 leaf of gelatine	cream
150 g (5 oz) bitter	grated chocolate
chocolate	
2 egg whites	

Blend the gelatine with 1 tablespoon of cold water and leave it to soften for 10 minutes.

Break the chocolate into small pieces and melt it in a double saucepan, or a bowl over a pan of hot water, stirring all the time. Leave the chocolate to cool, stirring it occasionally. Whisk the egg whites until stiff.

Heat the gelatine through, stirring constantly, until it dissolves. Fold in 1-2 tablespoons of double cream. Whip the remaining cream until it is almost stiff, then add the gelatine solution, whisking briskly. Add the melted chocolate and carefully fold in the egg whites.

Transfer the chocolate mousse to individual dishes and garnish with grated chocolate.

CALIFORNIAN FRUIT SALAD

Serves 4-6

350 g (11 oz) fresh
pineapple
350 g (11 oz) peaches
10 g (¼-½ oz) fresh root
ginger

2 vanilla pods
350 g (11 oz) raisins
3 cloves
350 g (11 oz) brown sugar
500 ml (18 fl oz) white rum

Peel the pineapple and take out the core. Blanch the peaches, then refresh them in cold water. Skin and stone them. Chop the fruit and peeled root ginger. Split the vanilla pods lengthways and add them to the chopped fruit with the raisins and cloves. Dissolve the sugar in the rum and pour it over the fruit. Seal the container very tightly and leave the fruit to marinate in a cool place for 3-4 hours.
Serve with vanilla ice-cream.

FRUITS OF THE FOREST SALAD

Serves 2

250 g (8 oz) fruits of the
forest, e.g. raspberries,
blackberries,
blackcurrants
100 g (3½ oz) sugar
40 ml (generous 1 fl oz)

brandy
250 ml (8 fl oz) double
cream
80 ml (2½ fl oz) fruit
liqueur

Pick over the fruits, then wash and drain them well. Dissolve the sugar in the brandy, pour it over the fruit and leave them to marinate for 30 minutes. Whip the cream until it forms soft peaks, fold in the fruit liqueur, and carefully fold in the fruit. Serve well chilled.

Below: *Californian fruit salad*

Above: *Exotic meringue with raspberry mousse*

EXOTIC MERINGUE WITH RASPBERRY MOUSSE

Serves 4

4 kiwi fruit
4 peach halves, tinned in syrup
4 ready-made meringues
200 ml (7 fl oz) double

cream
1 tbsp caster sugar
100 g (3½ oz) raspberries.

*P*eel the kiwi fruit, slice them and arrange them on top of the meringues with the peach halves.
To make the raspberry mousse: Whip the double cream and caster sugar until it forms soft peaks. Purée the raspberries to obtain 2 tablespoons of pulp, then pass it through a sieve and fold it into the cream. Put the raspberry mousse into a piping bag fitted with a star-shaped nozzle and pipe rosettes of cream onto the peaches.

BAKED APPLES

Serves 4-6

1 kg (2 lb) apples, e.g.
Cox's Orange Pippins
150 g (5 oz) sugar

100 g (3½ oz) raisins
50 g (2 oz) butter
ground cinnamon

*P*eel, core and slice the apples thinly. Butter a soufflé dish and arrange one-third of the apples on the base, then add 3 tablespoons of sugar, 50 g (2 oz) raisins and 25 g (1 oz) butter and sprinkle them with cinnamon to taste.

Continue layering the ingredients, finishing with a layer of apples. Sprinkle the top with sugar and dot with butter. Press the apples down well. Cover with a sheet of foil and bake them in the oven at 200-225°C (400-425°F, Gas Mark 6-7) for about 1 hour. Leave them to cool, then turn them out.
Serve with custard (see page 422).

FRUIT AND CREAM MERINGUES

Serves 4

2 egg whites
100 g (3½ oz) caster sugar
6-8 apricots
400 ml (14 fl oz) apricot
liqueur

3 kiwi fruit
2 tbsp sugar
150 ml (5 fl oz) double
cream

Whisk the egg whites until they are very stiff, then gradually fold in the caster sugar. Fill a piping bag fitted with a star-shaped nozzle with the egg whites. Place a sheet of baking parchment on a baking sheet and pipe 4 spirals, 8-10 cm (3-4 inches) in diameter onto the baking parchment, then pipe rosettes around the edge of each. Bake the meringues in the oven for 1 hour at 160°C (325°F, Gas Mark 3).

Leave the meringues to dry for several hours. Slice the apricots in half, and stone and slice them. Cook them in the apricot liqueur for about 5 minutes, then drain them and reserve the syrup. Peel and slice the kiwi fruit, combine them with the apricots and sugar and leave them to marinate.

Arrange the fruit on top of the meringues. Whip the double cream and sugar until it forms soft peaks, then fold in the apricot syrup. Pipe the whipped cream onto the meringues and fruit and serve immediately.

MIRABELLE PLUMS WITH CRANBERRY CREAM

Serves 4

500 g (1 lb) mirabelle
plums
50 g (2 oz) sugar
250 ml (8 fl oz) double

cream
250 g (8 oz) cranberry
preserve

Wash the plums, slice them in half and stone them. Bring 125 ml (4 fl oz) water to the boil with the sugar and cook the plums in it for 2-3 minutes until they are almost translucent. Leave the plums to cool, then drain them.

To make the cranberry cream: Whip the double cream until it forms soft peaks. Drain the cranberries and fold them carefully into the cream. Arrange the plums in individual dishes and top them with the cranberry cream.

PERSIMMONS MELBA

Serves 4

4 ripe persimmons
4 scoops of vanilla ice-
cream
100 g (3½ oz) raspberry
jelly

20 ml (generous 1½
tablespoons) of orange
liqueur
grated chocolate

Wash and dry the persimmons. Remove the leaves but leave the stalk. Slice the fruits into quarters but do not cut all the way through, so that they can be opened out in a star shape.

Put the persimmons into individual dishes, put a scoop of ice-cream in the centre of each, blend together the raspberry jelly and orange liqueur and pour it over the persimmons. Decorate with grated chocolate.

Left: *Fruit and cream meringues*
Right: *Persimmons Melba*

FRUITS OF THE FOREST WITH SABAYON SAUCE

Serves 6

300 g (10 oz) strawberries
300 g (10 oz) blackberries
300 g (10 oz) raspberries
zest of 1 lime, grated
1-2 tbsp lime juice
30 g (1 oz) sugar
2 tbsp eau-de-vie or

schnapps
6 egg yolks
4 tbsp white wine
250 ml (8 fl oz) double
cream
2 tbsp apricot liqueur
1 tsp ground cinnamon

Wash the fruit and put it in a large bowl. Add the lime zest and juice, sugar and eau-de-vie, cover and leave to marinate.

To make the sabayon sauce: Whisk together the egg yolks, white wine, cream, apricot liqueur and cinnamon in a double saucepan, or a bowl over a pan of hot water, until the sauce is smooth, creamy and thick and warmed through. Pour the sauce over the fruits of the forest.

MORELLO CHERRIES LA CRÈME

Serves 4

500 g (1 lb) fresh Morello
cherries or 450 g (15 oz)
tin Morello cherries in
syrup
30 g (1 oz) butter
2 tbsp sugar
40 g (1½ oz) flaked

almonds
4-5 tbsp cherry eau-de-
vie
2 tbsp double cream
vanilla or chocolate ice-
cream

Wash the fresh cherries, remove the stalks and pit them, or drain the tinned cherries. Melt the butter in a frying pan and brown the sugar in it. Add the cherries and almonds and heat them through, stirring all the time.

Flame the cherries using the cherry eau-de-vie. Fold in the cream and bring to the boil. Arrange scoops of ice-cream on 4 dessert plates and garnish with the flamed cherries.

Above: *Fruits of the forest with sabayon sauce*
Right: *Pineapple à la crème*

PINEAPPLE LA CRÈME

Serves 4

1 fresh pineapple
3-4 tbsp white rum
250 ml (8 fl oz) double cream

2-3 tbsp caster sugar
1 tsp vanilla essence or orange oil
1 pomegranate

Slice the pineapple in half a few centimetres (couple of inches) below the crown. Loosen the skin with the help of a long, pointed knife, scoop out the flesh with a spoon, and remove the core. Dice the flesh finely, pour the rum over it, cover and leave it to marinate for about 6 hours. Whip the cream until it forms soft peaks, gradually fold in the caster sugar, then add the vanilla essence or orange oil, and fold in the pineapple flesh. Fill the pineapple shells with the cream mixture and serve the rest in a dish. Slice the pomegranate in half, scoop out the seeds and use them to garnish the pineapple cream.

EXOTIC FRUIT FLAMBÉE WITH PINEAPPLE ICE-CREAM

Serves 4

1 small pineapple
100 g (3½ oz) caster sugar
2 tbsp lemon juice
250 ml (8 fl oz) double cream
1 kiwi fruit
1 mango, weighing about 150 g (5 oz)

100 g (3½ oz) fresh dates
100 g (3½ oz) strawberries
40 g (1½ oz) butter
3 tbsp sugar
125 ml (4 fl oz) orange juice
2 tbsp orange liqueur
2 tbsp white rum

Peel the pineapple and chop it finely, reserve one quarter and purée the rest. Combine the pineapple purée with the caster sugar and lemon juice. Whip the cream until it forms soft peaks and fold in the pineapple purée. Pour the mixture into a large bowl and put it in the freezer for 5 hours, stirring the ice-cream briskly every 20-30 minutes to break up the ice crystals.

Peel and slice the kiwi fruit. Peel the mango, remove the stone and chop the flesh finely. Slice the dates in half, stone them, then cut them in half again. Hull the strawberries and wash them, then cut them into halves or quarters. Melt the butter in a frying pan, add the sugar, and caramelize it, stirring all the time. Add the orange juice and stir until a thick sauce forms, then fold in the fruit, including the reserved pineapple flesh, and orange liqueur.

Heat the rum in a small saucepan, set light to it and pour the burning rum over the fruit. Divide the fruit amongst 4 dessert plates and garnish with 2 scoops of the pineapple ice-cream.

RHUBARB COMPTE

Serves 4

500 g (1 lb) rhubarb
100 g (3½ oz) sugar

1 sachet of vanilla sugar

Wash the rhubarb and cut it into chunks 2 cm (¾ inch) in length. Put the rhubarb in a saucepan, sprinkle it with the sugar, then add the vanilla sugar as soon as the juices start to thicken, and bring to the boil.

Cover and cook until the rhubarb is tender. Leave the stewed fruit to cool completely. Taste, and add more sugar of necessary.

RHUBARB WITH ORANGE SABAYON SAUCE

Serves 4-6

3-4 oranges
100 g (3½ oz) sugar
750 g (1½ lb) rhubarb
3 eggs
3 tbsp orange liqueur

1 tbsp lemon juice
15 pistachio nuts, chopped
zest of 1 unwaxed orange, grated
salt

Squeeze the oranges and bring 300 ml (10 fl oz) of juice to the boil with the sugar. Wash and trim the rhubarb, cut it into 5 cm (2 inch) chunks and cook them in the orange syrup for 4-5 minutes. Drain the rhubarb and reduce the juice. Pour it over the rhubarb and refrigerate.

Whisk the eggs with a pinch of salt, the orange liqueur and lemon juice in a double saucepan, or a bowl over a pan of hot water, until the sauce is smooth, creamy and slightly thickened, then take the pan off the heat and continue whisking until the sauce is cold. Pour the sauce over the rhubarb and garnish with chopped pistachio nuts and grated orange zest.

Left: *Exotic fruit flambée with pineapple ice-cream*
Below: *Rhubarb with orange sabayon sauce*

BANANAS WITH ALMOND SNOW

Serves 4

4 bananas	50 g (2 oz) sugar
juice of ½ lemon	50 g (2 oz) ground
1 egg white	almonds

Slit the banana skins in half lengthways and drizzle them with the lemon juice.

Whisk the egg white until stiff. Gradually add the sugar, a spoonful at a time, whisking all the time, then gradually whisk in the almonds. Fill a piping bag fitted with a star-shaped nozzle with the almond meringue, decorate the bananas with it and place them on a baking sheet. Cover them with a sheet of foil and cook them under the grill for 5 minutes.

Right: Fromage frais with seasonal fruits
Below: Pineapple meringues

PINEAPPLE MERINGUES

Serves 4

2 pineapples, each	2 tbsp rum
weighing 800 g (1½ lb)	4 egg whites
300 g (10 oz) fromage	2 tbsp caster sugar, sieved
frais	glacé cherries
1 tbsp sugar	

Cut the pineapples, and leaves, in half lengthways, scoop out the flesh and dice it finely. Fold the diced pineapple into the fromage frais, add the sugar and rum, and transfer this mixture to the pineapple halves. Whisk the eggs until stiff, then gradually whisk in the caster sugar. Fill a piping bag with the meringue and pipe it on top of the pineapples.

Put the pineapples in the oven at 100°C (200°F, Gas Mark ¼) and bake for about 5 minutes, or until the meringues brown slightly. Garnish with glacé cherries.

FROMAGE FRAIS WITH SEASONAL FRUITS

Serves 3-4

200 g (7 oz) fromage frais
6 tbsp orange juice
1 tbsp caster sugar
½ sachet vanilla sugar
seasonal fruit, e.g.

strawberries, cherries,
apricots, grapes, pears,
apples, mangoes, melons
lemon juice

*B*eat together the fromage frais and orange juice, caster sugar and vanilla sugar, then refrigerate it. Wash 100 g (3½ oz) of your chosen seasonal fruit and pat it dry or peel it as necessary. If you are using pears or apples, drizzle the lemon juice over them to stop them discolouring. Chop the fruit roughly, if necessary, and thread it onto skewers.

Serve with the orange-flavoured fromage frais.

GOOSEBERRY MERINGUES

Serves 4

500 g (1 lb) gooseberries   2 egg whites
250 g (8 oz) sugar

Wash, top and tail the gooseberries and bring them to the boil with 150 g (5 oz) sugar and 1 tablespoon of water. Simmer them until soft, then drain them, reserving the juice.

To make the meringue: Whisk the egg whites until stiff, then fold in the remaining sugar, a spoonful at a time, and transfer the mixture to a piping bag. Cover a baking sheet with foil and pipe spirals of meringue onto it for the meringue bases, and rosettes for the meringue tops. The bases should be about 7 cm (2½-3 inches) in diameter and the tops about 2 cm (¾ inch) high.

Place the baking sheet in the oven and bake the meringues at 100°C (200°F, Gas Mark ¼) for 50 minutes.

Leave them to cool, then fill them with the stewed gooseberries.

CHERRY SOUFFLÉ

Serves 4

300 g (10 oz) stale bread	grated
500 ml (18 fl oz) milk	1 kg (2 lb) cherries
50 g (2 oz) butter	3 tbsp cherry eau-de-vie or
4 eggs, separated	schnapps
75 g (3 oz) sugar	ground cinnamon
zest of 1 unwaxed lemon,	butter

Cut the bread into thin slices, heat the milk until lukewarm and soak the bread in it. Cream the butter until light and fluffy, then gradually beat in the egg yolks, sugar, cinnamon and lemon zest. Add the bread and stir well. Wash, de-stalk and pit the cherries, combine them with the eau-de-vie, then fold them into the bread mixture. Whisk the egg whites until stiff and fold them into the cherry mixture. Butter a soufflé dish, transfer to the cherry mixture to it, dot with butter and sprinkle with a little cinnamon and sugar.

Bake the soufflé in the oven at 150ºC (300ºF, Gas Mark 2) for an hour.

The soufflé should be served piping hot.

RASPBERRY TRIFLE

Serves 4

500 g (1 lb) raspberries
5 tbsp raspberry eau-de-vie or schnapps
120 g (4 oz) meringues

400 ml (14 fl oz) double cream
1 sachet of vanilla sugar

Pour the eau-de-vie over the raspberries. Crush the meringues roughly. Whip the double cream and vanilla sugar until it forms soft peaks. Layer the ingredients in a large glass dish, finishing with a layer of raspberries.

Serve well chilled.

APPLE SNOW

Serves 4-6

8 apples
2 egg whites

100 g (3½ oz) caster sugar

Peel, quarter and core the apples and cut them into slices. Bring them to the boil with a little water, cover and simmer for 5-6 minutes. Drain them, then purée them.

Whisk the egg whites until stiff, then fold in the sugar and vanilla sugar. Fold the meringue into the stewed apple, and transfer to individual dessert dishes.

Serve with little macaroon biscuits.

Below: *Cherry soufflé*
Left: *Gooseberry meringues*

SUBLIME PERSIMMON MERINGUES

Serves 4

4 ripe persimmons
4 tbsp rum
4 egg whites

2 tbsp sugar
1 tsp praline

Wash the persimmons, remove the leaves but leave the stalks. Cut them into segments but do not cut them all the way through, so that they open out in the shape of a star, then arrange them in an oven-proof dish, base downwards. Pour the rum over the persimmons.

Whisk the egg whites until very stiff, then fold in the sugar. Fill a piping bag with the meringue mixture and pipe the meringue into the middle of the persimmons. Put the dish under the grill and grill the meringues for 5-7 minutes, or until the meringue starts to brown.

Transfer the persimmons to individual dishes, sprinkle them with the praline and serve immediately.

BANANAS WITH CHOCOLATE

Serves 8

8 bananas
4 tbsp lemon juice
4 tbsp pistachio nuts,
chopped

6-8 tbsp milk
100 g (3½ oz) chocolate
150 ml (5 fl oz) double
cream

Peel the bananas, drizzle them with the lemon juice and sprinkle them with the chopped pistachio nuts. Bring the milk to the boil, add the chocolate, broken into squares, and heat it without boiling, stirring from time to time, until a thick sauce forms.

Pour the chocolate sauce onto 8 plates. Arrange the bananas on top. Whip the cream until it forms soft peaks, pipe it onto the plate with the bananas, and garnish it with chopped nuts.

ALCOHOLIC FRUIT SALAD

Serves 6

2 bananas
2 apples
2 tbsp lemon juice
125 g (4 oz) grapes
2 oranges
4 apricots
2 tbsp sugar

500 ml (18 fl oz) double
cream
2-3 tbsp Grand Marnier
30 g (1 oz) chopped
hazelnuts
vanilla sugar

Peel and slice the bananas. Peel, quarter and core the apples, then chop them. Drizzle the lemon juice over the fruit. De-seed the grapes. Peel the oranges and remove the pith, then chop the segments. Wash and stone the apricots and cut them into quarters. Fold the sugar and vanilla sugar into the fruit, then transfer them to a large glass dish.

Fold the Grand Marnier and nuts into the double cream. Pour the cream over the fruit and serve with shortbread or brandy snap biscuits.

Left: *Sublime persimmon meringues*
Right: *Bananas with chocolate*

ORANGE SEGMENTS WITH AVOCADO PURÉE

Serves 4

4 oranges
2 avocados
juice of 1 orange
2 tbsp sugar

vanilla sugar
1 tbsp Grand Marnier
maraschino cherries

Peel and segment the oranges, reserving the juice. Arrange the segments in individual dessert dishes and refrigerate them.

slice the avocados in half lengthways and stone them, then scoop out the flesh. Purée the avocado flesh with the orange juice, sugar, vanilla sugar and Grand Marnier in a blender or food processor. Transfer the purée to a piping bag and pipe it onto the orange segments. Garnish with maraschino cherries.

Serve with shortbread or other sweet biscuits.

PINEAPPLE BOATS

Serves 4

1 fresh pineapple
200 g (7 oz) sugar

1 vanilla pod

PINEAPPLE WITH RASPBERRY CREAM

Serves 4

250 g (8 oz) raspberries	3 tbsp caster sugar
250 ml (8 fl oz) double cream	1 fresh pineapple

Purée the raspberries, then push the purée through a sieve. Whip the cream until it forms stiff peaks, then fold in the raspberry purée and caster sugar.
Slice the pineapple and leaves lengthways into 8 sections, then carefully remove the core. Separate the flesh from the skin, slice each big segment of pineapple into little slices, and arrange them on the pineapple shells.
Serve the raspberry cream separately.

Left: *Orange segments with avocado purée*
Below: *Pineapple with raspberry cream*

Put the pineapple and leaves into 4 pieces lengthways, then remove the core. Cut the flesh away from the skin with a sharp knife and cut it into 2 cm (¾ inch) thick slices.

Bring 125 ml (4 fl oz) water to the boil with the sugar and split vanilla pod. Add the sliced pineapple, bring to the boil and simmer for 3 minutes.

Drain the pineapple slices on a rack. Bring the syrup to the boil again and boil it until the syrup starts to caramelize, then remove the vanilla pod. Arrange the pineapple shells on individual plates. Dip the slices of pineapple into the caramel, drain them quickly and arrange them in the pineapple shells.

HAZELNUT PARFAIT

Serves 8

150 g (5 oz) hazelnuts, finely chopped
350 g (11½ oz) sugar
7 egg yolks
1 whole egg

100 g (3½ oz) good quality chocolate
500 ml (18 fl oz) double cream
squares of chocolate

---

*T*o make the praline, put the hazelnuts on a baking sheet or in a dry frying pan and toast them for 5-8 minutes. Caramelize 100 g (3½ oz) sugar and fold in the hazelnuts. Spread the praline over a buttered baking sheet or marble board and leave it to set, then crush it finely.

Bring 250 ml (8 fl oz) water to the boil with 250 g (8 oz) sugar and simmer for about 7 minutes, until a syrup forms. Whisk together the whole egg and egg yolks, stir in the hot sugar syrup, whisking all the time, until a smooth, creamy mixture forms, then stand the bowl in cold water and continue whisking until the mixture has cooled. Fold the praline into the custard. Melt the chocolate in a double saucepan, or a bowl over a pan of hot water.

Whip the cream until it forms soft peaks, then fold 2 tablespoons of cooled chocolate into the cream. Briskly stir the remaining chocolate into the custard, then transfer the mixture to a large bowl and freeze it for 6 hours, stirring occasionally to break up the ice crystals. Arrange scoops of ice-cream on individual dessert plates, garnish with squares of chocolate and serve immediately.

RUM AND RAISIN ICE-CREAM

Serves 4

1 unwaxed lemon
200 g (7 oz) sugar
200 g (7 oz) raisins
4 tbsp white rum
200 ml (7 fl oz) double cream

½ sachet powdered gelatine
250 ml (8 fl oz) lemon juice
2 egg whites

---

*W*ash the lemon in very hot water and zest it. Bring 500 ml (18 fl oz) water to the boil, add the lemon zest and sugar and simmer it for 3-5 minutes, then strain off the lemon zest, reserving the syrup. Pour the white rum over the raisins and leave them to macerate. Whip the cream until it forms soft peaks and fold in the raisins. Blend the gelatine with 4-5 tablespoons of lemon juice, leave it to soften for 10 minutes, then heat it, stirring constantly, until completely dissolved.

Whisk the egg whites until stiff. Fold together the lemon syrup, the cream and raisins, remaining lemon juice, egg whites and warm gelatine and refrigerate. Stir carefully one last time before the dessert starts to set, then pour into individual moulds and freeze.

Before serving, dip the moulds into very hot water, then turn out the ice-creams into dessert dishes. Serve with chocolate sauce.

MONA LISA SUNDAE

Serves 6

750 ml (1¼ pints) toffee-and-almond ice-cream
chocolate sauce

200 ml (7 fl oz) double cream
bitter chocolate

---

*P*lace scoops of ice-cream on chilled dessert plates. Pour a pool of chocolate sauce around the ice-cream and garnish with the cream and chocolate.

Serve with mini chocolate rolls.

Left: *Hazelnut parfait*
Right: *Rum and raisin ice-cream*

ICED RASPBERRY PARFAIT

Serves 4

500 g (1 lb) raspberries
2 eggs, separated
125 g (4 oz) sugar
2 tbsp lemon juice

500 ml (18 fl oz) double
cream
toasted, flaked almonds

Purée the raspberries, then push them through a sieve. Whisk the egg yolks and sugar together until the mixture turns pale, then add the lemon juice. Whisk the egg whites until stiff, fold them into the yolk mixture, then fold this mixture and the cream carefully into the raspberry purée.

Transfer the mousse to a large dish or individual ramekins, cover with foil and freeze for 3-4 hours. Before serving, dip the dish or ramekins briefly in hot water, run a knife around the top of the dish, then turn out the parfait. Sprinkle with the toasted almonds.

SUNDAE HÉLÈNE

Serves 7-8

1½ litres (2½ pints)
pistachio ice-cream
500 g (1 lb) apricots,
tinned in syrup
raspberry jelly or

preserve
350 ml (12 fl oz) double
cream, whipped
flaked almonds

Arrange scoops of ice-cream on chilled dessert plates. Drain the apricot halves and place one on top of each scoop of ice-cream. Melt the raspberry jelly or preserve on a gentle heat and pour it over the apricots, then decorate with the whipped cream and flaked almonds.

ICE-CREAM AU GRATIN WITH ORANGES

Serves 6-8

4 oranges	1 sachet of vanilla sugar
125 g (4½ oz) sugar	500 ml (18 fl oz) vanilla ice-
3 tbsp Grand Marnier	cream
2 eggs, separated	16 sponge fingers

Peel the oranges and slice them into thin rounds. Sprinkle them with 25 g (1 oz) sugar, pour the Grand Marnier over them and leave them to marinate. Whisk the egg whites until stiff. Mix 100 g (3½ oz) sugar and the vanilla sugar together and fold it, a spoonful at a time, into the egg whites. Fill a piping bag fitted with a star-shaped nozzle with 2 tablespoons of meringue. Stir the two egg yolks into the remaining meringue. Arrange the ice-cream in a large, oval oven-proof dish. Break 9 of

Above: *Sundae Alexandra*
Left: *Raspberry parfait*

the sponge fingers in half, soak them in the juice from the marinated oranges and arrange them around the ice-cream. Layer the remaining biscuits on top of the ice-cream. Spread the egg mixture over the sponge fingers and ice-cream, pipe meringue decorations on top and place under a hot grill for 3-4 minutes.

Arrange the marinated orange slices on top of the ice-cream.

SUNDAE ALEXANDRA

Serves 5-6

750 ml (1¼ pints) vanilla-and-hazelnut ice-cream	500 ml (18 fl oz) double cream, whipped
4-6 tbsp advocaat	chopped hazelnuts
	chopped pistachio nuts

Place scoops of ice-cream in a chilled sundae dish. Pour the advocaat around the ice-cream and decorate with the whipped cream and chopped nuts.

above: *Pineapple and strawberry dessert*
Right: *Espresso sundae*

SUMMER'S DREAM SUNDAE

Serves 6-7

750 ml (1¼ pints)
blackcurrant sorbet

250 ml (8 fl oz) double
cream
1 sachet of vanilla sugar

Put a scoop of sorbet on a dessert plate. Whip the cream for 30 seconds, then fold in the vanilla sugar and continue whipping until the cream forms soft peaks. Garnish the ice-cream with the whipped cream and blackcurrants. Serve with wafer or shortbread biscuits.

APHRODITE'S DREAM

Serves 4

1 mango
2 tbsp Grand Marnier
500 ml (18 fl oz) pistachio
ice-cream

250 ml (8 fl oz) double
cream, whipped
shelled pistachio nuts

Wash the mango, cut it in half, remove the stone and chop the flesh, then drizzle it with the Grand Marnier.

Serve the pistachio ice-cream with the chopped mango, garnished with whipped cream and pistachio nuts.

HAWAIIAN SUNDAE

Serves 4

4 slices of pineapple in
syrup
500 ml (18 fl oz) lemon
sorbet

250 ml (8 fl oz) double
cream, whipped
wafer biscuits

Arrange the slices of pineapple on chilled dessert plates (put them in the freezer for 5 minutes before you need them). Arrange one or two scoops of sorbet on top of each slice of pineapple. Decorate with the whipped cream and garnish with the wafer biscuits.

PINEAPPLE STRAWBERRY DESSERT

Serves 4

16 large strawberries
20 ml (1½ tbsp)
Maraschino
4 slices of pineapple,
tinned in syrup

250 ml (8 fl oz) strawberry
ice-cream
30 g (1 oz) toasted, flaked
almonds

Wash the strawberries and slice them in half. Drizzle the Maraschino over them and leave them to marinate. Drain the slices of pineapple and arrange them on dessert plates. Put a scoop of strawberry ice-cream on top of each slice of pineapple, then add the strawberries. Sprinkle the desserts with the toasted, flaked almonds and serve immediately.

DREAM BANANAS

Serves 4

2-3 bananas
lemon juice
500 ml (18 fl oz) chocolate
ice-cream
300 ml (10 fl oz) double

cream, whipped
grated chocolate
cherries
lychees

Peel and slice the bananas and arrange them on dessert plates. Drizzle the lemon juice over them. Cut the ice-cream into 8 slices and arrange 2 slices on top of each serving of banana. Decorate the dessert with the whipped cream and garnish with grated chocolate, cherries and lychees.

ESPRESSO SUNDAE

Serves 4

4 egg yolks
100 g (3½ oz) sugar
3 tbsp Amaretto
125 ml (4 fl oz) strong
coffee

750 ml (1¼ pints) vanilla
ice-cream
grated chocolate
brandy snaps or similar

Whisk together the egg yolks and sugar in a double saucepan, or in a bowl over boiling water, until they turn pale. Stir in the Amaretto and coffee, and whisk for a further 5 minutes. Arrange scoops of ice-cream in sundae dishes and pour the sabayon sauce over them. Garnish with grated chocolate.

Serve immediately with the brandy snaps.

CHATEAU ROYAL SUNDAE

Serves 4-6

6-8 tbsp chocolate sauce
1-2 tbsp brandy
2 tbsp double cream
1 tbsp stem ginger,
chopped
500 ml (18 fl oz) hazelnut
ice-cream

pistachio nuts, chopped
sliced banana
mandarin segments
cherries
brandy snaps or similar
biscuits

Combine the chocolate sauce, brandy, cream and ginger. Pour it into chilled sundae dishes. Arrange scoops of ice-cream on top. Decorate the ice-cream with whipped cream and garnish with chopped nuts and fruit. Serve with the brandy snaps.

CAPRICE

Serves 4

4 tbsp chocolate sauce
750 ml (1¼ pints) toffee
ice-cream
250 ml (8 fl oz) double

cream, whipped
almonds
brandy snap biscuits

Pout the chocolate sauce into chilled sundae dishes.
.Arrange 3 scoops of ice-cream in each dish. Decorate
with the whipped cream and garnish with almonds and
brandy snaps.

VANILLA ICE-CREAM

Serves 4

2 egg yolks
75 g (3 oz) sugar
½ vanilla pod

250 ml (8 fl oz) double
cream

Whisk the egg yolks and sugar until the mixture turns
pale, then add the essence from the vanilla pod. Whip
the cream until it forms soft peaks and fold it into the egg
mixture. Transfer the mixture to an ice-cream container
and freeze for 3-4 hours. Arrange scoops of ice-cream in
4 sundae dishes.

Serve with sweetened forest fruits and wafer biscuits.

FRUIT SALAD WITH CHOCOLATE AND VANILLA ICE-CREAM

Serves 6-7

500 g (1 lb) strawberries
2 tbsp sugar
3 kiwi fruit
2 bananas

lemon juice
500 ml (18 fl oz) vanilla-
and-chocolate ice-cream,
e.g. chocolate chip

Wash the strawberries, hull them, slice them in half and
sprinkle them with the sugar. Peel the kiwi fruit and
bananas, slice them into rounds and drizzle the lemon
juice over the bananas. Put the fruit into a glass
dish. Arrange scoops of ice-cream on top
of the fruit and serve immediately.

Below: *Fruit salad with
chocolate-and-vanilla
ice-cream*

Above: *Olympic sundae*

OLYMPIC SUNDAE

Serves 4

750 ml (1¼ pints) pistachio
ice-cream
6 stewed apricots

strawberry purée
250 ml (8 fl oz) double
cream, whipped
ground almonds

Place 2 scoops of ice-cream in each of 4 chilled sundae dishes. Arrange half an apricot on top of each serving, and pour the strawberry purée over the top. Decorate with the whipped cream and ground almonds.

PEACHES CARDINAL

Serves 4

750 ml (1¼ pints) toffee
ice-cream
250 ml (8 fl oz) double
cream, whipped
4 peach halves, tinned in

syrup
raspberry purée
toasted almonds, chopped
wafer biscuits

Divide 12 scoops of ice-cream between 4 chilled sundae dishes. Decorate the ice-cream with the whipped cream. Drain the peach halves and arrange them on top of the ice-cream. Pour the raspberry purée over the peaches and top with the toasted almonds. Garnish with the wafer biscuits.

RHINEGOLD SUNDAE

Serves 4

400-500 g (13 oz-1 lb) black
grapes
500 ml (18 fl oz) chocolate
ice-cream

250 ml (8 fl oz) double
cream, whipped
chopped hazelnuts
wafer biscuits

Wash the grapes, slice them in half and de-seed them. Put 4 sundae dishes into the freezer for 5 minutes to chill them. Dice the ice-cream and arrange it in the chilled sundae dishes with the grapes. Garnish with the whipped cream, chopped nuts and wafers.

FIRE AND ICE FIESTA

Serves 4

500 ml (18 fl oz) milk
pinch of salt
4 tbsp sugar
zest of ½ unwaxed lemon,
grated

125 g (4 oz) pudding rice
2 eggs, separated
500 ml (18 fl oz) block of
ice-cream
lemon juice

Ad the salt to the milk and bring it to the boil with
2 tablespoons of sugar, the lemon zest and rice. Leave the
rice to swell for about 20 minutes. Fold the egg yolks into
the warm rice, and leave to cool.

Transfer the rice to 4 oven-proof dishes and chill it. Cut
the ice-cream into blocks and arrange them on top of the
rice. Whisk the egg whites with the remaining sugar
until very stiff and fold in the lemon juice. Pipe the
meringue on top of the ice-cream. Cook the meringue
under a very hot grill for about 5 minutes, then serve
immediately.

COFFEE PARFAIT

Serves 6

60 g (2 oz) ground coffee
1-2 tsp instant coffee
150 g (5 oz) sugar
3 egg yolks
pinch of salt

500 ml (18 fl oz) double
cream
crystallized fruits
coffee beans or chocolate
flakes

Pour 250 ml (8 fl oz) boiling water over the ground
coffee, add the instant coffee and leave to infuse for
15 minutes, then filter it. Bring 100 ml (3½ fl oz) water to
the boil with the sugar and simmer to form a stock syrup.
Whisk the egg yolks until foaming, stir in the hot sugar
syrup and whisk until a thick custard forms. Add the
coffee and salt to the custard.

Whip the cream until it forms soft peaks, then fold it into
the custard. Transfer the ice-cream mixture to a suitable
container and freeze for 3-4 hours. Turn the ice-cream
out onto a chilled serving dish. Decorate with crystallized
fruit, coffee beans or flaked chocolate.

Serve with meringues.

Below: *Fire and ice fiesta*

Above: *Apricots with chocolate ice-cream*

APRICOTS WITH CHOCOLATE ICE-CREAM

Serves 4

8-12 apricots
knob of butter
50 g (2 oz) flaked almonds
4-6 tbsp sugar

500 ml (18 fl oz) chocolate
and vanilla ice-cream
4 tbsp coffee liqueur

Blanch the apricots in boiling water, refresh them in cold water, skin them, slice them in half, stone them, then cut them into quarters. Melt the butter and fry the almonds, then add the sugar and melt it, stirring all the time.

Add the apricots, cover them and cook for about 5 minutes, then leave them to cool. Arrange scoops of ice-cream on top of the apricots, drizzle the coffee liqueur on top and serve immediately.

VANILLA AND STRAWBERRY PARFAIT WITH SABAYON SAUCE

Serves 4-6

1 vanilla pod
150 ml (5 fl oz) double cream
salt
8 eggs, separated

60 g (2½ oz) caster sugar
500 g (1 lb) strawberries
3 tbsp orange liqueur
250 ml (8 fl oz) port

Split the vanilla pod in half lengthways and scrape out the essence. Bring the cream to the boil with the vanilla essence and a pinch of salt. Whisk 4 egg yolks with 30 g (1 oz) sugar until they turn pale, then gradually stir in the hot cream. Leave the mixture to cool. Whisk 2 egg whites with the remaining sugar until stiff and fold them into the custard. Pour the custard into a savarin mould (capacity 1 litre (1¾ pints)) and freeze for 5 hours, stirring occasionally. Wash and hull the strawberries and slice them in half. Sprinkle them with a little extra sugar, add the orange liqueur and leave them to marinate.

To make the port sabayon: Whisk 4 egg yolks with the port and a pinch of salt in a double saucepan, or in a bowl over a pan of boiling water, until a smooth, creamy sauce forms. Turn the parfait out onto a chilled serving dish. Arrange the strawberries in the centre and pour the port sabayon over. Serve immediately.

PAPAYA SORBET

Serves 4

1 papaya, weighing about 500 g (1 lb)
100 ml (3½ fl oz)

grapefruit juice
40 g (1½ oz) caster sugar
sparkling wine

Slice the papaya in half, de-seed it and scoop out the flesh with a spoon. Purée the flesh with the grapefruit juice and sieved caster sugar. Pour the papaya purée into a suitable container and freeze for 2-3 hours (the sorbet should not set completely). Place scoops of sorbet in champagne flutes. Top up the glasses with sparkling wine. Serve immediately.

FRUIT ICEBERG

Serves 2

125 g (4 oz) fromage frais
1 tsp lemon juice
juice of ½ an orange
1 tbsp sugar

250 ml (8 fl oz) fruit-flavoured ice-cream
30 g (1 oz) popcorn

Combine the fromage frais, lemon juice, orange juice and sugar, then divide the mixture between 2 dessert dishes. Divide the ice-cream in half and arrange it on top of the fromage frais. Sprinkle popcorn over the top.

PEACH MELBA

Serves 4

300 g (10 oz) frozen raspberries
4 peach halves, stewed

500 ml (18 fl oz) vanilla ice-cream
double cream

Defrost the raspberries and purée them in a blender or food processor. Whip the cream until it forms soft peaks. Drain the peaches and slice them, but do not cut all the way through. Press down lightly on the peach half to form a fan shape. Dice the ice-cream and divide it amongst 4 sundae dishes, then top each with half a peach. Pour the raspberry sauce over the top. Decorate with whipped cream and serve immediately.

Left: *Vanilla and strawberry parfait with sabayon sauce*
Right: *Papaya sorbet*

KIWI FRUIT SUNDAE

Serves 4

6 kiwi fruit	cream
½ tsp vanilla sugar	4 scoops of pistachio ice-
1 tbsp orange preserve	cream
1 tbsp orange liqueur	4 scoops of strawberry
4 scoops of vanilla ice-	ice-cream

Peel the kiwi fruit. Chop 4 of them into small pieces, then mash them with a fork, and combine them with the vanilla sugar, orange preserve and orange liqueur. Slice 2 kiwi fruit in half lengthways, then slice them.
Arrange the 3 types of ice-cream in 4 sundae dishes, pour the kiwi fruit sauce over and garnish with slices of kiwi fruit. Serve immediately.

Below: *Melon sorbet*

MELON SORBET

Serves 2

1 melon, weighing about 1	sugar
kg (2 lb)	2 tbsp lemon juice
60-80 g (2-3 oz) caster	dry sparkling wine

Slice the melon in half, de-seed it and cut away the flesh from the skin. Dice some of the flesh, slice some into segments, cover and refrigerate it. Purée the rest, fold in the caster sugar and lemon juice. Freeze the purée for 5 hours, stirring occasionally. Serve the sorbet in the melon shells, pour the sparkling wine on top, and garnish with the diced and segmented melon. Serve immediately.

WILLIAMS PEAR SUNDAE

Serves 6

500 ml (18 fl oz) vanilla ice-	schnapps
cream	150 ml (5 fl oz) double
3 Williams pears, poached	cream
3 tbsp pear eau-de-vie or	30 g (1 oz) dark chocolate

Drain the pears and slice them in half. Put the ice-cream in a shallow dish. Arrange the pears on top of the ice-cream, and pour the eau-de-vie over them. Whip the cream until it forms soft peaks. Melt the chocolate in a double saucepan or in a bowl over a pan of hot water, then carefully fold in the whipped cream. Decorate the ice-cream and pears with the chocolate ganache.

Serve immediately with wafer or shortbread biscuits.

VANILLA ICE-CREAM ON A BED OF BLACKBERRIES

Serves 2

125 g (4 oz) milk curds or	125 g (4 oz) blackberries
fromage frais	250 ml (8 fl oz) vanilla ice-
1 sachet vanilla sugar	cream
20 g (¾ oz) sugar	cornflakes

Combine the curds, vanilla sugar, sugar and blackberries and divide the mixture between 2 dessert plates. Dice the ice-cream roughly and arrange it on top of the fruit. Sprinkle with cornflakes and serve immediately.

Right: *Williams pear sundae*

GOLDEN BISCUITS WITH CRANBERRY CREAM

Serves 6

100 g (3½ oz) almond paste
120 g (4 oz plus 1 tbsp) caster sugar
3 eggs
25 g (1 oz) flour
pinch of ground cinnamon
125 g (4 oz) fresh or tinned cranberries

125 ml (4 fl oz) cranberry juice
1 tsp powdered gelatine
1 tbsp crème de cassis or blackcurrant liqueur
1 tsp grated zest of an unwaxed lemon
120 ml (4 fl oz) double cream

Work together the almond paste, 50 g (2 oz) caster sugar and 1 egg in a food processor. Add the sieved flour and cinnamon, cover and leave to rest for about 3 hours.

Roll out the dough and cut out 10 circles, each 10 cm (4 inches) in diameter, and place them on an oiled baking sheet. As the dough is brittle when cooked, make 2 extra circles. Bake the dough in a preheated oven at 180ºC (350ºF, Gas Mark 4) for about 5 minutes, until the dough has browned slightly. Lift the circles off the baking sheet immediately and leave them to cool on a rack. Sprinkle them with 20 g (1 tablespoon) of sieved caster sugar and caramelize them under the grill.

To make the cranberry cream: Bring the cranberry juice and cranberries to the boil, take them off the heat, cover and leave them to cool. Blend the gelatine with 2 tablespoons of cold water and leave it to soften for 10 minutes. Separate the 2 remaining eggs and whisk the

yolks with 50 g (2 oz) caster sugar until the mixture turns pale. Add the blackcurrant liqueur and lemon zest, then the stewed cranberries, taking care to reserve 4 tablespoons. Reheat the gelatine, stirring all the time until it dissolves, then fold it into the custard mixture and refrigerate it.

Whip the cream until it forms soft peaks, fold it into the cranberry mixture and refrigerate it again. Fill a piping bag with the cranberry cream and pipe it onto 5 biscuits. Garnish with the reserved cranberries, and top with the remaining biscuits, caramelized side uppermost, pressing down on them lightly.

Variation: You could substitute blackcurrants or redcurrants for the cranberries.

FRUITS OF THE FOREST PANCAKE

Serves 4

4 eggs
1 tbsp sugar
½ tsp salt

4 tbsp milk
4 tbsp oat flakes
2 knobs of butter

Whisk all the ingredients together briskly, except the butter. Melt some of the butter in a frying pan, pour in one quarter of the batter and fry the pancake until golden on both sides, adding a little more butter before turning it.

Keep the pancake warm. Continue making pancakes until the batter is used up. Serve with sugared strawberries, blackcurrants, raspberries, cranberries, redcurrants or whipped cream flavoured with orange liqueur.

Left: *Golden biscuits with cranberry cream*
Above right: *Crêpes Suzette*

CRÈPES SUZETTE

Serves 6

50 g (2 oz) flour	250 ml (8 fl oz) milk
1 egg	100 g (3½ oz) butter
2-3 tbsp caster sugar	3 oranges
250 ml (8 fl oz) double cream	6 tbsp Grand Marnier

Sift the flour into a large bowl, break the egg into the centre, then add 1 tablespoon of caster sugar and the cream and milk. Whisk briskly until a smooth batter forms, then leave to rest for about 30 minutes. Melt the butter in a frying pan, pour in a small amount of batter and swirl it around the pan until it coats the base thinly, then fry it on both sides. Make 6 pancakes in all and set aside.

Peel 2 oranges, remove the pith and cut them into ½ cm (¼ inch) thick slices.

To make the orange butter: Blend 50 g (2 oz) softened butter with the grated zest of 1 orange and 1-2 tablespoons of caster sugar.

Melt a little of the orange butter in a flambée pan or heavy-based frying pan, reheat one of the pancakes on both sides, fold it into a triangle, arrange on a warmed plate and keep it hot. Repeat the process for the remaining pancakes.

Melt the remaining orange butter in the frying pan, add the slices of orange and cook them over a low heat. Push the orange slices into the centre of the pan, arrange the folded pancakes around the side, and reheat quickly. Pour the Grand Marnier over the pancakes and oranges and set light to it.

Serve the flamed pancakes and oranges with vanilla ice-cream.

SPONGE OMELETTE WITH PLUM CREAM

Serves 4

2 eggs, separated	4 tbsp plums, stoned
60 g (2½ oz) sugar	ground cinnamon
40 g (1½ oz) flour	1-2 tbsp brandy
30 g (1 oz) cornflour	grated zest of an unwaxed
150 ml (5 fl oz) double	lemon
cream	icing sugar

Whisk the egg yolks with half the sugar until the mixture turns pale. Whisk the egg whites with the remaining sugar until very stiff. Sift the flour and cornflour into the egg yolk mixture and fold in carefully, then fold in the egg whites.

Oil a baking sheet and dust it with flour. Shape the mixture into 4 circles, each 15 cm (6 inches) in diameter and bake them at 250°C (475°F, Gas Mark 9) for 5 minutes, then take them out of the oven and lift the omelettes off the baking sheet.
Purée the plums roughly in a food processor. Whip the cream until very stiff, then fold in the plums, cinnamon, brandy and lemon zest. Garnish the sponge omelettes with the plum cream and sprinkle with icing sugar.

Below: *Sponge omelette with plum cream*
Right: *Pancake Nelson*

PANCAKE NELSON

Serves 4

5 kiwi fruit	½ sachet vanilla sugar
5 fresh dates	12 sponge fingers
2 tbsp Maraschino	3 eggs, separated
2 tbsp orange juice,	100 g (3½ oz) caster sugar
freshly squeezed	
1 tbsp sugar	

Peel the kiwi fruit and slice them in half lengthways, then slice them. Reserve a few slices for decoration. Skin the dates, slice them in half lengthways and stone them. Pour the Maraschino and orange juice over the fruit, add the sugar and vanilla sugar and put the fruit in the refrigerator to marinate.

Arrange the sponge fingers in a shallow oven-proof dish and cover them with the marinated fruit and the juice. Whisk the egg yolks and caster sugar together until the mixture turns pale, then whisk the egg whites until stiff and fold them into the yolk mixture. Pour the egg mixture over the fruit. Bake the omelette in a preheated oven at 200°C (400°F, Gas Mark 6) for 12-15 minutes. Garnish the omelette with the reserved kiwi fruit. Serve immediately.

GOURMET SOUFFLÉ CONSTANCE

Serves 2

4 eggs, separated	almonds
75 g (3 oz) sugar	butter
25 g (1 oz) cocoa powder	1 tbsp breadcrumbs
75 g (3 oz) ground	

Whisk the egg whites until stiff. Whisk the egg yolks and sugar together until the mixture turns pale, then pour the whites on top of the yolk mixture. Sieve the cocoa powder on top of the egg whites, then add the almonds and fold all these ingredients carefully into the yolk mixture. Butter a soufflé dish, pour the soufflé mixture into it and sprinkle the breadcrumbs on top.

Bake in a preheated oven at 180°C (350°F, Gas Mark 4) for 25 minutes.

Serve with whipped cream or custard.

GLOSSARY

Even if everyone has their own secret ingredient to help make a recipe extra special, we all need to know the basics of culinary "jargon". This glossary will help you to understand what is meant by blanching vegetables, de-glazing cooking juices, making a roux and other terms which will give you a little more insight into the culinary arts.

Angostura: A bitter essence based on rum and the juice from the bark of a South American shrub.

Bain-marie: To cook or reheat food by placing it in a double saucepan, with boiling water in the bottom pan, or in a container which is either stood in a roasting tin filled with boiling water, or placed over a saucepan of boiling water.

Beurre manié: Equal quantities of butter and flour kneaded together, used to thicken gravy, sauces, soups and stews.

Beurre noisette: Butter which is melted and cooked until it turns light to dark brown, as required. Sometimes flavoured with lemon juice or wine vinegar.

Bind: To thicken, to give an even consistency to a sauce or soup.

Blanch: To boil something for a relatively short time to soften it (cabbage, for example), or to seal it (meat or vegetables) or to make it easier to remove the skin (for example, tomatoes, in which case 30 seconds is long enough).

Bouquet garni: A bunch of herbs, usually made up of parsley, thyme and bay leaf.

Braise: To cook slowly in a covered receptacle.

Chinois: A fine, conical-shaped strainer.

Court-bouillon: A seasoned stock in which fish is cooked.

Deglaze: To collect the cooking juices from the base of a frying pan or saucepan by dissolving them in a little water or another liquid.

Dressed: Food which has been prepared for cooking or serving, particularly poultry and fish, by cleaning, gutting, trimming, etc.

Ganache: A mixture of melted chocolate and cream which can be used as a sauce, or allowed to cool and used as a spreadable filling or topping for cakes, etc.

Herbes de Provence: A mixture of herbs, usually dried, commonly used in French cooking and particularly associated with recipes from the Provence region of France, hence the name. The mixture usually includes basil, parsley, thyme and oregano.

Julienne: Different vegetables which are cut into very thin matchsticks.

Lard: To wrap lean meat, usually with thin slices of bacon, for the purpose of preventing the meat from drying out during cooking and to impart flavour from the bacon fat.

Lardon: Diced bacon, often quite fatty, which is either rendered to release the fat as a flavouring for other ingredients, or fried until crisp and used as a garnish for a range of dishes, including salads.

Line: To cover the inside of a baking tin or dish with pastry.

Lovage: An aromatic herb originating from Persia.

Macerate: To soften or break up (fruit, etc.) by soaking in wine or other liquid.

Maraschino: A liqueur made from the marasca cherry.

Marinate: Leave to soak in a liquid, for example wine, to which herbs, spices and other ingredients have been added, to impart flavour and to tenderize.

Reduce: To boil so that the substance becomes more concentrated.

Refresh: To rinse or immerse food in cold water, pasta or vegetables, for example, which have been blanched or cooked in boiling water, to stop them cooking further and to help retain the colour and flavour.

Render: To fry bacon in a dry pan, releasing the fat which is then used for frying other ingredients, thus imparting the rich bacon flavour to the dish.

Reserve: To put to one side until needed for use later on in the recipe.

Roux: A mixture of flour and butter cooked together on a low heat until the flour starts to take on colour and which is used as a base for sauces, soups and gravies.

Sauté: To fry in fat until the substance turns golden brown in colour.

Seal: To fry quickly in fat at a high temperature to seal in the juices and flavour.

Skim: To remove the scum or froth from the surface of a liquid.

Soak: To immerse in cold water, with regard to meat and fish, for the purpose of removing blood and any impurities.

Steam: To cook over boiling water or with a little water in a closed receptacle.

Sweat: Cook over a low heat in a closed receptacle.

Work: To beat with a spatula or to whisk.

ALPHABETICAL LIST OF RECIPES